Jason Lang

Biomedical Informatics in Translational Research

Artech House Series
Bioinformatics & Biomedical Imaging

Series Editors
Stephen T. C. Wong, The Methodist Hospital and Weill Cornell Medical College
Guang-Zhong Yang, Imperial College

Advances in Diagnostic and Therapeutic Ultrasound Imaging, Jasjit S. Suri, Chirinjeev Kathuria, Ruey-Feng Chang, Filippo Molinari, and Aaron Fenster, editors

Biological Database Modeling, Jake Chen and Amandeep S. Sidhu, editors

Biomedical Informatics in Translational Research, Hai Hu, Michael Liebman, and Richard Mural

Genome Sequencing Technology and Algorithms, Sun Kim, Haixu Tang, and Elaine R. Mardis, editors

Life Science Automation Fundamentals and Applications, Mingjun Zhang, Bradley Nelson, and Robin Felder, editors

Microscopic Image Analysis for Life Science Applications, Jens Rittscher, Stephen T. C. Wong, and Raghu Machiraju, editors

Next Generation Artificial Vision Systems: Reverse Engineering the Human Visual System, Maria Petrou and Anil Bharath, editors

Systems Bioinformatics: An Engineering Case-Based Approach, Gil Alterovitz and Marco F. Ramoni, editors

Biomedical Informatics in Translational Research

Hai Hu
Richard J. Mural
Michael N. Liebman

Editors

ARTECH HOUSE

BOSTON | LONDON
artechhouse.com

Library of Congress Cataloging-in-Publication Data
A catalog record for this book is available from the U. S. Library of Congress.

British Library Cataloguing in Publication Data
A catalogue record for this book is available from the British Library.

ISBN-13: 978-1-59693-038-4

Cover design by Igor Valdman

© 2008 ARTECH HOUSE, INC.
685 Canton Street
Norwood, MA 02062

10 9 8 7 6 5 4 3 2 1

To the patients,
whose quality of life we strive to improve!

Contents

Preface

There are multiple definitions of "Biomedical Informatics." We have taken one that broadly defines this multidisciplinary subject as the management and usage of biomedical information encompassing clinical informatics, public health informatics, and bioinformatics. This definition is increasingly important as new concepts and technologies enter into medical practice and related basic research, and require new types of information management and data analysis that relies on sophisticated statistical and computational technologies.

In particular, this book focuses on the application of biomedical informatics for translational research. Translational research is often seen as the rapid inclusion of the results of basic biological research into clinical practice, (i.e., "bench to bedside"). We have found that it is equally important to have clinical needs feeding into the framing of basic research questions, more of a "bedside – bench – bedside" cycle which further requires a strong biomedical informatics base. The need for merging genomic, proteomic, and other "omic" data into the study of human diseases requires using computational and statistical technologies due to the sheer volume of the involved data. From the clinical perspective, it requires the identification of clinically relevant questions, and supports the application of the results from research back into clinical practice. From the molecular study perspective, it involves the application of advanced analytical technologies in the study of human bio-specimens. From the informatics perspective, it involves management of the large data sets generated in the study. From the data analysis perspective, it involves deployment of existing computational and statistical methods and algorithms, and the development of new methods to extract knowledge from the underlying data.

Our vision of biomedical informatics was formed and reduced to practice beginning in 2003 at the Windber Research Institute. In June 2004, Drs. Liebman and Hu presented some of our results at the Cambridge Healthtech Institute's Conference on Bioinformatics. The presentations drew the attention of Mr. Wayne Yuhasz, the Executive Acquisition Editor of the Artech Publishing House, who subsequently contacted us and initiated this book project. In late 2005, the editorial team was strengthened by the addition of Dr. Mural. In preparing the manuscript for this book, the editors divided their responsibilities as follows; Liebman was responsible for Chapters 1 and 11, Mural was responsible for Chapters 4 and 6, Hu was responsible for Chapters 7, 8, 9, and 10, Mural and Hu were jointly responsible for Chapters 2, 3, and 5, and Hu was responsible for all the administrative work associated with this book project.

As the editors, we sincerely thank all the contributors of this book who all work in the frontiers of biomedical informatics and translational research amongst different component fields. We highly appreciate the organizational support of the

Windber Research Institute. We are also very grateful to the funding from the U.S. Department of Defense to the Clinical Breast Care Project and the Gynecological Disease Program for which the Windber Research Institute is one of the major participants, which provided us with the opportunity to conceive, develop, and implement a biomedical informatics infrastructure, which in turn served as a rich resource especially when examples were needed to illustrate our points on biomedical informatics in this book. The funds for these two projects are managed through Henry Jackson Foundation for the Advancement of Military Medicine, Rockville, MD, USA.

Finally, we thank Mr. Wayne Yuhasz of Artech House, Inc., for his initiation of this project, and for his advice and patience throughout the development and completion of the manuscript.

Hai Hu,
Richard J. Mural,
Michael N. Liebman
July, 2008
Windber, PA

CHAPTER 1

Biomedical Informatics in Translational Research

Michael N. Liebman

This book's goal is to present the elements of and relationships among "omics"-based approaches and clinical data perspectives while establishing the critical need to understand, define, refine, and address actual clinical needs. A critical need exists to address the real issues that arise when a physician is faced with a patient and the need to make clinical choices that will impact the patient, the patient's quality life, and the patient's family. Bridging this gap between the clinical need and the available technologies, clinical data, and clinician input is the role that biomedical informatics can play in driving the evolution of patient care in the postgenome era.

Translational research and *personalized medicine* have become buzzwords that follow on the aspirations of systems biology and the postgenome era. They emphasize the need to apply high-resolution and high-throughput technologies to medical applications as they were originally conceived, intended, and funded. These terms, however, have evolved with diverse definitions as molecular and clinical researchers, clinicians and patients, venture capitalists and investment bankers, and the popular press have all attempted to identify the value proposition that should evolve from the overall investment in genomics, proteomics, metabolomics, and "omics" projects in general. In general, the development of "omics"-based technologies and their "integration" into systems biology have approached the complex problems of health care from a technology-focused, bottoms-up approach. The transition from the fundamental application of these approaches into true clinical utility remains elusive as outlined next.

The generation of data far exceeds the ability to convert it into useful clinical value, and, unfortunately, this trend continues in spite of weekly, even daily, reports of the discovery of new disease-related genes and so forth. In Figure 1.1, data is converted into information when redundancies are removed and it is "cleaned" to remove spurious results; information becomes knowledge when its interpretation leads to new discoveries (e.g., biomarkers, pathways, gene correlations); and knowledge evolves to clinical utility when it is finally incorporated into the actual practice of medicine (e.g., biomarkers become diagnostics and, eventually, causal diagnostics). Within this context, unfortunately, the gap between data/information and clinical utility continues to grow with time.

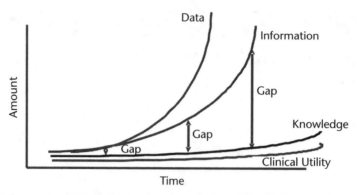

Figure 1.1 Relationship of data to information, knowledge, clinical utility, and the increasing gap between technology and science.

A significant opportunity has presented itself in which data generation can be accomplished within a top-down approach, but this requires using clinician insight and clinical data to identify and prioritize the relevant questions and use them to drive experimental design. The integration of this clinical perspective with "omics"-based data represents the field of *biomedical informatics* as described in this book. In this manner, it becomes essential to stratify the complexity of the disease as well as to stratify the molecular characteristics of the patient to provide new insight into the concepts and characteristics associated with the disease process as separate from those associated with the patient who is exhibiting the disease. The ultimate goal of these actions is to improve patient care and quality-of-life issues for the patient and his or her family. This goal cannot be achieved without a close link between the clinician and clinical perspective, which must drive the genomic, genetic, epidemiologic, and proteomic research.

This book is intended to present the components and their relationship from both "omics"-based approaches and clinical data perspectives, while establishing the critical need to understand, define, refine, and address the clinical needs that appear when a physician is faced with a patient and the need to make clinical choices.

In constructing this book, perhaps the first questions to address are "What is *biomedical informatics*?" and "How does it differ from *bioinformatics* and *medical informatics*? To establish the framework for this book and for this book to succeed, other terms also require examination and definition: *systems biology, translational medicine* or *research,* and *personalized medicine.* This book is not intended to be simply a series of definitions, but rather a presentation of the attempt to integrate a wide range of both clinical and molecular views and perspectives of the patient into a single, coherent patient-centric view. The goal of this reorientation is to enable the patient, her clinical history and state, the physician, and the molecular and/or clinical researcher to be better equipped to handle the data, information, and potential knowledge that results from the application of the advanced technologies of both omics and diagnostics, to identify and tackle real clinical problems along the path toward improving the patient's quality of life.

To define biomedical informatics, we probably have to examine how we view disease. The evolution from risk (genetics/genotype) to disease (expressed phenotype) should be viewed as a continuum, not as distinctly separable states, and disease itself should be viewed as an ongoing process, not a state fixed in time. This is an important distinction from the current application of diagnostics and therapeutic intervention and will impact the drug development process. Biomedical informatics requires access to longitudinal patient medical histories, not simply clinical trial data.

If we add clinical data to current bioinformatics practices, we establish the following relationships:

Clinical observations + Molecular/genetic information → Clinical correlations
Clinical observations + Biological process/pathway knowledge → Clinical mechanism

Clinical correlation points us in the right direction, but the clinical mechanism directs us to the best target for diagnostic or therapeutic development. Biomedical informatics is the catalyst for the conversion from correlation to mechanism. Although bioinformatics provides the fundamental knowledge about general biological processes, it is biomedical informatics, with the inclusion of clinical observations, that enables this knowledge to be brought to bear on drug and diagnostic development and, ultimately, clinical practice. Its value cannot be underestimated.

1.1   Evolution of Terminology

A simple Google search indicates incredible activity in the areas discussed thus far, with more than 1,990,000 hits for "personalized medicine" (compared to more than 293,000,000 for "medicine"), more than 1,910,000 for "translational medicine or research," and more than 146,000,000 for "systems biology." This probably reflects the diversity in interpretation and application of these terms rather than deep, focused efforts along specific research tracks. More importantly, these concepts have generally evolved from a focus on technology rather than a focus on clinical need, although their stated goals are directed to both understanding the fundamental science and improving patient care. An ongoing problem that exists within the scientific community is the perception that more data means more knowledge. This reflects an incomplete appreciation of the significant chasm between data and knowledge, and the even greater gap that exists when we evaluate knowledge in terms of clinical utility.

Several operational definitions are used in this book and it is important to understand their context as we examine molecular-based technologies, clinical observations and limitations, and clinical decision making. Whereas it is critical to understand these concepts individually, it is their synergies that will provide the basis for improving patient care and quality of life.

1.1.1   Translational Research

Translational research is focused on the conversion of laboratory results into clinical utility, but to be successful, *translational research must actually start in the clinic and not at the lab bench*. This critical change is necessary because good translational research must begin with the identification, elucidation, and communication of *clinically significant problems* into the laboratory for research and resolution. The only true measure of success of this targeted research is in terms of what translates into the clinic. Although this may seem logical, examples of such true successes are somewhat limited because the driver of much of academic research still focuses on research that may be significant for enhancing our understanding of biology, but does not necessarily transcend into addressing more direct clinical needs [1–5].

Chapter 2 addresses the clinical perspective that is necessary to support this view of translational research, and Chapter 3 discusses the critical aspects of sample and data collection and the quality control issues needed to support clinically based research.

1.1.2 Systems Biology

Systems biology is most commonly interpreted as the aggregation and integration of multiple approaches to analyze and define a system, that is, the "omics" perspective, and then analysis of the behavior of the system based on these perspectives. This bottom-up approach can only bring together those views that are available through the application of existing (and evolving) technologies. It is easy to see that this approach can be limited by the expectation that these technologies will provide a complete picture of the entity being studied rather than multiple views, each with its own contextual limitation. Of course, these technologies are neither comprehensive enough to provide a complete picture of a patient, nor can they necessarily produce data of equivalent quality or content. A more suitable approach to systems biology may involve a top-down approach, first examining the behavior of the intact system (e.g., a patient with or without disease symptoms), to more fully identify the critical question and then determine the technology or technologies most appropriate to addressing these questions. It is clear, however, that all results must be integrated into a comprehensive data model [6, 7]. In the case of biomedical informatics, this model should be patient-centric to enable the exploration of relationships among the multiple views presented by the different technologies. It should be clear that this top-down approach aligns directly with the translational medicine definition given earlier.

Chapter 4 provides a general overview of the range of data in the "omics" fields, as well as issues related to experimental design and implementation. Chapter 5 focuses on issues specifically related to genomic studies, and Chapter 6 presents the proteomic perspective.

1.1.3 Personalized Medicine

Personalized medicine has focused on optimizing treatment to maximize efficacy and minimize risk (i.e., therapeutic medicine), using the genetic makeup of the patient. However, per the Wikipedia website, "Medicine is … concerned with maintaining or restoring human health through the study, diagnosis, treatment and possible prevention of disease and injury." So, ideally, personalized medicine should incorporate and promote a significant component of *preventive* medicine, thus aligning more closely with the non-U.S. clinical perspective in which prevention is a major focus of health care that is frequently based on a single-payer system. More importantly, restricting the approach to only include genetic information may significantly limit its application to clinical practice and its ability to support broader research goals. Within the frameworks of translational research and systems biology as stated earlier, however, personalized medicine can evolve to achieve its broadest goals, the improvement of patient care [8].

The key to developing personalized medicine as previously described involves data tracking, data integration, and data analysis (e.g., visualization and data mining). These specific topics are covered in Chapters 7, 8, and 9. A key element to this integration and analysis involves the development of a patient-centric data model and its potential implementation across both the research and clinical domains.

Some of the challenges facing biomedical informatics include the following:

1. Patient records are not universally available in electronic form.
2. The data is soft data; that is, clinical observations may be qualitative in nature.
3. Quantitative results may require significant detail about the underlying test and reagents used.
4. Medical terminology may be ambiguous across different specialties.
5. Patient confidentiality must be maintained.
6. Patient consent must be obtained to use data in a particular study.
7. Diseases as we know them today are typically composites of multiple subtypes that reflect an individual's genetic makeup and response.
8. Diseases are frequently observed well beyond their initiation, which results in comorbidities and the reduced ability to provide effective treatments.
9. Disease etiologies require synchronization of patient records, which is not currently available for most diseases.
10. Methodologies evolve as do standards of care, practice guidelines, diagnostic procedures, and so forth. Many of these have analogies in the bioinformatics domain.

Chapters 10 and Chapter 11 focus on examples that tie together the components laid out in the earlier chapters. Chapter 10 focuses on the Clinical Breast Care Project (CBCP) as an example of the integration of the clinical and molecular infrastructures to support a broad-based research program ranging from clinical data and tissue collection to molecular characterization and analysis in terms of the translational research model addressed earlier, but in a bottom-up approach.

Chapter 11 focuses on an example of the top-down approach, in which the problems associated with clinical decision making for patient treatment in breast cancer are viewed from the perspective of successes and gaps in our appreciation of the full scope of patient–physician issues. Additional examples of the clinical perspective are presented about stratifying individuals in their transition toward menopause and about examination of disorders in blood coagulation.

Confronted with an emphasis on treatment rather than prevention, these activities have focused on the development of diagnostics and/or therapeutics to directly impact treatment rather than understanding the fundamental aspects of the underlying diseases or the physiological (and psychological) state of the patient. It is readily observed that breast cancer appears/behaves differently in premenopausal versus postmenopausal women. Is this the same disease in a developmentally different host or does it reflect different diseases beyond estrogen receptor (ER) and progestrone receptor (PR) status? Also, statistical evidence relates risk for breast cancer to smoking, alcohol use, and body weight factors.

Are these risks uniform throughout a patient's lifetime? Not likely! For example, the breast undergoes developmental changes continuously during the *in utero* to postmenopause transition (Figure 1.2), and the mechanistic basis for risk is probably related to differences in gene expression, protein expression, protein modification, and so forth that will accompany these developmental changes. Biomedical informatics approaches this problem by analyzing the clinical data epidemiologically to determine what level of exposure at what age may be most critical for establishing risk from one or more of these factors and then combining this with molecular characterization of the underlying physiological changes (Figure 1.3). In this manner, more than a simple correlation between these risk factors and breast disease can be realized because the molecular processes, including upregulation and downregulation of the gene/protein pathway, can be identified; these are potentially mechanistically related to observed risk. This enhances the likelihood for identifying new diagnostics as well as therapeutics and perhaps, more importantly, establishing a more highly refined basis for making lifestyle and environmental choices for the patient and the physician.

The complexity of the underlying biological relationship between patient and disease has not been adequately addressed by translational research, systems biology, or personalized medicine to date and requires refocusing their potential to describe these underlying processes. A fundamental aspect of this complexity is the fact that disease, although frequently described in terms of "disease state," actually represents a process that evolves over time, through a integrative relationship involving the patient's genetics and his interaction with lifestyle and environmental factors, always starting significantly before any symptoms may appear.

Genetic risk + Lifestyle/environment/exposure [$F(t)$] → Disease

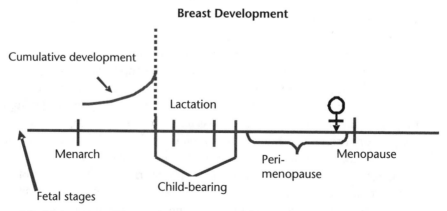

Figure 1.2 Major stages of breast development in a woman's lifetime.

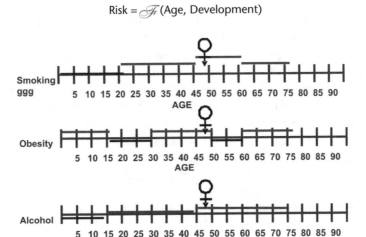

Figure 1.3 Assessment of critical lifestyle risk factors over a patient's lifetime.

The key to tackling this complex relationship comes from the integration of the approaches defined earlier, but the essential requirement is to define separately the characteristics of the patient from those of the disease.

Patients possess intrinsic characteristics, that is, those derived from their genetic makeup and its expression in their underlying physiological structures, and extrinsic factors such as their lifestyle and environmental exposures (e.g., physical activity, smoking behaviors, alcohol consumption). The disease represents a pattern of actions that interact with and are modified by these characteristics. Thus the conundrum is how to identify and separate the extensible definitions of disease from those that are dependent on the patient in terms of intrinsic and extrinsic characteristics. Thus, the presentation of disease exceeds the simple sum of its parts, namely, the patient and the disease process. For biomarkers/diagnostics to be effective in specifying targets or levels for appropriate intervention, it becomes critical to interpret and resolve the complexity of the disease–patient interaction.

To better define the patient, we have been developing a personalized health record (PHR) [9] that spans the life history of the patient and treats the data in a chronological record including, but not limited to, family history (at a genetic analysis level), history of diagnoses/illnesses, treatments and response, and lifetime exposure to environmental and lifestyle risk factors (e.g., smoking, body mass index, alcohol consumption).

A key difference in establishing a personalized health record versus an electronic medical record is that the PHR is temporally focused; that is, it creates a timeline for the patient around all clinical, lifestyle, and environmental parameters, while most electronic medical records (EMR) focus on specific medical incidents. The PHR provides the base to both represent and model temporal data and relate it accurately to the patient. This is critical to understanding the underlying physiological state of a patient, which includes co-occurring disease or treatment, as well as lifestyle and environmental factors, all of which may impact diagnosis, prognosis, and response to treatment.

An essential complement to the PHR in establishing its utility for clinical decision making involves the need to be able to model a patient with respect to both qualitative and quantitative time relationships and for the purpose of identifying critical co-occurrence information about diseases and risks. This enables a physician to both represent the detailed history of a specific patient and to also compare/search the database for other patients with similar patterns of disease for use in evaluating treatment options. The examination of co-occurrence of disease [10] or systemic problems is thus examined from both an epidemiologic perspective as well as a mechanistic perspective, using pathway databases and pathway simulation/reasoning methodologies to support the evaluation of genotypic variation or drug interactions in the patient.

Enhancing the accuracy in defining disease is extremely difficult because of the tendency to group potential disease subtypes under simple classifications, for example, breast cancer. Among the elements critical to more accurately define a disease subtype is the need to identify quantifiable characteristics, such as disease progression or subpathologies, which can readily complement the current trend toward stratification using gene expression technology alone. Utilization of the concepts of disease progression and disease process as noted should be invaluable for measuring and analyzing clinical parameters longitudinally—not just at time of diagnosis. Note that most diagnostics/biomarkers have been developed because of their correlative relationship with a disease diagnosis or state, not because of a quantifiable recognition of their mechanistic relationship to disease symptoms and so forth. Optimally, we need to define disease stratification as the longitudinal path or vector through all clinical parameters that can be observed for a patient and which may occur in multiple dimensions, each one reflecting a clinical observation. The CBCP (see Chapter 10) measures more than 600 clinical parameters and additional molecular descriptors longitudinally; thus, a patient can be algorithmically represented as moving through a 600-dimensional space!

Disease stratification involves identifying the significant clusters of this longitudinal progression, and the concomitant reduction of dimensionality necessary to describe the disease pathway. Disease staging, then, is observation of how far along a disease path a patient has progressed [11], although clinical ambiguities may be present when two patients exhibit similar diagnostic values but are on different disease paths. This can result from the limitations of using a correlative relationship with the biomarker and the fact that these patients may be at different time points along their separate disease paths that overlap in one or more dimensions (clinical parameters). Conversely, two patients may appear "diagnostically" different although they are on the same disease path but have been observed at different disease stages. This dilemma is faced by physicians daily and its resolution relies on the experience and knowledge of the practitioner. To truly develop diagnostics, biomarkers, and the area of personalized medicine, it will be critical to analyze and interpret the longitudinal nature of disease in a more quantifiable manner to reflect its true complexity.

This process of stratification of the patient versus stratification of the disease is not one that is readily solvable with current patterns of patient information/record keeping, sole dependency on genomic information, and so forth, but will require extensive, recursive modeling of the complexity of the relationship that truly defines the patient–disease relationship.

There also must be an evaluation, based on issues of quality of life for the patient and his or her family, access to technology, and cost–benefit analysis of the application, to determine for which diseases and which patients this analysis will become critical. These issues will quickly move beyond the question of access to technology to touch on cultural and ethical boundaries and sensitivities that currently exist. But the reality of personalized medicine and the development of effective diagnostics that truly support improvement of quality of life for the patient must anticipate and deliver on the integration of all of these factors to become truly effective. Biomedical informatics, as outlined in this book, will be an enabler of these changes.

References

[1]   Mathew, J. P., et al., "From Bytes to Bedside: Data Integration and Computational Biology for Translational Cancer Research," *PLoS Comput. Biol.*, Vol. 23, No. 2, February 2007, p. e12.

[2]   Littman, B. H., et al., "What's Next in Translational Medicine?" *Clin. Sci. (Lond.)*, Vol. 112, No. 4, February 2007, pp. 217–227.

[3]   The Translational Research Working Group (NCI/NIH) defines translational research as follows: Translational research transforms scientific discoveries arising from laboratory, clinical, or population studies into clinical applications to reduce cancer incidence, morbidity, and mortality." Available at http://www.cancer.gov/trwg/TRWG-definition-and-TR-continuum.

[4]   Wikipedia. "Translational Medicine."

[5]   Liebman, M. N., "An Engineering Approach to Translation Medicine," *Am. Sci.*, Vol. 93, No. 4, July/August 2005, pp. 296–300.

[6]   Huang, S., and J. Wikswo, "Dimensions of Systems Biology," *Rev. Physiol. Biochem. Pharmacol.*, Vol. 157, 2006, pp. 81–104.

[7]   Liebman, M. N., "Systems Biology: Top-Down or Bottom-Up?" *Bio. IT World*, March 2004.

[8]   Sikora, K., "Personalized Medicine for Cancer: From Molecular Signature to Therapeutic Choice," *Adv. Cancer Res.*, Vol. 96, 2007, pp. 345–369.

[9]   Hu, H., et al., "Biomedical Informatics: Development of a Comprehensive Data Warehouse for Clinical and Genomic Breast Cancer Research," *Pharmacogenomics*, Vol. 5, No. 7, 2004, pp. 933–941.

[10] Maskery, S. M., et al., "Co-Occurrence Analysis for Discovery of Novel Patterns of Breast Cancer Pathology," *IEEE Trans. on Information in Biomedicine*, Vol. 10, No. 3, July 2006, pp. 1–7.

[11] Liebman, M. N., "Information Processing Method for Disease Stratification and Assessment of Disease Progression," European Patent EP1399868.

CHAPTER 2

The Clinical Perspective

Lee Bronfman, Craig D. Shriver, and Emily Gutchell

2.1 Introduction

Biomedical informatics research begins with clinical questions: How can the growth of a tumor be stopped? How do certain diseases metastasize? Is there a less invasive way than surgical biopsy to determine the presence of breast cancer? The questions begin broadly and become very specific: Which women at high risk of developing breast cancer will benefit from the use of tamoxifen and which will not? What is the optimal combination of chemotherapy for a breast cancer that has metastasized to the bones? Why does Herceptin work for some breast cancer patients but not others?

It is within the clinical setting that the need for biomedical research is revealed, and to this setting that the advancements of biomedical research return. No one truly needs to be convinced of the need for clinical research. There is intrinsic agreement that as human beings we have extraordinary needs for quality health care. Although debates ensue regarding how research is conducted, it is rarely debated that research is an essential enterprise and that it should be conducted with the highest level of integrity. A research project that meets the highest standards will begin with a well-devised plan for launching the project from the clinical setting. In the competitive biomedical informatics research environment of today, a successful research project integrates the normal flow of clinical processes with the unique demands of research. Health care clinics conducting biomedical research are likely to be busy, with thousands of patient visits a year. Clinical research staff must accomplish their work within the normal clinic business of the day, which poses many challenges. A biomedical research project that is well integrated at the health care clinic setting exhibits the following qualities:

- Clinicians and clinic staff are well oriented to the goals of the research.
- Clinic staff are well trained in the processes related to the research.
- The actions of leadership support the research mission.
- An organized, well-documented process is followed to obtain a patient's informed consent to participate in research.

- Biospecimens are collected, temporarily stored, transported to, and permanently stored at the biorepository in which they will reside in such a way that the specimen is preserved for optimal immediate and future research.
- Well-designed data management systems serve and support the biomedical informatics platform of the project and are continually well maintained and managed. Clinical research staff managing biomedical information have appropriate, ongoing training in the informatics systems they use. Access to these systems is secure and limited to essential staff.
- Well-defined quality assurance processes are in place to monitor informed consent and the collection, storage, and transmission of all biomedical data collected, including biospecimens.

This chapter discusses important clinical perspectives involved in implementing and maintaining a biomedical research project. Important individual issues within the clinical health care setting are discussed first: ethics, privacy protection, subject consent, and quality assurance. Research protocol development and implementation are discussed later in the chapter. Although this chapter is intended to be useful to all biomedical researchers, it is focused operationally on the U.S. environment of regulation in health care research.

2.2   Ethics in Clinical Research

A basic discussion of ethics in biomedical research begins with two key documents, the Nuremberg Code and the Declaration of Helsinki [1, 2]. The Nuremberg Code was developed in 1947 amid the findings of a Nuremberg military tribunal that addressed the war crimes of a group of Nazi physicians. The Nuremberg Code is a directive of 10 ethical principles of research involving human subjects and is the first official offering of formal guidelines on the subject. Nearly 20 years later, the Declaration of Helsinki was introduced by the World Medical Association and adopted at the 18th World Medical Assembly in Helsinki, in June 1964. Adding to the core principles of the Nuremberg Code, it also outlines basic principles for ethical research. Amendments to the Declaration of Helsinki have been adopted five times between 1975 and 2000. Since then, notes of clarification have additionally been adopted. In themselves, the many revisions to the Declaration of Helsinki reflect the complex challenges of developing a comprehensive code of ethics for human use research. Regulations and guidelines are continually reevaluated for unforeseen gaps as well as the unintended consequences of overregulation exposed by the needs of researchers and human subjects today.

In the United States, it was not until 1974 that federal legislation was adopted to protect human subjects in medical research. The act was called the National Research Act [3]. The legislation charged a commission, the National Commission for Protection of Human Subjects of Biomedical and Behavioral Research, with addressing the need for federal guidelines and mandates to protect human subjects. In 1979 that commission produced the Belmont Report [4]. The Belmont Report is a summary of ethical principles intended to provide national guidelines to all those involved in human subject research. The Belmont Report focuses on three basic ethical concepts in research: respect for persons, beneficence, and justice. Also legislated by the National Research Act was the establishment of institutional review boards (IRBs) for reviewing research involving human subjects. The Department of Health and Human Services (DHHS) Office for Human Research Protections (OHRP) is the oversight body for IRBs in the United States. Federal regulations governing the protection of human subjects, under the statutory authority of the OHRP, can be found in Title 45, Part 46, Subparts A, B, C, and D, of the *Code of Federal Regulations* (CFR) [5]. Subpart A defines basic human subject protections that 15 other departments and agencies within the federal government also adopted. Because the language of Subpart A is identically reproduced in each of their different chapters of the CFR, it is referred to as the Common Rule [6].

Returning to the international scene, another document addressing human subject protections in biomedical research was published in the early 1990s. In an effort to address unique concerns of human subject protections for research conducted in developing countries, the World Health Organization collaborated with the Council for International Organizations of Medical Sciences (CIOMS), to publish the *International Ethical Guidelines for Biomedical Research Involving Human Subjects* in 1993, and again in 2002 [7].

IRBs and institutional ethics committees (IECs) exist to protect the rights and the welfare of human subjects participating in research. These oversight bodies require assurances that staff involved in research are trained in the ethics of human subject protection. Many IRBs require research staff to complete established trainings, usually offered online. References to available trainings in human subject protection can be found later in Section 2.8.2.

2.3   Regulatory Policies for Protecting a Research Subject's Privacy

Regulatory policies for safeguarding the privacy of personal information vary among countries and have an impact on the use of data in research. Privacy policies governing personal data originate from different perspectives, such as banking, e-commerce, business, and health care, in different countries. Regardless, safeguarding the privacy of research subjects is an aspect of ethical practice that is now highly legislated. Researchers in Canada are impacted by the Personal Information Protection and Electronic Document Act [8]; researchers in the European Union, by the European Union Directive on Data Protection [9]. Researchers in the United States must comply with the Health Insurance Portability and Accountability Act (HIPAA) [10].

HIPAA was enacted to address many disparate needs of health care consumers and government agencies such as protecting employee health insurance when workers changed or lost their jobs, reducing waste and fraud, and simplifying administrative processes. One of the many mandates of HIPAA produced the HIPAA Privacy Rule, which requires agencies to protect an individual's health information [11]. The Privacy Rule is administered through DHHS's Office for Civil Rights. Although HIPAA was enacted in 1996, the HIPAA Privacy Rule was implemented in April 2003.

Among the many mandates of the HIPAA Privacy Rule, it sets standards that limit the use and disclosure of protected health information (PHI) for research purposes. The Privacy Rule does not replace or modify the Common Rule or any of the other human subject protections in the CFR. The Privacy Rule works with these other regulations to increase human subject protections. The intent of the HIPAA Privacy Rule is to protect the privacy of individually identifiable health information by establishing conditions for its use and disclosure. All "covered entities" are subject to the HIPAA Privacy Rule. A covered entity is a health care provider, health plan, or health care clearinghouse. Researchers working within or collaboratively with covered entities become bound by provisions of the Privacy Rule as well. Thus, many researchers must obtain written permission from study enrollees, in the form of a HIPAA authorization, before the enrollee's protected health information can be used in research.

An enrollee's PHI is any information that can identify the individual. This includes the following 18 identifiers: names, locations smaller than a state, dates that relate directly to an individual, telephone and fax numbers, e-mail addresses, Social Security numbers, medical record numbers, prescription numbers, health plan beneficiary numbers, other account numbers, certificate/license numbers, vehicle identification numbers, serial numbers, license plate numbers, device identifiers/serial numbers, web URLs and IP addresses, biometric identifiers such as fingerprints and voiceprints, photographic images, and any other unique identifying number or code. Given this exhaustive list and the nature of clinical and demographic data collected for biomedical research projects (such as dates of birth, zip codes, dates of medical diagnostic tests and procedures, and family medical histories), it is likely that the biomedical researcher will need to obtain written HIPAA authorization from research subjects.

For protocols collecting very limited PHI, a researcher may elect to use a limited data set as defined by the Privacy Rule. A limited data set is one in which all of the following identifiers pertaining to the research participant, as well as the participant's relatives, employers, and household members, have been removed from the recorded data: names, addresses (town, city, state, and zip codes are aspects of addresses that may remain in a limited data set), telephone and fax numbers, e-mail addresses, Social Security numbers, medical record numbers, health plan beneficiary numbers, account numbers, certificate/license numbers, vehicle identification numbers, serial numbers, license plate numbers, device identifiers/serial numbers, web URLs and IP addresses, biometric identifiers such as fingerprints and voiceprints, and full-face photographic images and any comparable images.

If using a limited data set, written authorization from the research subject is not required. However, a data use agreement between the covered entity and the researcher is required, ensuring that specific safeguards will be taken with the PHI that remains within the data set. The IRB may require evidence of the data use agreement in the protocol submission or may require a reference to the data use agreement within the informed consent document. Informed consent is covered in the next section.

A final consideration for researchers is to use only de-identified health information, as defined by the Privacy Rule, for which there are no restrictions on use and discloser. There are two ways to de-identify health information:

1. Remove all of 18 unique identifiers (listed earlier) specified by the Privacy Rule, thereby assuring no information can identify the individual.
2. Statistically deidentify information whereby a statistician certifies that there is a very small risk that the information could be used to identify the individual.

In most cases, biomedical informatics researchers will have a need for robust data sets that do include some elements of personally identifiable data, and thus must obtain a HIPAA authorization from research subjects. HIPAA authorization is different from, but may be combined with, the informed consent document. It must be for a specific research study. A single, general HIPAA authorization for all research within an organization is not permitted. It must contain core elements and required statements as mandated by the Privacy Rule. The National Institutes of Health provides user friendly guidance on the core elements and required statements at http://privacyruleandresearch.nih.gov/authorization.asp. Additionally, the requirements are published in the *Code of Federal Regulations*, Title 45, Part 164.508(c) and (d).

The HIPAA authorization does not need to be reviewed by the IRB or privacy board, unless it is combined with the informed consent document, in which case the IRB will review it as part of informed consent. The HIPAA authorization form need not expire, and the fact that it does not must be stated. All research participants must receive a signed copy of their HIPAA authorization.

2.4   Informed Consent

Informed consent must be obtained from every research subject. This is a federal requirement mandated by the CFR, Title 21, Part 50, Section 50.25, and Title 45, Part 46, Section 116. The intent of the regulation is to provide research subjects with all of the necessary information needed to make an informed decision about whether or not to participate in the research. There are many required elements in a consent form. Each is listed within the code noted above. Among them, of key importance to the biomedical researcher are a description of the study's research purposes and procedures, identification of any procedures in the protocol that are considered experimental, a disclosure of alternative treatments that may be of benefit to the patient, the expected duration of a subject's participation, a description of any reasonably foreseeable risks, a statement describing the extent to which confidentiality of records will be maintained, and, where appropriate, a statement of significant new findings that developed during the course of the research, which could impact the subject's willingness to continue to participate. Additionally, patients must be informed about the types of data that will be collected for the research project, how it will be privately and securely stored, and how it will be analyzed.

Many IRBs recommend that consent forms be written at an eighth-grade reading level. This becomes challenging when genomic and proteomic investigations are the goal of the researcher. Mark Hochhauser, Ph.D., is a readability consultant and advocates the use of plain English for consent forms. He recommends including a table of contents in a consent form and following a question and answer format [12].

Microsoft Word offers functions for calculating readability scores for a document. These can be optionally displayed when using the Spelling and Grammar tools. A student's or children's dictionary can also be a useful tool. It is important that the consent form be written in the language that the research subjects use; therefore, more than one language version of the consent form may be necessary.

Be sure to include all of the required elements as outlined in the CFR in your informed consent document. These are likely to be reviewed carefully by the IRB.

An excerpt from the informed consent document used by the Clinical Breast Care Project (CBCP) is shown below. CBCP is a biomedical research collaboration between Walter Reed Army Medical Center in Washington, D.C., and Windber Research Institute in Windber, Pennsylvania. The CBCP seeks to decrease morbidity and mortality from breast cancer and breast disease by providing patients with state-of-the-art clinical care, including advances in risk reduction. The CBCP is also committed to a translational research goal of rapidly translating research findings into clinical practice. The CBCP has a state-of-the-art biospecimen repository to which research subjects contribute blood and tissue samples. Multiple questionnaires containing clinical data are collected on each patient and biospecimens are, thus, extensively annotated. Researchers use the repository to conduct proteomic and genomic research. Clinical data are analyzed in response to proteomic and genomic analysis and findings. Biomedical informatics scientists develop informatics structures and expand the informatics environment on which the research relies for rapid translation into the clinical environment. Given the challenges of adequately describing research with many goals in easy-to-understand language, the section of the informed consent document used by the CBCP that describes the study is two pages long. The following is an excerpt from that section:

> The tissue and blood samples will undergo the primary research studies as described in the next paragraphs.

> This breast tissue can be used for many types of laboratory research looking at cell changes during breast cancer development, identification of risk factors that lead to breast cancer, learning why and how breast cancer spreads to lymph nodes, and breast tissue biology. Some of this type of research on tissue is genetic research. These research studies may include examination of the gene markers of the breast cells or lymph nodes, as well as other parts of the breast cells.

> The primary research uses of the blood and tissue samples are to study the genetic makeup, protein changes, and to look for other research markers that may be associated with breast disease. This information will be analyzed and stored in a computer database using your assigned code number.

> Any remaining blood and tissue samples left over after these studies are done will remain frozen indefinitely until needed for approved research projects. There may be future uses of the remaining frozen samples of your blood that are not known to us at this time. If other research is to be conducted using these samples, this research also will only be conducted after the samples have been stripped of all identifiers. It is not possible at this time to predict all the potential future research uses of the samples. You will be given the opportunity at the end of this consent form

to indicate if you will allow your blood and tissue samples to be used for future unknown breast disease research.

Although not required by the CFR, an important item on a consent form for proteomic and genomic research, and biomedical research in general, is an option to consent for future research. If approved by the IRB, this will allow researchers to conduct proteomic and genomic research in the future without having to obtain a second consent from the subject. Many ethicists and, in fact, most patients prefer this approach to consenting in advance for related, but presently unknown, future research on specimens and data collected now. It avoids a cold call from the research team in what might be years after the patient has successfully completed a course of treatment for the disease and readdressing a difficult time in order to obtain an updated consent; such a call could cause needless emotional turmoil. If the patient should die of his or her disease, and the research team then inadvertently contacts the family, this too could have significant emotional effects on all concerned. Enlightened IRBs, especially those with good patient or layperson representation, understand this important point about allowing the patients to consent now for future unknown research uses of their donated biospecimens and data. For studies that employ future use consenting, a reliable process must be in place that identifies to the appropriate study personnel in a timely manner which participants' data may not be used for future research. In the experience of the CBCP, only about 2% of the participants refuse to consent to future use research.

Obtaining consent from patients for future research uses of their clinical data, including imaging data, as well as their biospecimens could prove pivotal to the success of a biomedical research project in the genomic age.

2.5   Collecting Clinical Data: Developing and Administering Survey Instruments

The array of clinical data collected by a biomedical research project will depend on the goals of the project. Representatives from the clinical setting and the research setting will be involved in determining what information needs to be collected. Some consulting firms specialize in the development of research survey instruments. These firms offer expertise in instrument development, optimal interviewing formats given the characteristics of the instrument, training of staff for standardized administration of the instrument, and data collection and data management services. American Institutes for Research (http://www.air.org/), RTI International (http://www.rti.org/), and RAND Survey Research Group (http://www.rand.org/srg/) are organizations that offer survey development consultation. If a project requires a lower cost solution, companies such as ObjectPlanet (http://www.objectplanet.com/), Apian (http://www.apian.com), and PREZZA Technologies (http://www.prezzatech.com/biz/company/) offer software for designing and implementing surveys.

Many research projects develop their own survey instrument(s). It is helpful to convene a multidisciplinary task force to successfully compile all data elements necessary for the project. Staff with expertise along the continuum of collecting, processing, storing, and analyzing data to be collected should be consulted. These are clinical experts and scientists, business administrators at the organizations involved in the research, research specialists adept at consenting and administering questionnaires to research subjects, information technology (IT) specialists in programming, web services, and database management, and data quality specialists. Each of these knows something helpful about obstacles and solutions for successfully obtaining and securing data at their organization and/or their level of enterprise.

Data acquisition can easily become a lofty goal. The ideal to pursue the most complete and accurate information available should be tempered with an understanding of the realities of data collection. Research participants range in their abilities to give reliable, thorough information. Not all participants can answer an extensive survey in one interview. It is helpful to prioritize essential information needed by the project from nonessential information in keeping a survey from becoming too exhaustive for the participants. Consider other venues such as electronic medical records within the health care informatics system from which data can be drawn, keeping in mind that patients must be informed about and agree to the data being collected about them. The following are example data types collected in the CBCP: family cancer histories, dates of menarche and menopause, hormone replacement therapy use and duration, hormonal birth control use and duration, pregnancy and birth histories, intake of tobacco, alcohol, fat, caffeine, and underarm cosmetic use and duration. Additionally, diagnosis and treatment data are collected, such as mammogram dates and findings, ultrasound dates and findings, CT scans, x-rays, bone scans, PET scans, MRI, chemotherapy, radiation therapy, hormonal and endocrine adjuvant therapies, pathologic diagnoses from biopsies, lumpectomies, mastectomies, and so forth.

The method by which the survey instrument will be administered must be chosen. Although there are many ways to administer a research questionnaire (mail, Internet, telephone, computer, chart abstraction, focus groups, and so on), the personal, one-on-one interview conducted by qualified and trained staff may yield the highest quality data. Once the content of the instrument has been established, the reliability of the responses it generates depends on the instrument being administered the same way to every respondent. This reliability is achieved by standardizing administration across interviewers [American Institutes for Research, personal communication, January 2004].

To standardize administration across interviewers, training is required. Providing staff with professional training on administering the survey will clarify difficult or confusing questions, establish trust between interviewer and interviewee, empower research staff to confidently administer the survey, and result in better data collection. It may allow for a longer, more extensive survey instrument to be reliably completed by minimizing the questionnaire fatigue that patients experience when filling out lengthy research tools.

2.6 Issues Important to Biomedical Informatics

2.6.1 Data Tracking and Centralization

A biomedical informatics study collects many data for multiple purposes. Demographic data on participants are essential for managing the demands of daily research in the health care clinic. A data tracking system is needed to keep track of all such data. Different types of data need to be tracked in different ways. For example, data of a PHI nature, such as names, addresses, phone numbers, medical record numbers, and dates of birth, are often elements that should be readily available to clinic staff but blinded to researchers (with some exceptions such as date of birth that are allowed in the "limited data set" defined in Section 2.3.). Non-PHI data, such as dates and results of diagnostic tests, procedural interventions and outcomes, medical therapies and outcomes, personal medical histories, social histories, family histories of certain illnesses, stress levels, caffeine intake, x-ray images, ultrasound images, tissue and blood biospecimens, should all be properly tracked (refer to Chapter 7), and ideally are all subsequently centralized into a database of a data warehouse nature (refer to Chapter 8), to enable researchers to analyze them synergistically as much as possible. The data and findings generated by research scientists in bench practice comprise another data domain that should be integrated with the whole to allow comprehensive data analysis.

A clinical data tracking system needs to cover many aspects of clinical data and biospecimen collection issues. The system not only needs to track normal clinical data collection, specimen annotations, and lab values and test results, but also needs to properly handle possible erroneous events such as an illegible value, an incorrectly transcribed value, a misunderstood survey question, a preliminary report finding differing from the final report finding, a clinical lab system temporarily not available, and a missing specimen—these are all examples of the need for checks and balances in the processes of data collection, data entry, data quality control, and data transmission, storage, and reporting. Well-executed data management processes that provide effective stewardship at each step along the way contribute to an essential and solid foundation for the research project. A more comprehensive discussion of clinical data tracking is provided in Chapter 7.

The clinical team at the health care facility is responsible for the initial collection of most biomedical data gathered on the patient. Staff members, often research nurses with clinical expertise, administer the survey(s) or questionnaire(s) associated with the research, and collect further medical information such as lab values and test results. Once collected, either the same staff, or different staff manage the tasks of quality review and data entry of what can be multiple data instruments. After data entry is complete, another round of quality review/quality control tasks should be implemented to ensure the data have been entered accurately and thoroughly.

2.6.2   Deidentifying Data

Questionnaires, medical images such as mammograms and ultrasound images, and biospecimens will need to be deidentified to the extent stated on the informed consent and HIPAA authorizations. Yet, these data must also be tracked in an organized fashion for proper data management. A research-specific ID number—not the subject's Social Security number or hospital number or other personal identifier—needs to identify all biospecimens and data collected for each enrolling individual. The project must plan for how a research subject's ID number will be assigned, where and how the connection between the assigned ID number and the subject's name will be stored, and who, besides the principal investigator, will have access to this information.

To this end, a database containing the patient's demographic information that is needed by clinic staff, as well as the patient's unique, research-specific ID number must be maintained in a secure way. Access to it should be password protected and available to essential staff only. Documents containing both the patient's name and unique research ID number should be used and viewed only by essential staff in the clinic. Paper files requiring storage that link the participant's name with his or her research-specific ID number should be locked and viewed only by essential staff. Such files should be shredded when disposal becomes necessary. All data that will be entered into the biomedical informatics platforms, and analyzed for research purposes must contain the research-specific ID number of the patient, and must not contain other patient identifiers such as names or medical record numbers, assuming this level of deidentification has been promised to the patient within the informed consent. Thus, the researchers conducting research analysis will see only a research ID for the patient, but those clinical research staff who need the information will have access to both the patient's name and research ID number.

Biospecimens and questionnaires require a tracking barcode or unique identifier of their own. That identifier links to the research subject's specific ID number and also links to the date these data are collected. This becomes essential when multiple surveys, images, and biospecimens from one research subject are collected throughout the lifetime of the project. One participant may have five yearly mammograms on file in the biomedical informatics repository. Each mammogram needs to be identified as belonging to that unique patient (research-specific ID number), and each needs to be identified as a unique data element of its own, associated with the date it was obtained (e.g., a unique barcode ID number that maps back to the research-specific ID number and the date the mammogram was obtained).

2.6.3 Quality Assurance

The clinical team will need to communicate closely with the data management staff that receive and review the questionnaires, biospecimens, and other clinical data such as mammograms and ultrasound images. It is vital to have open communication channels for resolving discrepancies, as well as electronic data tracking tools for making changes to data collected. Neither medical charting, nor the processes of retrieving medical and social histories from patients are 100% reliable.

The process of obtaining as accurate and complete a data record as possible from a patient can require much back and forth between data collectors and data reviewers, depending on the volume of patients participating in the research study, the volume of data collected, and the precision with which data is collected. For example, a research nurse may record that a mammogram was completed on a patient the same day she completed a research questionnaire, but forgets to include the actual mammogram result on the questionnaire. The research staff conducting the quality review of the questionnaire identifies the missing value and must communicate with the research nurse to obtain it.

At the CBCP, the Windber Research Institute developed a user-friendly online data tracking tool that streamlines the process of identifying, communicating, and resolving discrepancies in clinical data collected. The tool is called the Quality Assurance Issue Tracking System (QAIT) [13]. There are thousands of enrollees in the CBCP so far, and the project collects many hundreds of data elements from each enrollee. Without precise methods for correcting errors, the project would lose vital data strength and compromise its ability to conduct excellent research. The QAIT provides secure online communication between the data entry technicians and the quality specialists who review all the questionnaires for completeness and accuracy before data are entered. The process is straightforward. When an issue requires clarification or correction based on standard operating procedures, it is entered into the QAIT by a data entry technician. A quality reviewer then opens that issue in the QAIT, via secure online access, and assesses what needs to be done to resolve the issue. This may require verifying information in a medical record or verifying information through the research nurse who initially collected it. When the quality reviewer successfully resolves the issue, the resolution is entered into the QAIT. That issue is then closed by a data entry technician. The steps, dates, and times along the way are recorded electronically by the QAIT. At any given moment, the current stage of the issue's progress is easily identified by the users. When the issue is resolved, the data entry technician enters the correct value into the clinical data tracking system CLWS, which is described in more detail in Chapter 7.

These processes are the standard operating procedures for quality checks and balances using the QAIT, before ultimate data entry into the CLWS. Once data are entered, further quality checks are applied in the form of a computer program called QA Metrics, which implements hundreds of established quality assurance (QA) rules to flag discordant data, given their relationship to each other. In addition to data problem resolution, the QAIT provides reports that enable management to better supervise, train, and track proficiency of staff involved in the data collection and quality assurance processes. Figure 2.1 depicts a list of issues that require clarification and/or correction by users of the QAIT.

2.6.4   Data Transfer from the Health Care Clinic to the Research Setting

The biomedical information collected within the clinical setting must become available to the research specialists and scientists who will use and analyze the information. This may involve manual and/or electronic transfer of information. It may be a matter of entry into the data tracking systems and repositories that are on site or a matter of shipping to sites where the data and specimen management systems are located. Regardless, quality control practices that ensure the integrity of clinical data and biological specimens during transfer are of paramount importance.

Quality control methods for transferring biological specimens to the repository are covered in Chapter 3. As previously discussed, all clinical data should undergo quality review before being cleared for data entry. The data entry processes themselves should also have a quality oversight component. If the data tracking system is one whereby data entry occurs directly, such as a survey administered electronically on the Internet, with no opportunity for quality review before data entry, it is necessary for quality control procedures to begin at the point after which the data is entered, but before it is analyzed by the researchers.

WRI Shared Resources

Jun 4, 2007 – Monday
provided by Biomedical Informatics Group

Home | (C)LWS QA | My Profile | Log out

Emily Gutchell

- Core QA
- questionnaires
- report
- search
- QA summary
- recent issue/FU
- help

Display setting: ok
0. All >
Active all >

Number	Barcode	CBCP Number	Questionnaire Date	Last QA Date	Version	Status
1. [+]	00006BFP	100000146	04/12/2007	05/29/2007	Follow-up (04/14/2003)	Data Entry
2. [+]	000029W6	000200134	04/04/2007	05/29/2007	Follow-up (04/14/2003)	Data Entry
3. [+]	00006S1P	000000592	04/03/2007	05/25/2007	Follow-up (04/14/2003)	Data Entry
4. [+]	00006KBG	000000100	04/03/2007	05/25/2007	Follow-up (04/14/2003)	Data Entry
5. [+]	00006S1N	100000707	04/02/2007	06/04/2007	Follow-up (04/14/2003)	Ready for QA [Claim for QA]
6. [+]	00006BD7	000400014	02/20/2007	06/01/2007	Follow-up (04/14/2003)	Ready for QA [Claim for QA]
7. [+]	00006BC2	100001126	01/29/2007	06/01/2007	Core questionnaire (04/14/2003)	Ready for QA [Claim for QA]
8. [+]	00006BDV	100000357	01/22/2007	05/30/2007	Follow-up (04/14/2003)	Data Entry
9. [+]	00006BBT	100001128	01/09/2007	05/31/2007	Core questionnaire (04/14/2003)	QA: Ismail Del (no pending issue)
10. [+]	00006BD6	000400006	12/08/2006	06/01/2007	Follow-up (04/14/2003)	Ready for QA [Claim for QA]
11. [+]	00006BD8	000400021	08/28/2006	06/01/2007	Follow-up (04/14/2003)	Ready for QA [Claim for QA]

Figure 2.1 The list of current issues being generated in the QAIT online tool used by the Clinical Breast Care Project. Notice the status column. Issues that are ready for a quality specialist to respond to are marked "Ready for QA." Issues that are still being formulated by a data entry technician are marked "Data Entry." Issues that have been resolved by a quality specialist are marked "QA: (no pending issue)" along with the quality specialist's name.

The challenge of the quality review process is to ensure that the clinical data collected are as accurate and complete as possible. An organized data management system such as the QAIT tool described earlier, which tracks corrections and changes to data, is invaluable for maintaining integrity when processing clinical data. Coordination of the quality review takes continual involvement and oversight. A standard operating procedure that details the quality control process that clinical data undergo may be essential for projects that collect many clinical data elements.

2.7   Standard Operating Procedures

Written policies and procedures can greatly assist in ensuring standardized adherence to regulations, guidelines, local policies, and institutional directives. Standard operating procedures (SOPs) provide staff with easy-to-locate guidance. They should be living documents that are developed, shared with appropriate staff, reviewed, and revised periodically. The format of SOPs should be standardized. Staff can then rely on the existence of SOPs within a familiar format that is easy to find within the clinic and/or research setting.

Each SOP should be titled with the subject or standard it addresses. It should then state why the organization has this standard and who must comply with it. Finally, the steps of the procedure should be clearly delineated. A biomedical research project will require an SOP for the collection, storage, and shipping of biospecimens. Also important is an SOP for gaining informed consent from patients. It is also useful to have an SOP for receiving, reviewing, and entering questionnaire data. Figure 2.2 shows the table of contents for a SOP that delineates how the core questionnaire from the CBCP is processed after it has been administered to a research participant.

SOPs define the scope of practice for an individual or a program. They provide guidelines for new members of the team. They document roles and responsibilities for the research team, and they set the standards of good practice for the operation of the research project. It is worthwhile to keep these benefits in mind when faced with how time consuming it is to write useful SOPs and the fact that they must be periodically reviewed and updated to reflect changes. Make every effort to write SOPs that can be, and are, enforced in practice. Deviations from them may not be viewed kindly by an auditor.

2.8   Developing and Implementing a Research Protocol

The research protocol must be developed and submitted to the IRB affiliated with the organization where the research will be conducted, and must be approved prior to the beginning of any research. As previously discussed, IRBs exist to ensure that research conducted within the organization is well designed and without undue risk to participants, and that human subjects are protected from unethical practices. Augmented by implications of the genomic era, as well as regulatory mandates to protect personal health information, protecting privacy has also become an important concern to IRBs. The specific requirements for writing and submitting a

Contents

1	Purpose	4
2	Scope	4
3	Roles	4
3.1	WRI	4
3.2	Walter Reed Army Medical Center	4
4	Data Entry and QA Procedures at WRI	4
4.1	Receiving Questionnaires	4
4.2	Data Entry and QA	5
4.3	Data Entry Completion Time	5
4.4	Applying QA Matrix to Reconciled Data	5
5	QA Procedure at WRAMC	6
5.1	Procedure for Receiving and Logging Questionnaires at WRAMC	6
6	Quality Control	7
6.1	QA Record	7
6.2	Hard Copy Monitor	7
6.3	Completed QA Criteria	7
6.4	Questionnaire Maintenance and Use Procedure	7
7	Patient withdrawal	7
7.1	Questionnaires	7
7.2	Tissue Repository	7
8	Date Entry Rules for Core and Follow up Questionnaires	8
8.1	General Rules	8

Figure 2.2 Table of contents for a SOP used in the Clinical Breast Care Project to standardize the way research questionnaires are processed.

research protocol to an IRB are unique to any given organization, yet because the goals of an IRB are the same everywhere, the required elements of a protocol are fairly consistent. Organizations such as the U.S. Food and Drug Administration (http://www.fda.gov/oc/gcp/guidance.html#guidance), the Office for Human Research Protections (http://www.hhs.gov/ohrp/education/#activities), the National Institutes of Health (http://clinicalcenter.nih.gov/researchers/training/ippcr.shtml), and the Society of Clinical Research Associates (http://www.socra.org) offer courses and educational material on developing clinical research protocols. Reed and Jones-Wells [14] suggest that a protocol can be thought of as a blueprint for what is to be done, how it is to be done, and who is to assume ultimate responsibility for it. In an effective protocol, these three basic questions of what, how, and who are fully addressed.

2.8.1 Developing a Research Protocol

The cover page of a protocol includes the title of the study; the name, title, and contact information of the principal investigator, associate investigators, or collaborators; and, if required, medical monitor information. Figure 2.3 shows a sample cover page for a protocol.

The *principal investigator* (PI)is the individual primarily responsible for the actual execution of the clinical investigation. He or she is responsible for the conduct of the study, obtaining the consent of research subjects, providing necessary reports,

1. __PROTOCOL TITLE:__ Tissue and blood repository for molecular, biochemical and histologic study of breast disease

2. __PRINCIPAL INVESTIGATOR:__
> [Name of Principal Investigator]
> [Title of Principal Investigator]
> Phone:
> Fax:
> Email:

3. __ASSOCIATE INVESTIGATORS:__
> [Name of Associate Investigator 1]
> [Title of Associate Investigator 1]
> Phone:
> Fax:
> Email:

> [Name of Associate Investigator 2]
> [Title of Associate Investigator 2]
> Phone:
> Fax:
> Email:

> [Name of Associate Investigator 3]
> [Title of Associate Investigator 3]
> Phone:
> Fax:
> Email:

4. __COLLABORATING PERSONNEL:__
> [Name of Collaborating Personnel 1]
> [Title of Collaborating Personnel 1]
> [Address of Collaborating Personnel 1]
> Phone:
> Email:

Responsibility: Carry out successful receipt of de-identified donor specimens transferred to the research and tissue banking facility, and to manage and oversee the scientific experiments and handling of results of all studies involving the said specimens at said facility.

> [Name of Collaborating Personnel 2]
> [Title of Collaborating Personnel 2]
> [Address of Collaborating Personnel 2]
> Phone:
> Email:

Responsibility: Act as onsite Principal Investigator at the collaborating clinical center for the tissue and blood repository and high-throughput research initiatives as described in this protocol.

5. __MEDICAL MONITOR__: Minimal risk study, medical monitor not required.

Figure 2.3 Sample cover page of a protocol to study breast disease by collecting biological specimens from research subjects at two different clinical sites, and storing and analyzing the specimens at a research facility.

and maintaining study documents. Some or all of these responsibilities can be, should be, and often are delegated to other trained professionals with the requisite expertise, under the supervision of the PI. The PI is usually affiliated with the institution where the research is to be conducted; if that is not the case, however, an administrative point of contact will be identified.

Associate investigators are other key personnel involved in the governance of the study who are affiliated with the sponsoring institution. For the example of a protocol to study breast disease, these may be a breast surgeon, a pathologist, a medical oncologist, a radiation oncologist, a radiologist, and so forth.

Collaborating personnel are all other key personnel involved in the governance of the study that come from outside the sponsoring institution. In the example, the collaborating personnel identified could be the vice president of the research facility where the biorepository is located, and the breast surgeon consenting patients to the protocol at the second site.

A medical monitor is a physician who monitors the study from a medical safety perspective and is not involved in any way with the research study. When a study is assessed to pose greater than minimal risk to its subjects, a medical monitor will likely be necessary. The responsibilities of a medical monitor include:

1. Periodic review of research files, medical records, and so on;
2. Review of annual progress reports, adverse events, protocol deviations;
3. The ability to terminate the study or participation in the study if there is concern about the welfare of enrolled subjects.

Many research studies only pose minimal risk to participants and may not require a medical monitor. Minimal risk to human subject participants is defined within the CFR: "Minimal risk means that the probability and magnitude of harm or discomfort anticipated in the research are not greater in and of themselves than those ordinarily encountered in daily life or during the performance of routine physical or psychological examinations or tests" [15].

The body of a research protocol should be composed of the following sections, or variations thereof:

Objectives

The objectives of the protocol are stated, including the research hypothesis if any. Research objectives should be consistent with the Plan and Data Analysis sections. The medical application or medical importance and usefulness of the results of the study are often cited in the objectives.

Background and Significance

The Background and Significance section of a protocol is necessary to justify the need for the project and explain the rationale. It includes a summary of relevant literature. Making this section easy to understand, especially to those outside of the specialty of the study, is important.

Plan and Data Analysis

The protocol's plan is comprised of many subsections that together delineate the broad scope of processes and methodologies that will be implemented by the protocol. Each subsection must be addressed briefly. This assures the IRB that the plan for implementing the protocol has been thoroughly conceived. The subsections include, but may not be limited to:

- Study design;
- Recruitment methods, with inclusion and exclusion criteria for subject participation;
- An estimate of the sample size planned for the study;
- Anticipated start date and expected completion date of the study;
- Data collection practices, including types of data collected as well as practices for ensuring patient confidentiality, including processes for handling PHI as defined by HIPAA;
- Data analysis practices, that is, a general description of how the data collected will be analyzed and by whom.

When a study includes the collection and storage of human biological specimens, additional information will be required. Such information will include but may not be limited to:

- Obtaining informed consent for future use of specimens and clinical data;
- Specimen collection procedures;
- Specimen shipping procedures;
- Specimen storage procedures;
- Specimen confidentiality, and how it will be maintained;
- Who will have access to specimens;
- Length of time specimens will be stored;
- Withdrawal and destruction of specimens.

The research office associated with the IRB that will approve your protocol may have valuable guidelines and/or standard formats for submitting the plan, as well as other sections of the protocol.

References
Include a section of references that have been cited in the protocol.

Budget
The budget for the research project is submitted with the protocol. Individual IRBs usually provide their own specific, required budget formats.

Attachments Relevant to the Research
The IRB will require copies of documents to be used in conducting the research such as consent forms, questionnaires/survey instruments, brochures describing the research, and marketing material. If additional, collaborative protocols or grant proposals are affiliated with the project, these will be required by the IRB.

Developing a protocol is a time-consuming, labor-intensive undertaking. There will be many drafts, revisions, and consultations with associate investigators before a final document is submitted to an IRB. Once the review process begins with the IRB, correspondence and communication will require additional clarification and revision before a final version is approved. Although all IRBs must adhere to the Common Rule, individual IRBs may function quite differently from one another. It behooves the principal investigator and study coordinator to become familiar with the requirements of their IRB. Attention to detail in this phase of research will prove beneficial as the study is conducted.

After the IRB has granted initial approval of a research protocol, a yearly, continuing review will be required. The IRB will provide the format for what is called a Continuing Review application. This is likely to include a progress report of the number of enrollees during the past year, as well as the duration of the study, changes in such things as survey instruments, consent forms, or any changes to the protocol's activities that require approval from an IRB. If any significant events requiring regulatory reporting have occurred, the original report to the IRB of the event is included in the progress report.

2.8.2 Implementing the Research Protocol

Once the protocol, consent form, questionnaire/survey instrument(s), and HIPAA authorization have been approved by the IRB, and the biomedical informatics systems and repositories are functioning to receive data and specimens, a planned implementation of the research protocol can take place. Clinical staff responsible for specimen acquisition need training in exactly how specimens will be obtained, transported within the clinic, stored temporarily, and shipped to the repository. Team planning and "dry runs" for every aspect of the acquisition process, but with no actual specimen, should be considered. This will help ensure that the first batch of biological specimens sent to the repository location will not be compromised due to unforeseen problems. Similar "dry runs" should be done with subject enrollment and clinical data management.

All staff responsible for obtaining informed consent, administering survey instruments to subjects, and conducting quality oversight on the biomedical information collected will need to be thoroughly knowledgeable about the protocol and proficient in their respective specialties. Completion of a live or online course in the protection of human subjects is recommended for all staff directly involved in the research and is required by many IRBs. Courses may be offered through professional organizations such as the Society of Clinical Research Associates [16]. The Office for Human Research Protections and the National Cancer Institute offer free web-based resources for human subjects training [17, 18]. Information about international codes and ethics for human subject protections is also covered by these sources. The Collaborative IRB Training Initiative (CITI), out of the University of Miami, provides a comprehensive selection of educational modules for biomedical and social and behavioral researchers. Continuing education modules are also offered as a refresher to ensure that the research staff remains competent in the area of Human Subject Protection [19]. Staff responsible for consenting subjects to the protocol, as well as completing the questionnaire/survey instrument, should be encouraged to keep track of any issues or problems experienced with the consent form or the survey instrument. Staff meetings are a good forum to discuss "best practices" in administration of the instrument and consenting of subjects. Also discuss any questions frequently asked by subjects to help determine which questions on the survey may need special attention and clarification. This will augment reliability and standardization of both the administration of the survey instrument and the obtaining of informed consent. A successful biomedical informatics research initiative will include a solid orientation and continuing education programs for staff.

2.9 Summary

In summary, preparing the documents and the processes for ensuring a well-run protocol is a time-consuming endeavor that requires collaboration from many experts. The administration of the protocol must be planned, the formal protocol written, and the informed consent and HIPAA authorization documents written. A survey instrument must be developed. Approval from the IRB of the organization(s) conducting research must be obtained. All staff participating in research activities must be trained for their unique roles in the study as well as in research ethics, including the protection of human subjects. Data management systems for ensuring integrity and confidentiality of biospecimens and clinical data must be developed, implemented, and continually managed. Quality oversight and ongoing staff education must be conducted with regularity. Biospecimens and clinical data must be successfully transferred from the clinic setting to the setting in which the scientific research will be carried forward.

References

[1] "The Nuremberg Code," available at http://www.hhs.gov/ohrp/references/nurcode.htm.

[2] World Medical Association, http://www.wma.net/e/policy/b3.htm.

[3] U.S. Congress, House of Representatives, Bill H.R. 7724, Public Law 93-348, July 12, 1974.

[4] "The Belmont Report," available at http://www.hhs.gov/ohrp/humansubjects/guidance/belmont.htm.

[5] U.S. Department of Health and Human Services, http://www.hhs.gov/ohrp/humansubjects/guidance/45cfr46.htm.

[6] U.S. Department of Health and Human Services, http://www.hhs.gov/ohrp/45CFRpt46faq.html.

[7] Council for International Organizations of Medical Sciences (CIOMS), http://www.cioms.ch/frame_guidelines_nov_2002.htm.

[8] "The Personal Information Protection and Electronic Document Act," available at http://www.privcom.gc.ca/legislation/02_06_01_e.asp.

[9] "Eur-Lex, Directive 95/46/EC of the European Parliament and of the Council of 24 October 1995 on the Protection of Individuals with Regard to the Processing of Personal Data and on the Free Movement of Such Data," available at http://eur-lex.europa.eu/LexUriServ/LexUriServ.do?uri=CELEX:31995L0046:EN:HTML.

[10] "Public Law 104-191," available at http://aspe.hhs.gov/admnsimp/pl104191.htm.

[11] "Summary of the HIPAA Privacy Rule," available at http://www.hhs.gov/ocr/privacysummary.pdf.

[12] Hochhauser, M., "Informed Consent Reading, Understanding and Plain English," SoCRA Source, Issue 42, November 2004, pp. 24–26.

[13] Zhang, Y., et al., "QAIT: A Quality Assurance Issue Tracking Tool to Facilitate the Enhancement of Clinical Data Quality" (submitted for publication).

[14] Reed, E., and A. Jones-Wells, "Writing a Clinical Protocol: The Mechanics," in *Principles and Practice of Clinical Research*, J. I. Gallin (Ed.), San Diego, CA: Academic Press, 2002, p. 439.

[15] *Code of Federal Regulations*, Title 45 Public Welfare; Subtitle A; Department of Health and Human Services, Part 46, Subsection 46.102.

[16] Society of Clinical Research Associates, http://www.socra.org.

[17] U.S. Department of Health and Human Services, Office for Human Research Protections, http://www.hhs.gov/ohrp/education/#materials.

[18] "National Cancer Institute, Human Participant Protections Education for Research Teams," available at http://cme.cancer.gov/clinicaltrials/learning/humanparticipant-protections.asp.

[19] "CITI Collaborative Institutional Training Initiative," available at http://www.citiprogram.org.

CHAPTER 3

Tissue Banking: Collection, Processing, and Pathologic Characterization of Biospecimens for Research

Jeffrey Hooke, Leigh Fantacone, and Craig Shriver

This chapter provides an overview of tissue banking practices and is intended to serve as a guide that can be adapted, as appropriate, to the mission and scientific needs of individual biospecimen resources. Details about laboratory methods and procedures can be found elsewhere [1]. The principles set forth in this discussion are based on a model developed by the Clinical Breast Care Project (CBCP), a joint breast cancer research project between Walter Reed Army Medical Center and Windber Research Institute that was established in 2001. Although the focus of the CBCP is breast disease, the principles described herein can be applied, with only slight modifications, to other organ systems as well.

3.1 Introduction

3.1.1 A Biorepository's Mandate

In today's era of high-throughput genomic and proteomic research, there is a demand for high-quality and well-annotated tissue. Unfortunately, human specimens when available are often unsuitable for genomic and proteomics research because of the type of preservation method (i.e., formalin-fixed paraffin-embedded tissue instead of frozen tissue) and the absence of supporting clinical and demographic data. Although emerging technologies for retrieval of ribonucleic acid (RNA) and protein from formalin-fixed paraffin-embedded (FFPE) tissue may permit the use of these samples for genomics and proteomics research, the lack of uniform tissue acquisition procedures and standardized protocols for specimen handling may limit the usefulness of many biologic specimens and preclude comparisons of research results obtained at different institutions. Finally, the type of informed consent obtained from many biorepositories is not sufficiently robust to allow the unrestricted use of these specimens for long-term follow-up.

The goal of a biorepository is to increase the quantity and variety of high-quality samples. All types of biospecimens (diseased and nondiseased tissue, blood and its various components, bone marrow, and so on) are potentially useful for research, and great care must be exercised to ensure that they are handled in a manner that will not compromise their value. The discussion that follows outlines the components required for establishing and managing a successful biorepository in today's high-throughput world of translational genomics and proteomics research.

3.1.2   Overview of Current Tissue Banking Practices

Human tissue repositories have existed in the United States in one form or another for more than 100 years. These repositories are located at a variety of sites including the Armed Forces Institute of Pathology (AFIP), the National Institutes of Health (NIH) and its sponsored facilities, other federal agencies, diagnostic pathology laboratories, academic institutions, hospital-based research laboratories, commercial institutions, and nonprofit organizations. These tissue collections are diverse, ranging from large multisite operations to informal collections in a researcher's freezer [2].

The National Pathology Repository, located at the AFIP, is perhaps the largest collection of pathology material in the world, housing more than 50 million tissue-mounted slides and 30 million paraffin-embedded tissue blocks [3]. The tissue repositories supported by the NIH are smaller than those of the AFIP, but the NIH is the largest funding source for tissue repositories. For example, the National Cancer Institute (NCI), a component of the NIH and the federal government's principal agency for cancer research, supports a variety of research initiatives including the Cooperative Human Tissue Network (CHTN) [4], the Clinical Trial Cooperative Group Human Tissue Resources [5], and the Specialized Programs of Research Excellence (SPOREs) [6]. Collectively, the tissue repositories of university- and hospital-based laboratories represent the oldest and largest collection of tissue specimens in the United States, with some paraffin-embedded tissue blocks dating back more than a century [2].

In many countries, government-sponsored biorepository initiatives have been established, particularly in recent years, to help understand and manage the health care needs of their people. The Swedish National Biobanking Program is a nationwide collaboration that was created to "increase the quality, usefulness, efficiency, and accessibility of Swedish biobanks for health-related research as well as for clinical care and treatment" [7]. The Swedish program has at least 10 unique biobanks, with a total collection estimated between 50 and 100 million samples [8]. Similar projects exist in Canada, Norway, and the United Kingdom. The UK Biobank, started in 2007, is a large, long-term study in the United Kingdom, which is investigating the contributions of genetic and environmental exposures to the development of disease. The biobank plans to collect blood and urine samples, along with extensive clinical and demographic data, from 500,000 volunteers ages 40 to 69. These patients will be followed for 25 years [9].

One of the best known private industry endeavors is led by deCode Genetics in Iceland. Created in 1996, deCode has created a bank of genetic samples from 100,000 volunteers. Its mission is to identify human genes associated with common diseases using population studies and to apply the knowledge gained to guide drug discovery and development. So far, the company has isolated genes believed to be involved in cardiovascular disease and cancer [10].

3.2   Consenting and Clinical Data Acquisition

Whereas biospecimens used by basic researchers may require only limited clinical information, biospecimens collected for translational research (e.g., target identification or validation) require more in-depth associated clinical data, such as medical and family histories, treatment, and clinical outcomes data. All data collected must be entered into the repository's biomedical informatics system, where it can be integrated with data from the genomics and proteomics research platforms. Uniform, approved protocols must be used to enroll donors and obtain biospecimens. Donor consent and authorization to utilize blood and tissue samples is typically done by dedicated personnel such as nurse case managers and research nurses, who have received appropriate training in the consenting process and in the rules and regulations governing the use of human subjects in research, and can act on behalf of the principal investigator in the consenting process. The study coordinators must describe the study to the patient, obtain consent, and, whenever possible, complete the study-specific questionnaire with the donor.

Potential participants should be given information related to the kinds of biospecimens that may be taken and the kinds of studies the samples will be used for. Note that in a clinical setting potential participants for tissue and blood donation typically present with an imaged or palpable lesion that needs further evaluation. As a result, disease-negative patients cannot be prospectively enrolled as control subjects. Should tissue samples be collected from a patient with no pathologic findings, the samples can be used as controls. The consent for the collection and utilization of specimens should be explicit and separate from the routine surgical consent. Donors should be given ample opportunity to ask questions and to decline participation if they choose. At every stage, personnel should make the potential donors feel comfortable and emphasize that their confidentiality and health care needs are not compromised. Once all clinical data have been collected, they must be entered into the repository's biomedical informatics system. Procedures for ensuring accurate data entry are crucial. Accurate data entry is accomplished by using standardized terminology and forms. Automated techniques to flag discrepancies and track errors and reconciliation also help to ensure the integrity of the information being collected. The consenting process and issues related to it were discussed in greater detail in Chapter 2.

3.3   Blood Collection, Processing, and Storage

Peripheral blood is an attractive sample source for biomedical research because a minimally invasive procedure is all that is required to collect a sample (i.e., a simple blood stick versus a tissue biopsy). The spectrum of genetic and physiological events associated with tumors and other diseased states can be potential targets for molecular detection in the blood of patients. The analysis of blood RNA, for example, holds promise for noninvasive gene expression profiling, and the discovery of tumor-derived deoxyribonucleic acid (DNA) in the plasma of cancer patients has provided an alternative method for cancer detection, monitoring, and prognosis [11, 12].

Blood samples should be collected as early in the diagnosis as possible. Samples collected in vivo (while cancerous tissue is still present within the body) are best for these molecular studies. In particular, blood samples taken prior to biopsy are ideal since tissue has not yet been manipulated and the circulating blood has not been subjected to medical agents and physiological responses associated with surgical procedures. The amount of blood that is drawn from a patient and the types of collection tubes that are required depend on the specific objectives of a researcher. In each case, it is imperative that the entire process from sample collection to analysis be standardized so that reliable and reproducible results are achieved. Nurses, phlebotomists, and laboratory personnel play critical roles in this process.

In contrast to DNA and protein—both of which are relatively stable in blood preparations—RNA is unstable in vitro and poses unique technical challenges. Enabling technologies such as quantitative reverse transcriptase polymerase reaction (RT-PCR) and microarrays require high-quality, highly purified RNA samples. Preparing such samples is difficult due to the presence of endogenous RNAs that easily degrade the RNA and to the induced expression of certain genes after the blood is drawn. Both RNA degradation and in vitro gene induction can lead to an underestimation or overestimation of gene transcript number. Fortunately, techniques such as the PAXgene Blood RNA System (QIAGEN Inc.) now exist that allow for the isolation, stabilization, and purification of cell-associated blood RNA. This technology has allowed even isolated laboratories that lack RNA-handling expertise to venture into the arena of gene expression profiling.

For biorepositories involved in cancer research, two or three tubes of blood may be required; however, the actual amount of blood that is drawn should be limited to meet the objectives of the particular study. Three blood tubes in common usage are the serum tube (BD Vacutainer with red closure), the plasma tube (BD Vacutainer with green closure), and the PAXgene RNA tube. For genomic and proteomic-based applications, the tubes are utilized as follows:

- *Serum tube:* Fractionated into serum and clot. Serum used for analysis of blood proteins. Clot used for a variety of downstream DNA analyses.
- *Plasma tube:* Fractionated into plasma and cell fraction. Plasma used for analysis of blood proteins and identification of plasma-associated DNA. Cell fraction used for cell-associated DNA studies.
- *PAXgene RNA tube:* Used exclusively for the isolation and stabilization of RNA.

Both the serum and plasma tubes are fractionated into their components using a centrifuge, the components aliquotted into cryovials, and then placed into a −80°C mechanical freezer. The PAXgene tube is incubated at room temperature for at least 2 hr (overnight is best) to allow complete lysis of blood cells, before processing or freezing. At all times standard operating procedures must be adhered to. For blood collection, the standard procedure is to fill collection tubes in a set order (serum, plasma, RNA), followed by inversion of the tubes to allow proper mixing with the reagent in each tube (serum tube: clot activator; plasma tube: sodium heparin; PAXgene RNA tube: RNA stabilizing reagent). In the case of the PAXgene RNA tube, failure to completely fill the PAXgene tube or failure to invert the tube following collection may result in inadequate RNA yield [13]. Standard procedures for processing blood samples should detail the appropriate supplies to be used, centrifugation speed and times, aliquot volumes, storage temperatures, and shipping specifications (Figure 3.1). A bar-coding system to track the samples from the time of collection through the time of storage and utilization is advantageous. The frozen blood samples can be maintained on site in a −80°C freezer or transported via overnight service (e.g., FedEx or private courier) to another site in a carefully packaged container containing dry ice. Standardized and carefully monitored shipping procedures should be integrated with a biorepository's informatics system whenever possible.

3.4   Tissue Collection, Processing, Archiving, and Annotation

3.4.1   Tissue Collection

Most existing biorepositories collect tissue from patients undergoing surgery or other diagnostic procedure. A typical scenario for tissue collection is as follows: Prospective patients are counseled and informed consent is obtained for tissue sam-

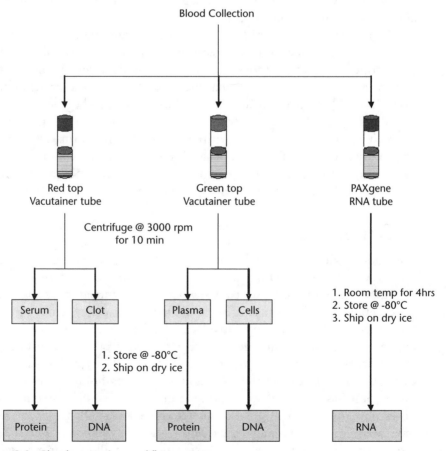

Figure 3.1   Blood processing workflow.

ple archiving and experimental use. A research nurse or other trained repository personnel monitors the operating room (OR) schedule to determine when the patient's surgery is going to occur from which tissue will be collected. The surgeon removes the tissue according to whatever surgical procedure is indicated, and the tissue is sent to the pathology laboratory. Once in the laboratory, the pathologist or pathologist assistant examines the tissue and takes what is necessary for patient diagnosis and determines what portion of the specimen is in excess and can be released to the repository. The portion of the specimen intended for the repository is immediately given to trained repository personnel who begin processing the specimen for preservation and storage.

As with blood, RNA in tissue is susceptible to ischemia-induced injury and can rapidly degrade once it is removed from the patient. Therefore, it is important that the tissue be placed in a plastic bag, which is then placed in a container of slush ice and rapidly transported to the laboratory for processing. If multiple tissue samples (e.g., tumor and suspicious lymph nodes) are obtained, it is unacceptable to batch the specimens—each tissue sample must be taken to the pathology laboratory as soon as it is removed. For quality assurance purposes, the warm ischemia interval (the time period based on when a tissue sample is removed from a patient to the time of cryopreservation) should be carefully monitored. Because tissue-banking activities often deviate from the routine day-to-day activities of an OR, it is useful to engage in active dialogue with the surgical team and to provide frequent in-services about tissue handling procedures.

To protect patient confidentiality and to comply with federal patient privacy regulations, all clinical samples collected for research should be deidentified. Deidentified samples are those that have had all identifiers or codes removed such that the ability to identify particular individuals, via clinical or demographic information, would be extremely difficult for the researcher. The deidentification process starts first with the patient, who should be assigned a unique patient-specific research number, and continues with the data collection forms and clinical samples. Deidentification is readily accomplished by a scannable barcode system, which links each sample to a particular patient and tracks the specimens and associated information throughout their lifetime in the repository.

3.4.2 Tissue Processing

The prioritization of patient diagnosis over collection of specimens for research purposes is vital to ensuring that patient care is not compromised. As such, it is imperative that the surgically excised specimen be examined by a pathologist. It is unacceptable practice for a surgeon to aid in the process by removing a portion of a tumor or other lesion intraoperatively, as the disruption of the specimen may hamper pathologic assessment of lesion size, margins, or other diagnostically important characteristics. Once the sample arrives in the laboratory, the pathologist examines the specimen in the fresh state, records all relevant pathologic information, and inks the specimen as appropriate to assess margins. Tissue is harvested for research purposes only after the pathologist has determined that all diagnostic requirements have been satisfied. If removing tissue for research will compromise the diagnostic integrity of the specimen (e.g., the lesion is very small or near a surgical margin), then tissue archiving must be avoided and the specimen processed entirely for histologic evaluation.

In addition to lesional tissue (e.g., tumor), it is good practice to harvest adjacent grossly normal tissue as well. In all cases, a mirror image section of the harvested tissue should be obtained and processed for microscopic examination so that the tissue composition of the research sample can be verified. This is particularly important for heterogeneous tissues such as the breast. For example, a single 4-micrometer-thick tissue section of breast may harbor a variety of pathologic processes, such as fibrocystic changes, microcalcifications, and intraductal hyperplasia, in addition to the targeted lesion (i.e., tumor) (Figure 3.2). Additionally, even grossly normal breast tissue may contain important pathologic lesions that are detected only by careful microscopic examination. Diagnostically important lesions of the breast that are often invisible to the naked eye include lobular carcinoma in situ, ductal carcinoma in situ, and even some invasive lesions, particularly invasive lobular carcinoma. For these reasons, it is critical that every tissue sample harvested—cancerous or normal—be characterized microscopically.

3.4.3   Tissue Archiving and Storage

There are several obstacles to high-throughput molecular analyses of tissue samples, beginning with the types of fixation and embedding. For most diagnostic laboratories, tissue specimens are processed using formaldehyde-based (e.g., formalin) fixation, which provides excellent preservation of tissue morphology. Although well suited for diagnostic pathology laboratories, formaldehyde fixation induces extensive protein and nucleic acid cross-linking and makes recovery of biomolecules tenuous at best. These samples are not satisfactory for high-through-

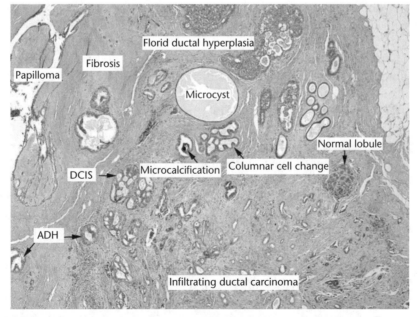

Figure 3.2   Tissue heterogeneity. A multitude of pathologic processes are present in this single microscopic field from a hematoxylin and eosin (H&E)–stained slide of breast (4× objective; approximate field width: 5.5 mm). DCIS: ductal carcinoma in situ, ADH: atypical ductal hyperplasia.

put expression methodologies such as cDNA microarrays or two-dimensional polyacrylamide gel electrophoresis (2D-PAGE). Therefore, a crucial need exists for processing methodologies that produce good histologic detail and also allow recovery of mRNA and protein of sufficient quantity and quality for molecular profiling studies. Currently the best tissue preservation method that fulfills this requirement is OCT embedding, followed by rapid freezing. OCT (Optimal Cutting Temperature compound; Tissue-Tek) is a cryosolidifiable compound used commonly in pathology laboratories. A tissue sample selected for research is placed in a plastic cryomold and topped with OCT; the entire apparatus is allowed to rapidly freeze on dry ice or in a liquid medium such as cooled isopentane or liquid nitrogen. Tissue sections are then cut in a cryostat and mounted onto special slides. This approach not only retains tissue morphology, but allows investigators to perform high-throughput molecular analyses on all of the various biomolecules in a sample.

As previously discussed, breast tissue is heterogeneous. A single section of tissue can contain multiple cell types, including invasive carcinoma cells, preinvasive intraductal carcinoma cells, benign ductal epithelial cells, myoepithelial cells, leukocytes, fat cells, endothelial cells, and connective tissue fibroblasts. Laser microdissection is a relatively new technology that allows cells of interest to be isolated from a tissue-mounted slide, thus creating a pure cell population. Molecular studies can then be performed, reducing contamination by bystander cells and producing more reliable results [14]. OCT-embedded tissue is especially well adapted to this technique because it allows the tissue to be sectioned directly on a microtome and provides good histologic detail.

At our institution stock tissue is created by freezing excess tissue directly in liquid nitrogen. These flash frozen specimens can be converted into OCT sections if required or can be utilized for studies that do not require histologic analysis (e.g., measurement of exogenous chemicals).

Although not well suited for molecular profiling studies, formalin fixed paraffin embedded tissue represents a valuable and vast resource. FFPE tissue is useful for a variety of applications including the targeting of proteins, RNA, and DNA by means of immunohistochemistry, in situ hybridization, and fluorescence in situ hybridization (FISH), respectively. A specific application of FFPE tissue is the analysis of allelic imbalance/loss of heterozygosity (AI/LOH) in tumors. Also, because of the excellent tissue morphology, FFPE tissue can be utilized for laser microdissection to analyze selected populations of cells.

Utilization of paraffin blocks for research depends on various factors such as storage guidelines issued by regulatory agencies, medicolegal issues, and database management. Clinically acquired FFPE tissue is usually stored for 10 years as mandated by the College of American Pathologists (CAP). Many pathology groups discard the blocks after that time. To prevent this loss, many repositories are now archiving and utilizing these discarded blocks for research. With approval by an institutional review board (IRB), it is also possible to utilize FFPE tissue that is within that 10-year period providing the diagnostic integrity of the tissue block is not adversely affected by the research process.

With regard to storage, there is no consensus on the optimal storage condition. Storage for frozen specimens (OCT-embedded or snap frozen) ranges from −80°C in mechanical freezers to −190°C in the vapor phase of liquid nitrogen. Storage at lower temperatures (i.e., −190°C) may help preserve the molecular integrity of the specimens for long-term storage. FFPE tissue blocks and tissue microarrays should be stored under conditions that protect them from extremes of temperature or other damage (e.g., humidity). Many biorepositories use barcoded inventory systems to track specimen location. Establishing SOPs for biospecimen storage and using a barcoding inventory system ensure that specimens are stored appropriately and are accessible for distribution when necessary.

Once specimens are placed into storage, it is necessary to monitor storage conditions and to maintain equipment in good working order. Most repositories utilize a monitored central alarm system, have electric backup or liquid nitrogen backup, and maintain extra freezers to allow for quick transfer of specimens in the event of equipment failure. Professional periodic maintenance is recommended. Finally, periodic checks on stored biospecimens (e.g., testing RNA integrity) help to ensure the quality and integrity of the samples distributed to researchers.

When shipping frozen tissue samples, the same principles that were described for transporting blood apply. It is especially important that the frozen samples be packed in sufficient dry ice to cover the specimen vials and that an overnight courier service be used if possible to prevent thawing damage. Standardized shipping procedures that are integrated with the repository's bioinformatics system aid in tracking all shipments. Biospecimens sent to the repository from satellite sites and samples sent from the repository to researchers can be efficiently tracked using a barcoded inventory system.

3.4.4 Pathologic Characterization of Tissue Samples

For each tissue sample entered into a repository, a base set of pathologic data is required. Pathologic annotation of specimens should ideally include site of origin (e.g., breast), primary diagnosis (e.g., infiltrating ductal carcinoma), secondary descriptors (e.g., well differentiated), pathologic stage, additional diagnostic studies (e.g., estrogen and progesterone receptor analysis), and associated histopathologic findings (e.g., fibrocystic changes, intraductal hyperplasia, microcalcifications). Although many repositories rely on blinded surgical pathology reports to gather this information, a data collection form with common data elements and standardized terminology is preferred. Additionally, central review of H&E-stained slides when available ensures accurate, consistent pathologic data, eliminates problems associated with interobserver variability, and provides a valuable tool for oversight of the quality of the tissue samples collected.

The amount of pathology information that is collected by a repository depends on the specific needs of the repository and on the level of support provided by pathologists. At the Clinical Breast Care Project, a federally funded military–civilian collaboration based at Walter Reed Army Medical Center, each case—benign or malignant—undergoes extensive histopathologic evaluation by the CBCP-dedicated pathologist. All diagnostic slides (H&E sections, immunohistochemical stains) are reviewed, including the matched H&E sections that are mirror images of the submitted research samples. The relevant information is recorded on a standardized 12-page data collection form, followed by entry of the data into the repository's bioinformatics system. The data collection form has a unique identifying number linked to the patient and details surgical and pathologic data as described below:

1. A procedure summary that includes a list of all surgical procedures and respective dates.
2. A summary of all pathologic diagnoses including inflammatory/reactive lesions, benign lesions, papillary lesions, biphasic tumors, hyperplasias, in situ carcinomas, invasive carcinomas, and metastases. The current CBCP ,master list includes 130 diagnoses (Figure 3.3).
3. Expanded sections for recording details of atypical lesions, in situ carcinoma, and invasive carcinoma.

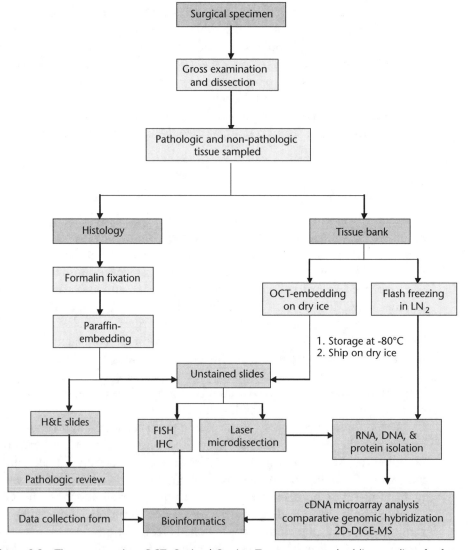

Figure 3.3 Tissue processing. OCT, Optimal Cutting Temperature embedding medium for frozen tissue specimens; LN$_2$, liquid nitrogen; H&E, hematoxylin and eosin; FISH, fluorescence in situ hybridization; IHC, immunohistochemistry; LCM, laser capture microdissection; 2D-DIGE-MS, two-dimensional difference in-gel electrophoresis and mass spectrometry.

4. A summary of results from ancillary studies (e.g., ER, PR, HER-2/*neu*).
5. A summary of lymph node involvement, including size of metastatic deposits.
6. Sections for recording distant metastasis and American Joint Committee on Cancer (AJCC) pathologic stage.
7. A sample attribute form for recording characteristics of research samples, including preservation method, location of lesion, warm ischemia time, diagnosis, and so forth.

A schematic representation of tissue processing, archiving, and annotation is illustrated in Figure 3.3. As with blood collection and processing, standard operating procedures must be strictly adhered to during this process. Diagnostic requirements must be met before research tissue is harvested; therefore, standard procedures should require that tissue samples be kept on site for a specified time before transport to another site or use for research. The tissue will then be available for recovery and paraffin embedding should it be needed for further diagnostic evaluation. To minimize specimen contamination separate blades should be used for sectioning tumor and benign tissue samples; separate ink bottles and single use cotton tipped applicators should be used for inking margins. Effective standard operating procedures also reduce ischemia time and eliminate interobserver variability in histologic evaluation and recording of pathologic data.

3.5 Conclusion

In summary, research biorepositories represent the critical element in any successful translational clinical/research program. Without access to well-defined, carefully collected, properly consented human biospecimens, the field of research will be forever limited to inadequate cell lines and mouse models, and the promise of robust biomedical informatics programs and capabilities will never be fully realized. Attention to detail at all levels of biospecimen acquisition will result in a treasured resource of outstanding quality that meets all federal requirements for consenting and research.

References

[1]   Snell, L., and P. Watson, "Breast Tissue Banking: Collection, Handling, Storage, and Release of Tissue for Breast Cancer Research," in *Breast Cancer Research Protocols*, Totowa, NJ: Humana Press, 2006, pp. 3–24.

[2]   Eiseman, E., and S. B. Haga, *Handbook of Human Tissue Resources: A National Resource of Human Tissue Sample,* Santa Monica, CA: The RAND Corporation, MR-954-OSTP, 1999.

[3]   "National Pathology Repository," available at http://www.afip.org/Departments/repository/npr.html.

[4]   Cooperative Human Tissue Network, http://www-chtn.ims.nci.nih.gov.

[5]   "NCI Specimen Resource Locator," available at http://cancer.gov/specimens.

[6]   "Specialized Programs of Research Excellence (SPOREs)," available at http://spores.nci.
       nih.gov.

[7]   "The Swedish National Banking Program," available at http://www.biobanks.se/docu-
       ments/RapportBiobanksprogrammet.pdf.

[8]   "Biobanks: Accelerating Molecular Medicine Challenges Facing the Global Biobanking
       Community," available at http://www-03.ibm.com/industries/healthcare/doc/content/bin/
       Biobanks_Accelerating_Molecular_Medicine.pdf.

[9]   UK Biobank, http://www.ukbiobank.ac.uk.

[10] deCode Genetics, http://www.decode.com.

[11] Garcia, J.M., et al., "Extracellular Tumor DNA in Plasma and Overall Survival in Breast
       Cancer Patients," *Genes Chromosomes Cancer*, Vol. 45, July 2006, pp. 692–701.

[12] Huang, Z. H., L. H. Li, and D. Hua, "Quantitative Analysis of Plasma Circulating DNA at
       Diagnosis and During Follow-Up of Breast Cancer Patients," *Cancer Lett.*, Vol. 243,
       November 8, 2006, pp. 64–70.

[13] "PAXgene Blood RNA Kit Handbook 06/2005," available at http://www.preanalytix.com.

[14] Lehmann, U., and H. Kreipe, "Laser-Assisted Microdissection and Isolation of DNA and
       RNA," in *Breast Cancer Research Protocols*, Totowa, NJ: Humana Press, 2006, p. 66.

Biological Perspective

Richard J. Mural

CHAPTER 4

This chapter is designed to give the reader a very basic understanding of some of the biological and biochemical principles behind the technologies that generate much of the data that are used in the high-throughput biology, "omics," which forms the experimental side of translational research. Readers with an information technology background should find this chapter and some of its references useful in forming a better appreciation of the basics of the science that generate these data. An attempt will also be made to point out types of data that may have technical issues or that might easily be overinterpreted. Readers with a strong background in molecular biology can skip this chapter and proceed to the next chapter.

4.1 Background for "Omics" Technologies

The goal of translational research is to move the findings of basic research into the clinical setting where they can have an impact on the standard of care, increase the efficiency and efficacy of care, and improve patient outcomes. Frequently this involves trying to improve the identification of the disease state (diagnostics) and the prediction of the course of disease (prognostics) or the response to therapy (including limiting adverse responses) for an individual using various "omics" technologies.

Modern high-throughput molecular biology, often referred to as "omics" as in genomics, proteomics, transcriptomics, and so forth, is based on a number of technological developments in molecular biology and biochemistry that have occurred during the past 30 years. To understand the data that are generated by these methods and put these data into context, the following section provides a primer on some of the basic principles of modern molecular biology. (A number of excellent texts exist for students at all levels including [1]. Those interested in more details and a deeper understanding of this material are referred to such texts.)

4.2   Basic Biology and Definitions

4.2.1   A Historical Perspective

The discoveries in the basic biological sciences that enabled the development of translational research in biomedicine were all made during the last 100 to 150 years. The elucidation of the basic laws of inheritance was worked out by the Austrian monk Gregor Mendel in the 1860s. (Accounts of Mendel's discoveries and his rules can be found in a variety of basic textbooks. One can also find translations of Mendel's original work online at http://www.esp.org.) One of the ironies in the history of biological sciences is that Mendel's work had no impact on the development of biology in the 19th century. It was not until the turn of the 20th century, after independent rediscovery of Mendel's work by three different scientists [2–4], that the science of modern genetics really began. The history of the early years of genetics has been related in numerous accounts and texts [5].

Though tremendous progress was made in both the practical and theoretical aspects of the field, it took 50 years to establish the physical basis of heredity. By the mid 1940s the work of Avery, McLeod, and McCarty [6] had established that DNA was the molecule that encoded genetic information, and the determination of the structure of DNA by Watson and Crick in the early 1950s [7] led to the explosive growth of molecular biology. At a time when millions of genetic variants can be mapped to the human genome in a matter of weeks, it is interesting to note that when Watson and Crick worked out the structure of DNA in 1953, not a single human gene had been mapped and the number of human chromosomes was not accurately known. Fifty years after the discovery of the double helix, the "complete" sequence of the human genome was determined.

Clearly, our understanding of disease, its variability in different individuals, and the variation in response to drugs and other therapies that is seen among individuals as well as finding diagnostic and prognostic markers for disease are powerfully driven by genetics and our understanding of the biology of DNA.

4.2.2   Biological Processes

In a biological sense, it is information that is passed between the generations. In reality, information is the only thing passed between generations. A 100-ton blue whale starts life as a single cell, weighing less than a milligram, that is the fusion of a sperm cell from its father and an egg cell from its mother, which together create a full set of genetic information for a blue whale. This is that only material transferred between the generations and it is the information contained in the DNA that engages the developmental program that leads to the creation of a new individual.

The fact that genetic information is written as a code, totally analogous to computer codes (although for DNA and RNA it is base 4 rather than binary), has led many to propose that biology is, in fact, an information science. Although this is true, the functioning of organisms, biological machines, also requires manipulations and transformations of matter (physics and chemistry) and the capture, transformation, and storage of energy.

There are some basic transactions that are needed to support life and that, therefore, must be properties of molecules that are the physical basis of life. The genetic material must be able to make an accurate copy of itself, for example, in a process called replication. Based on the evidence and its physical properties, DNA not only qualifies for, but clearly is the molecule that stores and transmits genetic information. Its structure even suggests how replication can be accomplished as Watson and Crick point out, as a poignant afterthought, in their Nobel Prize–winning publication [7].

DNA can be thought of as an archive of information and as such it does not participate actively in the production of cellular components. Instead, DNA is copied through the process of transcription into RNA, which transfers the information stored in the DNA to the primary structure (amino acid sequence) of proteins. One of the primary ways in which genetic information is converted into biological activity is through the translation of the information copied from the DNA to RNA into the order of amino acids that make up a protein (polypeptide). This basic informational and biochemical transformation is referred to as the central dogma of molecular biology that "DNA makes RNA makes protein." As with many dogmas, numerous exceptions have been found to this rule, but in general it is true to say that in biological systems information flows from DNA to RNA to protein.

Some other terms in common usage in both popular and scientific discourse regarding translational research merit brief definition and clarification.

4.2.3   Some Definitions

Gene. In the last 100 years or so, the concept of a gene has undergone an evolution from a purely theoretical construct to a more or less well-defined sequence of bases in a DNA molecule. The definition of a gene has changed many times over the years, and there is still no completely accepted common definition [8]. Conceptually, the gene is the basic functional unit of inheritance. That said, a gene may ultimately encode one or more proteins or a functional RNA molecule. The coding region of a gene may span only a few hundred bases or it could extend for more than a million bases. There are also sequences in the DNA, some near the coding portion of the gene, but others that may be tens of thousands of bases away that control the expression of the gene; that is, when and how much the gene is transcribed. These complexities make it difficult, if not impossible, to point to the precise beginning and end of a gene. This problem is more than an academic exercise because how a particular sequence is assigned to a gene is fundamental to the interpretation of data generated by many of the technologies used in high-throughput biology such as microarrays. Part of the difficulty in comparing gene expression data generated on different platforms comes from differences in assigning sequences to genes.

Genotype and *phenotype.* Two other concepts that are important to understanding and interpreting the data used in translational research are *genotype* and *phenotype.* These concepts are intertwined and often confused. They are also confounded with other concepts such as complex traits and the debate about the relative importance of genetics and environment. The term *phenotype* refers to the observed state of a trait, or traits, of interest. Simple examples are features such as hair or eye color. Other phenotypes include blood type, variation in measurable biochemical function of any given enzyme, or a complex series of features such as those associated with Down syndrome.

The term *genotype* refers to the state of the gene or group of genes that influence the trait(s) of interest. Genes can vary in many ways from individual to individual. Gross alternations can include deletion or duplication; in the case of Down syndrome, for instance, an entire chromosome (HSA21, human chromosome 21) can be duplicated, which can have major phenotypic consequences. Many of the gross alterations of the genome are not compatible with life and the phenotype of such a genotype is early embryonic death.

Changes in the DNA sequence of genes are another source of genotypic variation that may or may not affect the phenotype of the individual harboring such a variant. Single nucleotide polymorphisms (SNPs) are positions (bases) in the genomic DNA that may vary between individuals. The frequency of the variant alleles, the particular base at the variant position on the given chromosome, can vary greatly in different populations. Most of these variants have no detectable phenotype and are referred to as silent, but some can cause a change in the information encoded in a gene. Such polymorphisms are usually referred to as *mutations* if they cause a change in phenotype. In the simple case where a polymorphism exists as one of two alternative bases, two alleles, the chromosome harboring the variation can have one of two genotypes.

Though the phenotype is a function of genotype it is also influenced by the environment. Individuals with the genetic disorder phenylketonuria (PKU) are unable to properly metabolize the essential amino acid phenylalanine [9]. This can have serious consequences including mental retardation. The treatment is to limit phenylalanine in the diet, that is, to change the environment. Thus, an individual with the genotype that leads to a deficiency in an enzyme that metabolizes phenylalanine can have a severe phenotype in an environment rich in phenylalanine, but be essentially normal in an environment with reduced phenylalanine.

4.3 Very Basic Biochemistry

4.3.1 DNA

DNA is a double-stranded polymer built up of four nucleotides (bases): adenine (A), thymine (T), guanine (G), and cytosine (C). Each of these consists of a nitrogenous base either a purine (A and G) or a pyrimidine (C and T). Each of these is attached to a five-carbon sugar, deoxyribose, which forms the backbone of each strand through a phosphate linkage between the sugars of each nucleotide.

Critical to the ability of DNA to replicate itself and thus transmit genetic information between cellular and organismal generations are the rules by which bases in one strand pair with bases on the other strand. The bases in each strand, which are on the interior of the double helix, are hydrogen bonded to one another, and the stereochemistry of these hydrogen bonds dictates that A always pairs with T and G always pairs with C. Thus, if one knows the sequence of bases in one strand, then one can determine the sequence of the other strand. To write down the complement of a strand with the sequence AACGTGCGGA, one can write:

A-T
A-T

C-G
G-C
T-A
G-C
C-G
G-C
G-C
A-T

Note also that the individual strands of the DNA polymer have polarity; that is, they have a chemically distinguishable directionality. In addition, the polarity of one strand is opposite to the other:

5′ A-T 3′
A-T
C-G
G-C
T-A
G-C
C-G
G-C
G-C
3′ A-T 5′

This directionality is indicated by the labeling of the ends as 5′ or 3′. (These correspond to positions on the 5 carbon ring of the deoxyribose sugar, the details of which can be found in any basic biochemistry text.) By convention, sequences are written from left to right in the 5′ to 3′ direction. The two strands that we have been discussing would be written in text as 5′-AACGTGCGGA-3′ and 5′-TCCGCACGTT-3′. (*Note:* Although sequences are written out in the text following this convention, the labels 5′ and 3′ are usually dropped.)

In the laboratory DNA is water soluble and quite stable. Because most enzymes that degrade DNA have an absolute requirement for divalent cations, magnesium (Mg^{2+}) or manganese (Mn^{2+}), most buffers for storing DNA contain chelating agents such as ethyldiamine tetraacetic acid (EDTA). These buffers are also mildly basic because DNA is somewhat acid labile and has improved solubility in basic solution.

4.3.2 RNA

The linear sequence of bases in the DNA encodes the majority of the genetic (i.e., heritable) information in the cell. The best understood biological code is the genetic code, which specifies the sequence of amino acids in proteins. This code converts the sequence of bases in the DNA into the sequence of amino acids in proteins. DNA is copied to RNA by the process of transcription. As will be discussed later, control of transcription is a key cellular regulatory process. RNA is the molecule that is the substrate for translation, the process by which the genetic code is translated into protein. In eukaryotes, that is, organisms whose cells have membrane-bound nuclei, the RNA that is translated into protein, referred to as messenger RNA (mRNA),

DNA Sequencing

The technology behind the most widely used method for DNA sequencing was developed by Frederick Sanger in 1975 [15] and for this work he shared the 1980 Nobel Prize in chemistry (his second). Broadly, this method is referred to as *sequencing by synthesis* and involves modifying the *in vitro* DNA synthesis reaction so that the products yield information about the sequence of the DNA template being copied. By adding modified dNTPs (dideoxy dATP, dideoxy dTTP, dideoxy dCTP, and dideoxy dGTP) that stop the elongation of the newly synthesized DNA strand when they are incorporated (chain termination) into the strand DNA synthesis mix, the products consist of a series of DNA strands each terminating at one of the modified bases.

These products can be resolved by electrophoresis, and because the terminating base can be labeled with a fluorescent dye, the DNA sequence of the newly synthesized strand can be read directly from the gel. For example, if the newly synthesized strand contained the subsequence AGTCGA, the shortest product seen on the gel would end in an A, and being labeled with the dye corresponding to ddATP could be identified by its corresponding color; the next would end in a G, with its color; the next with a T; and so forth. Thus, the sequence is directly read. This process has been highly automated and a modern DNA sequencing instrument can generate nearly a million bases of DNA sequence per day. Next generation instruments are being developed—some using modifications of sequencing by synthesis, others using totally different technologies—that will increase the output by orders of magnitude.

From an informatics perspective, DNA sequence data presents a number of challenges in large part in just managing and presenting the data. The volume of data, both the raw data that must be generated to determine the sequence of an individual and the final sequence that might be used for a "personalized" approach to medicine, is very large. The diploid (that is, from both sets of chromosomes) DNA sequence of an average person contains about 6 billion bases. When individual DNA sequences become cheap enough to be part of a standard personal medical record, the data handling problem will be very large. The sequence data for 100,000,000 people would be 10^{17} bases and could require petabytes of storage. Realizing the potential of DNA sequencing in personalized medicine and translational research will remain a challenge for the foreseeable future.

undergoes extensive processing before it is transported into the cytoplasm where it undergoes translation.

RNA is a single-stranded polymer built up of four nucleotides (bases): adenine (A), uracil (U), guanine (G), and cytosine (C). Each of these consists of a nitrogenous base of either a purine (A and G) or a pyrimidine (C and U). RNA is very similar to DNA with the exception that the pyrimidine uracil is substituted for thymine. Each of these is attached to a five-carbon sugar, ribose, which forms the backbone of the strand through a phosphate linkage between the sugars of each nucleotide.

The genetic code, which was cracked in the 1960s [10], is read three bases at a time so it is a triplet code. DNA and RNA are each made up of four types of bases, which if read three bases at a time yield 64 (4^3) triplet combinations. Each of these triplet combinations is referred to as a *codon*. Naturally occurring proteins are made up of 20 amino acids, thus there are more available codons, 64, than there are amino acids to code for. A number of amino acids are encoded by more that one codon. In fact, 61 codons specify the 20 naturally occurring amino acids and the 3 remaining codons are used as punctuation; that is, they signal "stop" to the machinery of protein synthesis (Table 4.1). These termination codons, UAA, UAG, and UGA (TAA, TGA, and TAG in DNA), signal stop to the translation machinery. A detailed description of protein synthesis, a process that involves several hundred macromolecules (RNAs, proteins, nucleotides, and so forth), is beyond the scope of this chapter and the reader is referred to a molecular biology text [1].

In addition to its role as the "messenger" in the translation of the genetic code into protein, RNA is involved in a number of important cellular functions both structural and catalytic. RNA has roles in the process of RNA splicing and in several other important processes that regulate gene expression. Recently, a number of small RNAs have been discovered that play an important part in gene regulation. A number of large RNA transcripts that do not appear to encode protein have also been discovered, but their role is not yet known [11].

Compared to DNA, RNA is a very liable molecule. Ribonucleases (RNAases) are ubiquitous and very stable enzymes that require no cofactors. Because of this, the isolation of intact RNA is technically challenging. Many of the new technologies that are at the foundation of translational biomedical research depend on measurement of (quantitation of) RNA, and the quality of these data can be compromised by the problems of dealing with RNA. This is an important caution to anyone trying to interpret these data.

Table 4.1   Codon Table

First Position	Second Position U		C		A		G		Third Position	
	UUU	Phe	UCU	Ser	UAU	Tyr	UGU	Cys	U	
U	UUC		UCC		UAC		UGC		C	U = Uracil
	UUA	Leu	UCA		UAA	Stop	UGA	Stop	A	C = Cytosine
	UUG		UCG		UAG		UGG	Trp	G	A = Adenine
	CUU		CCU	Pro	CAU	His	CGU	Arg	U	G = Guanine
C	CUC		CCC		CAC		CGC		C	
	CUA		CCA		CAA	Gln	CGA		A	Phe (F) = Phenylalanine
	CUG		CCG		CAG		CGG		G	Leu (L) = Lecine
	AUU	Ile	ACU	Thr	AAU	Asn	AGU	Ser	U	Ile (I) = Isoleucine
A	AUC		ACC		AAC		AGC		C	Met (M) = Methionine
	AUA		ACA		AAA	Lys	AGA	Arg	A	Val (V) = Valine
	AUG	Met	ACG		AAG		AGG		G	Ser (S) = Serine
	GUU	Val	GCU	Ala	GAU	Asp	GGU	Gly	U	Pro (P) = Proline
G	GUC		GCC		GAC		GGC		C	Thr (T) = Threonine
	GUA		GCA		GAA	Glu	GGA		A	Ala (A) = Alanine
	GUG		GCG		GAG		GGG		G	Tyr (Y) = Tyrosine

His (H) = Histidine
Gln (Q) = Glutamine
Asn (N) = Asparigine
Lys (K) = Lysine
Asp (D) = Aspartic acid
Glu (E) = Glutamic acid
Cys (C) = Cysteine
Trp (W) = Tryptophane
Arg (R) = Arginine
Gly (G) = Glycine

Polymerase Chain Reaction

One of the critical enabling technologies that has fueled the revolution in biomedical science is the polymerase chain reaction (PCR) for which Kary Mullis won the 1993 Nobel Prize in chemistry [13]. This process allows the exponential amplification of DNA (or RNA). This makes it practical to detect and characterize DNA and RNA sequences that exist at very low concentration (in theory a single copy) in any biological sample.

The technique depends on the specificity of nucleic acid hybridization, which can best be visualized by considering the denaturation/renaturation of DNA. Recall that DNA is a double-stranded polymer held together by complementary base pairing. Raising the temperature will disrupt the hydrogen bonding between the strands and allow the strands to separate. When a solution of single-stranded DNA is cooled, the complementary strands will find one another and reform the double helix. The specificity of base pairing makes this a process with very high fidelity; under controlled conditions only exactly matching strands will renature.

DNA synthesis was first carried out *in vitro* (that is in a test tube) in 1957 by Arthur Kornberg [14] (for which he shared the 1959 Nobel Prize). This process requires an enzyme, DNA polymerase, the four nucleotide triphosphates (dATP, dTTP, dCTP, and dGTP), various cofactors, the DNA template, and a primer. DNA polymerases are ubiquitous (found in every cell) and varied. In PCR a DNA polymerase from a thermophilic bacterium (one that lives at temperatures exceeding 60°C) is used. Artificial primers (synthetic DNA sequences complementary to a portion of the target sequence) for each strand are added to the DNA synthesis reaction and the mixture is cycled between synthesis and denaturation temperatures, exponentially amplifying the target sequence. RNA is first copied into cDNA (complementary DNA) using a viral enzyme (RNA-dependent DNA polymerase; also known as reverse transcriptase), and then the same procedures are followed as for DNA. This technology is absolutely critical for DNA sequencing, gene expression analysis and many other techniques used in translational research.

4.3.3 Proteins

Proteins are not only the product of translation of messenger RNA, they are also structural and functional workhorses of the cell. Most cellular chemistry is catalyzed by proteins (enzymes), which are the key mediators of cellular metabolism. Proteins are the primary structural molecules of the cell. They also control the movement of other molecules in and out of the cell. Signaling from the cell exterior to interior, inside the cell, and between cells is also mediated by proteins.

Physically, proteins are polymers of amino acids. Twenty amino acids found in nature are used in the construction of proteins. Chemically, these amino acids are very diverse, resulting in a wide range of functional possibilities for proteins. Functional proteins are often complexes of one or more kinds of proteins. It is the diver-

Microarrays

A number of high-throughput techniques characterizing DNA and RNA utilize microarray technology. The basis for these methods is the specificity of nucleic acid hybridization as discussed in the box titled "Polymerase Chain Reaction." Microarrays have been developed to quantify the amounts of a particular DNA or RNA sequence in a mixture of nucleic acids. The mixture is interrogated by labeling the nucleic acid found in the mixture, usually by PCR, and hybridizing to a probe or set of probes specific to the species of interest. The amount of hybridization is proportional to the concentration of the species of interest in the mixture.

The advantage of microarray techniques is that the concentration of many species can be determined simultaneously by fixing many probes to a surface in a grid (array) in which the location of each probe is fixed and, hence, the hybridization signal at that position is a readout of the concentration of the species interrogated by that probe. The spots for a given probe can be very small, hence the needs for microarrays. Hundreds of thousands to more than a million features might be present on a single array. Copy number variation and gene expression analysis are two types of measurements that use this approach and they will be discussed in detail in Chapter 5.

Another type of analysis that is based on the same basic technology is the determination of single nucleotide polymorphisms or specific sequence (genetic) variants. Although the method used is similar to that described earlier, that is, an array of probes to which a mixture of labeled DNA is hybridized, the hybridization property being exploited is quite different. For short probes (20 to 25 bases), the requirement for an exact match between the probe and the sequence being interrogated is very stringent. Conditions can be established so that a mismatch of even one base will greatly reduce the signal. This specificity allows the technique to distinguish been two or more possible bases at a given position. The signal in this analysis is based on the specificity of the hybridization, not the quantity of the target species. This allows a single DNA sample to be simultaneously genotyped for hundreds of thousands of variants. These types of experiments will be discussed in Chapter 5.

sity of chemistry and structure that has enabled proteins to evolve into the vast array of functions that enable and enrich life.

Humans are estimated to have more than 100,00 different proteins. (Although the human genome contains about 25,000 protein encoding genes, alternative splicing of mRNA and other forms of post-translational processing of proteins yields more kinds of proteins than genes that encode them [12].) They are found intercellularly and in most body fluids. The concentrations of individual proteins vary by orders of magnitude.

All of these properties of proteins make them important targets for study of disease processes because they can be both markers of disease and targets for pharmacological therapeutics. Their great diversity and chemical heterogeneity make the isolation, quantitation, and identification of proteins technically challenging. In addition, unlike DNA and RNA, no technology is available to amplify proteins found in biological specimens. This is a tremendous disadvantage when trying to characterize or identify rare proteins in a mixture of interest.

4.4   Summary

A basic understanding of the molecular biology and biochemistry behind the various "omics" technologies is important to the practitioner of translational biomedical informatics. Understanding the benefits and limitations of the various technologies is critical to designing systems that can integrate the data derived from these methods and to designing systems that ensure data quality and consistency in projects where large volumes of diverse and complex data are used to try to understand disease processes or, ultimately, to influence clinical decisions. Further reading in these areas, particularly in some of the texts suggested in the References section, is well worth the time of the serious reader.

References

[1]   Alberts, B., et al. *Molecular Biology of the Cell*, 4th ed., London: Garland Science, 2002.

[2]   Correns, C. G., "Mendels Regel über das Verhalten der Nachkommenschaft der Rassenbastarde," *Berichte der Deutschen Botanischen Gesellschaft*, Vol. 18, 1900, pp. 158–168. First published in English as Correns, C. G., "Mendel's Law Concerning the Behavior of Progeny of Varietal Hybrids," *Genetics*, Vol. 35, No. 5, Part 2, 1950, pp. 33–41.

[3]   De Vries, H. "Sur la loi de disjonction des hybrids," *Comptes Rendus de l'Academie des Sciences (Paris)*, Vol. 130, 1900, pp. 845–847. First published in English as De Vries, H., "Concerning the Law of Segregation of Hybrids," *Genetics*, Vol. 35, No. 5, Part 2, 1950, pp. 30–32.

[4]   Tschermak, E., "Über Künstliche Kreuzung bei Pisum sativum," *Berichte der Deutsche Botanischen Gesellschaft*, Vol. 18, 1900, pp. 232–239. First published in English as Tschermak, E., "Concerning Artificial Crossing in Pisum sativum," *Genetics*, Vol. 35, No. 5, Part 2, 1950, pp. 42–47.

[5]   Sturtevant, A. H., *History of Genetics*, Woodbury, NY: Cold Spring Harbor Laboratory Press, 2001.

[6]   Avery, O. T., C. M. MacLeod, and M. McCarty, "Studies on the Chemical Nature of the Substance Inducing Transformation of Pneumococcal Types: Induction of Transformation by a Desoxyribonucleic Acid Fraction Isolated from Pneumococcus Type III," *J. Exp. Med.*, Vol. 79, 1944, pp. 137–158.

[7]   Watson, J. D., and F. H. C. Crick, "Molecular Structure for Deoxyribose Nucleic Acid," *Nature*, Vol. 171, 1953, pp. 737–738.

[8]   Scherrer, K., and J. Jost, "The Gene and the Genon Concept: A Functional and Information-Theoretic Analysis," *Molecular Systems Biology*, Vol. 3, 2007, pp. 1–11.

[9]   Scriver, C. R., "The PAH Gene, Phenylketonuria, and a Paradigm Shift." *Hum. Mutat.*, Vol. 28, 2007, pp. 831–845.

[10] Nirenberg, M. W., and J. H. Matthaei, "The Dependence of Cell-Free Protein Synthesis in E. coli upon Naturally Occurring or Synthetic Polyribonucleotides," *Proc. Natl. Acad. Sci. USA*, Vol. 47, 1961, pp. 1588–1602.

[11]   Mattick, J. S., and I. V. Makunin, "Non-Coding RNA." Hum. Mol. Genet., Vol. 15, 2006, pp. R17–R29.

[12]   Black, D., "Protein Diversity from Alternative Splicing: A Challenge for Bioinformatics and Post-Genome Biology," *Cell*, Vol. 103, 2000, pp. 367–370.

[13]   Saiki, R. K., et al., "Enzymatic Amplification of Beta-Globin Genomic Sequences and Restriction Site Analysis for Diagnosis of Sickle Cell Anemia," *Science*, Vol. 230, 1985, pp. 1350–1354.

[14]   Lehman, I. R., et al., "Enzymatic Synthesis of Deoxyribonucleic Acid. I. Preparation of Substrates and Partial Purification of an Enzyme from *Escherichia coli*," *J. Biol. Chem.*, Vol. 233, 1958, pp. 163–170.

[15]   Sanger, F., S. Nicklen, and A. R. Coulson, "DNA Sequencing with Chain-Terminating Inhibitors," *Proc. Natl. Acad. Sci. USA*, Vol. 74, 1977, pp. 5463–5467.

CHAPTER 5

Genomics Studies

Yaw-Ching Yang and Henry Brzeski

5.1 Introduction

A change in the base sequence of an individual's DNA can cause a change in the mRNA sequence, which may, in turn, affect a protein's sequence and functionality (see Chapter 4). Changes in protein functionality may, in turn, affect a cell's metabolism and hence the functioning of an individual's cells, tissues, or organs. Such changes can be present in a cell that has acquired a mutation during the lifetime of the individual (somatic) or it may be present in the genetic material the individual received at conception (germ line). For this reason it is important to consider the source of the DNA that will be used for any experiments that investigate changes in DNA sequences that may be associated with disease. For instance, if the purpose of an experiment is to analyze tumor cells that have acquired mutations that render them refractory to growth regulation, then it is essential to isolate DNA from the tumor (where cells have acquired the mutation) and not from blood cells that contain the patient's unaltered germ line sequence. The corollary is also true, namely, if an experimenter is attempting to discover genetic differences that predispose individuals to a disease, it would be preferable to work with cells that do not contain any mutations caused by the disease; that is, it is better to work with cells that have the germ line sequence. In some instances it may be possible to use blood cells, although in doing so the researcher must bear in mind that the DNA comes from white blood cells and these cells have undergone genomic rearrangements to form the immunoglobulin and T-cell receptor genes so these cells would not be suitable when working with patients with leukemia.

Alterations in a DNA sequence can affect (1) a gene's regulatory regions (e.g., a promoter, silencer, splice signals, mRNA stability signals) or (2) the protein coding sequence of the DNA. Either type of mutation can lead to alterations in the functionality of the gene. In the first case, it is likely that the alterations in the DNA sequence will affect the level of mRNA produced from the gene, whereas in the second case, the level of mRNA produced will usually not be affected but its functionality might be. However, if the mutated mRNA regulates the functionality of other genes, then the level of expression of the regulated genes will be affected. Alternatively, if mRNA produces a protein that fails to function, it is highly likely that the cell will modify its metabolism by underexpressing or overexpressing other genes to compensate for the defect. For this reason, different technologies and software have been developed to analyze the results of different experimental protocols. Because changing the functionality of regulatory genes can affect the level of expression of downstream genes, only through careful analysis of gene networks can such a change be discovered. The loss of functionality will be seen in the variation of downstream-regulated genes, but these do not, per se, carry any mutations in them although alteration of their expression level may contribute to the observed pathology.

A number of genomic technologies have been developed to acquire information at the DNA and mRNA levels from human tissues and other biological specimens. The technologies that will be addressed in this chapter are DNA sequencing, array-based comparative genome hybridization, single nucleotide polymorphism (SNP) analysis, and gene expression analysis. All of these technologies require purification or amplification of the relevant nucleic acid (DNA or mRNA) sequence(s) from all other sequences present in the cell prior to analysis. This is now routinely performed using the polymerase chain reaction (see Chapter 4) [1]. After amplification the sequence can be analyzed using the technologies just mentioned.

Understanding the basic experimental details of the methods to be discussed in this chapter is important for further analysis because researchers must take into account how the experiment was performed and how the results were obtained. Each of these techniques provides a different—and incomplete—measure of the state of the genome and transcriptome, so using a broad spectrum of methods is important for developing a complete picture of the genome as it relates to disease status. In this chapter, we also discuss two translational medical research case studies that utilize some of these technologies.

5.2 Genomic Technologies Used for DNA Analysis

5.2.1 DNA Sequencing

Until recently, the methodology of finding DNA sequence alterations by sequencing DNA was predominantly gel based and labor intensive [2]. This technology has the advantages that it provides a detailed view of a gene sequence without any selection preconditions (except the choice of PCR primers) and allows for the identification of all sequence changes in the defined region.

Although the initial sequence determination is automated, the analysis of this sequence is a more manual process because, in many cases, the important functional regions of the protein(s) of interest are not known. Having initially identified DNA sequence variations specific to the affected population and subsequently identified that these sequence differences affect protein functionality, it is then necessary to relate protein function to physiological and metabolic effects. Ultimately this information may relate the molecular information to the etiology of the disease and provide insights into how to improve patient treatment. Some of these genes may have properties that make them potential drug targets.

5.2.1.1   DNA Sequencing Technology

Sequencing technology has changed dramatically since the 1970s. The chemical sequencing method developed by Maxam and Gilbert [3] and the plus–minus method developed by Sanger and Coulson [4] in the mid-1970s were the first rapid sequencing methods. But in the late 1970s, they were replaced by the chain-terminator method developed by Sanger, Nicklen, and Coulson [2], which was even more efficient and rapidly became the method of choice. In 1985, Mullis and colleagues [1] developed the polymerase chain reaction, a technique to replicate small amounts of DNA. PCR not only revolutionized genomic research, but also allowed for the automation of the sequencing process. Using a combination of PCR, dye-termination methods, and capillary electrophoresis, modern automated DNA sequencing instruments (DNA sequencers) generally sequence up to 96 samples per run and perform as many as 24 runs a day. The two major providers of DNA sequencers, Applied Biosystems (ABI) and General Electric Healthcare (GE), both provide a wide range of sequencers with capacities of 1 to 96 capillary.

When the starting material is genomic DNA (as apposed to cloned DNA), sequencing reactions start with PCR, followed by cleanup and resuspension before loading onto the sequencer. The PCR reaction begins with denaturation of the DNA templates, followed by annealing with primers (chemically synthesized, single-stranded DNA fragments, between 18 and 25 base pairs long) complementary to the start and end of the target sequences. This is followed by the extension step, during which the DNA polymerase copies the DNA template. This procedure (denaturizing, annealing, and extension) is repeated many times (usually 30 to 35 cycles) and ends with a final elongation step. Primers are designed depending on the target gene sequences. A primer should be highly specific to the target region and with the correct guanine/cytosine (GC) content so as not to interfere with PCR procedures (namely, maintaining melting and annealing temperatures at reasonable values).

The raw files from the sequence output are usually used to build trace files and sequences in text format (in 600 to 800 base lengths) and then analyzed using different software. Trace files usually come with QA data, generated by the software, that allow interpretation of the quality of the sequence (Phred scores). Any cell will contain two copies of a DNA sequence, one maternal and one paternal. If these are identical (i.e., the cell is said to be homozygous for that sequence), then the software that calls the sequence is relatively reliable and the sequence found in the text file is usually correct. However, it is possible that an individual is heterozygous for the sequence of interest (i.e., she or he received a different version of the gene of interest from the mother and father), in which case two bases will be found to exist at the same position in the DNA strand. This is one of the important reasons for determining new DNA sequences, but it is not easy to determine from the text file, so it becomes necessary to visually examine trace files to find these heterozygous bases because they can be difficult to pick up when using autoanalysis software.

5.2.1.2   Biomedical Informatics Requirements

Sequencing technology is mature and has been widely used in medical research for many different purposes over many years. Many bioinformatics tools are available for sequence data analysis. The most important issues are the storage and tracking of the huge amount of sequencing data for research purposes. Laboratory information management systems (LIMSs) and data warehouses are the two critical tools in this respect. Details of these informatics tools, sequence analysis software and LIMS, will be discussed in Chapter 7 and 8, respectively.

5.2.1.3   Future Directions

Although sequencing technology has been around for more than 30 years and the technology is relatively mature and easy to use, there is still room for further improvement. New technology is focusing on developing higher throughput by increasing the speed and capacity of automated sequencing machines, lowering the amount of DNA needed for a sequencing reaction, and reducing the cost.

A few new sequencing technologies are available now. The Pyrosequencing method developed by Ronaghi and Nyrén is based on the "sequencing by synthesis" principle [5]. The method allows sequencing of a single strand of DNA by synthesizing the complementary strand along it and detecting which base was actually added at each step. Both Solexa technology (Illumina, San Diego, CA, USA) and 454 technology (454 Life Science, Branford, CT, USA) are based on this principle and achieve a higher throughput and lower cost for DNA sequencing. The main challenge of this technology is assembling the much shorter reads (up to 36 base pairs for Solexa and 200 to 300 for 454) for each run. Both companies have developed their own bioinformatics tools for sequence assembly.

The Applied Biosystems SOLID System is another new technology that is available (Applied Biosystems, Foster City, CA, USA). This methodology is based on sequential ligation with dye-labeled oligonucleotides. Its procedure begins with library preparation followed by emulsion PCR/bead enrichment. These enriched beads are then modified to allow covalent bonding onto glass slides. The key advantage of this system is the ability to accommodate increasing densities of beads per slide. These slides are then loaded into the SOLID analyzer for the ligation reaction and data detection and analysis. Even though this system produces only 25 to 35 bases per read, it can generate 1 to 1.5 gigabases per slide due to its high bead density.

The nanopore technology that is currently under development at Harvard University aims to sequence a human genome in 2 hr at a cost of less than $1,000. This technology is based on passing DNA thru a tiny hole not much larger than a DNA molecule in a thin, solid-state membrane. The technique involves detecting changes in the nanopore's electrical properties caused by the passage of the single DNA molecule. More information about this developing technology can be obtained from publications [6–9] and the following website: http://www.mcb.harvard.edu/branton.

5.2.2   Genotyping

5.2.2.1   Array Technologies

Most of the subsequent analytical methods discussed in this chapter involve chip technology so this will be explained in general terms using the Affymetrix SNP chip technology as an example. Any subsequent differences will be pointed out during the relevant introduction. Because all genomic sequences are well characterized, it is possible to build a chip that screens for these sequences. Currently, Affymetrix SNP chips contain 1.3 million features on a 5-in. × 5-in. quartz wafer, on which oligos (probes) are synthesized *in situ* using a masking technology similar to that used in the electronics industry.

The DNA to be assayed (target) is fluorescently labeled and incubated with the chip. During incubation of the labeled target with the probes on the chip, sequences in the target hybridize with the probes where there is complementarity (i.e., if two short oligos are placed on adjacent features and these oligos are identical except that each contains one of the alternative bases of the SNP, then the target DNA will bind to only that feature which contains the relevant SNP sequence). The bound target DNAs are detected by scanners, and software is used to deconvolute which probe (gene) is where and how much labeled target has bound to the probe. The extent of hybridization is quantified and this allows the determination of a Boolean value ("yes, the sequence is present" or "no, it is not in the case of SNPs"). Alternatively, by calculating the fluorescent intensity, we can obtain a measure of relative copy number. Then, using commercially available software (GDAS/Merlin), it is possible to look for links between multiple SNPs and particular diseases and thus identify genetic loci that are linked to and perhaps causative of the disease.

Now that the current sets of chips carry such a large number of SNPs, it is no longer necessary to have a group of related individuals in order to carry out this strategy (although this helps). However, as mentioned elsewhere in this book, identifying causative mutations is difficult in many diseases because a patient may experience many symptoms caused by differing mutations, hence the patients should be stratified as rigorously as possible to facilitate this sort of analysis.

Genotyping by Sequencing

Currently, automated sequencers can produce large amounts of data in a short time, which has, in certain cases, made sequencing a viable option for SNP genotyping especially when identifying multiple SNPs in a small region. It is possible to detect SNPs in a target DNA region by comparing the sequence data between diseased and unaffected samples. Detailed information about sequencing technology is provided in the previous section. If a study encompasses only a few genes, then sequencing might be the most efficient method for SNP analysis.

The typical protocol begins with identification of genes of interests through a literature search or by identifying candidate genes as described earlier. The region of interest is then identified using, for example, UniSTS/ensemble software by matching the SNP to DNA sequences. PCR primers are designed for this region, which are then amplified and sequenced as described earlier. Sequencing results obtained from the affected individual can then be compared with reference samples, such as a database like GenBank [25], a reference [26], or unaffected tissue [27], to identify SNPs that may be related to the condition under investigation.

Primer Extension

Primer extension is a method used to measure the amount of a specific RNA transcript or to map the 5' end of DNA or RNA fragments. It is an enzyme-based method that has been modified to detect SNPs. The first step is to design or purchase primers that are specific for each SNP. To detect the SNP, the SNP primer is first hybridized to the target DNA, and then a sequencing reaction is performed to extend the primer by only a single base. This incorporated single base is fluorescently labeled and can be detected in a normal sequencing run and thus determines the SNP allele. In studies that require only a small number of genes and few samples, this will be the method of choice since the cost is low, but the procedure is relatively time consuming. To increase the throughput, multiplexing is a simple option. However, to reach a higher throughput, this procedure can be combined with microarray technology by arraying primer extension probes on slides. In this way, many SNPs can be genotyped at once. But this method still cannot achieve the throughput of SNP arrays (see later discussion).

Another major development in high-throughput genotyping of SNPs involves the combination of primer extension followed by matrix-assisted laser desorption/ ionization time-of-flight mass spectrometry (MALDI-TOFMS). Because the molecular weights of all methylated and unmethylated DNA bases differ, the modified nucleotide can be identified by determining the mass increase of the primer using mass spectrometry. This is a platform that is not gel based and is amenable to multiplexing and automation. This assay consists of three steps: PCR amplification, primer extension, and then mass spectrometric analysis. However, analysis of oligonucleotides using MALDI-TOFMS is very sensitive to metal ion contamination. Therefore, sample purification for mass spectrometric analysis is essential for reliable results. In most protocols, solid-phase purification methods are used that can be manual and time consuming. Ion-exchange resins have been developed as a simpler method for sample conditioning prior to MALDI-TOFMS analysis. These resins can be purchased in a 96-well format, which allows for high-throughput analysis and automated cleanup.

SNP GeneChip Arrays

Several different SNP platforms are based on chip technology including the Affymetrix SNP GeneChip arrays and Illumina BeadChip arrays. We focus here on the Affymetrix system. The Affymetrix SNP GeneChip array is a hybridization-based SNP detection method. Affymetrix uses its own patented technology, which directs synthesis of DNA oligonucleotide probes on the SNP GeneChip arrays. The same technology is used in the GeneChip expression arrays.

These genotyping SNP chips were designed using a whole genome approach to detect the large number of SNPs in the human genome. They have evolved from 10K SNP arrays to 100K arrays to the third generation 500K arrays, which consist of 500K SNP markers on two chips. The next generation of Affymetrix SNP arrays will have the capacity to detect 1 million SNPs and is currently available.

Because a huge amount of probes are on a single chip, it is difficult to achieve optimal hybridization conditions for every probe. To increase the sensitivity and specificity of array performance, each SNP maker includes several redundant probes and mismatch controls. Although hybridization-based oligonucleotide microarrays have a relatively lower specificity and sensitivity, the scale of SNPs that can be interrogated is a major benefit. This technology is ideal for high-throughput research projects, but is relatively expensive. However, the price per chip has been going down and the product's performance has been improved. Data generated from these three generations of the Affymetrix genotyping SNP array has been used in linkage and association studies, whole genome association analysis, and copy number variation studies.

5.2.2.2   Technological Assessment of Genotyping

There are many types of genetic variation, such as point mutations, deletions, insertions, and translocations. Determination of the genetic variation between samples is referred to as *genotyping,* a process that is used to determine the genetic constitution of a sample of interest using molecular biological assays. In theory, the most comprehensive genotypic analysis would involve analysis of an individual's entire DNA sequence. In practice, this analysis is usually restricted to tens of genetic loci. In most studies, only a fraction of sample genotypes is determined due to the huge size of the genome and the limitation of the technologies available; however, not every study requires such large-scale genotyping. Different genetic variations occur at different rates in the population and require different assays for study. Therefore, many different technologies have been developed depending on the aim and scale of the research. Most genetic variations that do not include chromosomal rearrangement are due to the fact that, over the period of evolutionary time, individuals have acquired, and passed on to their progeny, single base changes (SNPs) or insertions/deletions (indels) in their DNA that may or may not affect gene functionality. However, these abundant, easily assayed genetic variations are very powerful genetic markers.

Because the interest in SNPs has increased dramatically during the past few years, many SNP genotyping technologies have been developed including molecular beacons and SNP microarrays. Initially SNPs were assayed using enzymatic-based methods such as restriction fragment length polymorphism (RFLP); however, it is now more common to use primer extension assays. The simplest, but most arduous, method is based on sequencing. This chapter describes the basic technology of these three platforms (sequencing, primer extension, and SNP arrays), but will describe the Affymetrix system in detail.

The human DNA sequence is highly variable and it is thought that there is one base variation in every 300 bases. These base variations are known as single nucleotide polymorphisms. These SNPs are fixed in the population and are stably inherited from generation to generation and occur universally throughout the human genome. The best available information indicates that less than 2% of the human genome codes for protein and, although there are many theories as to the function of the remainder, it is not known for certain. If a SNP occurs in a coding region, it can potentially change the protein sequence; however, because the genetic code is degenerate, a change in DNA sequence does not always change the protein sequence and, if it does, then the change is usually for a similar amino acid, generally rendering the change in the DNA sequence benign. Hence, it is unusual for a SNP to affect protein function. Nevertheless, SNPs are found to be associated with various human diseases [10–12] and are proving to be of particular interest in pharmacogenomics [13–16].

However, the power of SNPs lies less in their ability to predict changed protein sequences and more in the fact that they are (1) numerous, (2) ubiquitous, (3) stably inherited, and (4) very well characterized. At the time this book was written, the Single Nucleotide Polymorphism Database (dbSNP; http://www.ncbi.nlm.nih.gov/projects/SNP) release 127 contained 11,825,732 validated SNPs and, therefore, provides a fairly evenly distributed set of markers across the entire human genome. For this reason, one aim of biomedical informatics is to find a link between a SNP and a particular disease symptom or outcome, thus identifying genetic loci that are linked to a specific clinical trait even though the mutation giving rise to the SNP per se may not cause changes in gene expression (e.g., it may occur in a noncoding part of the gene or may even lie in an adjacent, unaffected gene). Hence, the SNP is a stable genetic marker that may not necessarily be causative of the disease, but provides an indication of an adjacent locus that is. This ability to link SNPs to a genetic locus led to the establishment of the HapMap project in which SNP distribution was assessed for five different ethnic groups [17] and has since been used to find relationships between SNPs and various diseases [18, 19].

Another important event in gene expression is the processing of mRNA. As described in Chapter 4, after transcription the precursor mRNA is processed and a large percentage of it is discarded. This processing follows specific rules (most of which are well characterized; e.g., splicing predominantly takes place between AGGT sequences that flank the 5' and 3' ends of the intron) and this results in the removal of variable lengths of precursor mRNA, which are not important for the function of the coded protein. However, it is possible for one gene to give rise to multiple proteins through a process known as alternative splicing in which different exons are mixed and matched to provide similar proteins with slightly different functionalities. There are many reports in the literature of such events [20]. Because this is controlled by the DNA/mRNA sequence, alterations in the DNA sequence can lead to altered splicing and production of proteins with altered functionality. For instance, if the AGGT splicing signal is mutated, the cell may well find an alternative (cryptic) splice site and use this instead, giving rise to a protein with altered functionality and so giving rise to disease [21–24].

Because these SNPs are well characterized, it is possible to build a chip that screens for these SNPs (currently a 500K SNP chip is commercially available). The following is true for SNP chips and is generally true for other chip-based technologies described later.

5.2.2.3 Affymetrix Genotyping SNP Assay Workflow

Affymetrix named their genotyping SNP array assay process *whole genome sampling analysis* (WGSA). It includes a few key steps: restriction enzyme digestion, adapter ligation, PCR amplification, fragmentation, and hybridization (Figure 5.1).

The Affymetrix protocols start with 1 μg of DNA that is divided into four tubes (250 ng of DNA per tube) for the restriction enzyme digestion, which cuts genomic DNA into different sized fragments that allow the specifically designed adapter to bind. After heat inactivating the restriction enzymes, adapter ligation is performed using T4 DNA ligase. Specific primers for the PCR amplification are embedded in these adapters. After another heat step to inactivate the DNA ligase, a specific PCR

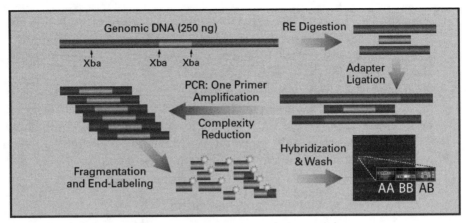

Figure 5.1   GeneChip mapping assay overview. (Courtesy of Affymetrix.)

program is run to amplify DNA fragments that are between 200 and 1,100 base pairs (bp) long. This step reduces the DNA complexity and produces enough DNA for hybridization. The PCR products are purified using the QIAquick PCR purification kit (Qiagen), quantified, fragmented using DNase1, and then labeled with biotin. The reduced size of DNA fragments ensures that hybridization to the 25mers probes is achieved more efficiently.

Labeled DNA fragments are then injected into GeneChip arrays for overnight hybridization and then washed and stained in an Affymetrix Fluidic station 450 using preinstalled Affymetrix protocols. The final step is to scan the arrays on an Affymetrix Scanner 3000 with default settings. The scanned images are analyzed using GeneChip Genotyping Analysis software (GTYPE), which generates Microsoft Excel files that include the calls for each marker. The raw data file can be imported into other software such as Merlin and Viria (Agilent) for further analysis

5.2.2.4   QA/SOP Issues

The most important factor that affects the quality of SNP results is the quality of the sample DNA. Both sequencing and primer extension technologies have been applied in research for a long time and are relatively mature and easy to accomplish. Most primers designed for genotyping are well studied, and once the optimized condition for these primers been achieved, the failure rate is relatively small. However, running the Affymetrix GeneChip genotyping arrays requires precise and careful handling.

Three quality control/quality assurance (QC/QA) steps are used to check the quality of the reactions. The first step occurs after the PCR step, at which time an aliquot is run on an agarose gel. The resulting lengths of the PCR products must be in the range of 200 to 1,100 bp. The second QC/QA step occurs after PCR product purification and elution when the product is quantified and normalized; this step is critical for hybridization. Purified and diluted PCR products are quantified by measuring the optical density (OD) at 260, 280, and 320 nm. A typical average sample OD260 is 0.5 to 0.7. The OD260/OD280 ratio should be between 1.8 and 2. The sample is discarded if this metric falls outside of this range. The OD320 measurement should be very close to zero (0 ± 0.005). The third QC/QA step involves electrophoresis of the PCR products on an agarose gel after fragmentation. The average size should be less than 180 bp and only samples with the correct length distribution should be used for the array hybridization.

The results of image analysis of each Affymetrix SNP array contain a quality report file. It provides the call rate (percentage of determined genotypes in the samples) of each chip. For the 100K and 500K SNP chips, the call rate should be above 95% and 93%, respectively. However, for amplified DNA samples, call rates would be lower but should be above 90% for both types of chips.

5.2.2.5 Biomedical Informatics Requirements

Many commercial software packages are available for genotyping data analysis such as GeneSpring GT (Agilent), Genemapper (ABI), and Exemplar (Sapio Sciences). In addition, freely distributed software is available that has been developed by academic institutions. This includes DHIP Linkage (Harvard University) and GENEHUNTER-MODSCORE (Philipps University Marburg, Germany). Most of this software provides different data analysis methods and visualization tools.

Commercial data analysis software tends to have more embedded statistical methods and better data presentation tools. In addition, the packaged software usually covers all steps from raw data import through data analysis and presentation to functional genomic analysis. Free software, in contrast, usually covers only some of these capabilities, so users of free software have to gather a few different packages to obtain tools for conducting an entire analysis. Other key challenges include the storage of millions of data points and keeping track of all samples and procedures. Most labs use a laboratory information management system for this purpose. LIMS will be discussed in detail in Chapter 7.

5.2.2.6 Future Directions

High-density SNP detection is very straightforward and provides extensive coverage at relatively low expense. New generation SNP chips contain more than 1.8 million probes on a single chip and the unit cost continues to drop. This is enabling many more researchers to carry out whole genome association studies. Data generated from these SNP markers can be used not only for genotyping analyses, but also for loss of heterozygosity (LOH) and copy number variation studies.

5.2.3 Array-Based Comparative Genomic Hybridization

Many forms of chromosomal copy number variation are found in a genome such as deletions or amplification of part of, or even entire, chromosomes. It is also possible for fragments of DNA to have been moved between chromosomes, leading to equal (balanced translocations) or unequal (unbalanced translocations) exchange of genetic information between paternal and maternal chromosomes. Chromosomal copy number aberrations are often associated with diseases and can be useful molecular markers in prediction of response to therapies and disease outcomes [28–30]. Array-based comparative genomic hybridization (aCGH) is a high-throughput technology designed to detect all of the above-mentioned chromosomal copy number aberrations. At least 10 different aCGH systems are available with different throughput rates and different methodologies.

5.2.3.1 Technological Assessment of Chromosomal Rearrangements

In the case of aCGH analysis, the DNA probe is attached covalently to a glass substrate; however, this DNA is a large sequence prepared by PCR unlike the small, synthetic oligo used in SNP chips or microarrays. Analysis involves hybridization of DNA from a patient to the chip to assess the presence of that particular probe sequence. However, unlike SNP analysis where single base changes are involved, in the case of aCGH, deletions can be of varying lengths that are usually clustered around a defined sequence so the sequence attached to the glass chip is usually far longer (1,500 to 2,000 bases) than that used on a SNP chip (25 to 50 bases).

In addition, the technology examines variations in copy number, and chip technology does not allow for quantitative assessments between chips; therefore, the aCGH uses two differently labeled DNAs, which are applied to the chip at the same time. One (the reference) is obtained from blood, whereas the second is obtained from the diseased tissue and is labeled differently. After hybridization the signal from each DNA is compared and the areas showing a biased hybridization ratio are deemed to be amplified or deleted.

This technology does not use a high density of probes and the areas targeted for assessing amplifications or deletions are derived from areas previously reported in the literature. Therefore, the same warning is necessary for aCGH as for PCR amplification; namely, the chip assays 50,000 loci, so detection of amplification or equivalence on these 50,000 loci can be stated, but it does not provide any amplification or deletion status on the remainder of the genome.

5.2.3.2 Example Platform

In this section, we focus on the BAC aCGH chips developed at Roswell Park Cancer Institute (RPCI) [31, 32]. The RPCI human 19K BAC array is comprised of about 19,000 RPCI-11 BAC clones that are all well annotated for gene content [31, 32]. This 19K array has a 160-kilobase resolution and includes many known tumor suppressor genes and oncogenes. These gene probes are generated by ligation-mediated PCR as described by Snijders et al. [32] and Nowak et al. [33]. Each gene probe is printed in duplicate on a single slide together with positive and negative control probes. All aCGH arrays are printed in the RPCI microarray core facility using 10K Microspot pins and a MicroGrid ll TAS arrayer (BioRobotics) on amino-silanated glass slides (Schott Nexterion type A+). This is a two-color hybridization system that utilizes experimental and control samples that are labeled with two different dyes, and then hybridized to the same chip.

The choice of control for each test sample is project dependent. In most cases, pooled samples from either cytogenetically normal males or females are used. For example, samples run in a laboratory studying breast cancer can use control DNA from normal males. This allows the sex difference to act as an internal control and the expected X and Y chromosomal copy number variation monitors the overall quality of the aCGH experiment. This method provides the flexibility of comparing results with other experiments performed earlier or later. In some studies, DNA from disease tissues is directly compared to DNA from normal tissue of the same patient, thus providing an exact picture of disease-specific mutations in that particular patient.

The aCGH technology is based on random primer labeling and hybridization of genomic DNA to aCGH arrays (Figure 5.2). It is a 3-day process with DNA labeling on day 1, DNA cleanup and hybridization on day 2, and post-hybridization washing and scanning on the final day. It is very important to use only high-quality, accurately quantified genomic DNA for the labeling. Amplification of DNA from small samples is possible, but results might be less reliable. Details of the procedure are provided next.

A total of 1 μg of genomic DNA is used for each sample (test and reference). DNA is first random primed using the BioPrime Labeling Kit in a thermocycler. After denaturing of the DNA/primer mixture, the test sample is labeled with Cy5 dCTP and the reference sample is labeled with Cy3 dCTP overnight (16 hr) at 37°C. On day 2, the labeled DNA is cleaned up using a Qiagen MiniElute PCR Cleanup Kit to remove unincorporated nucleotides and then concentrated by ethanol precipitation. The DNA pellet is resuspended in hybridization buffer and added to the aCGH arrays. Hybridization takes place either in a GeneTAC HybStation or manually in hybridization cassettes (Corning) placed in a water bath for 16 hr at 55°C. On the final day, the slides are washed and fixed prior to scanning. The arrays are scanned using an Axon GenePix scanner 4200A. Image analysis and quantification are carried out using commercially available image analysis programs such as Imagene v6.0.1 (BioDiscovery Inc.) or GenePix Pro (Molecular Device).

Image analysis of aCGH chips is performed in an identical manner to the analysis of two-color expression microarrays (see later discussion). First, the image is used

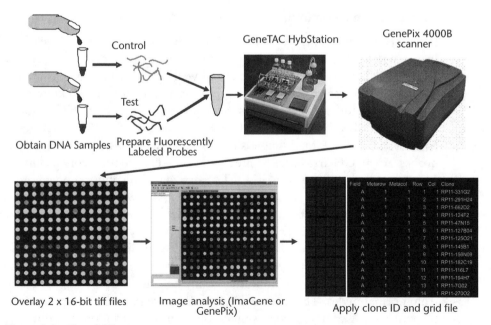

Figure 5.2 The aCGH process.

to generate raw signal intensity data that can be further analyzed to identify potential copy number variations. In most software, two pseudo-colored images test (Cy5-red) and reference (Cy3-green), are aligned first to produce a single composite image. A grid is aligned over the arrayed spots and automatically adjusted to the size and shape of the spots. A corresponding BAC ID file is integrated into the grid that indicates the BAC identification of each spot. Any irregular spots are identified and flagged to avoid contamination of data.

The software then extracts signal intensity using proprietary segmentation algorithms specific to the software being used, which involves calculation of signal intensity (1) inside the spot, (2) around the spots (buffer zone), and (3) in the background. Usually, mean or median signal intensity and background for both samples at each spot are generated by the software. The software calculates the mean signal intensity by subtracting the mean background signal intensity from the original spot intensity. A negative spot signal is possible due to higher background signals. The Cy5 and Cy3 signals are then normalized because they may not be evenly represented from both samples on the same array due to labeling or hybridization variations. (The detailed normalization method is described on the RPCI website at http://www.roswellpark.org/Site/Research/Shared_Resources/Microarray_and_Genomics_Resource.) The final normalized $\log_2$ ratio for each BAC clone is the average of the $\log_2$ ratios from replicate spots. The data are then imported into Microsoft Excel with mapping information from the University of California, Santa Cruz (UCSC) genome browser (http://genome.ucsc.edu).

5.2.3.3   QA/SOP Issues

It is important to use only good-quality array results for data analysis. Therefore, proper QA/QC standards have to be established to ensure the integrity of data. For RPCI aCGH technology, the QA/QC process starts with chip production. Each batch is checked for spot quality by test hybridizations of selected chips from the beginning, middle, and end of each print run. Samples used for these test hybridizations are male and female pooled reference DNA.

For chips to be acceptable, all scanned images have to be clean without missing spots and without spots having irregular shapes. Background signal intensities for both Cy3 and Cy5 on each chip have to be below 200 with an average signal intensity above 2,000. The percentage of positive calls for each chip has to be above 92% (using the Hyb oven) and 95% (using the Static hyb method). If the chips fail to meet these criteria, the whole batch will only be used as test chips—they will not be available for actual experiments. These same standards are also applied to experimental results. Only chips meeting the criteria just listed can be used for further data analysis. The most important factor that dictates the arrays results is the quality of the sample DNA. Therefore, only high-quality DNA (A260/280 ratio between 1.8 and 2.2) should be used.

5.2.3.4   Biomedical Informatics Requirements

Initial analysis of the data is platform specific and some of this analysis will be described in Section 5.3.2.1. To further expedite the aCGH data analysis process,

RPCI has developed a fully automated software package (aCGHViewer) specific for their BAC aCGH arrays as a conduit between the aCGH data tables and a genome browser [34]. It allows rapid identification of copy number aberrations across the whole genome and on a chromosome-by-chromosome basis (Figure 5.3). In addition, aCGHViewer is linked to the UCSC or the National Center of Biotechnology Information (NCBI) genome browser that allows the user to query the gene content in the regions of interest. It operates on all major computer platforms and is freely available at http://falcon.roswellpark.org/ aCGHview.

Effective biomedical informatics analysis of aCGH data is necessary because of the different data sets involved. It involves (1) a large number (up to 50,000) of genetic loci, (2) the genetic loci are found at varying chromosomal positions, (3) the extent of duplication/deletion is variable between loci, and (4) the loci involve different genes with different functionalities. To analyze these data with a translational goal, it is necessary to identify which loci are affected, the extent of duplication/deletion, the number of chromosomes affected, whether other genes lie between the duplicated/deleted loci for which no probe exists, which metabolic pathways are affected and their relationship to disease symptoms, and ultimately patient outcome. Therefore, this analysis not only requires access to in-house data on patient samples, but also requires access to data available in the public domain concerning metabolic pathways, protein–protein interactions, and gene regulatory networks.

5.2.3.5 Oligo-Based aCGH Platform

In addition to the BAC clone-based aCGH platform, there are oligo-based aCGH platforms that use long oligos (50mer to 85mer). The Nimblegen (NumbleGen,

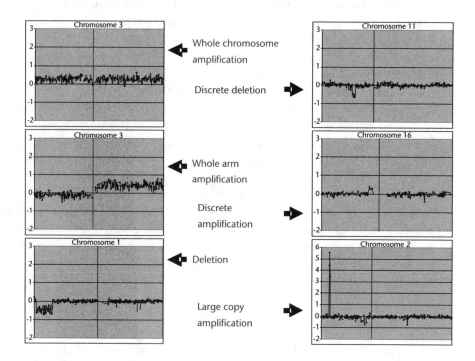

Figure 5.3 Possible outcomes of aCGH analysis.

Madison, WI, USA) platform is an example. Nimblegen high-capacity arrays contain 385,000 probes on a single glass slide. This high-density feature enables design of a human whole genome aCGH array with 6-kb resolution and thus provides a picture of genome-wide copy number changes. In addition, its technology can be used in a more focused study, such as a single chromosome or a region. This fine-tiling array with probes as dense as 10-bp spacing provides ultra-high-resolution detection of small deletions and amplifications, as well as breakpoint mapping to less than 500-bp intervals. The oligo-based aCGH platform generally provides higher density and resolution than the BAC clone. However, its basic procedure and data analysis are similar to analysis methods using the BAC clone-based aCGH platform.

5.3   Genomic Technology Used for RNA Analysis

5.3.1   Real-Time PCR

Many different methods were used for the quantification of mRNA prior to the development of microarrays, namely, Northern blotting, ribonuclease protection assays (RPA), in situ hybridization, and PCR. However, those methods are best at detecting the presence or absence of specific RNAs and are not suitable for quantitative measurement. Among them, PCR is the most sensitive and technically simple method and requires less RNA. PCR is a method that exponentially amplifies DNA sequences from a genomic DNA template, and the products of the PCR reaction are detected by electrophoresis on an agarose gel followed by ethidium bromide staining. For this reason, PCR is good at the detection of the presence or absence of a specific DNA but not for quantitative measurement. Reverse transcription PCR (RT-PCR) was later developed to measure mRNA by converting mRNA into complementary DNA (cDNA), which then serves as a DNA template for the PCR reaction. However, when the procedure was developed, it also used agarose gel electrophoresis and ethidium bromide staining as the detection method, which is not suitable for quantitative measurement. Subsequently, quantitative reverse transcription real-time PCR (qRT-PCR) was developed. In principle, real-time PCR instruments allow the measurement of the fluorescence of the DNA produced after each PCR cycle, and the relative amount of fluorescence detected when the DNA or cDNA amplification is exponential can be used for quantitative measurements [35].

Detection of the production of double-stranded DNA is achieved either specifically (using specially designed probes) or nonspecifically using SYBR green. Therefore, it is important to keep in mind the detection process when analyzing data from such experiments. Using probes, such as TaqMan (Applied Biosystems, Foster City, CA, USA), will provide quantification data on the gene under analysis, whereas using SYBR green simply shows the progress of an amplification reaction without definitive information on its specificity. SYBR green is a dye that binds to double-stranded but not single-stranded DNA. It is frequently used in real-time PCR reactions. Other methods, using specially developed PCR primers, can be used to detect the product during real-time PCR, but are not discussed here. However, many of the principles discussed later in this chapter apply to any real-time PCR reaction.

5.3.1.1 Data Analysis Methods

Several methods are commonly used for quantification of alterations in mRNA levels using real-time PCR [36, 37] including the standard curve method [35], the Pfaffl method [38], and the delta-delta CT method [39]. This section discusses only the Pfaffl method as used by the ICycler (Bio-Rad) real-time PCR instrument. After the PCR reaction, all of the necessary values required for calculation of target gene expression are provided in a Microsoft Excel spreadsheet. All PCR reactions for target and control (housekeeping) genes are carried out in triplicate. Examination of the progress of the amplification (increase in fluorescence) shows the process to be sigmoidal. The point at which amplification can be detected (the point at which the sigmoidal curve increases over baseline) is known as the threshold cycle (Ct). It is directly related to the concentration of DNA present in the original analyte and is the parameter used in all subsequent calculations.

The first step is to determine the difference in the Ct's (delta C_T or ΔCt) of the target gene between experimental and control samples. The fold change of target gene Ct between experimental and control samples is termed the efficiency. The same calculation is then performed for the control housekeeping genes. The ratio between these two efficiencies is the overall expression difference for the target gene between the experimental and control samples.

5.3.1.2 Biomedical Informatics Requirements

Quantitative RT-PCR is a relatively low throughput technology that usually does not generate thousands of data points. The main concern of biomedical informatics support is not in the data analysis, but in the data and sample tracking and storage. Again, this issue will be addressed in the Chapter 7 (LIMSs) and Chapter 8 (data warehouses).

5.3.1.3 Future Directions

In the near future, qRT-PCR is still the choice of technology for low-throughput gene expression studies and will continue to serve as the confirmation tool for microarray expression profile results (see Section 5.3.2). The main focus of the technology development is in increased throughput, improved accuracy, and reduced time. These are especially necessary for many diagnosis assays, which are the main clinical application of this technology, for example, qRT-PCR assays for detection of smallpox virus [40], methicillin-resistant *Staphylococcus aureus* [41], and *Mycoplasma genitalium* [42]. These assays all provide quick and reliable results indicating the presence or absence of the pathogen in patients.

5.3.2 Microarrays

Both SNP chips and aCGH measure the status of the cell's DNA; however, this will not affect a cell if this DNA is not expressed. Hence, a third type of chip has been used to measure the extent of expression of discrete genes. Microarray technology is similar to that described earlier for SNP chips except that, in this case, gene transcripts (mRNA) are extracted from a cell or tissue of interest, converted into DNA, used to generate labeled aRNA, and hybridized to a DNA chip to determine the amount of each transcript (mRNA) present in a cell.

The chip is constructed in a similar fashion to that described earlier for SNP chips, and the probes are constructed to monitor known human genes found in GenBank (~25,000). After scanning, quantification, and deconvolution, the results consist of relative levels of expression of each of the genes on the chip. Biomedical informatics analysis will not only show the relative levels of expression of each gene, but, by correlating the expression levels with SNP, aCGH, and metabolic pathway data, will allow a systems biology approach to the analysis. This will provide clues as to which common pathways are affected, rather than the discrete gene information provided by the three separate analyses described earlier, and it should accelerate the development of patient treatment methodologies.

When DNA microarray technology was first introduced in the mid-1990s, it was expensive, the protocols were difficult to follow, and the results were inconsistent in many cases. However, the potential of detecting thousands of genes at the same time has made it an indispensable tool in many projects and has led to exponential growth in its use. This interest in DNA microarrays has led to advances in the technology that have made it more affordable and reliable.

5.3.2.1   Array Technologies

The principle of microarrays relies on nucleic acid hybridization between complementary DNA strands. The sequence of one of these strands is known (the probe) and is attached to the microarray; the other is the sample that is labeled (the target). Two major DNA sources are used as probes on microarrays, oligonucleotide and cDNA. Oligonucleotide microarrays are constructed using either short (15- to 30-bp) or long (50- to 75-bp) oligonucleotides. These oligonucleotide probes can be directly synthesized on arrays (Affymetrix) or synthesized separately and then spotted onto glass arrays (Agilent and GE).

The cDNA microarray is constructed by spotting DNA fragments that were generated by a PCR reaction (100 to 500 bp) onto glass arrays. The range of probes per chip is from a few hundred to 45,000 or more. Many microarray cores in universities and research institutes produce their own in-house arrays. Extensive setup and testing are required before these homemade array facilities can become fully functional and provide consistent high-quality arrays. However, they are generally less expensive than commercially available arrays and the ability to individualize the arrays makes them more flexible. In recent years, more and more commercial microarray platforms have reduced their price for academic users and are providing more flexible custom arrays.

For spotted arrays, at least nine arrayers from different companies are available on the market. The basic principle of these arrayers is very similar in that they use pins to deposit the DNA or oligonucleotides onto glass slides by touching the surface. Two major types of pins are used in these arrays, the quill-based pin and the pin-and-ring system. Both require many adjustments to produce consistent spots and the pins need to be replaced relatively often. Ink-jet technology (Hewlett-Packard) is a nontouch method that "shoots" probes onto the glass surface. It produces very consistent and high-quality spots, but is more expensive. Both

Agilent and GE use this technology for their arrays. The microarray core at Albert Einstein College of Medicine in the Bronx, New York, has established and used its own array system since 1998. Many aspects of making cDNA microarrays and protocols for spotting arrays can be found at its website: http://microarray1k.aecom. yu.edu.

In most spotted arrays, the two-color or two-channel method is used. Both control (labeled with Cy3) and test (labeled with Cy5) samples are cohybridized onto the same array. In most studies, samples are run on microarrays at least in duplicate. Therefore, a dye swap (test sample labeled with Cy5 on one chip and with Cy3 on the other) is usually performed to control for variations introduced by the labeling with two different dyes rather than due to variations in gene expression.

The basic workflow begins with total RNA or mRNA annealed with oligo-dT primers followed by first strand cDNA synthesis by reverse transcription. In this step, fluorescent dyes, Cy3 and Cy5, are incorporated into cDNA targets. After cDNA cleanup and concentration, the sample is hybridized to the array overnight at a specific temperature that is suitable for each type of array. Arrays are then washed with different stringency buffers, spun dry, and then scanned. Many scanners available such as Axon (Molecular Device), ScanArray (PerkinElmer), and DNA Microarray Scanner (Agilent). All of them have different models that are designed for different throughputs and laser requirements. Depending on the spot density, arrays can be scanned at either 5- or 10-μm resolution. In some cases, only a single dye is used on arrays. The workflow is the same for this single-channel method, using only one sample on each chip, but the data analysis will be very different.

Scanned images are analyzed using image analysis software that is provided with each scanner. The software packages differ in the details of their operation, but the basic principle is very similar. All of them overlay the two images (Cy3-green and Cy5-red) to form a single composite image. A grid with the spot information (Gene ID) is applied to the image and automatically adjusted to each spot. In most image analysis procedures, all irregular spots are flagged with different symbols to indicate the reason, such as signal intensity too low, spots run into each other, or speckles on the spots. If required, data generated from these contaminated spots can be discarded prior to further analysis.

Most software provides many values in the output raw data files including the mean and median of signal and background intensity. In most studies, the final spot signal intensity is given by subtracting the mean background signal intensity from the median signal intensity. However, this is very subjective and other methods are also used. After all of the raw data have been generated, data analysis identifies the differentially expressed spot (genes) among different sample groups. This is discussed later in this Section 5.3.2.5.

5.3.2.2 Example Platform

There are many commercial providers of oligonucleotide microarrays such as Affymetrix (GeneChip arrays) and Agilent (DNA microarray). Agilent microarrays contain long oligonucleotides and use the two-color method. Affymetrix arrays contain short oligonucleotides and use a one-color method (one sample per chip). This section uses Affymetrix as an example to show the workflow. Only high-quality

RNA should be used for microarray experiments. Most laboratories use an Agilent 2100 Bioanalyzer to check RNA integrity and only samples with an RNA integrity number (RIN) above 6 are used. Although Affymetrix has its own labeling reaction kit, the Ambion Message Amp II Biotin Enhanced Kit is used in this laboratory because it performs more consistently. The procedure in this laboratory uses the Ambion protocol for RNA amplification followed by the Affymetrix hybridization protocols for all GeneChip array procedures (Figure 5.4).

Briefly, 1 μg of total RNA is used for reverse transcription to produce single-strand cDNA (using oligo-dT primers) followed by second strand synthesis to form double-strand cDNA. After cDNA purification, biotin-labeled aRNA target is produced by an *in vitro* transcription (IVT) reaction using the cDNA template.

After aRNA purification, an aliquot of the labeled aRNA is run on Agilent's Bioanalyzer as a quality check and another aliquot is quantified using the Nanodrop UV/Vis spectrophotometer (Nanodrop). Only high-quality aRNA with a yield of more than 10 μg is fragmented and hybridized to Affymetrix GeneChip arrays overnight (18 hr) in a temperature-controlled hybridization oven. After hybridization, GeneChip arrays are loaded onto a Fluidic Station 450 for washing and staining using the standard Affymetrix procedure. After the final wash, the GeneChip arrays are scanned using the Affymetrix GeneChip Scanner 3000 G7. Scanned images are analyzed using Affymetrix data analysis software (GDAS) to generate the raw data.

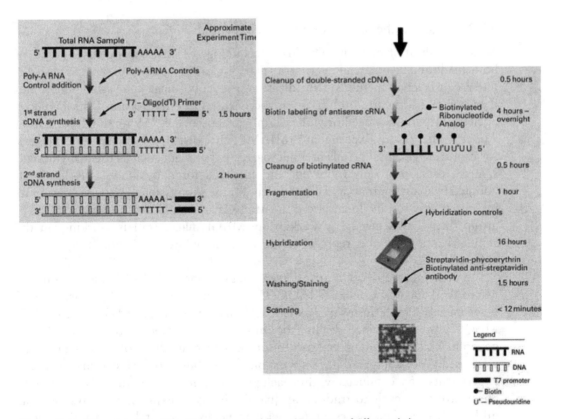

Figure 5.4   Affymetrix GeneChip Expression workflow. (Courtesy of Affymetrix.)

5.3.2.3   QA/SOP Issues

Many factors affect the quality of microarray results. The most important factor is the quality of the RNA samples. RNA degrades far more readily than DNA. Handling of RNA samples requires more care and precision. Therefore, only high-quality RNA (A260/280 ratio between 1.8 and 2.2) should be used. The Agilent Bioanalyzer is one of the most powerful instruments available for detecting DNA/RNA quality. All RNA samples run on gene expression microarray chips required quality checks using the Agilent Bioanalyzer. In most cases, the RIN of each sample must be above 6 for the microarray experiment.

Each company has its own rigid QA/QC protocols to ensure that its products produce consistent high-quality results. End users have to follow the SOP provided by their chip provider in order to obtain the consistent results reported by the supplier. On the Affymetrix platform, the products of cRNAs are run twice on the Bioanalyzer to ensure it is of good quality. Only samples with the correct length distribution are used for the array hybridization.

For Affymetrix platforms, the image analysis results of each chip include a quality report file. It states the call rate (the percentage of probes that are expressed in the samples), the results of positive and negative controls, average the signal intensity, the 3' and 5' expression ratio of the same housekeeping genes, and many other parameters that can be further used in determination of the quality of chip results. Only chips that have passed the factory threshold recommendation should be used in further data analysis.

5.3.2.4   MIAME Checklist and Platform Comparison

No standardization exists in microarray technology because many different types of homemade and commercial microarray platforms are available, all of which use different construction methods, hybridization protocols, image analysis methods, and data analysis software. In 2001, the Microarray Gene Expression Data (MGED) Society (http://www.mged.org/index.html) proposed the "Minimum Information About a Microarray Experiment" (MIAME) checklist that provides a framework for capturing essential details in a microarray experiment such as the array design, samples used, protocols followed, and methods for data analysis. It has been adopted by many journals as a requirement for the submission of papers incorporating microarray results. In addition, the MicroArray and Gene Expression (MAGE) group (http://www.mged.org/Workgroups/MAGE/mage.html) is working on the standardization of the representation of gene expression data and relevant annotations.

In September 2006, Nature Biotechnology reported [43–49] results from the MicroArray Quality Control (MAQC) Consortium, which studied performance of seven microarray platforms that included Affymetrix, Agilent, and GE systems. This MAQC project combined results from more than 100 reports from 51 academic, governmental, and commercial institutions in which hundreds of microarray chips were used. They compared not only the platforms, but also the locations where the experiments were conducted within each platform. In addition, they also compared the microarray result to traditional quantitative gene expression assays, such as qRT-PCR. Their data suggested that, with proper experimental design and analysis, all of these different platforms are reliable and compatible with each other and are in line with qRT-PCR.

5.3.2.5   Data Analysis Issues

Microarrays and other technologies are in their infancy and there are still many issues to resolve concerning how to interpret results from these high-throughput experiments and how to interpret the outcomes. In a critical review of published microarray experiments [50], the authors examined microarray data from 90 papers published between 2000 and 2004. They were compared with respect to their statistical analysis and their stratification with regard to clinical cancer outcome. In the case of translational research, it is clearly the outcome-related genes that are of primary interest and these are the genes addressed in this paper. The authors' main concern was related to the occurrence of "false-positive" results, which, when using a P value of <0.05 on a microarray containing 10,000 genes gives rise to 500 false-positive signals by chance alone. Therefore, the authors suggested that a P value of <0.001 when performing such an analysis would be more appropriate. The authors preferred the far more stringent Benjamini–Hochberg method [51] using a 10% level to restrict the false discovery rate. The papers quoted here conform to the guidelines set out in [50], although they also use other analysis criteria (such as support vector machines) that are not addressed in the paper. As experimental and analytical methods improve over time, the classification criteria will also change so the examples quoted next should be regarded more as examples of principle rather than suggested practice.

5.3.2.6   Biomedical Informatics Requirements

A few commercially available software packages are available for microarray data analysis such as GeneSpring (Agilent), GeneSifter (GeneSifter), Spotfire (Spotfire), and Resolver Expression Data Analysis System (Rosetta Inpharmatics). In addition, software has been developed by academic institutions that is freely distributed, such as DCHIP [52], Clustering, and TreeView. These software packages provide basic data analysis methods and visualization tools. It should be possible to obtain reliable identification of genes that are differentially expressed between experimental and control samples using any one of the software packages just mentioned. Most of the packages also include some statistical tests that can be used for more detailed analysis. Once the differentially expressed genes have been identified, the next step is to make sense of their biological meaning before it can be related to patient outcome and used in translational research. A few software packages are available commercially for pathway analysis, such as Ingenuity (Ingenuity), Explain (Biobase), and PathwayAssist (Iobion). Detailed analysis methods will be discussed in Chapters 8 and 9.

5.3.2.7   Future Directions

Microarray technology has become one of the most popular and powerful technologies in genomic research and has become a standard technology in translational research. With the completion of the Human Genome Sequencing Project, the esti-mate of human protein coding genes is between 20,000 and 25,000. Most of the cur-rent whole genome microarrays cover almost all of these transcripts. Alternatively, it is possible to obtain microarrays that focus on specific diseases or pathways, and it is also possible to have custom arrays prepared for those projects with special requirements. The major developments will take place in sample preparation, which will allow the use of smaller samples that have been archived for other purposes. Such samples were not prepared with RNA analysis in mind and so the RNA quality will be suboptimal, for example, FFPE samples that are isolated using microdissected, laser-captured samples. Companies such as NuGEN are focusing on the amplification of RNA for microarray experiments from as little as 1 ng of total RNA.

More than 60% of human genes undergo alternative splicing and yield hun-dreds of thousands of functionally distinct transcript variants. In addition, many disease-causing point mutations affect RNA splicing. Hence, the need for arrays capable of detecting these splicing events has increased dramatically in the last few years. The Affymetrix Exon array is one of the platforms designed to target these splicing events. It has an increased number of probes that target individual exons of most gene sequences and so can identify expression levels of individual exons, which, together with novel analysis algorithms, has allowed the detection of correct and incorrect splicing events.

Another new and highly focused microarray application for gene expression has emerged in the last few years that goes beyond traditional analyses. It is known as genome-wide location analysis and also called ChIP-on-Chip (chromatin Immunoprecipitation-on-chip). This powerful new platform is used for exploring transcriptional activities by allowing the determination of the precise location on the genomic DNA sequence where a regulatory protein is bound. These binding sites may indicate regions of DNA containing regulatory sites for methylation, histone modification, DNA replication, modification, and repair and so help in the identifi-cation of target genes involved in development and disease progression. Such an approach has been used in research into various diseases such as diabetes, leukemia, and breast cancer.

5.3.3   Chips for Alternative Splicing Analysis (GeneChip Exon)

The number of genes in the human genome has been estimated by the Human Genome Sequencing Project as between 20,000 and 25,000, which is considerably lower than the 100,000 to 150,000 estimated based on expressed sequence tag (ESTs). Though the number of protein coding genes is less than expected, it is quite possible that the diversity of proteins made in the human body may well be as high or higher than the number anticipated from the high number of genes estimated before the sequencing of the human genome. Alternative RNA splicing is thought to be the major cause for this diversity. This, of course, suggests that the old paradigm of "one gene, one protein" (and one function) is an oversimplification.

RNA splicing is a posttranscriptional process that occurs prior to translation. It is an essential, highly regulated, and complex step. A gene is first transcribed into a premessenger RNA (pre-mRNA) that contains multiple exons and introns. During

RNA splicing, introns are removed and exons are retained to form the mature mRNA. Because of the existence of many exons and introns in premRNA, different combination of exons can be retained in the mature mRNA, thus creating a diverse array of mRNAs. This is the process referred to as alternative RNA splicing [53]. It is estimated that between 50% and 75% of human genes undergo alternate splicing, yielding hundreds of thousands of mature mRNAs that may encode proteins with many distinct functions.

Alternate splicing can occur in either coding or noncoding regions. If it includes the coding region, it will affect the final protein sequence and structure, whereas alternate splicing of the noncoding regions might change regulatory regions and hence affect the level of protein expression. The association between alternate splicing and cancer has become a new focus point in cancer research [24, 54, 55].

5.3.3.1   Array Technology

To study alternate splicing events in a high-density, high-throughput manner, Affymetrix has developed a line of products that includes GeneChip Exon Arrays and the Whole Transcript (WT) Sense Target Labeling Assay. The GeneChip Human Exon 1.0 ST Array contains about 45,000 genes with an average of 10 exons per gene and four probes per exon. This probe set design enables not only expression analysis but also analysis of alternate splicing. The WT Sense Target Labeling Assay is made specifically for the Exon arrays. It utilizes a random priming strategy with end-point DNA fragmentation and labeling. The basic workflow of the assay is discussed next.

One microgram of total RNA is mixed with control poly-A RNA and subjected to rRNA reduction. After RNA cleanup and concentration, the first round of cDNA synthesis is carried out, after which in vitro transcription is conducted overnight to produce cRNA. Following cRNA cleanup on the second day, second-round first-strand cDNA synthesis is carried out using random primers with 8 μg of cRNA. This cRNA/cDNA hybrid is treated with RNase H to remove cRNA followed by a cDNA cleanup step. Fragmentation and terminal labeling of the cDNA generates a target for alternative splicing analysis where 5.5 μg of cDNA is injected into arrays for overnight hybridization. Day 3 involves standard washing, staining, and scanning of arrays.

Because this is a relatively new technology and there are about 1.4 million data points per sample, data analysis is very challenging. New algorithms have been developed and further development is in progress. It is expected that easier and more accurate analysis methods will be available in the near future; for now, however, the method recommended by Affymetrix is sufficient. Detailed information about the Affymetrix data analysis algorithms can be found in an Affymetrix technical note available at their website (http://www.affymetrix.com).

5.3.3.2   Biomedical Informatics Requirements

Because this is a relatively new application of gene array technology, very few commercial software packages are available. In addition to Affymetrix's own software, XRAY (Biotique) and Partek Genomics Suite (Partek) are two packages targeted specifically at splicing analysis. With the millions of data points generated for each sample, tracking and storage are always key issues in biomedical informatics support.

5.3.3.3 Future Directions

The potential to detect splicing events makes this technology an important tool for gene expression analysis. Together with traditional expression microarrays and DNA genotyping data, this technology turns genomic research into a complete package for biomedical studies. New developments are aimed at making this technology more automated and more affordable to researchers.

5.4 Translational Research Case Studies

We have described genomic technologies that are used in translational medical research. We have selected two cases to demonstrate the applications of these technologies. The two cases presented in the following subsections both use aCGH and microarrays as the analytical technologies. As mentioned earlier in this chapter, changes in gene expression may be due to loss of function of a regulatory gene/protein that is expressed at normal levels. For this reason, the changes are not detectable in microarray analysis, although the effects of these mutations are seen in changes in expression of all downstream genes. Therefore, the aCGH/microarray combination type of analysis gives an indication of not only those pathways (genes) that are disrupted but it also, by identifying amplified/deleted chromosomal loci that are causative of the changes in gene expression, indicates the primary lesions that may be responsible for the disease.

Obviously, these two approaches are complementary and provide one example of the power of biomedical informatics in translational research since informatics is able to pool the results from these independent assays and analyze them to provide maximal benefit for the patient. This combination is seen here between different genomic technologies, but is obviously not limited to them, and later in the book case studies will be presented that pool more disparate data sets to the same end. Such an analysis is important because, although genes are easy to measure, it is their products (activated proteins) that finally affect a cell's metabolism.

These approaches have certain benefits when performed in isolation; however, their true translational benefits are displayed when performed in combination as can be seen in the cases presented. Case 1 represents a review of a series of separate microarrays and aCGH experiments performed by different groups on different samples, so it provides a more generalized view of gene expression and locus involvement, yet it also includes a correlation of locus with transcript, which indicates that there is some relationship between the two. Case 2 is a single study on pancreatic adenocarcinoma in which microarray analysis and an aCGH study were performed on the same tissue and identifies the benefits of using this type of strategy.

5.4.1   Case 1

In the original classic paper by Fearon and Vogelstein [56], colorectal cancer was proposed to progress by a pathway that proceeded from early adenomas through intermediate and late adenomas to adenocarcinoma. It was proposed that, as the tumor advanced through the earlier stages, it acquired more mutations and its growth became more aggressive (although this is now considered to be more restricted to tumors originating in the distal part of the colon). It appears that colon tumors originating proximal or distal to the splenic flexure contain mutations caused by either microsatellite instability (MSI) or chromosomal instability (CIN), respectively. These two types of mutational events have different prognoses (CIN is poorer than MSI). Hence, it is important to understand the types of mutations present in a patient with colon cancer so that treatment may be adjusted accordingly depending on the prognosis.

In [57], the authors reviewed published data from more than 30 publications reporting microarray data from colon cancer tissues or cell lines in humans or mice. They identified 128 genes reported in three or more papers as being differentially expressed between colorectal adenomas and carcinomas when compared to normal mucosa. They also identified a small number of genes showing differential expression in patients with a good or poor prognosis and a different set that varied between patients with CIN or MSI [58, 59], but there was less consistency between the papers analyzed.

They then repeated the analysis using aCGH data reported for the same types (but different cases) of colorectal cancer. Because aCGH technology was developed more recently, there are fewer published reports but, nevertheless, they were able to identify a similar increase in genetic alterations during progression from the adenoma to the carcinoma stage, in agreement with the original suggestions of Fearon and Vogelstein. Array-based CGH analysis also showed differences in chromosomal loss between tumors classified as CIN or MSI in that CIN or MSI tumors tend to show genomic alterations at mutually exclusive chromosomal loci.

This paper illustrates the power of combining clinical data with multiple genomic assays, but suffers from the fact that this involves an analysis of multiple results performed by different groups using different DNA/RNA preparation procedures, on samples that were acquired from different surgeries under different conditions. Nevertheless, the results are indicative of the potential of this type of approach because the authors are able to identify data indicating that the changes in gene expression are linked to chromosomal gain or loss.

5.4.2   Case 2

Most cases of pancreatic adenocarcinoma present very late, such that the tumor is usually very advanced on diagnosis. This probably accounts for the fact that the 5-year survival rate for those patients undergoing surgery is <5% [60]. As with other cancers, advanced stages of the disease are associated with multiple chromosomal aberrations many of which are consistently reported in different studies. This consistency of reporting indicates that these aberrations are probably involved in disease progression. As with other cancers, the number of mutations and their location is, generally, inversely related to a patient's outcome. As mentioned previously, chromosomal loss leads to loss of genes and, subsequently, alterations in gene expression. Therefore, the two studies (aCGH and microarray analysis of gene expression) provide complementary data: aCGH reports the chromosomal regions that have been amplified or deleted, biomedical informatics identifies the genes located in the affected regions, microarrays identify the genes whose expression is affected, and biomedical informatics relates the genes to their metabolic function. This information is then correlated with patient outcome. In addition, many metabolic pathways in cells are interconnected, so deleting one gene is likely to lead to changes in multiple pathways.

A recent report [61] presented both aCGH and microarray gene expression data from the same tissue and then examined it to see if it correlated with patient outcome. This analysis showed that those tumors associated with a more malignant clinical determination had more chromosomal aberrations. Secondly, certain chromosomal loci (from aCGH data) were consistently amplified or deleted in more malignant cases of adenocarcinoma. Thirdly, certain differentially expressed genes (from microarrays) were also found to be associated with poorer patent prognosis. Finally, comparison of the aCGH and microarray data showed that the differentially expressed genes were often found in the chromosomal regions identified as being amplified or deleted. Of these regions a small number were found to be associated with patient prognosis. This raises the hope that not only can this set of tools be used for identifying a particular treatment regimen that will be optimal for patient survival, but it may also allow the development of a personalized drug treatment based on underexpressed or overexpressed genes.

5.5 Summary

This chapter focused on obtaining data from the analysis of gene structure and expression in human specimens. The methodologies described here include DNA sequencing, DNA copy analysis using array comparative genomic hybridization, genotyping using SNPs, gene expression analysis using microarrays, gene expression analysis using PCR, and chips for alternative splicing analysis.

For each methodology, the fundamentals of the technology were described, followed by examples of how the method is used and an outline of the experimental procedure. Other issues such as QA/SOP considerations, biomedical informatics requirements, and future directions of the technologies were also discussed wherever appropriate. Two case studies were presented to illustrate how the genomic technologies can be applied to translations research.

References

[1]   Saiki, R. K., et al., "Primer-Directed Enzymatic Amplification of DNA with a Thermostable DNA-Polymerase." *Science*, Vol. 239, 1988, pp. 487–491.

[2]   Sanger, F., S. Nicklen, and A. R. Coulson, "DNA Sequencing with Chain-Terminating Inhibitors," Proc. Natl. Acad. Sci. USA, Vol. 74, 1977, pp. 5463–5467.

[3]   Maxam, A. M., and W. Gilbert, "New Method for Sequencing DNA," Proc. Natl. Acad.Sci. USA, Vol. 74, 1977, pp. 560–564.

[4]   Sanger, F. and Coulson, A. R., "Rapid Method for Determining Sequences in DNA by Primed Synthesis with DNA-Polymerase," *J. Molecular Biol.,* Vol. 94, 1975, pp. 441-&.

[5]   Ronaghi, M., M. Uhlen, and P. Nyren, "A Sequencing Method Based on Real-Time Pyrophosphate," *Science,* Vol. 281, 1998, pp. 363, 365.

[6]   Wang, H., et al., "DNA Heterogeneity and Phosphorylation Unveiled by Single-Molecule Electrophoresis," *Proc. Natl. Acad. Sci. USA,* Vol. 101, 2004, pp. 13,472–13,477.

[7]   Deamer, D. W., and D. Branton, "Characterization of Nucleic Acids by Nanopore Analysis," *Acc. Chem. Res.,* Vol. 35, 2002, pp. 817–25.

[8]   Wang, H., and D. Branton, "Nanopores with a Spark for Single-Molecule Detection," *Nat. Biotechnol.,* Vol. 19, 2001, pp. 622–623.

[9]   Kasianowicz, J. J., et al., "Characterization of Individual Polynucleotide Molecules Using a Membrane Channel," *Proc. Natl. Acad. Sci. USA,* Vol. 93, 1996, pp. 13770–3.

[10] Schork, N. J., D. Fallin, and J. S. Lanchbury, "Single Nucleotide Polymorphisms and the Future of Genetic Epidemiology," *Clin. Genet.,* Vol. 58, 2000, pp. 250–264.

[11] Emahazion, T., et al., "SNP Association Studies in Alzheimer's Disease Highlight Problems for Complex Disease Analysis," *Trends Genet.,* Vol. 17, 2001, pp. 407–413.

[12] Tost, J., and Gut, I. G., "Genotyping Single Nucleotide Polymorphisms by MALDI Mass Spectrometry in Clinical Applications," *Clin. Biochem.,* Vol. 38, 2005, pp. 335–350.

[13] Guzey, C., and Spigset, O., "Genotyping as a Tool to Predict Adverse Drug Reactions," *Curr. Top. Med. Chem.,* Vol. 4, 2004, pp. 1411–1421.

[14] Pirmohamed, M., and Park, B. K., "Genetic Susceptibility to Adverse Drug Reactions," *Trends Pharmacol. Sci.,* Vol. 22, 2001, pp. 298–305.

[15] Marsh, S., Kwok, P., and McLeod, H. L., "SNP Databases and Pharmacogenetics: Great Start, But a Long Way to Go," *Hum. Mutat.,* Vol. 20, 2002, pp. 174–179.

[16] McCarthy, J. J., and Hilfiker, R., "The Use of Single-Nucleotide Polymorphism Maps in Pharmacogenomics," *Nat. Biotechnol.,* Vol. 18, 2000, pp. 505–508.

[17] Gibbs, R. A., et al., "The International HapMap Project," *Nature,* Vol. 426, 2003, pp. 789–796.

[18] Tian, L., et al., "Sequencing Complex Diseases with HapMap," *Genetics,* Vol. 168, 2004, pp. 503–511.

[19] Ribas, G., et al., "Evaluating HapMap SNP Data Transferability in a Large-Scale Genotyping Project Involving 175 Cancer-Associated Genes," *Hum. Genet.,* Vol. 118, 2006, pp. 669–679.

[20] Johnson, J. M., et al., "Genome-Wide Survey of Human Alternative Pre-mRNA Splicing with Exon Junction Microarrays," *Science,* Vol. 302, 2003, pp. 2141–2144.

[21] Karni, R., et al., "The Gene Encoding the Splicing Factor Sf2/Asf Is a Proto-Oncogene," *Nat. Struct. Mol. Biol.,* Vol. 14, 2007, pp. 185–193.

[22] Wang, L., et al., "Alternative Splicing Disrupts a Nuclear Localization Signal in Spleen Tyrosine Kinase That Is Required for Invasion Suppression in Breast Cancer," *Cancer Res.,* Vol. 63, 2003, pp. 4724–4730.

[23] Spena, S., Tenchini, M. L., and Buratti, E., "Cryptic Splice Site Usage in Exon 7 of the Human Fibrinogen B Beta-Chain Gene Is Regulated by a Naturally Silent SF2/ASF Binding Site Within This Exon," *RNA,* Vol. 12, 2006, pp. 948–958.

[24] Gautschi, O., et al., "Cyclin D1 in Non-Small Cell Lung Cancer: A Key Driver of Malignant Transformation," *Lung Cancer,* Vol. 55, 2007, pp. 1–14.

[25] Chen, G. G., et al., "Single Nucleotide Polymorphism in the Promoter Region of Human Alpha-Fetoprotein (AFP) Gene and Its Significance in Hepatocellular Carcinoma (HCC)," *Eur. J. Surg. Oncol.,* Vol. 33, 2007, pp. 882–886.

[26] Elahi, E., et al., "Intragenic SNP Haplotypes Associated with 84dup18 Mutation in TNFRSF11A in Four FEO Pedigrees Suggest Three Independent Origins for This Mutation," *J. Bone Miner. Metab.,* Vol. 25, 2007, pp. 159–164.

[27] Kohaar, I., et al., "TNFalpha-308G/A Polymorphism as a Risk Factor for HPV Associated Cervical Cancer in Indian Population," *Cell Oncol.*, Vol. 29, 2007, pp. 249–256.

[28] Brodie, S. G., et al., "Multiple Genetic Changes Are Associated with Mammary Tumorigenesis in Brca1 Conditional Knockout Mice," *Oncogene*, Vol. 20, 2001, pp. 7514–7523.

[29] Carrasco, D. R., et al., "High-Resolution Genomic Profiles Define Distinct Clinico-Pathogenetic Subgroups of Multiple Myeloma Patients," *Cancer Cell*, Vol. 9, 2006, pp. 313–325.

[30] Bell, D. R., and Van Zant, G., "Stem Cells, Aging, and Cancer: Inevitabilities and Outcomes," *Oncogene*, Vol. 23, 2004, pp. 7290–7296.

[31] Cowell, J. K., and Nowak, N. J., "High-Resolution Analysis of Genetic Events in Cancer Cells Using Bacterial Artificial Chromosome Arrays and Comparative Genome Hybridization," *Adv. Cancer Res.*, Vol. 90, 2003, pp. 91–125.

[32] Snijders, A. M., et al., "Assembly of Microarrays for Genome-Wide Measurement of DNA Copy Number," *Nat. Genet.*, Vol. 29, 2001, pp. 263–264.

[33] Nowak, N. J., et al., "Genome-Wide Aberrations in Pancreatic Adenocarcinoma," *Cancer Genet. Cytogenet.*, Vol. 161, 2005, pp. 36–50.

[34] Shankar, G., et al., "aCGHViewer: A Generic Visualization Tool for aCGH Data," *Cancer Inform.*, Vol. 2, 2006, pp. 36–43.

[35] Bustin, S. A, "Absolute Quantification of mRNA Using Real-Time Reverse Transcription Polymerase Chain Reaction Assays," *J. Mol. Endocrinol.*, Vol. 25, 2000, pp. 169–193.

[36] Lee, L. G., Connell, C. R., and Bloch, W., "Allelic Discrimination by Nick-Translation PCR with Fluorogenic Probes," *Nucleic Acids Res.*, Vol. 21, 1993, pp. 3761–3766.

[37] Livak, K. J., et al., "Oligonucleotides with Fluorescent Dyes at Opposite Ends Provide a Quenched Probe System Useful for Detecting PCR Product and Nucleic Acid Hybridization," *PCR Methods Appl.*, Vol. 4, 1995, pp. 357–362.

[38] Pfaffl, M. W., "A New Mathematical Model for Relative Quantification in Real-Time RT-PCR," *Nucleic Acids Research.*, Vol. 29, 2001, p. 45.

[39] Livak, K. J., and Schmittgen, T. D., "Analysis of Relative Gene Expression Data Using Real-Time Quantitative PCR and the 2(-Delta Delta C(T)) Method," *Methods*, Vol. 25, 2001, pp. 402–408.

[40] Sofi Ibrahim, M., et al., "Real-Time PCR Assay to Detect Smallpox Virus," *J. Clin. Microbiol.*, Vol. 41, 2003, pp. 3835–3839.

[41] Huletsky, A., et al., "New Real-Time PCR Assay for Rapid Detection of Methicillin-Resistant *Staphylococcus aureus* Directly from Specimens Containing a Mixture of Staphylococci," *J. Clin. Microbiol.*, Vol. 42, 2004, pp. 1875–1884.

[42] Svenstrup, H. F., et al., "Development of a Quantitative Real-Time PCR Assay for Detection of *Mycoplasma genitalium*," *J. Clin. Microbiol.*, Vol. 43, 2005, pp. 3121–3128.

[43] (2006). Making the most of microarrays. Nat Biotechnol 24, 1039.

[44] Canales, R. D., et al., "Evaluation of DNA Microarray Results with Quantitative Gene Expression Platforms," *Nat. Biotechnol.*, Vol. 24, 2006, pp. 1115–1122.

[45] Frueh, F. W., "Impact of Mircoarray Data Quality on Genomic Data Submissions to the FDA," *Nat. Biotechnol.*, Vol. 24, 2006, pp. 1105–1107

[46] Guo, L., et al., "Rat Toxicogenomic Study Reveals Analytical Consistency Across Mircoarray Platforms," *Nat. Biotechnol.*, Vol. 24, 2006, pp. 1162–1169.

[47] Patterson, T. A., et al., "Performance Comparison of One-Color and Two-Color Platforms within the MircoArray Quality Control (MAQC) Project," *Nat. Biotechnol.*, Vol. 24, 2006, pp. 1140–1150.

[48] Shi, L., et al., "The MicroArray Quality Control (MAQC) Project Shows Inter- and Intraplatform Reproducibility of Gene Expression Measurements," *Nat. Biotechnol.*, Vol. 24, 2006, pp. 1151–1161.

[49] Tong, W., et al., "Evaluation of External RNA Controls for the Assessment of Microarray Performance," *Nat. Biotchnol.*, Vol. 24, pp. 1132–1139.

[50] Dupuy, A., and Simon, R. M., "Critical Review of Published Microarray Studies for Cancer Outcome and Guidelines on Statistical Analysis and Reporting," *J. Natl. Cancer Inst.*, Vol. 99, 2007, pp. 147–157.

[51] Hochberg, Y., and Benjamini, Y, "More Powerful Procedures for Multiple Significance Testing," *Statistics Med.*, Vol. 9, 1990, pp. 811–818.

[52] Li, C., and Wong, W. H., "Model-Based Analysis of Oligonucleotide Arrays: Expression Index Computation and Outlier Detection," *Proc.Natl. Acad. Sci. USA,* Vol. 98, 2001, pp. 31–36.

[53] Lopez, A. J., "Alternative Splicing of Pre-mRNA: Developmental Consequences and Mechanisms of Regulation," *Annu. Rev. Genet.*, Vol. 32, 1998, pp. 279–305.

[54] Bignell, G., et al., "Sequence Analysis of the Protein Kinase Gene Family in Human Testicular Germ-Cell Tumors of Adolescents and Adults," *Genes Chromosomes & Cancer*, Vol. 45, 2006, pp. 42–46.

[55] Yousef, G. M., et al., "Identification of New Splice Variants and Differential Expression of the Human Kallikrein 10 Gene, a Candidate Cancer Biomarker," *Tumor Biol.*, Vol. 26, 2005, pp. 227–235.

[56] Fearon, E. R., and Vogelstein, B., "A Genetic Model for Colorectal Tumorigenesis," *Cell,* Vol. 61, 1990, pp. 759–767.

[57] Cardoso, J., et al., "Expression and Genomic Profiling of Colorectal Cancer," *Biochim., Biophys.Acta–Rev. Cancer,* Vol. 1775, 2007, pp. 103–137.

[58] Gervaz, P., Bucher, P., and Morel, P, "Two Colons–Two Cancers: Paradigm Shift and Clinical Implications," *J. Surg. Oncol.*, Vol. 88, 2004, pp. 261–266.

[59] Goel, A., et al., "Characterization of Sporadic Colon Cancer by Patterns of Genomic Instability," *Cancer Res.*, Vol. 63, 2003, pp. 1608–1614.

[60] Alexakis, N., et al., "Current Standards of Surgery for Pancreatic Cancer," *Br. J. Surg.*, Vol. 91, 2004, pp. 1410–1427.

[61] Loukopoulos, P., et al., "Genome-Wide Array-Based Comparative Genomic Hybridization Analysis of Pancreatic Adenocarcinoma: Identification of Genetic Indicators That Predict Patient Outcome," *Cancer Sci.*, Vol. 98, 2007, pp. 392–400.

CHAPTER 6

Proteomics

V. S. Kumar Kolli

6.1 Introduction

Proteins are ubiquitous in nature and are fundamental to life. They are the molecular machines that perform a multitude of functions critical to the cell. The expression of proteins in a cell is dynamic and changes over time and with the physiological state of a cell. There is a great deal of interest in cataloging the changes in protein expression with respect to changing physiological conditions and external stimuli. Knowledge of the patterns of protein expression associated with a biological state and changes in the biological state will lead to an understanding of how proteins communicate with each other in transforming the information through the dynamic networks that they build by associating into multiprotein complexes. These are organized into pathways and they respond to changing conditions and perform vital functions at the cellular level and also regulate gene expression.

Alterations in the protein expression and structure will cause interruptions in the normal intercellular communication and lead to abnormal (diseased) phenotypes. Display of such alterations in the proteome requires high-throughput comprehensive protein separation and protein identification tools. This chapter provides readers with an overview of how information pertaining to proteins is collected from clinical samples and how this molecular information may be translated into knowledge that can improve the health and outcomes of patients with debilitating diseases.

Techniques for sequencing proteins were developed well before the development of DNA sequence analysis, and the first biopolymer to be completely sequenced was a protein, insulin [1]. This molecule had been the trendsetter in the 20th century for the advancement of sequence analysis technology and biotechnology. Insulin, as the first therapeutic protein, laid the foundation for the development of protein databases. A proposal to catalog all human proteins and determine their location, concentration, structure, and interacting partners was debated in the early 1980s utilizing the then recently developed two-dimensional gel electrophoresis technique (2DGE). The plan was never implemented, partly for political reasons, and because of the lack of mature, sensitive technology for identifying the proteins in a high-throughput way. Ultimately, human genome sequencing emerged as the preferred approach for cataloging human genes, and this work enabled the proliferation of new technologies in high-throughput analysis, involving hardware and software, and innovations and improvements in the lab automation procedures.

The release of the complete draft of the human genome [2, 3] at the beginning of the 21st century has opened new avenues for addressing biological and medical questions using genome information as a framework. Although the list of genes does not provide details about how the cells function under different conditions, the genome-wide sequence information enabled the massive parallel analysis of gene expression to study cellular physiology. The gene chips that were developed to rapidly map the gene expression profiles of various cell types, tissue types, physiological states, and states resulting from certain environmental cues have generated large amounts of information about gene functions, gene regulation, and gene interaction dynamics. Genome-wide transcript analysis has shown poor correlation [4] with the levels of the gene's end product, protein, which actually performs the function at the cellular level. This poor correlation has been attributed to differences in translational efficiency, turnover rates, half-life stabilities, compartmentalization of proteins, and post-translational modifications of proteins. Consequently, the techniques to design, characterize, and measure protein levels have moved to center stage in functional genomics to illuminate the properties of biological systems that are not obvious by DNA or mRNA sequence analysis alone.

The invention of two novel ionization techniques, matrix assisted laser desorption ionization (MALDI) [5] and electrospray ionization (ESI) [6], in the early 1990s fueled the application of mass spectrometers to address the structural problems of large biopolymers such as proteins, and the technique of mass spectrometry has evolved along with demands from the field of biology and biomedicine for a more versatile technique for handling the current high-throughput analysis of proteins in the postgenome era.

Modern medicine has hinged on disease diagnostics, and diagnostic pathology has revolutionized the ways in which diseases are detected and how responses to therapies are monitored and predicted. Although diagnostic pathology techniques recognize the patterns or stages of the disease, outcomes of disease intervention are often poor due to the lack of knowledge about the molecular mechanisms that underlie the disease. Advances in molecular biology and molecular profiling techniques have pushed diagnostic pathology to greater heights to classify the diseases based on their molecular profiles and to understand the disease mechanisms associated with the disease phenotypes. The molecular profiling of disease specimens will bring new approaches in diagnosing diseases, in improving therapeutic efficacy, and in opening new avenues for individualized diagnostics and individualized medicine.

To harness the power of molecular profiling research on diseased specimens, the development of tissue and biologics resources across the world is increasing, and the informatics resources used to track and retrieve the annotated information pertaining to the specimens are also evolving to enhance the quality of information that can be provided to benchside scientists and to bedside clinicians to expedite translational research for better patient care.

As mentioned previously, proteins are the building blocks of cells and tissues, and derangements in the protein levels can be displayed through the high-throughput analysis of diseased specimens and comparison of these with profiles from normal specimens to unravel the molecular mechanisms that initiate disease and drive its progression, through the identification of biomarkers associated with the disease.

In this chapter, we describe the analysis of samples that potentially carry information that reflects the changing molecular patterns associated with the disease and how to use this technology to discover biomarkers for disease.

6.2 Clinical Specimens

6.2.1 Body Fluids

The importance of body fluids for disease diagnosis has been proposed since Hippocratic times when diseases were attributed to the imbalance of the constituents of four humors: blood, phlegm, yellow bile, and black bile [7]. Modern medicine has developed diagnostic tests that monitor the levels of proteins and correlate their abnormal quantities to the disease conditions. Recently developed molecular profiling techniques are further probing into body fluids to uncover the potentials of these specimens in disease diagnostics, disease classification, and applications in early disease detection.

Because body fluids comprise the secretions of various tissues in the body, the direct assessment of gene expressions through the analysis of mRNA is not possible in the case of body fluids. Consequently, proteomics has become central to the qualitative and quantitative analysis of proteins in body fluids to relate them to pathophysiological conditions.

Owing to the importance of the characterization of body fluids in understanding human physiology and in discovering biomarkers, the proteomes of several body fluids have already been analyzed in the postgenome era and their proteins have been cataloged to provide reference knowledge about various human body fluids [8], such as plasma/serum, urine, cerebrospinal fluid, saliva, bronchoalveolar lavage fluid, synovial fluid, nipple aspirate fluid, tear fluid, breast milk, and amniotic fluid. The methods developed in sample collections and methods of proteome profiling will leverage this research to capture biomedical molecular information for improved diagnostics and therapeutics.

6.2.1.1 Blood

Blood is a liquid tissue and a medium for transporting signaling molecules, nutrients, and oxygen and for exchanging metabolic wastes, thus maintaining homeostasis at the systemic level. Stoichiometric disturbances in the major constituents of blood reflect malfunctions of the organs or the presence of a disease; hence, the analysis of plasma/serum, the noncellular component of blood, has drawn considerable attention as a target for developing protein diagnostics.

As blood perfuses through the body, it is in direct contact with the tissues such that any aberrant secretions of proteins from the tissues or factors released by apoptic/necrotic activities of cells due to presence of cancer are carried into the circulation. A comprehensive and complete analysis of circulating blood proteins from healthy and diseased states may provide a window for detecting early markers of disease. It has been estimated that more than 10,000 proteins/peptides are present in the plasma/serum, yet only 22 proteins, mostly the proteins secreted from liver and antibodies from the immune cells, make up 99% of proteins in plasma/serum [9]. Analysis of the remaining 1% low in abundance, though highly important proteins is an analytical challenge to the discovery of biomarkers. Several approaches have been developed for selective removal of highly abundant proteins to facilitate the identification of low-abundance plasma/serum proteins by decreasing the dynamic range [10]. There is also growing evidence that the abundant carrier proteins in the blood enrich the protein fragments that are shed from diseased cells in the body, and avoid their clearance from kidneys, thus increasing their utility as potential disease markers. Adding to the complexity of a plasma/serum sample, environmental factors such as food intake and its influence on the physiological conditions of the blood may have large effects on the concentrations of proteins in the blood and may complicate biomarker discovery. Sample handling and preparation are also known to have confounding effects on the interpretation of proteomic results.

The Human Proteome Organization (HUPO), an organization that aims to catalog all human proteins and to develop SOPs for proteomics, has conducted a pilot project on human plasma and serum samples. From the outcomes of this pilot project obtained from 35 labs across the world, the HUPO has issued recommendations for procuring, storing, and analyzing plasma and serum samples. This study has identified more than 3,000 proteins from the plasma proteome [11] using various proteomics platforms, and the protein information and protocols are serving as templates for developing targeted approaches and improving analytical methods for identifying diagnostic markers from various disease-related clinical samples.

6.2.1.2 Urine

Urine is an easily accessible, noninvasive clinical sample. Molecular profiles from urine can be correlated to pathologic conditions, and its composition and profiles of the analytes may mirror pathophysiological processes occurring in the body. Urine has been used as a clinical sample since ancient times to check for abnormalities by physical observations, estimation of protein content, and levels of sugar. These observations can be used to monitor the changing physiological condition of the body. Conventional biochemical methods trace only one or few analytes to diagnose disease condition(s), whereas modern analytical methods can characterize the complete composition of urine and may provide biomedical information that can subclassify the disease conditions and lead to better treatments. Because urine is an ultrafiltrate of blood, the analysis of urine samples may complement the analysis of plasma/serum and may give better clues about disease states.

Urine specimens have potential diagnostic value with regard to diseases associated with the urogenital system and can be used to indirectly assess cardiac and diabetes-related diseases. Studies on profiling the urine proteome revealed that more than 1,000 proteins are present in urine [12] and several techniques are being developed to optimize the sample collection protocols and analytical methods to minimize the preanalytical and technical variations in assessing urine samples for disease diagnostics.

6.2.1.3   Cerebrospinal Fluid

The fluid that circulates within the central nervous system (CNS) is cerebrospinal fluid (CSF) and it acts as a cushion to protect the brain from shocks. CSF is produced by the choroid plexus and is a medium that provides nutrients, communication, and removal of metabolic wastes from the cells of the CNS. This liquid bathes the CNS tissue, so it can be of diagnostic value because it can reflect biochemical changes that distinguish normal and pathophysiological conditions [13]. Molecular profiling techniques are emerging for analyzing CSF specimens to investigate the physiology and the onset of CNS tumors and neurodegenerative diseases such as multiple sclerosis, Alzheimer's, Parkinson's, and Huntington's disease. The biomedical information generated from these specimens comprising various CNS-related pathologies may provide new ways to diagnose CNS diseases and to develop new therapeutics.

6.2.2   Tissue

Tissue specimens from diseased tissues have been the mainstay for disease diagnosis in cancer and other diseases. The utility of clinical tissue samples for molecular profiling research is increasing because they carry rich information pertaining to stage and condition of the disease. Advancements in radiological imaging technology have improved the detection of lesions or benign tumors in the human body and are enabling molecular research to be performed on these benign samples. Comparative molecular profiling research using clinical tissue specimens collected at different stages of disease along with the normal tissues will unlock the mechanisms that underlie the disease initiation and progression and will provide a set of molecular tools to screen, diagnose, and classify neoplastic diseases.

Several hypotheses have been put forward regarding the initiation of cancer mainly involving gene mutations [14], genome instability [14], and epigenetics [15]. Errors can accumulate in the cell's genes, disrupting normal cellular processes and leading to a clonal expansion of the mutated cell, which can evolve into a malignant form with the acquired characteristics of invasiveness and the ability to metastasize. This transformation of a cell also brings changes in the extracellular matrix that surrounds the cell by eliciting mechanisms that favor the growth advantage of neoplastic cells to colonize the tissue. Given the interplay of molecules at the interface of the cell and stroma during the neoplastic transformation, the characterization of factors that are present in the stroma may give further insights into the disease mechanisms.

Histopathology techniques have been the mainstay for diagnosis, classification, and staging of cancer and related diseases. They are the primary predictor of prognosis or outcomes of disease from histological classification. However, evidence is accumulating to suggest that histologically similar tumors can have clinically different behaviors and different outcomes. Outcome prediction will be further worsened if the cancer cells are poorly differentiated, and there is an urgent need to explore alternate ways to classify poorly differentiated cancers because these tumors are highly aggressive. This behavior is attributed to differences in the molecular networks that underlie the tissues and that govern the phenotypic expressions of diseases and the response to therapy. Consequently, molecular profiling techniques are making inroads into diagnostics to better classify and subclassify the disease (cancer) based on the molecular compositions of lesions or tumors. The use of gene expression profiles from breast cancer tissue specimens has successfully subclassified these tumors. Although there is a technological advantage in transcript analysis, the annotation of diseased tissues through proteomics is gaining momentum as changes in protein dynamics directly dictate the disease phenotypes through the networks that they build and control.

The tissue specimens that are collected at different stages of a disease can provide a snapshot of protein expression patterns that reflect the disease phenotypes and may shed light on the protein pathways involved in the transformation of a "normal" tissue to a malignant tissue. In spite of the wealth of biomedical information that can be gleaned from tissues, the molecular analysis of tissues is hampered by the heterogeneous population of cells that constitute the tissue. The recently developed technique of laser capture microdissection (LCM) can help reduce this heterogeneity by allowing the harvesting of a relatively homogeneous population of neoplastic cells [16] from the background cells comprising normal cells, stromal cells, and inflammatory cells in the sample through direct microscopic visualization and dissection. This enables molecular profiling of the harvested cells, which helps to map the molecular pathways that are associated with the disease phenotypes.

The ability to amplify nucleic acids (DNA and RNA) allows their recovery from various tissue samples that were collected and preserved using various protocols, thus favoring genomic analysis over proteomic analysis. Coupling of LCM techniques with high-performance and ultrasensitive liquid chromatography/mass spectrometry (LC/MS) instruments for tissue protein profiling along with the improvements in the protein sample preparation using single-tube methods and even the development of protein extraction procedures for recovering proteins from FFPE specimens have greatly increased the utility of proteomic analysis of diseased tissues. Millions of FFPE specimens have been preserved across the world, and the improvements in the proteomics protocols will tap into this treasure to mine the biomarkers from FFPE. Preliminary proteomics profiling [17] on these samples revealed that the quality of FFPE samples is comparable to that of flash frozen tissue samples.

6.3 Proteomics Technologies

Currently, the major focus in the application of proteomic techniques to clinical samples is the discovery of biomarkers that have a predictive or prognostic value through the comparative analysis of normal and diseased specimens. There is a paradigm shift happening in these research areas. Biomarkers have traditionally been examined one at a time, but with the advancement of high-throughput proteomic technologies, it has become possible to examine the expression of several proteins simultaneously. Biomarker discovery requires high-resolution methods to display protein profiles that identify the proteins whose expression is altered. With the recent advancements in high-throughput protein profiling technologies, the visualization of global protein expression has been enabled, and improvements in the technology and development of new methods are being based on the knowledge acquired from the pilot studies of biological samples.

Proteomics technology integrates three major analytical components: separation, quantitation, and identification. Separation is the key component in proteomics. It decreases the dynamic range of complex protein mixtures and allows the detection of low-abundance important proteins, which could be potential biomarkers. Recently, several platforms have been developed for multistep separation of proteins that exploit the physical and chemical characteristics of proteins to fractionate the proteins/peptides for proteomic analysis. We describe next some of the major proteome profiling workflows that combine the proteome extraction methods [18] from various clinical specimens to generate information that can be of predictive value for clinical outcomes, disease progression, therapeutic response, and understanding the underlying disease mechanisms. Currently, no single proteomic technique can provide all of the relevant information from pathologic samples to correlate with the clinical outcomes. These techniques are generally complementary and, along with tools to integrate the protein/peptide information with the patient clinical information, will add to the power of translational research.

6.3.1   Two-Dimensional Gel Electrophoresis

The 2DGE technique has been a powerful one for simultaneously resolving thousands of proteins and quantitating differences in protein abundance. Since its introduction in 1975 [19], this technique has been incrementally improved for better separation, visualization, and protein identification (through coupling with mass spectrometry). Given the resolving power of 2DGE, this technique has been widely used in profiling the proteins that are specific to a cell type, tissue type, or body fluid [20]. The inherent power of this technology to display large numbers of proteins simultaneously and detect differences in protein expression and post-translational modifications has enabled the comparative study of proteomes between normal and diseased states.

In 2DGE, proteins are separated based on charge in the first dimension (isoelectric focusing, IEF) and molecular mass in the second dimension (sodium dodecyl sulfate–polyacrylamide gel electrophoresis, SDS-PAGE). These properties are orthogonal and efficiently use the separation space; they also offer a good display of a few thousand proteins. The samples can be run in a wide variety of available dimensions of immobilized pH gradient strips (first dimension) and the SDS-PAGE gels (second dimension). To improve the spatial resolution of protein spots, the pH ranges of the first dimension can be varied or large-format gels can be used in the second dimension.

To visualize the proteins, the gels are stained with a variety of staining reagents whose sensitivity and dynamic range differ in capturing the descriptive and quantitative information. The most commonly used dye, Coomassie blue, has a poor sensitivity (25 ng protein/spot) and two orders of dynamic range compared to the most sensitive, silver stain, with <1 ng protein/spot sensitivity but with a poor linear dynamic range (~1 order of magnitude). The fluorescent stain Syproruby has sensitivity comparable to silver stain with an improved dynamic range (~3 orders of magnitude) for better quantitative analysis.

To derive quantitative information, stained gels are scanned on a densitometer or fluorescent scanner to measure spots for comparative analysis of protein samples. This type of profiling requires running each sample separately on one gel for comparative analysis. It is technically very difficult to duplicate the gel running conditions between samples, which drastically limits the superimposition of images across the samples and limits the utility of this type of analysis.

The introduction of cyanine fluorescent dyes (Cy3 and Cy5) for labeling proteins made it possible to run a pair of samples within the same gel under identical conditions and to measure the relative quantities of proteins between the samples [21]. The application of the differential ingel electrophoresis (DIGE) technique was further improved by Amersham Inc., which developed a 2D DIGE platform to determine the statistically significant protein expression alterations that correlate with the disease or experimentally induced changes in cells [22]. A third dye (Cy2), which was introduced by Amersham, enables an internal standard (which is a pooled sample comprised of equal amounts of protein from each sample involved in the DIGE study) labeled with Cy2 to be included on each gel and allows multiple gels to be linked for accurate quantitative protein expression analysis between the samples. The DIGE technique improved the sensitivity (0.025 ng /protein spot) and dynamic range (~4 orders of magnitude) over the conventional 2DGE technique and the ability to multiplex the samples in the DIGE design reduced the number of gels that needed to be run.

The DIGE gels are scanned on a Typhoon variable-mode imager to acquire the images for the protein sample labeled with each dye, and the images are registered for protein quantitative analysis across the samples to discern the altered expression of proteins between the healthy and diseased states. These fluorescent dyes do not interfere with protein identification by MS because only one lysine per protein molecule is labeled (minimal labeling dyes) and most commonly an unlabeled protein sample is also loaded along with the labeled protein and the gel is poststained with Coomassie blue or Syproruby for picking the spots. The differentially expressed spots whose coordinates are mapped to the coordinates of preparative gel or poststained DIGE gel spots are used to generate a pick list and the spots are excised from the gel to identify the proteins of interest. The identification of protein spots from the DIGE workflows utilizes a robotic workstation to prepare the samples for MS analysis by MALDI- TOFMS or liquid chromatography with tandem mass spectrometry (LC/MS/MS).

The ability of the 2DGE technique to fractionate proteins to discrete spots in a 2D gel made it possible to apply a multitude of analyses on the separated proteins to derive the information pertaining to protein isoforms and post-translational modifications (mainly phosphorylation and glycosylation) of proteins. This also provides a means to probe for the presence of antigens associated with the diseased specimens using the antibodies. For example, the proteins separated on a 2D gel can be sequentially stained with various fluorescent dyes [23] to detect phosphoproteins (Pro-Q diamond), glycoproteins (Pro-Q Emerald), and total proteins in a biological sample (Sypro). This parallel analysis using multiple stains will allow determination of the global functional protein expression differences between the clinical samples. This global knowledge will aid in designing downstream analyses for a more targeted approach to identify protein interactions and pathways involved in the diseased state. Another advantage of fractionating intact proteins in a 2D gel is that they are available for probing with the antibodies/autoantibodies for antigen identification.

The aggressive cytokeratin isoforms that are associated with poor clinical outcomes in the lung adenocarcinoma were identified by a combination of 2DGE and 2D Western blots workflows [24]. Several reports have stressed the importance of profiling host humoral immune responses to developing cancer in the human body and 2D Western blots of proteins displayed on a 2D gel facilitate this type of screening to identify novel cancer antigens from established cancer cell lines or directly using the cancer tissue specimens. This type of screening was demonstrated with breast cancer cell lines using sera from breast cancer patients [25] for identifying tumor antigens.

Despite the advantages offered by 2DGE in profiling clinical samples to associate distinct protein patterns or altered protein expressions with pathologic conditions, this method suffers from several shortcomings. Problems detecting low-abundance proteins; underrepresentation of extremely acidic, basic, and hydrophobic proteins; and problems detecting proteins with high and low molecular weights are among these shortcomings. In addition the method is laborious and plagued with run-to-run variation, which confounds matching spots between runs. Nonetheless, 2DGE is the only technique that has a high-resolution capacity to provide visualization of more than 1,000 intact protein spots in one experiment. The 2DGE technique alone and its multiplexed DIGE version have been used to profile various types of clinical samples, including serum/plasma, CSF, urine, and several types of cancer tissue specimens in order to identify markers associated with disease conditions by differential proteomics [26–30]. To give an example, the 2DGE protein patterns from 24 patients with B-cell chronic lymphocytic leukemia (B-CLL) discriminated the patients based on the clinical variables and identified the altered expression of several classes of proteins: redox enzymes, heat shock protein, and disulfide isomerase associated with the shorter survival [31]. The recently introduced saturation labeling technique using fluorescent dyes improved the profiling of scarce tissue samples using very minute amounts of protein (<5 μg) and recent reviews anticipate further improvements to the 2DGE workflows [32].

6.3.2 MALDI-TOF

The ability to ionize intact large nonvolatile biopolymers using the MALDI technique has impacted biology and biomedicine in addressing the structural analysis of proteins [5]. Unlike ESI, MALDI is a static technique in which the analyte of interest is mixed with an UV absorbing organic compound and spotted on a target for laser irradiation to generate the ions from an analyte. The suitability or compatibility of a time-of-flight (TOF) analyzer in recording the ions associated with each laser pulse exploited this combination further during the last decade. That, along with improvements in the speed of electronics, have helped MALDI evolve into a most robust, sensitive, and very high throughput platform for proteomic applications.

The MALDI-TOF technique has been widely used in conjunction with the 2DGE workflows to identify the proteins mainly by peptide mass fingerprinting (PMF). The front-end NanoLC separation process, which is the key for online ESI/LCMS shotgun proteomics, has been adapted to collect fractions directly onto the MALDI target plates and has demonstrated the capabilities of LC/MALDI in proteomic applications such as biomarker discovery [33]. The added advantage of this time freezing of elution peaks on the target is that it is not subject to time constraints when analyzing the components, so detailed analyses can be performed on the interesting peptides. The spotted plates can be archived for MALDI-MS analysis and this decoupling of separation from high-performance MALDI-TOF/TOF MS instruments enables several workflows to be interfaced to MALDI-MS for protein identification.

The attributes of a MALDI-TOF instrument and its ability to interface with the method-oriented front-end parallel sample preparation has led to the application of this type of MS instrument for high-throughput profiling of blood sera from healthy and diseased individuals to look for biomarker patterns. The seminal work of Petricoin and colleagues [34] demonstrated that peaks obtained from the surface-enhanced laser desorption and ionization (SELDI)-TOF analysis of clinical samples can be used as discriminators to classify disease states and that prediction models can be built based on the SELDI-TOF data for applications in the early detection of cancer. Several front-end peptide fractionation techniques have been developed that employ a wide variety of functionalized (SELDI) surfaces [35] or functionalized magnetic beads [36] with hydrophobic, hydrophilic, anion exchange, cation exchange, and immobilized metal or antibody affinity capture to selectively enrich a subset of proteins/peptides from biological samples for SELDI-TOF and MALDI-TOF profiling. These fractionation methodologies have been automated for robotic handling of samples from parallel processes to spotting the samples along with matrix onto high-density target plates, making this a robust platform for the analysis of hundreds of samples per day in a high-throughput fashion for direct marker analysis from body fluids. Currently, this SELDI/MALDI-TOF technique is being explored to hunt for the peptide signatures from various biological fluids that distinguish disease states using advanced pattern recognition tools.

Despite its usefulness in rapidly revealing pattern differences between sample groups of interest, this method is limited to detecting patterns of peptides with a mass range of 1 to 20 kDa due to sensitivity issues at high mass range and the size of peptides that can be analyzed by TOF/TOF sequence analysis for the ultimate identification of discriminators. However, this technique has shown great promise just using pattern differences as a biomarker for distinguishing among samples, although there has been much debate about the reproducibility of the patterns across a different set of samples and the association of these serum patterns to disease.

A more detailed study of serum samples from patients with three different solid tumors and nonsolid tumor controls by Villanueva et al. [37] shed further light on the origin of low molecular weight peptides. The study concluded that the formation of most of the discriminatory peptides was due to the action of complement and ex vivo exoproteases with a small number of cancer-specific discriminators. Although this study showed evidence for ex vivo formation of low molecular weight peptides, evidence has accumulated from other reports that protein fragments from the cells and tissues that are produced in vivo due to tumor-related processes such as apoptosis, tumor-stromal interaction, vascularization, and immune responses to cancer cells are enriched on carrier proteins and circulate in the blood without being filtered by the kidney. Selective enrichment methods for these carrier-bound factors from Alzheimer's [38] and ovarian cancer [39] sera were demonstrated, and MALDI-TOF analysis distinguished the diseased samples from controls in both cases. Sequence analysis of peptides from the ovarian cancer sera revealed that the albumin associated peptides were derived from the low-abundance proteins that are involved in cellular proliferation, cancer, and cancer signaling pathways. The complete map of peptides in the serum and the carrier-protein-associated peptides achieved by means of high-throughput MALDI-TOF can provide information that may reflect changing patterns in the blood due to disease and may give clues to early disease detection.

Given the gentle desorption of intact analytes from surfaces by UV laser beams with spot widths of ~50 μm, the MALDI technique has drawn considerable attention in the applications of imaging MS to directly analyze tissue proteins and their spatial distribution in a tissue section [40, 41]. The direct analysis of pathologic tissue samples will enable the identification of patterns associated with disease free from the confounding secondary effects of environment and lifestyle that exist in the analysis of body fluids such as serum. To achieve MALDI-MS imaging, a tissue section 5 to 20 μm thick is cut from a frozen tissue block and mounted onto a conductive MALDI target plate. The matrix is deposited on the dried tissue section either as individual spots or as a homogeneous layer depending on the spatial resolution required for the analysis. The proteins are desorbed from each spot upon laser irradiation, and a spectrum of ions is recorded for each laser shot by TOF analysis. The target is rastered to collect data points from all areas and the ion densities from each spot (or pixel) are mapped to get an ion image from each tissue section. The peptide/protein molecular weight–specific patterns are constructed from each pixel or spot to correlate their expression with the disease state or outcome and these patterns may be useful in subclassifying the histological findings.

6.3.3 Liquid Chromatography Mass Spectrometry

The combination of liquid chromatography and mass spectrometry is emerging as an alternative and complementary technique to the 2D DIGE technique for profiling the complex mixture of proteins from clinical samples. The gel-free analysis of complex protein mixtures by mass spectrometry has been possible with an ESI source due its dynamic nature of sample introduction for spray ionization. This property allowed the coupling of LC with the ESI source for online LC/ESI/MS analysis. Several mass spectrometers with different mass analyzer configurations are available for high-throughput proteomics and a variety of front-end protein fractionation methods have been coupled to the LC/MS instrumentation to cover the wide dynamic ranges of protein concentrations in proteome samples. The most widely used workflow to profile the proteins using the LC/MS/MS instrumentation is the so-called bottom-up or shotgun approach [42] for protein analysis.

6.3.3.1 Shotgun Proteomics

In this workflow technique, the extracted protein mixtures from the biological samples are treated with an endoprotease, usually trypsin, and the peptide mixtures are analyzed by an online LC/MS/MS for protein characterization. The LC/MS/MS analysis begins with a sample injection onto a reverse phase C18 column, which separates the peptide mixture over a period of time as solvents are pumped through the column by the high-performance liquid chromatography system. The separated peptides are ionized by nanoESI and sequentially introduced into the mass spectrometer. This dynamic process generates an ion chromatogram with both intensity and time dimensions. For any given time point in the chromatogram, a spectrum of masses (mass-to-charge ratios of peptides) is registered and the complexity of the spectrum depends on the number of components eluted at that particular time.

To be successful with shotgun proteomics, all of the peptides detected in the MS full spectrum or survey spectrum have to be fragmented to obtain peptide sequence information. In a tandem MS or MS/MS analysis, a peptide ion of interest from a mixture of peptide ions is isolated in the first stage and fragmented by collisional activation using an inert gas to produce the fragment ion spectrum in the second stage. Because most modern mass spectrometers have the capability to select peptide ions for tandem MS analysis in a data-dependent mode, the peptides detected in the full-scan mode are selected for MS/MS based on the selection criteria, and the MS is switched between full MS and MS/MS modes. The consecutive acquisition of data points in these two stages can be used to derive semiquantitative protein information.

The cycle time of these alternate events depends on how fast the mass spectrometer collects these data points. The instruments with the faster scan rates and the data systems with the dynamic exclusion of peptides analyzed by MS/MS eliminate the redundant analysis and facilitate the selection of low-abundance peptides for MS/MS analysis by increasing the dynamic range. The newer hybrid mass spectrometers such as LTQFT and LTQ Orbitrap have faster duty cycles (5 times) compared to the first generation data-dependent LCQ ion trap and QTOF instruments and provide more proteome coverage for a given LC/MS run.

It is estimated that there will be as many as 100,000 protein species in a given cell type (the copy numbers of individual proteins may differ from 1 to 100,000) whose concentrations may be spread over 6 orders of magnitude; in the case of plasma/serum, for instance, the dynamic range of protein concentration is ~12 orders for ~10,000 proteins. On average, each protein will give 30 tryptic peptides upon trypsin digestion, and it is a formidable task to achieve deep proteome coverage due to undersampling by 1D LC/MS/MS even on high-performance instruments.

To reduce the complexity of peptides in the LC/MS/MS analysis, several prefractionation approaches have been used that will separate the proteins before the proteolysis [43] or after the proteolysis at the peptide level [44]. Among these approaches, online multidimensional LC/MS/MS is the most robust and high-throughput technique [42]. This technique separates the peptides based on charge in the first dimension and hydrophobicity in the second dimension. The technique uses an ion-exchange column upstream of a reverse phase (RP) column.

Although these approaches provide good coverage of the proteins in the sample, the overlap of protein IDs between these methods differs because each workflow favors the identification of a different subset of proteins in the sample. Alternatively, targeted fractionation of peptides carrying specific post-translational modifications (phosphorylation and glycosylation) or reactive functional groups such as sulfhydryl groups is also a common practice with shotgun proteomics to reduce the complexity of peptide mixtures and to increase its dynamic range while adding information on which proteins (peptides) are so modified. These methods generally do not affect the overall proteome coverage when based on the cysteinyl peptides, but this is not the case with the phosphopeptide and glycopeptide affinity capture procedures because proteins bearing these modifications in the proteome account for only 30% and 65%, respectively.

Multidimensional separation improves the proteome coverage, but these workflows are prone to variation. They also increase the analysis time and can cause sample losses at each step. Moreover, this workflow requires every biological replicate to be processed in the same labor-intensive manner and requires that MS/MS be used to characterize the peptides. This approach is not feasible for a clinical study, in which sample amounts are limited and protocols require a large number of samples to achieve statistical relevance. To circumvent these multiple separation stages and to improve the peak capacities for 1D RPLC, high-pressure LC systems have been built that utilize longer capillary columns packed with smaller particles (<2 μm) to achieve the high-resolution separation of peptides [45]. These setups improved the proteome coverage and the results obtained with 10-kpsi RPLC-LCQ MS/MS were comparable to the multidimensional protein identification technology (MudPIT) on LCQ [45].

To exploit the ability of the high-pressure (~ 20 kpsi) systems in extending the dynamic range of detection for identifying the low-abundance proteins from clinical samples, the proteomics group at Pacific Northwest National Laboratory (PNNL) has developed a robust proteomics approach that utilizes routine multidimensional LC/MS/MS to completely characterize a given sample system such as cells, tissue, or body fluid and validates the peptide identifications from the accurate mass and retention time recorded from a parallel multidimensional analysis on a high-performance Fourier transform ion cyclotron resonance (FTICR) instrument. The data from these two analyses will be matched to construct a database comprising accurate mass and time (AMT) tags [46]. The creation of an AMT database obviates the MS/MS analysis on subsequent, similar types of samples and increases the throughput with the improved dynamic range. The potential of AMT mapping resides in the ability of high-pressure LC systems to achieve reproducible 1D RPLC separations in conjunction with highly accurate mass measurements using FTICR MS. This setup demonstrated the identification of serum proteins ranging more than 6 orders of magnitude in concentrations without depleting the highly abundant proteins. The highly specialized instrumentation used to achieve such analytical capabilities is not currently available in the market, is expensive to build, and needs highly skilled personnel to maintain. The recently introduced nanoAcquity UPLC (Waters) system has demonstrated the high-resolution separations on peptide mixtures from a single chromatographic run and has the ability to use capillary columns packed with 1.7-μm particles (at >10 kpsi).

Other emerging technologies with the potential to provide robust, faster separations for proteomics applications are microfluidic chip technology [47, 48] and gas-phase separations based on ion mobility mass spectrometry [49, 50]. With these improvements in the instrumentation, robust platforms are being developed that achieve high reproducibility and throughput with broad dynamic range and accurate quantitation capabilities. These platforms may serve as diagnostic tools for the analysis of clinically relevant samples.

The potential of exploring proteomes with shotgun proteomics has been realized. This has allowed a wealth of qualitative information to be extracted from samples of clinical relevance. Now the most important area for further development of proteomics is to derive quantitative information (relative protein concentrations) for samples having different physiological states. The measured peptide intensity in an LC/MS run does not always reflect its actual abundance in the sample due to the variability in the ionization process by ESI and the ion-suppression effects caused by the coeluting peptides. As a result, run-to-run comparisons among samples to derive accurate quantitative information using peak intensities or peak areas are difficult.

To compensate for these variations, stable isotopes or mass tags are commonly used to label the peptides from one sample, and this labeled sample is mixed with the other sample for direct relative comparison in one LC/MS run. The isotopically distinguishable peptides will have the same chemical properties, so they will have similar chromatographic behavior and will ionize with the same efficiency. The mass spectrometer will resolve these two peptide species based on the mass difference, and the quantities of the peptides can be measured using peak areas.

Currently, several labeling strategies are employed for quantitative shotgun proteomics. These include the covalent labeling of proteins by isotope-coded affinity tagging (ICAT) [51, 52] and peptides by iTRAQ [53], ^{18}O exchange in the tryptic peptides in the presence of trypsin [54, 55], and metabolic labeling [56]. Other advantages of ICAT are the reduced complexity of tryptic peptides because of the pooling of the cysteine-containing peptides and that the samples experience the same variations during the digestion and extraction. The ^{18}O and iTRAQ methods are applied only on the proteolytically cleaved samples and thus control only the LC/MS variances. The iTRAQ method allows multiplexing of several samples [57] and the isobaric tag on fragmentation will allow the measurement of peptide quantities from the reporter ions in the MS/MS spectrum, which differ by a single mass unit.

Although these labeling strategies overcome the preanalytical and analytical variances in quantifying the proteins, their applications are limited to only two or a few (iTRAQ) samples. Methods are envisioned that are similar to those used in 2D DIGE workflows where the clinical samples are spiked with an ^{18}O-labeled tryptic peptide mixture obtained from pooling all the samples involved in the study, and the ^{16}O analyte/^{18}O standard ratios from each sample can be used for quantitative analysis [58]. Due to constraints such as the cost of stable isotopes, the large number of samples involved in the study, and the limited sample sizes from clinical sources that limit the labeling strategies for protein quantitation in translational research, the focus has shifted to label-free quantitation to attain greater flexibility and speed in the sample preparation by minimizing the steps in the sample process. A study conducted by the Association of Biomolecular Resource Facilities (ABRF) proteomics research group on less complex protein mixtures to compare quantitation methods revealed that the label-free analysis gave similar or better results than the isotope-labeled studies. Improvements in the nanoLC-ESIMS platforms, such as the ability to generate reproducible results and the development of statistical methods to measure the technical variations from the LC/MS data sets, are helping to develop LC/MS into a robust platform for protein quantification in clinical applications.

Despite the tremendous amounts of data generated by shotgun proteomics, most of the proteins are identified with only a few peptides, which limits the information that can be obtained regarding protein isoforms that might result from alternative splicing or posttranslational modifications (PTMs) of proteins. The splice variants and PTMs have been shown to be implicated in human diseases, and correlation of their forms and functions in the context of disease is very important in translational research. One way to examine the details of the state of intact proteins is to apply a top-down approach and measure the protein mass by MS and fragment it in a second MS step to obtain sequence information. This approach requires a very high resolution technique such as ESI-FTICR because the proteins masses can range from 5 to 200 kDa and require an electron capture dissociation (ECD) technique, which fragments the peptide backbone while leaving the PTMs intact. This method is still in its infancy and requires off-line protein separation to fractionate the sample into simple mixtures for top-down proteomics. Top-down proteomics on a chromatographic timescale was demonstrated recently using complex protein mixtures [59]. Currently, the size limit for sequencing of proteins by a top-down approach is ~30 kDa. This method holds great potential for characterizing histones and their modifications. The correlation of histone modifications to clinical outcomes has been recently observed [60] and it is clear that top-down proteomics will have a place in translational research.

6.3.3.2 Characterization of Posttranslational Modification of Proteins Using the Shotgun Approach

More than 200 protein PTMs [61] are known and they hold key functions in regulating most cellular processes. These modifications can affect a protein's hydrophobicity, charge, conformation, and location and also extend the range of its functions. The diversification of proteins due to PTMs increases the range of protein variants by 2 orders of magnitude over a genome encoding around 25,000 genes and emphasizes the outdated nature of the one gene–one protein hypothesis. Among these modifications the most important ones are protein phosphorylation and glycosylation, because these are involved in a variety of cellular processes. Characterization of these two functional subproteomes using global approaches is not currently feasible and requires a targeted approach to assess their importance.

Phosphorylation is a dynamic process that occurs on serine, threonine, and tyrosine residues and is controlled by kinases and phosphatases. This event plays an important role in cellular processes such as signal transduction, gene expression, cell cycling, peptide hormone response, and apoptosis [62]. It is estimated that at any given time one-third of the human proteome is phosphorylated. Phosphorylation site mapping and quantification give insights into the relationship between signaling networks and downstream biological responses. Deciphering the quantitative differences between the disease and normal states as well as the variation of phosphorylation site selection will provide a window into the network dynamics associated with each phenotype.

The presence of a negative phosphate group, which gives a poor response to ESI in the positive mode, and the substoichiometric levels of phosphorylation modification in a mixture of proteins necessitate the enrichment of phosphopeptides from the total protein digest for LC/MS/MS analysis. Several approaches for the enrichment of phosphopeptides have been described in the literature and these employ antibodies [63], immobilized metal ions [64, 65], or metal oxides [66]. Recent reports regarding the optimization of phosphopeptide enrichment procedures revealed that the use of TiO_2 shows superior performance over other methods. The enriched phosphopeptides are analyzed by an online LC/MS/MS on an ion trap to identify the peptide and the phosphorylation site. The phosphopeptides readily lose H_3PO_4 (–98 Da) and HPO_3 (–80 Da) under MS2 conditions and may not provide the sequence-specific ions for peptide identification. The data-dependant selection of these neutral loss ions for further fragmentation in MS3 will give more information for determining the sequence and location of the phosphate group. The recently introduced electron transfer dissociation (ETD) method has shown potential for characterizing the phosphopeptides because this technique preserves the phosphate group on the peptide backbone during tandem MS analysis [67].

Protein glycosylation is the most complex posttranslational modification in the eukaryotes, and glycans in the glycoproteins play important roles in protein folding, recognition and adhesion, intracellular transport, and protein degradation. Approximately 65% of the human proteome is glycosylated and most of the secretory and cell surface proteins are glycosylated. Carbohydrates are mainly attached to the side chains of asparagine, serine, and threonine residues in proteins, and based on the point of attachment they are classified as N-linked and O-linked glycoproteins. There is no known sequence motif for O-linked glycosylation in proteins, whereas there is a required motif for N-linked glycosylation (Asn-X-Ser/Thr). The structures of carbohydrates or glycans attached to the peptide side chains are dictated by a panel of glycosyltransferases and glycosidases present in the endoplasmic reticulum (ER) and Golgi apparatus. Glycosylation sites show micro- and macroheterogeneities for the same protein species, resulting in multiple protein isoforms. The varying degree of structural diversity exhibited by these molecules allows them to store biological information that will be decoded by complementary biological molecules in the context of cellular communication and interaction with the surrounding medium.

Oncogenic transformation of a cell may disrupt the cell's glycan synthesis machinery, which may result in the altered expression of glycans on the proteins of tumor cells. Alterations in the structures of glycans will disorder the normal functions of a cell at the cell–cell and cell–matrix interfaces, which may cause pathologies, and these altered structures may serve as biomarkers for the disease state. The potential of glycoproteins as diagnostic biomarkers, such as CA125, PSA, AFP, CA15-3, CA27-29, and Her2/neu [68], is apparent in several cancers, and the comparative profiling of glycoproteomes from diseased and normal specimens will further enhance the scope of diagnostic applications for cancer and enable improved clinical outcomes.

The characterization of glycosylation sites and the structures of glycans that modify proteins is very complex. The methods that were developed in conjunction with MS in characterizing glycoconjugates are being applied and improved to allow high-throughput analysis of glycoproteomes and glycomes. The differential capture of qualitative and quantitative information relating to glycosylation holds great promise in translational research. Approaches for glycosylation profiling of proteins exploit natural glycan moieties to capture the tryptic glycopeptides by one of two methods: serial/mixed lectin affinity or by modifying the glycans to an aldehyde reactive group by periodate and then conjugating them to the hydrazine beads. These procedures enrich the glycopeptides from the total protein digest mixtures, and the captured peptides are treated further with endoglycosidase to obtain the peptide portion of glycopeptides [69]. The glycan-stripped peptides are characterized by an online LC/MS/MS to identify the peptide sequences that were originally glycosylated.

While the lectin affinity enrichment allows N-glycans to be characterized after PNGase F cleavage, the periodate workflow destroys the glycans and it can be used to capture both N- and O-linked peptides. The O-linked glycopeptides pose great challenges in characterizing because there is no enzyme that cleaves all of the O-linked glycans, leaving the option of releasing them by chemical means such as reductive beta-elimination [70].

Although these methodologies provide a means for characterizing the glycosylation sites and glycan structures, the details of glycan heterogeneity at each site and their structures cannot be revealed because these methods cleave the link between glycan and peptide. The release of N-glycan in the presence of ^{18}O water can yield quantitative information about the N-glycosylation of these peptides [71]. The recently developed advanced hybrid MSs that use the ETD technique have demonstrated potential in characterizing the intact glycopeptides by an online LC/MS/MS [72], and these techniques will obviate the multistep workflows involved in the characterization of glycopeptides.

6.3.4   Protein Arrays

One emerging high-throughput technology is that of using microarrays to rapidly profile proteins from biological fluids and tissue lysates as a means of collecting molecular information relevant to pathologic conditions. To envision a gene expression type array to probe proteome-wide expression patterns, a diverse array of affinity reagents or antibodies that are specific for each expressed protein is required. The need to generate the antibodies [73] and affinity reagents to explore the human proteome was proposed to the HUPO council in 2005, and a draft of human proteome antibody initiative that has the goal of promoting and facilitating the generation of a set of well-validated antibodies for human proteins was formulated. This plan endorses the production of well-characterized antibodies (nonvariable regions) for the nonredundant human proteome (~23,000 proteins) and envisions a catalog of resources for human antibodies and an atlas of protein expression in normal and diseased tissues based on antibody proteomics (http://www.proteinatlas. org). This resource will also enhance specific targeted proteomic applications to help researchers gain knowledge about the composition of protein complexes using a combination of pull-down and MS profiling to decipher the pathologic protein networks in disease conditions.

Unlike linear sequence hybridization for DNA and RNA, protein interactions with cognate or complementary molecules are very complex due to the structural diversity of proteins. These interactions involve the tertiary or quaternary forms of proteins whose stability depends on a number of physiological parameters. These constraints pose numerous technical challenges in immobilizing the antibodies or proteins on the surfaces while retaining the specific fold conformations needed to interact with the proteins various partners.

To overcome these limitations, research has been done by several groups to optimize the protein content on chips and the parameters for surface selection for immobilization, array printing, protein labeling, and array reading [74, 75]. These efforts enabled the emergence of chip-based and bead-based protein arrays to facilitate the miniaturized ELISA-type assays in a massively parallel fashion to gain insights into the protein interactome. These methods have been developed to measure protein–antibody, protein–protein, protein–drug, and enzyme–substrate interactions under diseased and normal conditions for early cancer disease screening, cancer prognosis, and patient stratification.

Cytokines are produced by a wide variety of cells and these secreted proteins play an important role in innate immunity, apoptosis, angiogenesis, cell growth, and differentiation. The expressions of individual cytokines are altered in cancers, and the interplay between immune and tumor cells further alters their expression, which might be useful in determining the specific stage and grade of tumors. Profiling cytokines in the blood is believed to give clues to the pathophysiological changes occurring in the blood and may have diagnostic value in the early detection of cancer and cancer classification. The potential application of first generation protein arrays has readily been realized with the profiling of low-abundance cytokines (pg/mL) from cancer sera.

Several commercial vendors are supplying these antibody arrays and are working to develop them as diagnostic tools for cancer. Cytokine arrays are available in planar multidot format and solution phase bead-based format. Both formats use two antibodies for a sandwich-type assay of the qualitative and quantitative assay of cytokines.

The diagnostic power of cytokine signaling molecules along with the marker CA-125 was demonstrated with a multiplexed cytokine bead-based assay that discriminates ovarian cancer sera from control sera using a panel of cytokines [76]. A similar type of multipanel cytokine assay, which includes CA19-9, distinguished pancreatic cancer sera from the sera of healthy controls. The same panel showed high sensitivity and specificity for distinguishing sera from chronic pancreatitis from pancreatic cancer sera [77]. In a comprehensive study of cytokine, profiling of 259 archived plasma samples using planar membrane arrays of 120 cytokines identified 18 classifiers that discriminated Alzheimer's and control samples with 90% specificity [78].

Another important application of protein arrays that holds great promise is the early detection of cancer and the stratification of cancer patients by fingerprinting autoantibodies from the patient sera using well–defined, tumor-derived antigen arrays. It is known that the immune system recognizes the self-antigens expressed in tumors and elicits antibodies against these tumor antigens. Exploitation of these autoantibodies as serological diagnostic markers has been explored recently for several cancers [79]. As with DNA microarrays, the protein arrays will follow similar steps in the data analysis to derive the expressions or patterns between the clinical samples.

6.4   Analysis of Proteomics Data

Use of proteomics with clinical samples generates huge amounts of data and requires tools to keep track of the data obtained from various sample processing methods and data collection methods. Tools are also needed for preparation of proteomics data for downstream analyses such as estimation of the technical variation associated with each process using statistical tools. Ultimately, these data are used for the comparative analysis of proteomics data sets to distinguish healthy and diseased groups and for identifying markers that are associated with particular diseases. The complete description of integrated informatics tools that facilitate the high-throughput analysis of "omics" data will be discussed in the following chapters, so in this chapter we merely highlight the quantitative and qualitative aspects of data analysis involved in protein identification.

6.4.1   2D DIGE Data Analysis

The 2D DIGE workflow provides very high resolution, protein-centric information from clinical samples. Several commercial software tools such as DeCyder (GE Healthcare), PDQuest (Bio-Rad), and Progenesis (Nonlinear Dynamics) are available to process information derived from the protein spots for comparative analysis across the samples. These tools perform multiple tasks: spot detection, background subtraction, noise removal, normalization of spot maps, and alignment of spot maps across the data sets to transform the image data for quantitative and pattern analysis. The spots that show twofold expression differences (with statistical significance) between the two groups are picked robotically from the gels for qualitative protein identification by MS.

The most commonly used MS workflow with 2D DIGE is MALDI-TOF, which measures the masses of tryptic peptides from each gel spot. The peptide masses are compared to one of several protein sequence databases to identify the proteins using the peptide mass fingerprinting (PMF) approach. The most commonly used PMF search engines that correlate the experimental peptide masses to the in silico tryptic peptide masses are Profound [80] and Mascot [81]. These search engines are integrated with the data processing tools associated with the MALDI-TOF platforms. The data are preprocessed to remove the noise peaks and to select the monoisotopic peaks for PMF mapping. The successful identification of proteins from PMF depends on the mass accuracy, number of peptides mapped to the sequence, and the spot composition.

6.4.2   SELDI-TOF/MALDI-TOF Data Analysis

Data analysis of SELDI-TOF and MALDI-TOF profiles from the clinical samples focuses mainly on the identification of diagnostic profile features from the MS spectra that can be used to train algorithms to distinguish the groups of interest such as control from cancer samples or to distinguish between cancer stages.

MALDI-TOF profiles are prone to several sources of variations, some of which are inherent to the instrument used for collecting the data, to sample preparation steps, and also to the individual biological variation from individual clinical samples. All of these sources of variation will generate differences in the intensity of peptide peaks in the MS profiles. To eliminate or control for these variations, the data sets are processed to normalize the data from each profile before selecting diagnostic features. Among the steps that are used to make these corrections are baseline correction, background subtraction, noise detection, data smoothing, normalization, and peak detection and alignment. The preprocessed data are subjected to feature selection algorithms to develop a predictive model for discriminating the target condition (control or diseased).

Due to the high dimensionality of SELDI-TOF/MALDI-TOF proteomic profiles, in which the number of data points in the profiles is higher than the number of samples, data reduction techniques are used to reduce this high-dimensional data into a small set of highly discriminative features whose parameters can be readily estimated across the data sets [82]. Several analysis packages that perform univariate and multivariate analysis on the features to identify the classifiers and to develop predictive models from these classifiers are available, some of which are of academic (the caBIG -Q5 Probabilistic Classification algorithm), whereas others are commercial (Ciphergen Biosystems' Biomarker Patterns software and Bruker Daltonics' ClinProTools).

6.4.3 Shotgun Proteomics Data Analysis

While the 2D gel and SELDI-TOF data give descriptive information about the intact protein/peptide contents of biological sources, shotgun proteomics provides information at the tryptic peptide level. This makes the data analysis more complex because further analysis is needed to derive the information that describes the original protein content of the sample.

Because most LC/MS/MS platforms collect data in two stages, the data sets consist of intact peptide masses and the fragment ion masses specific to the selected peptide sequences. Several software tools have been developed to interpret the data collected at the two stages of the LC/MS/MS analysis. The preprocessing of data to derive quantitative information from the survey or full spectrum will follow more or less the same procedures mentioned for 2D gel and MALDI-TOF data. Additional tasks such as deconvolution of multiply charged ions, assembling the isotopic clusters into peptides and matching them with the theoretical natural isotope distributions, combining the intensities from different charge-state ions of the same peptide, and selecting the monoisotopic peaks are all required for LC/MS/MS data analysis. The visualization of LC/MS data in a 2D format that is analogous to a 2D gel image has been made possible with tools such as msInspect [83], SpecArray [84], DeCyderMS (GE Healthcare), and Rosetta Elucidator (Rosetta Biosoftware). These tools are bundled with various peak cleanup and peak alignment algorithms to derive label-free protein quantitation from LC/MS and LC/MS/MS data sets.

The power of shotgun proteomics technology lies in the ability to identify peptides through the correlation of MS/MS spectra of peptides to protein databases using database search programs such as Sequest [85], Mascot [81], Sonar [86], and X!tandem [87]. All of these programs match the MS/MS spectra to database sequences in a similar manner: First, experimental peptide masses are compared with the theoretical peptide masses derived from in silico enzymatic digestion of proteins in the database, and then the predicted fragment ions from the in silico fragmented peptides are compared with the experimental fragment ions for the subset of peptides in the peptide mass error window. Each program assigns a score that quantifies the degree of similarity between the two spectra, although the programs differ in the manner by which they calculate this score [88]. Whereas Mascot scores are calculated to have a statistical significance of 0.05 for matches, the Sequest program does not provide any statistical significance for its calculated correlation scores.

Given the large numbers of MS/MS spectra obtained from each sample by shotgun proteomics, it is very likely that incorrect or random matches are assigned to peptides and this necessitates a robust validation tool to filter incorrect peptide matches. Because of the difficulties involved with assigning correct matches, statistical methods [89, 90] have been developed to validate the peptide identifications derived from database search tools.

Searching of data sets with the forward and reverse protein databases is also being used to estimate the false identification rates. Reverse protein databases are essentially random sequence databases so any match is a false-positive and the number of matches can be used to predict a false-positive rate. The recently developed PROVALT tool has demonstrated the ability to assign a false discovery rate for protein identifications from Mascot search results using this method [91]. The database correlation retrieves only the information from the sequences entered in the databases. If there are any peptides with unknown modifications or peptides derived from the known protein variants, but not in the database, no match will be found in the database search. In such cases, the data can be probed with de novo sequencing algorithms to deduce the sequence or sequence tag of peptide for BLAST search, against more complete databases, to identify the protein(s) [92].

6.5 Summary

This chapter provided an overview of sources of clinical samples that carry biomedically relevant protein information and various proteomics technologies that have the potential to profile the samples to discern altered protein expression patterns associated with diseases for early detection and prognosis. Clinical proteomics is still in its infancy, and the pilot studies that are being conducted in the labs across the world are providing the baseline knowledge about sources of variation, technology suitability for a given case study, and sample selection criteria. These studies are paving the way for new approaches to using proteomics data to expedite translational research. Although the application of proteomics in clinical settings is mainly a discovery process, advancements in the technology that improve the reproducibility and dynamic range of these methods are showing great promise in developing these platforms into tools that will improve the diagnosis and treatment of disease.

References

[1] Stretton, A. O., "The First Sequence. Fred Sanger and Insulin," *Genetics*, Vol. 162, 2002, pp. 527–532.

[2]   McPherson, J. D., et al., "A Physical Map of the Human Genome," *Nature*, Vol. 409, 2001, pp. 934–941.

[3]   Venter, J. C., et al., "The Sequence of the Human Genome," *Science*, Vol. 291, 2001, pp. 1304–1351.

[4]   Greenbaum, D., et al., "Comparing Protein Abundance and mRNA Expression Levels on a Genomic Scale," *Genome Biol.*, Vol. 4, 2003, pp. 117.

[5]   Karas, M., and Hillenkamp, F., "Laser Desorption Ionization of Proteins with Molecular Masses Exceeding 10,000 Daltons," *Anal. Chem.*, Vol. 60, 1988, pp. 2299–2301.

[6]   Fenn, J. B., et al., "Electrospray Ionization for Mass Spectrometry of Large Biomolecules," *Science*, Vol. 246, 1989, pp. 64–71.

[7]   Anderson, N. L., and Anderson, N. G., "The Human Plasma Proteome: History, Character, and Diagnostic Prospects," *Mol. Cell Proteomics*, Vol. 1, 2002, pp. 845–867.

[8]   Zhang, Y., et al., "MAPU: Max-Planck Unified Database of Organellar, Cellular, Tissue and Body Fluid Proteomes," *Nucleic Acids Res.*, Vol. 35, 2007, pp. D771–D779.

[9]   Tirumalai, R. S., et al., "Characterization of the Low Molecular Weight Human Serum Proteome," *Mol. Cell Proteomics*, Vol. 2, 2003, pp. 1096–1103.

[10] Bjorhall, K., Miliotis, T., and Davidsson, P., "Comparison of Different Depletion Strategies for Improved Resolution in Proteomic Analysis of Human Serum Samples," *Proteomics*, Vol. 5, 2005, pp. 307–317.

[11] Omenn, G. S., et al., "Overview of the HUPO Plasma Proteome Project: Results from the Pilot Phase with 35 Collaborating Laboratories and Multiple Analytical Groups, Generating A Core Dataset of 3020 Proteins and a Publicly-Available Database," *Proteomics*, Vol. 5, 2005, pp. 3226–3245.

[12] Adachi, J., et al., "The Human Urinary Proteome Contains More Than 1500 Proteins, Including a Large Proportion of Membrane Proteins," *Genome Biol.*, Vol. 7, 2006, pp. R80.

[13] Tarnaris, A., Watkins, L. D., and Kitchen, N. D., "Biomarkers in Chronic Adult Hydrocephalus," *Cerebrospinal Fluid Res.*, Vol. 3, 2006, p. 11.

[14] Hanahan, D., and Weinberg, R. A., "The Hallmarks of Cancer," *Cell*, Vol. 100, 2000, pp. 57–70.

[15] Lund, A. H., and van Lohuizen, M., "Epigenetics and Cancer," *Genes Dev.*, Vol. 18, 2004, pp. 2315–2335.

[16] Bonner, R. F., et al., "Laser Capture Microdissection: Molecular Analysis of Tissue," *Science*, Vol. 278, 1997, pp. 1481–1483.

[17] Crockett, D. K., et al., "Identification of Proteins From Formalin-Fixed Paraffin-Embedded Cells by LC-MS/MS," *Lab. Invest.*, Vol. 85, 2005, pp. 1405–1415.

[18] Lundblad, R. L., "Sample Preparation for Proteomic Studies," in *The Evolution from Protein Chemistry to Proteomics: Basic Science to Clinical Application.* Boca Raton, FL: CRC press, 2006, pp. 161–194.

[19] O'Farrell, P. H., "High Resolution Two-Dimensional Electrophoresis of Proteins," *J. Biol. Chem.*, Vol. 250, 1975, pp. 4007–4021.

[20] Anderson, N. G., and Anderson, N. L., "Analytical Techniques for Cell Fractions. XXI. Two-Dimensional Analysis of Serum and Tissue Proteins: Multiple Isoelectric Focusing," *Anal. Biochem.*, Vol. 85, 1978, pp. 331–340.

[21] Unlu, M., Morgan, M. E., and Minden, J. S., "Difference Gel Electrophoresis: A Single Gel Method for Detecting Changes in Protein Extracts," *Electrophoresis*, Vol. 18, 1997, pp. 2071–2077.

[22] Marouga, R., David, S., and Hawkins, E., "The Development of the DIGE System: 2D Fluorescence Difference Gel Analysis Technology," *Anal. Bioanal. Chem.*, Vol. 382, 2005, pp. 669–678.

[23] Wu, J., et al., "Functional Characterization of Two-Dimensional Gel-Separated Proteins Using Sequential Staining," *Electrophoresis*, Vol. 26, 2005, pp. 225–237.

[24] Gharib, T. G., et al., "Proteomic Analysis of Cytokeratin Isoforms Uncovers Association with Survival in Lung Adenocarcinoma," *Neoplasia*, Vol. 4, 2002, pp. 440–448.

[25] Le Naour, F., et al., "Proteomics-Based Identification of RS/DJ-1 as a Novel Circulating Tumor Antigen in Breast Cancer," *Clin. Cancer Res.*, Vol. 7, 2001, pp. 3328–3335.

[26] Young, D. S., and Tracy, R. P., "Clinical Applications of Two-Dimensional Electrophoresis," *J. Chromatogr. A*, Vol. 698, 1995, pp. 163–179.

[27] Sharma, K., et al., "Two-Dimensional Fluorescence Difference Gel Electrophoresis Analysis of the Urine Proteome in Human Diabetic Nephropathy," *Proteomics*, Vol. 5, 2005, pp. 2648–2655.

[28] Somiari, R. I., et al., "High-Throughput Proteomic Analysis of Human Infiltrating Ductal Carcinoma of the Breast," *Proteomics*, Vol. 3, 2003, pp. 1863–1873.

[29] Hu, Y., et al., "Comparative Proteomic Analysis of Intra- and Interindividual Variation in Human Cerebrospinal Fluid," *Mol. Cell Proteomics*, Vol. 4, 2005, pp. 2000–2009.

[30] Kakisaka, T., et al., "Plasma Proteomics of Pancreatic Cancer Patients by Multi-Dimensional Liquid Chromatography and Two-Dimensional Difference Gel Electrophoresis (2D-DIGE): Up-Regulation of Leucine-Rich Alpha-2-Glycoprotein in Pancreatic Cancer," *J. Chromatogr. B Analyt. Technol. Biomed. Life Sci.*, Vol. 852, 2007, pp. 257–267.

[31] Voss, T., et al., "Correlation of Clinical Data with Proteomics Profiles in 24 Patients with B-Cell Chronic Lymphocytic Leukemia," *Int. J. Cancer*, Vol. 91, 2001, pp. 180–186.

[32] Wilson, K. E., et al., "Comparative Proteomic Analysis Using Samples Obtained with Laser Microdissection and Saturation Dye Labelling," *Proteomics*, Vol. 5, 2005, pp. 3851–3858.

[33] Pan, S., et al., "Application of Targeted Quantitative Proteomics Analysis in Human Cerebrospinal Fluid Using a Liquid Chromatography Matrix-Assisted Laser Desorption/Ionization Time-of-Flight Tandem Mass Spectrometer (LC MALDI TOF/TOF) Platform," *J. Proteome Res.*, Vol. 7, 2008, pp. 720–730.

[34] Petricoin, E. F., et al., "Use of Proteomic Patterns in Serum to Identify Ovarian Cancer," *Lancet*, Vol. 359, 2002, pp. 572–577.

[35] Tang, N., Tornatore, P., and Weinberger, S. R., "Current Developments in SELDI Affinity Technology," *Mass Spectrom. Rev.*, Vol. 23, 2004, pp. 34–44.

[36] Villanueva, J., et al., "Serum Peptide Profiling by Magnetic Particle-Assisted, Automated Sample Processing and MALDI-TOF Mass Spectrometry," *Anal. Chem.*, Vol. 76, 2004, pp. 1560–1570.

[37] Villanueva, J., et al., "Differential Exoprotease Activities Confer Tumor-Specific Serum Peptidome Patterns," *J. Clin. Invest.*, Vol. 116, 2006, pp. 271–284.

[38] Lopez, M. F., et al., "High-Resolution Serum Proteomic Profiling of Alzheimer Disease Samples Reveals Disease-Specific, Carrier-Protein-Bound Mass signatures," *Clin. Chem.*, Vol. 51, 2005, pp. 1946–1954.

[39] Lopez, M. F., et al., "A Novel, High-Throughput Workflow for Discovery and Identification of Serum Carrier Protein-Bound Peptide Biomarker Candidates in Ovarian Cancer Samples," *Clin. Chem.*, Vol. 53, 2007, pp. 1067–1074.

[40] Chaurand, P., Schwartz, S. A., and Caprioli, R. M., "Imaging Mass Spectrometry: A New Tool to Investigate the Spatial Organization of Peptides and Proteins in Mammalian Tissue Sections," *Curr. Opin. Chem. Biol.*, Vol. 6, 2002, pp. 676–681.

[41] McDonnell, L. A., and Heeren, R. M., "Imaging Mass Spectrometry," *Mass Spectrom. Rev.*, Vol. 26, 2007, pp. 606–643.

[42] Wolters, D. A., Washburn, M. P., and Yates, J. R., 3rd, "An Automated Multidimensional Protein Identification Technology for Shotgun Proteomics," *Anal. Chem.*, Vol. 73, 2001, pp. 5683–5690.

[43] Barnea, E., et al., "Evaluation of Prefractionation Methods as a Preparatory Step for Multidimensional Based Chromatography of Serum Proteins," *Proteomics*, Vol. 5, 2005, pp. 3367–3375.

[44] Shen, Y., et al., "Ultra-High-Efficiency Strong Cation Exchange LC/RPLC/MS/MS for High Dynamic Range Characterization of the Human Plasma Proteome," *Anal. Chem.*, Vol. 76, 2004, pp. 1134–1144.

[45] Shen, Y., et al., "Automated 20 kpsi RPLC-MS and MS/MS with Chromatographic Peak Capacities of 1000–1500 and Capabilities in Proteomics and Metabolomics," *Anal. Chem.*, Vol. 77, 2005, pp. 3090–3100.

[46] Smith, R. D., et al., "An Accurate Mass Tag Strategy for Quantitative and High-Throughput Proteome Measurements," *Proteomics*, Vol. 2, 2002, pp. 513–523.

[47] Li, J., et al., "Application of Microfluidic Devices to Proteomics Research: Identification of Trace-Level Protein Digests and Affinity Capture of Target Peptides," *Mol. Cell Proteomics*, Vol. 1, 2002, pp. 157–168.

[48] Xie, J., et al., "Microfluidic Platform for Liquid Chromatography-Tandem Mass Spectrometry Analyses of complex peptide mixtures," *Anal. Chem.*, Vol. 77, 2005, pp. 6947–6953.

[49] Henderson, S. C., et al., "ESI/Ion Trap/Ion Mobility/Time-Of-Flight Mass Spectrometry for Rapid and Sensitive Analysis of Biomolecular Mixtures," *Anal. Chem.*, Vol. 71, 1999, pp. 291–301.

[50] Valentine, S. J., et al., "Multidimensional Separations of Complex Peptide Mixtures: A Combined High-Performance Liquid Chromatography/Ion Mobility/Time-of-Flight Mass Spectrometry Approach," *Int. J. Mass Spectrom.*, Vol. 212, 2001, pp. 97–109.

[51] Chen, R., et al., "Quantitative Proteomic Profiling of Pancreatic Cancer Juice," *Proteomics*, Vol. 6, 2006, pp. 3871–3879.

[52] Stewart, J. J., et al., "Proteins Associated with Cisplatin Resistance in Ovarian Cancer Cells Identified by Quantitative Proteomic Technology and Integrated with mRNA Expression Levels," *Mol. Cell Proteomics*, Vol. 5, 2006, pp. 433–443.

[53] Aggarwal, K., Choe, L. H., and Lee, K. H., "Shotgun Proteomics Using the iTRAQ Isobaric Tags," *Brief Funct. Genomic Proteomic*, Vol. 5, 2006, pp. 112–120.

[54] Yao, X., et al., "Proteolytic 18O Labeling for Comparative Proteomics: Model Studies with Two Serotypes of Adenovirus," *Anal. Chem.*, Vol. 73, 2001, pp. 2836–2842.

[55] Yao, X., Afonso, C., and Fenselau, C., "Dissection of Proteolytic 18O Labeling: Endoprotease-Catalyzed 16O-to-18O Exchange of Truncated Peptide Substrates," *J. Proteome Res.*, Vol. 2, 2003, pp. 147–152.

[56] Ishihama, Y., et al., "Quantitative Mouse Brain Proteomics Using Culture-Derived Isotope Tags as Internal Standards," *Nat. Biotechnol.*, Vol. 23, 2005, pp. 617–621.

[57] DeSouza, L., et al., "Search for Cancer Markers from Endometrial Tissues Using Differentially Labeled Tags iTRAQ and cICAT with Multidimensional Liquid Chromatography and Tandem Mass Spectrometry," *J. Proteome Res.*, Vol. 4, 2005, pp. 377–386.

[58] Qian, W. J., et al., "Advances and Challenges in Liquid Chromatography-Mass Spectrometry-Based Proteomics Profiling for Clinical Applications," *Mol. Cell Proteomics*, Vol. 5, 2006, pp. 1727–1744.

[59] Parks, B. A., et al., "Top-Down Proteomics on a Chromatographic Time Scale Using Linear Ion Trap Fourier Transform Hybrid Mass Spectrometers," *Anal. Chem.*, Vol. 79, 2007, pp. 7984–7991.

[60] Seligson, D. B., et al., "Global Histone Modification Patterns Predict Risk of Prostate Cancer Recurrence," *Nature*, Vol. 435, 2005, pp. 1262–1266.

[61] Krishna, R. G., and Wold, F., "Post-Translational Modification of Proteins," *Adv. Enzymol. Relat. Areas Mol. Biol.*, Vol. 67, 1993, pp. 265–298.

[62] Pawson, T., and Scott, J. D., "Signaling Through Scaffold, Anchoring, and Adaptor Proteins," *Science*, Vol. 278, 1997, pp. 2075–2080.

[63] Rush, J., et al., "Immunoaffinity Profiling Of Tyrosine Phosphorylation in Cancer Cells," *Nat. Biotechnol.*, Vol. 23, 2005, pp. 94–101.

[64] Feng, S., et al., "Immobilized Zirconium Ion Affinity Chromatography for Specific Enrichment of Phosphopeptides in Phosphoproteome Analysis," *Mol. Cell Proteomics*, Vol. 6, 2007, pp. 1656–1665.

[65] Nuhse, T., Yu, K., and Salomon, A., "Isolation of Phosphopeptides by Immobilized Metal Ion Affinity Chromatography," *Curr. Protoc. Mol. Biol.*, Chapter 18, 2007, Unit 18.13.

[66] Cantin, G. T., et al., "Optimizing TiO2-Based Phosphopeptide Enrichment for Automated Multidimensional Liquid Chromatography Coupled to Tandem Mass Spectrometry," *Anal. Chem.*, Vol. 79, 2007, pp. 4666–4673.

[67] Mikesh, L. M., et al., "The Utility of ETD Mass Spectrometry in Proteomic Analysis," *Biochim. Biophys. Acta*, Vol. 1764, 2006, pp. 1811–1822.

[68] Zhang, H., et al., "Identification and Quantification of N-linked Glycoproteins Using Hydrazide Chemistry, Stable Isotope Labeling and Mass Spectrometry," *Nat. Biotechnol.*, Vol. 21, 2003, pp. 660–666.

[69] Kaji, H., et al., "Mass Spectrometric Identification of N-linked Glycopeptides Using Lectin-Mediated Affinity Capture and Glycosylation Site-Specific Stable Isotope Tagging," *Nat. Protoc.*, Vol. 1, 2006, pp. 3019–3027.

[70] Carlson, D. M., "Structures and Immunochemical Properties of Oligosaccharides Isolated from Pig Submaxillary Mucins," *J. Biol. Chem.*, Vol. 243, 1968, pp. 616–626.

[71] Kaji, H., et al., "Lectin Affinity Capture, Isotope-Coded Tagging and Mass Spectrometry to Identify N-Linked Glycoproteins," *Nat. Biotechnol.*, Vol. 21, 2003, pp. 667–672.

[72] Wuhrer, M., et al., "Glycoproteomics Based on Tandem Mass Spectrometry of Glycopeptides," *J. Chromatogr. B Analyt. Technol. Biomed. Life Sci.*, Vol. 849, 2007, pp. 115–128.

[73] Uhlen, M., and Ponten, F., "Antibody-Based Proteomics for Human Tissue Profiling," *Mol. Cell Proteomics*, Vol. 4, 2005, pp. 384–393.

[74] Cretich, M., et al., "Protein and Peptide Arrays: Recent Trends and New Directions," *Biomol. Eng.*, Vol. 23, 2006, pp. 77–88.

[75] Sanchez-Carbayo, M., "Antibody Arrays: Technical Considerations and Clinical Applications in Cancer," *Clin. Chem.*, Vol. 52, 2006, pp. 1651–1659.

[76] Gorelik, E., et al., "Multiplexed Immunobead-Based Cytokine Profiling for Early Detection of Ovarian Cancer," *Cancer Epidemiol. Biomarkers Prev.*, Vol. 14, 2005, pp. 981–987.

[77] Zeh, H. J., et al., "Multianalyte Profiling of Serum Cytokines for Detection of Pancreatic Cancer," *Cancer Biomark.*, Vol. 1, 2005, pp. 259–269.

[78] Ray, S., et al., "Classification and Prediction of Clinical Alzheimer's Diagnosis Based on Plasma Signaling Proteins," *Nat. Med.*, Vol. 13, 2007, pp. 1359–1362.

[79] Casiano, C. A., Mediavilla-Varela, M., and Tan, E. M., "Tumor-Associated Antigen Arrays for the Serological Diagnosis of Cancer," *Mol. Cell Proteomics*, Vol. 5, 2006, pp. 1745–1759.

[80] Zhang, W., and Chait, B. T., "ProFound: An Expert System for Protein Identification Using Mass Spectrometric Peptide Mapping Information," *Anal. Chem.*, Vol. 72, 2000, pp. 2482–2489.

[81] Perkins, D. N., et al., "Probability-Based Protein Identification by Searching Sequence Databases Using Mass Spectrometry Data," *Electrophoresis*, Vol. 20, 1999, pp. 3551–3567.

[82] Hauskrecht, M., et al., "Feature Selection for Classification of SELDI-TOF-MS Proteomic Profiles," *Appl. Bioinformatics*, Vol. 4, 2005, pp. 227–246.

[83] Bellew, M., et al., "A Suite of Algorithms for the Comprehensive Analysis of Complex Protein Mixtures Using High-Resolution LC-MS," *Bioinformatics*, Vol. 22, 2006, pp. 1902–1909.

[84] Li, X. J., et al., "A Software Suite for the Generation and Comparison of Peptide Arrays from Sets of Data Collected by Liquid Chromatography-Mass Spectrometry," *Mol. Cell Proteomics*, Vol. 4, 2005, pp. 1328–1340.

[85] Eng, J. K., McCormack, A. L., and John R. Yates, I., "An Approach to Correlate Tandem Mass Spectral Data of Peptides with Amino Acid Sequences in a Protein Database " *J. Am. Soc. Mass Spectrom.*, Vol. 5, 1994, pp. 976–989.

[86] Field, H. I., Fenyo, D., and Beavis, R. C., "RADARS, A Bioinformatics Solution That Automates Proteome Mass Spectral Analysis, Optimises Protein Identification, and Archives Data in a Relational Database," *Proteomics*, Vol. 2, 2002, pp. 36–47.

[87] Craig, R., and Beavis, R. C., "TANDEM: Matching Proteins with Tandem Mass Spectra," *Bioinformatics*, Vol. 20, 2004, pp. 1466–1467.

[88] Sadygov, R. G., Cociorva, D., and Yates, J. R., 3rd, "Large-Scale Database Searching Using Tandem Mass Spectra: Looking Up the Answer in the Back of the Book," *Nat. Methods*, Vol. 1, 2004, pp. 195–202.

[89] Fenyo, D., and Beavis, R. C., "A Method for Assessing the Statistical Significance of Mass Spectrometry-Based Protein Identifications Using General Scoring Schemes," *Anal. Chem.*, Vol. 75, 2003, pp. 768–774.

[90] Keller, A., et al., "Empirical Statistical Model to Estimate the Accuracy of Peptide Identifications Made by MS/MS and Database Search," *Anal. Chem.*, Vol. 74, 2002, pp. 5383–5392.

[91] Weatherly, D. B., et al., "A Heuristic Method for Assigning a False-Discovery Rate for Protein Identifications from Mascot Database Search Results," *Mol. Cell Proteomics*, Vol. 4, 2005, pp. 762–772.

[92] Taylor, J. A., and Johnson, R. S., "Implementation and Uses of Automated *de novo* Peptide Sequencing by Tandem Mass Spectrometry," *Anal. Chem.*, Vol. 73, 2001, pp. 2594–2604.

CHAPTER 7

Data Tracking Systems

Hai Hu and Leonid Kvecher

7.1 Introduction

In the preceding chapters, we have discussed the operational details of biomedical informatics research, including clinical data collection, specimen collection and tissue banking, and molecular studies at the genomic and proteomic levels. Collectively, those chapters described the types of data that are captured for this type of integrative research. How these data are captured, centralized, and applied to research and the tools needed for analyzing or mining the data are the topics discussed in the remainder of this book.

In this chapter, we focus on the data tracking system for biomedical informatics research. The four major sections focus on an overview of data tracking systems, system requirements, approaches for establishing the system, and the challenges of system deployment.

7.1.1 Definition of a Data Tracking System

We define a data tracking system as a computer software application that is used to systematically capture data generated across all platforms in an organization such as a laboratory or a research institute. In biomedical informatics research, such data platforms include clinical data collection, tissue banking, genomic research, and proteomic research (Figure 7.1). Within each data platform are multiple experimental platforms that collect or generate various types of data. For a given experimental platform, an experimental workflow is typically followed that implements a protocol or an experiment. At its lowest level, a data tracking system covers experimental workflows.

In this chapter we define a data tracking system as an extended version of a laboratory information management system (LIMS). A LIMS is generally a software system that is used in the laboratory to manage the tracking of samples, laboratory users, instruments, standards, and other laboratory functions. It may also manage such functions as invoicing, plate management, and workflow automation. In general, a LIMS does not track clinical data nor tissue samples as found in a biorepository. Though tissue sample management is being incorporated into LIMS systems, we use the term *data tracking system* to refer to the more inclusive information management system that includes clinical data and biospecimen tracking.

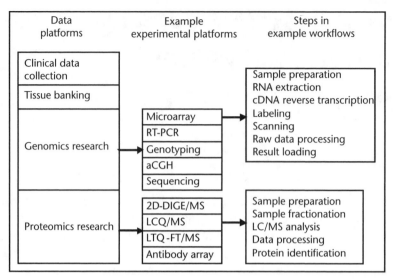

Figure 7.1   The coverage of a data tracking system for biomedical informatics research.

LIMS will be used to describe the more traditional laboratory information management system.

A data tracking system can be composed of functionally distinct modules, each being responsible for covering a specific data platform. The major modules correspond to major functions, such as clinical data collection, tissue banking, genomic research, and proteomic research, as shown in Figure 7.1. Each major module may then be composed of multiple experimental or data collection platforms, each being responsible for covering one specific type of experiment in the form of a workflow. A workflow is composed of multiple steps that cover the corresponding experimental or data collection steps. For example, one experimental platform in the genomic research module may be gene expression analysis using microarrays, with corresponding workflow steps of sample tracking, RNA preparation, cDNA reverse transcription, labeling, scanning, raw data processing, and final result loading.

7.1.2   Why Use a Data Tracking System?

Biomedical informatics research often deals with enormous amounts of data that are collected or generated through clinical exercises and genomic and proteomic experiments. The sheer volume of the data generated makes it impossible for any organization to rely on manual paper lab notebooks to keep track of experiments without using an electronic system. Accompanying data acquisition, QC/QA procedures are performed that also generate data that should be tracked. With a proper data tracking system, when a scientist uses the data for research he or she not only knows how the data are generated, but also the quality of the data.

When all of the relevant data are captured in a timely fashion in one electronic system, there are three different ways in which the researcher can design and carry out a study. In one approach, a study can be designed starting from the enrollment of subjects, including patients and controls, to collection of the clinical data and specimens and conducting of the molecular experiments, and then to analyzing data to obtain end results. In another approach, clinical data and specimen information that have already been collected can be utilized to design new molecular experiments to address new questions. Finally, after a critical mass of clinical data and experimental data have accumulated in a data tracking system, a researcher can make use of the existing stored data to design a new in silico experiment so that new relationships can be mined from the data without having to physically enroll new subjects and conduct new experiments.

As discussed in Chapter 1, we consider disease a process instead of a state. When a clinical study is designed as a longitudinal study, the data tracking system can capture all of the clinical and molecular study data chronically and thus provide valuable information for longitudinal disease studies. With data captured in one electronic tracking system, they are not subject to loss due to human error or unreconcilable formats. A comprehensive collection of the data into a centralized system will lay a solid foundation for the longitudinal study of disease.

A data tracking system is also a powerful tool for troubleshooting when problems with the data are encountered. With built-in QA procedures, a researcher can identify and correct operational errors early instead of at the stage of final data analysis. In addition, a data tracking system allows project leaders to easily check the status of a project, including specimen usage and the progress of the experiments. A researcher can keep track of the data collected or generated at multiple sites and report the results as needed. A data tracking system also allows for easy management and manipulation of the data for storage, such as in a data warehouse [1–3] or when moving them into any special data analysis software.

Note that the primary reason a data tracking system is needed for biomedical informatics research is to manage the large amount of data generated that can no longer be managed manually. We should understand that a data tracking system serves an established workflow better than serving a workflow in a research environment that is typically more dynamic. In some fields such as pharmaceutical industries, data tracking systems are needed to also satisfy the governing agency's regulatory requirements; that aspect of the functionality of data tracking systems is not the focus of our discussion here.

7.2   Overview of Data Tracking Systems

7.2.1   Historical Review

In providing a historical review, we focus on LIMS. Because biomedical informatics research is relatively new, there is little extra "history" in our definition of the data tracking system compared to that of the LIMS.

Biology and life sciences can be traced back more than 25 centuries ago to the 4th century B.C., when Aristotle classified 540 animal species and dissected at least 50 of them. He surely did not have a data tracking system or LIMS at his disposal. Until recent modern times, life scientists relied mainly on paper lab notebooks to describe their experiments, track experimental steps, record results, and prepare reports.

The first LIMSs were introduced near the beginning of the 1970s, thanks to the development of computer technology. These systems were typically one-off solutions; that is, a LIMS was usually specially designed for a specific laboratory to cover its specific operations and could not be generalized for use in a different laboratory.

The first commercial LIMS was not developed until the early 1980s. These systems were developed on centralized minicomputers. Heavy customization was required in order to serve a specific laboratory. Therefore, the cost of these systems was very high and their implementation was slow. As a result, not many institutions deployed these systems.

In the 1990s, LIMS migrated from minicomputers to PCs using a client–server architecture. Thanks to increased processing speeds and decreased costs, more organizations started transitioning from paper lab notebooks to electronic data capture. Technology also made it possible to develop LIMS that were more user friendly and cost efficient than in the past.

Currently, LIMS is an active service area with many companies providing commercial products. Of the LIMS products on the market, the majority rely on web-based architectures. In the recent years, XML-based LIMSs have become available as well. This technology enables LIMS to be more flexible and customizable. LIMSs have been applied in many industries including analytical chemistry, pharmaceuticals, quality assurance, petroleum, food and beverage, textiles, agricultural services, and environmental laboratories [4–9]. Serving in a research, manufacturing, or environmental testing setting in the United States, a LIMS typically enables compliance with GLP (Good Laboratory Practice), GALP (Good Automated Laboratory Practice), GMP (Good Manufacturing Practice), and GAMP (Good Automated Manufacturing Practice) guidelines as regulated by the Food and Drug Administration (FDA) and Environmental Protection Agency (EPA). A LIMS's electronic signature and audit trail should also meet FDA Guideline 21 CFR Part 11.

In general, LIMSs adequately serve industries with mature technologies in terms of tracking data, preparing reports, and enhancing productivity. When serving relatively new research fields such as biomedical informatics research, LIMSs face many problems and challenges.

7.2.2   Available Resources

Available resources for LIMSs include websites, books [10–13], peer-reviewed journal papers, and trade magazine articles [7–9, 14–19]. A good description of the historical development of LIMSs can be found at the website of LIMSource [20], which also lists about 150 LIMS companies. In addition, dozens of companies provide LIMSs that have been specialized for health care–related industries. Other websites such as LIMS Finder [21] also provide useful information on LIMSs. All LIMS companies also have their own websites, and a representative list of LIMS vendors is shown in Table 7.1.

7.2.3   Data Tracking Systems in the Life Sciences

Data tracking systems for the life sciences in general have been developed both as open source and commercial systems. In academic development, such systems include ones that aim to providing a lightweight software solution and ones that are

Table 7.1 Representative LIMS Vendors

Vendor	Product	Website
Affymetrix	GeneChip Operating Software (GCOS)	http://www.affymetrix.com/index.affx
Agilent Technologies	Agilent QC Client LIMS	http://www.agilent.com/
Applied Biosystems	SQL*LIMS	http://www.appliedbiosystems.com/ http://www.sqllims.com/
Bruker BioSpin	SampleTrack	http://www.bruker-biospin.com/
Cimarron Software	Scierra LWS	http://www.cimsoft.com/
Genologics	Proteus, Geneus	http://www.genologics.com/
LabVantage Solutions	Sapphire LIMS, LVL LIMS (Europe only)	http://www.labvantage.com/
LabWare	LabWare LIMS	http://www.labware.com/
Ocimum Biosolutions	Genchek, Biotracker, Genowiz, Pharmatracker, OptGene, Nutrabase, iRNAchek, Toxchek	http://www.ocimumbio.com/
PerkinElmer	Labworks LIMS	http://www.perkinelmer.com/
Thermo Electron	Nautilus LIMS, SampleManager LIMS	http://www.thermo.com/
VelQuest	SmartLab	http://www.velquest.com/

based on modular data structures that are well suited for data management in biomedical informatics research [22–25]. An example of such a system has been developed as part of the efforts of the caBIG program (cancer Biomedical Informatics Grid) initiated by the National Cancer Institute Center of Bioinformatics (NCICB) of the NIH. The system is called the cancer Laboratory Information Management System (caLIMS) [26]. Specialized data tracking system for biospecimens and proteomics are also under development and these will be discussed later in this chapter.

In the following subsections, we discuss the status of data tracking systems for the four major components of data collection for biomedical informatics research.

7.2.3.1 Clinical Data Collection

Ironically, few data tracking systems are available for clinical data collection in biomedical informatics research. Applications are available, though, for clinical trials, and for electronic medical records (EMR) and electronic health records (EHR). A discussion of clinical trials is beyond the scope of this chapter, however, EMR, EHR, and hospital information systems (HISs) are relevant to the scope of this book so we will provide a brief discussion of the relevant aspects of these systems.

An HIS cover the administrative, clinical, and financial aspects of a hospital including patient registration, diagnosis, treatment, and billing. An EMR is one of the important components of a HIS in a hospital system, and it can also function as an independent system in a clinic. An EMR replaces the paper medical record that the physician creates and maintains for a specific patient's visits. One single patient may have multiple EMRs maintained in multiple physicians' offices, and the collection of them, which is a longitudinal and aggregated record of the patient's health information, is called an EHR. When all patients' EHRs are available, following proper governing regulations, they will be of tremendous value to biomedical informatics research. Additional information on HIS/EMR/EHRs can be found in books [27], societies, and available websites [28] that are dedicated to these issues.

Even in this computer-dominated electronic era, the use of HIS/EMR/EHRs is very nonuniform. This is one of the three major challenges we see when using the clinical data in the electronic systems supporting biomedical informatics research. Being the world leader in computer-based information technology, the United States lags far behind Europe and some Asian countries in adopting these systems, and EMRs and EHRs are still not widely used by most health care providers. In many European countries where there are government-sponsored centralized health insurance programs, EMRs and EHRs are demonstrating the ability to enhance health care services in more than 90% of clinics and hospitals. When discussing biomedical informatics research in Europe, it is a natural assumption or at least a common thought that the clinical data should be from the HIS or EMR or EHR. But in the United States, for biomedical informatics research clinical data still have to be collected via special questionnaires.

The second challenge of using the data from HISs, EMRs, or EHRs for research is the diversity of the software on the market. These various software systems have been independently developed and do not share the same data structures or interfaces. Therefore, to use data from different systems, interfaces and parsers will have to be developed for each of them in order to include these data in research. Again this problem is more severe in the United States than in Europe.

The third challenge is the effect that the protection of patients' privacy has on using medical data for research purposes. Various regulations are in place for protecting patient privacy in the United States, Canada, Australia, and most European countries. Deidentification is critical to using patient data in these countries. Disease-specific information extraction or protection is another consideration. For example, an AIDS patient may be willing to provide data for a lung cancer study, but at the same does not want his or her AIDS information to be shared.

No mature commercial data tracking system is currently available for clinical data to be used in biomedical informatics research, probably because of the diversity of clinical data types and the fact that different research projects may need different types of clinical data. A proper data model that meets the needs of such diverse clinical data types has yet to be developed.

As an example of a clinical data tracking system for biomedical informatics research, we will briefly discuss the Clinical Laboratory Workflow System (CLWS) codeveloped by the Windber Research Institute (WRI) and Cimarron Software. The CLWS has answered the fundamental needs of the Clinical Breast Care Project, which was discussed in Chapters 1 through 3 and will be described in more detail in Chapter 10. This system tracks patient enrollment, questionnaire assignment, clinical data collection and QA, clinical specimen collection and processing, and double-blind data entry. This workflow can be integrated with other genomic and proteomic laboratory workflows. Figure 7.2 shows a screenshot of the CLWS with the workflow displayed on the left side of the screen and the data entry page on the right side of the screen.

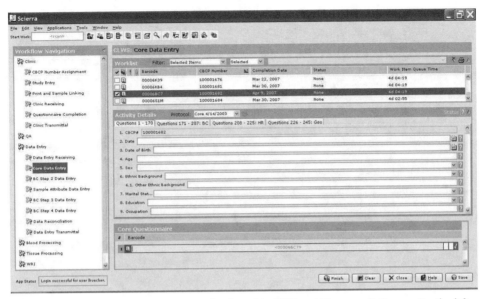

Figure 7.2 A screenshot of the CLWS codeveloped by WRI and Cimarron Software. On the left side of the screen is the workflow, including major steps of clinical activities, clinical data QA, clinical data entry, blood processing, and specimen processing. On the right side of the screen is the data entry page.

7.2.3.2 Tissue Processing and Banking

In biomedical informatics research, body fluids and solid tissues must be properly collected, processed, and stored to ensure the quality of specimens for genomic and proteomic experiments. Clinical specimen processing technologies were described in Chapter 3, and processed specimens are typically stored in vapor-phase liquid nitrogen freezers for long-term preservation.

The specific needs of tissue processing and banking are discussed later in Section 7.3.4.2. Commercial data tracking systems are available to serve this specific area [29]. A screenshot of one such system, Freezerworks, is shown in Figure 7.3.

As noted earlier, as part of the caBIG program, caTissue has been developed for biospecimen data tracking [30]. Although the whole system is still under development, an early version of this system been released for adoption as an open-source system.

7.2.3.3 Data Tracking for Genomics and Proteomics Studies

The importance of using LIMSs in genomics and proteomics studies has been acknowledged since the beginning of the Human Genome Project [16]. In fact, there are commercial LIMSs rooted from this project. Currently, there are a number of products, including open-source systems from academic institutes and commercial systems from LIMS companies covering genomic and proteomic research.

It is probably fair to say that the LIMS presence in academic labs really started at the turn of the century [31]. By early 2007, dozens of papers had been published in peer-reviewed journals indexed by PubMed regarding LIMS for genomic and proteomic studies. These include a system for DNA profiling [32], a system for a

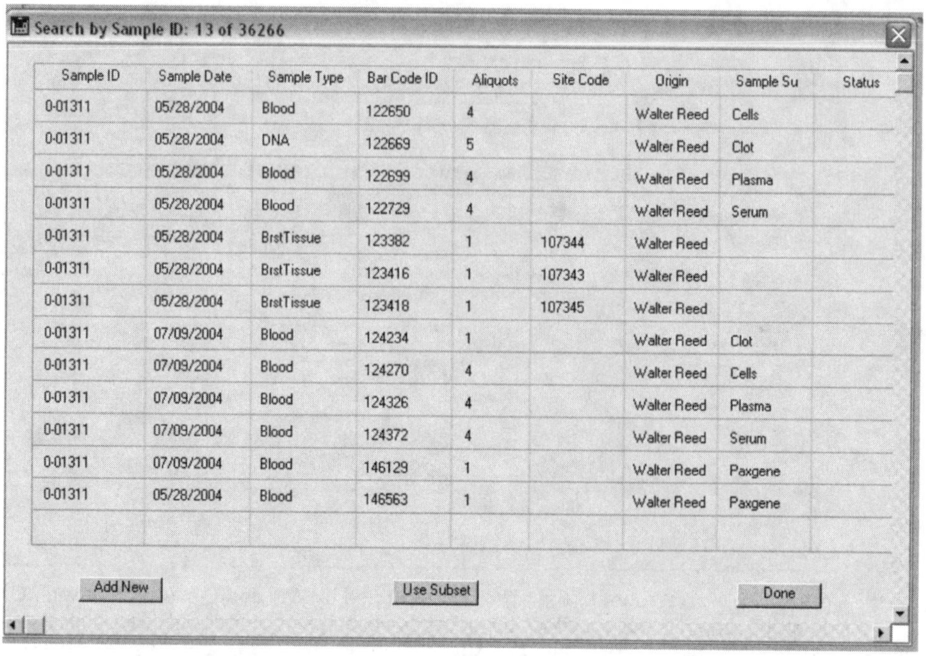

Search by Sample ID: 13 of 36266

Sample ID	Sample Date	Sample Type	Bar Code ID	Aliquots	Site Code	Origin	Sample Su	Status
0-01311	05/28/2004	Blood	122650	4		Walter Reed	Cells	
0-01311	05/28/2004	DNA	122669	5		Walter Reed	Clot	
0-01311	05/28/2004	Blood	122699	4		Walter Reed	Plasma	
0-01311	05/28/2004	Blood	122729	4		Walter Reed	Serum	
0-01311	05/28/2004	BrstTissue	123382	1	107344	Walter Reed		
0-01311	05/28/2004	BrstTissue	123416	1	107343	Walter Reed		
0-01311	05/28/2004	BrstTissue	123418	1	107345	Walter Reed		
0-01311	07/09/2004	Blood	124234	1		Walter Reed	Clot	
0-01311	07/09/2004	Blood	124270	4		Walter Reed	Cells	
0-01311	07/09/2004	Blood	124326	4		Walter Reed	Plasma	
0-01311	07/09/2004	Blood	124372	4		Walter Reed	Serum	
0-01311	07/09/2004	Blood	146129	1		Walter Reed	Paxgene	
0-01311	05/28/2004	Blood	146563	1		Walter Reed	Paxgene	

Add New   Use Subset   Done

Figure 7.3 A screenshot from of Freezerworks, a tissue banking solution developed by Dataworks [29]. Shown here is a sample search result for a particular subject. It includes subject ID, specimen collection date, specimen type, barcode, aliquot number, specimen code at the collection site (where applicable), collection site name, sample tube type (for blood samples), and status.

clinical cytogenetics lab [33], several systems for microarray experiment tracking [34–36], and several systems for genotyping [37–39]. For proteomic studies, several systems have been developed for protein structure analysis NMR and x-ray crystallography [40–44]. LIMS have also been developed to support gel-based protein separation and mass spectrometry–based protein identification technologies [45–47], including protLIMS, which is a proteomics LIMS developed as part of caBIG [48], although the authors do not have firsthand information on how these systems function.

Although data tracking systems or LIMS developed by academic organizations are usually free, they are typically less robust than a commercial product and lack professional support. The latter is common to open-source software, which fatally hinders such systems from being adopted by a mass data–producing laboratory or institute.

LIMS companies extending service to biomedical informatics or the life sciences typically do so by developing additional modules based on their products that were originally designed for non–life sciences areas, such as analytical chemistry or pharmaceutical industry. An example vendor is LabVantage [49]. New companies were incorporated as well to specifically develop data tracking systems for this area, and examples include Cimarron Software and Genologics [50, 51]. Because new companies did not have the burden (or treasure) of an existing LIMS structure, they were often able to design a new structure based on the new needs of biomedical informatics research and, thus, they have the potential to serve the area better. Figure 7.4

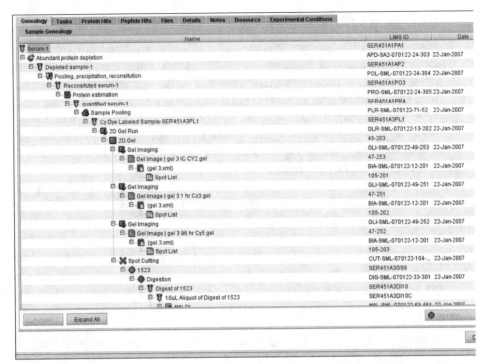

Figure 7.4   Screenshot of a proteomics study workflow in Proteus software. Major steps for 2D gel-based protein separation followed by mass spectrometry protein identification were shown with time stamps indicating the time the steps were performed. (*Courtesy of Genologics.*)

shows one example proteomics study workflow, which is a screenshot of Proteus software developed by Genologics.

Another kind of commercial LIMS arose from the need to support the experimental platforms that vendors offer for biomedical informatics research. One such example is the GeneChip Operating Software (GCOS) from Affymetrix [52], which was designed to support laboratories performing moderate- to high-throughput microarray analysis using the Affymetrix GeneChip technology. Other vendors of high-throughput technologies have also developed limited systems for tracking the data generated by their systems.

7.3   Major Requirements of a Data Tracking System for Biomedical Informatics Research

Multiple modules are needed in data tracking systems for biomedical informatics research, each covering a specific data platform that meets specific requirements as shown earlier in Figure 7.1. We know that, although some experimental platforms have been relatively mature with their requirements well defined, the field of biomedical informatics research in general is still in dynamic development. Thus, the requirements presented here speak only for the current requirements in the area, which will certainly evolve with time.

7.3.1 General Requirements

A major general requirement is the extensibility of the system. Extensibility refers to the ability to add new functions or modify the existing ones without having to make major changes to the infrastructure itself [53]. As a general requirement for IT products, extensibility is particularly important for data tracking systems for biomedical informatics research. The dynamic nature of the field often demands modifications of existing protocols and the addition of new experimental platforms and thus new protocols. The data tracking system needs to be modified accordingly without changing its backbone structure.

The data tracking system can be workflow based, because the workflow concept is relatively intuitive to end users. It should track the major operational steps, and capture the data generated by the instrument(s). The QA/QC results should be tracked as well.

An easily configurable system is especially desirable. System administrators should be able to assign role-based privileges to all users [54], for example, to allow the principal investigator to design the experiment, allow project managers to select the protocol and specimens to start the experimental workflow, and allow laboratory research associates to carry out the experiment following the workflow. A data tracking system should always store the data with a time stamp and user stamp, and such stamps can be very useful for troubleshooting.

Users with high privileges, such as the system manager or lab manager, should be allowed to develop a new workflow or revise an existing one by inserting a new step or deleting or modifying an existing step. In doing so, all the changes need to be audited for future reference. Meanwhile, the system should store the old data and the new data in such a way that, after necessary modifications, the reporting utility will be able to report both the old data and the new data in the same way, for example, by allowing nulls to be reported if a step is inserted or deleted. In addition, if the data in the tracking system are to be loaded into a data storage system such as a data warehouse, then, after proper modifications, the data exporting utility should be able to handle the old data and the new data the same way.

7.3.2 Front-End Requirements

Because end users of the data tracking system may have limited computer skills, it is important for the interfaces to be user friendly and intuitive. Most likely this is the only source of information the end users have to judge the quality of the system. If the end users do not like the system, chances are, it will not make it through the deployment stage.

Flexibility is also important in the user interface. This does not mean that all users should be able to modify the system, but privileged users should be allowed to do so as discussed earlier. The front end should also allow problem reporting and solving with a type of two-way mechanism instead of just a one-way reporting system as is seen in many LIMS where, when a problem occurs the workflow leads to a problem reporting step and ends there. In such cases, even when a solution to the problem is later found, the previously reported step cannot be corrected.

Barcode reading is necessary to keep track of the questionnaires, specimens, sample vials, plates, and so forth. Barcode reading steps should be properly planned so that important containers are tracked and, depending on the design philosophy, intermediate containers can be omitted to prevent the tracking from becoming cumbersome.

Reporting capability is crucial. The purpose of tracking the data is to retrieve and present them when needed. Reporting utilities may include canned reports and ad hoc queries. Canned reports are queries precoded by software engineers during the development stage following specified reporting requirements. Because the codes are optimized, these reports can be generated in a highly efficient manner. Ad hoc querying, a reporting utility that allows an end user to select the data elements to report by specifying the data criteria, should be supported. These reports are flexible, but may take some time to execute since the query is not optimized. Both types of reports are very important.

7.3.3   Back-End Requirements

The back-end structure should ensure the extensibility of the system with regard to the modification of the front-end workflows. Because a data tracking system is a transactional database, and many users may access it at the same time, it is important to ensure a high operational efficiency even at times when large data files are being captured or when resource-demanding queries are being executed.

There are a number of general IT back-end requirements; here we discuss only system backup and disaster recovery, which we consider to be extremely important. As a transactional database, the data should be backed up daily. One possibility is to perform an incremental backup daily, with a weekly, complete backup scheduled at a time when the tracking system is not in use, for example, during the weekend. Complete backup typically requires a system shutdown, which is inconvenient during working hours.

To ensure disaster recovery, the backup medium should be stored in a different physical location so that when a disaster occurs, the backup data can be safely restored as soon as new servers have been set up.

7.3.4   Field-Specific Requirements

We see two important general requirements for biomedical informatics research data tracking. First, the system needs to capture diversified types of data from many clinical and experimental platforms. Second, the system needs to handle data that are of a very large size, such as image files and microarray expression data. These two requirements need to be properly satisfied in order for the data tracking system to function well. For the first need, the only solution appears to be to develop coverage for each platform. Note that some experimental platforms share the same intermediate steps (for example, mRNA reverse transcription is a step in RT-PCR and in microarray gene expression analysis), so object-oriented data modeling is a good choice. At a minimum, the program should be of a modular structure so that experimental steps can be developed into submodules (or sub-submodules) to be reused in additional experimental platforms.

For the second need listed, debate is ongoing as to whether some types of large-size data should be loaded into the data tracking system or simply archived with its file location saved in the tracking system. Many people agree that images should be handled with the second approach, but there are different opinions about other data types such as the gene expression level data from microarray analysis. One opinion is to keep the original data file intact; another opinion is to parse the data file and load the expression signal intensity or even normalized intensity into the data tracking system so that when a research scientist requests it, the expression level data can be reported directly at the gene level and loaded into other data analysis software without having to be transformed from the original data file. Decisions on how to capture data from large files should be decided on a case-by-case basis.

7.3.4.1 Requirements for Clinical Data Tracking

Clinical data collection includes subject enrollment, questionnaire completion, specimen collection, data entry (if so designed), and quality assurance. The following steps and data types need to be captured in the data tracking system:

- Subject enrollment involves assigning a project-specific subject ID to protect the subject's privacy; consenting the subject using IRB-approved protocols, which may evolve with time; consenting the subject for future use of clinical data and specimens; handling the withdrawal of a subject from the study; and so forth.

- Questionnaire completion includes possible completion by patients, by nurses via interviews with the subject or chart auditing, by pathologists after a diagnosis is done, and possibly by other clinical staff as well. The questionnaires may be in hardcopy or electronic form. The questionnaires may contain questions about demographics, medical history, family history, lifestyle, risk factors, surgical information, pathological sample annotations, treatment information, and outcomes.

- Specimen collection and processing includes body fluid collection and subsequent processing; for example, blood samples may be processed into plasma and cells, and serum and clots. Solid tissues can be presented or preserved in several ways as discussed in Chapter 3.

- Medical image data include mammograms, x-ray images, ultrasonic images, MRI, and pathology slide images. These files are usually very large, and for each patient's visit a set of the files (for example, digital mammograms) is often generated. How to capture such data in the tracking system was discussed at the beginning of Section 7.3.4.

- Data entry will be an additional step if the questionnaires are completely manually instead of electronically.

- Quality assurance refers to measures deployed to ensure the integrity of the data. A SOP should be developed and followed for all the clinical steps. Major QA steps include visual inspection of the completed questionnaire, double data entry to reduce data entry errors, a computer program to check the data ranges and the consistency between the answers to related questions, and the correction of errors in the data tracking system. Regarding error handling, in a data tracking system there is typically a high barrier to modifying the data once committed. But for clinical data, because their collection involves a number of manual steps and because much of the data accuracy relies on subjects' memory, data errors are inevitable. It is not unusual for some of these data errors to be identified months after the data had been committed into the tracking system, and such mistakes need to be corrected. Thus, the data tracking system needs to have built into it an easy data correction utility for clinical data.

7.3.4.2   Requirements for Tissue Banking and Specimen Preparation

Tissue banking is the process of receiving clinical specimens from clinical sites and preserving them for molecular studies. A tissue banking facility is usually equipped with multiple freezers, bearing the same or different internal division structure. For this process, the data tracking system needs to deal with several special requirements:

- *Sample receiving.* A unique specimen ID should have been assigned when the specimen was collected, and if after receiving, the specimen is divided, child specimens should be assigned a unique ID as well. However, the relationship to the parental specimen should be maintained. The specimen ID should then link back to the subject ID for association with the clinical data including pathology annotations.
- *Freezer location management.* Depending on the specimen types, the freezers may be divided into different structures. Sometimes a defined structure of racks and shelves needs to be modified. The location management facility should allow for easy location assignment and checking in and checking out of specimens.
- *Specimen tracking.* When a specimen is not consumed completely by one experiment, the remaining sample needs to be tracked. The number of thaws also needs to be tracked because the quality of the specimen for gene expression and proteomic studies may be affected. The specimens should be split into aliquots for initial tissue banking so that when doing experiments only needed aliquots are taken out. This practice reduces the number of freeze–thaw cycles for the specimen.
- *Laser capture microdissection.* When performing surgery to remove the diseased tissue, the surgeon usually takes the surrounding tissue out as well to ensure a clear margin (i.e., to ensure no diseased tissue is left in the body). Sometimes the diseased tissues may be a small part of the whole specimen, and when doing experiments it will be necessary to isolate the diseased cells from the surrounding apparently normal tissues to enhance the detection of disease signals. A technology called laser capture microdissection (LCM) has been developed for this purpose in studies using tissues [55, 56]. Multiple tissue cryosections are often needed and isolated diseased cells can be pooled for molecular studies. The tracking system needs to capture such detailed tissue information for later data analysis steps.

7.3.4.3 Requirements for Genomics Experiments

As discussed in Chapter 5, genomics studies include both DNA and RNA technologies. The former includes DNA sequencing, SNP analysis, and aCGH. The latter includes gene expression microarray analysis, RT-PCR, and so forth.

From the data tracking point of view, genomic technologies can be classified into two groups, microarray-based and nonmicroarray-based. The microarray-based genomic studies require storage of thousands to hundreds of thousands of data points for a single experiment, and storage of the raw array images. The data points involved in nonmicroarray-based technologies are usually at a much smaller scale.

Sample preparation for genomic studies can involve many steps, but the technologies are relatively well established. It is important to properly track not only the parental samples such as the original OCT tissue block, but also the subsequent child samples derived from them, such as slices of tissues and DNA/RNA tubes from LCM as discussed in the preceding subsection. The intermediate products created during the experiment also need to be tracked if so desired (see Sections 7.3.2 and 7.4.2). The following major steps for several example genomic experimental platforms need to be tracked.

Gene Expression Microarray

- Specimen tracking.
- Total RNA preparation (RNA isolation kits).
- QA of RNA (Agilent Bioanalyzer).
- cDNA preparation.
- Labeling.
- Hybridization (Affymetrix GeneChip arrays).
- Scanning of the microarray. Handling of the raw image data was discussed earlier in this section.
- Image analysis to generate the raw signal intensity data.
- Loading of the raw data: Parse and load, load the raw data directly, or only input the raw data file location depending on the needs.

RT-PCR

- Specimen tracking.
- Total RNA preparation (RNA isolation kits).
- QA of RNA (Agilent Bioanalyzer).
- cDNA preparation.
- Primer selection and preparation.
- Programming and running of PCR (BioRad real-time PCR Instrument).
- Raw data processing and result loading.

Array CGH

- Specimen tracking.

- DNA extraction (DNA isolation kits).
- Labeling.
- Sample loading onto the aCGH chip.
- Scanning and image analysis for the raw data.
- Raw data processing and result loading.

Sequencing

- Specimen tracking.
- DNA extraction (DNA isolation kits).
- Sequencing (some instrument specific files and formats).
- Data file processing and loading.

As seen earlier, mRNA-based analyses involve total RNA preparation and reverse transcription, and then the samples are loaded onto the experimental platform. Similarly, DNA-based analyses involve DNA extraction and labeling (sometimes with DNA amplification, which is not discussed here), and then the prepared samples are applied to the experimental platforms. If the tracking system is of a modular structure, the modules from sample tracking to molecule preparation can be reused again and again, simplifying the development of the entire workflow. Of course, there might be some subtle differences in the sample preparation steps for different experiments using the same type of molecules, so the tracking modules will need to be developed in a generalized form for easy adaptation to different needs.

7.3.4.4   Requirements for Proteomics Experiments

Similar to genomic studies, for proteomic studies the specimen needs to be uniquely tracked to allow proper tracing of the information back to the clinical data of the donor. Multiple tissue types, including multiple blood sample subtypes, are involved in proteomic studies. However, sample preparation in proteomic studies is typically not as complicated as in genomic studies.

Protein expression studies are often carried out with different protein separation and identification technologies depending on the tissue type and the goal of study, as described in Chapter 6. As discussed there, proteomic technologies are not as mature as genomic technologies and, thus, flexibility of the tracking system is more important in proteomic studies. Data generated in different experimental steps, as well as the output files from the instruments and platform-specific data analysis software, should be captured in the tracking system. Data types from example proteomic experimental platforms that need to be tracked are described next. (More detailed description of these experimental platforms can be found in Chapter 6.)

2D-DIGE/MS

- Specimen tracking.
- Sample preparation.
- Protein labeling (with Cy2, Cy3 or Cy5) and sample pooling.

- First dimension separation (IEF).
- Second dimension separation (SDS-PAGE).
- Gel scanning (Typhoon 9400).
- Image cropping (Imagequant).
- Spot detection and BVA analysis.
- Match prep gel to BVA space and generate pick table.
- Spot-picking, digestion, and spotting using the robotic spot handler workstation.
- MS analysis: MALDI-MS (Ettan MALDI, ABI 4700, and Bruker ultraflex MALDI) or LC/MS of digested samples.
- Protein identification: Profound or MASCOT.

Nongel-Based Proteomics (LC/MS)

- Specimen tracking.
- Sample preparation.
- Sample fractionation (offline).
- LC/MS analysis of fractions.
- Data processing and protein identification (Xcaliber Home, Bioworks, SEQUEST, and MASCOT, using protein databases of IPI, Swiss-Prot/Trembl, or NCBI-nr).

Protein or Antibody Arrays

- Specimen tracking.
- Sample preparation.
- Array selection and preparation.
- Sample loading onto the array.
- Probing with sandwich-type assay or directly labeled proteins.
- Fluorescent scanning.
- Image processing and expression data file generation.
- Data file capturing by the tracking system.

7.3.5 Additional Points

A key implied requirement of a data tracking system for biomedical informatics research is to allow easy linking between the clinical data and molecular study data. In a patient-centric data model, a patient owns the clinical data and the specimens, and the molecular study data are properties of the specimens. A properly designed object model will certainly help meeting this implied requirement.

Analytical capability is typically not a requirement for a data tracking system, although it is normal for the analytical results from an instrument interface to be parsed and captured in the data tracking system. For example, in proteomics labs, the mass spectrometry identification of proteins through MALDI-TOF or Q-TOF analysis should be captured by the data tracking system. The logic why a data tracking system should not support data analysis, is that it is supposed to track the experimental data generated in the lab, with an audit trail such that any modifications of the captured data are tracked. If the experimental data are analyzed and tracked in the data tracking system, the recursive trial-and-failure process will definitely pose a major challenge to the audit trail. For a heavily used system, it is certainly not desirable to have data analysis compete for CPU time and BUS traffic.

7.4   Ways to Establish a Data Tracking System

So far we have discussed the requirements for a data tracking system. Next we explore how a data tracking system is established in a specific biomedical informatics research organization. Three approaches are possible: (1) Buy the system off the shelf, (2) develop the system from scratch, or (3) pursue a hybrid mode for which part of the system is purchased off the shelf and the rest is developed in house or with a partner.

Before making an implementation decision, one should first assess the specific needs of the organization, and then compare these needs to the capabilities of commercially available systems. The requirements outlined in the previous two sections should be of value to this assessment process. For example, if an organization focuses mainly on biomarker discovery using a gene expression microarray experimental platform or array-based genotyping platform, then there are several commercial systems from which to choose, and the best way to establish a data tracking system for such a need may well be to buy one off the shelf. On the other hand, if the organization uses the protein antibody array as the main experimental platform, then there is no system currently available on the market (although this may change with time), so the only way to satisfy this need is to develop one. If the organization operates on several data platforms, and the available commercial data tracking systems can satisfy some but not all the needs, then the organization may opt for a hybrid solution—to buy whatever is available and develop the rest.

7.4.1   Buy a System Off the Shelf

Although peer-reviewed papers and trade magazine articles are available on how to select a LIMS vendor and test or validate a LIMS product, the publications are in general either not up to date or focused on analytical chemistry or quality assurance but not on biomedical informatics research [7–9, 14, 15, 17–19]. Given this limitation in the literature, we suggest some criteria for identifying a commercial data tracking system for biomedical informatics research. These factors can be categorized as front-end technical features (factors 1–5), back-end technical structure features (factors 6–8), and general issues (factors 9–13) and they are discussed next:

1. *Is the workflow interface user friendly?* A cumbersome interface will discourage users from using the data tracking system. Having to work with a cumbersome interface daily will also negatively affect the performance of those working in the lab.

2. *Is the workflow flexible and can it be easily configured?* When a better experimental protocol is identified or developed, it may become necessary to alter the existing workflow for future experiments. Such flexibility should be a built-in feature in the system, even though, in practice, altering a workflow causes data management problems and thus should not happen more than occasionally.

3. *Is the coverage complete with regard to all of your institutional operations?* It is rare that an off-the-shelf data tracking system will cover all the operations in a comprehensive research entity, but the more complete the coverage by the product, the less the required customization.

4. *Is the coverage complete with regard to your specific experimental platform(s)?* For example, are all the data elements you will need for the next research and analysis steps covered? Are your QA procedures covered? Are the data from your analytical instrument properly captured?

5. *Is the reporting utility satisfactory?* For example, is the reporting utility easy to use? Does it give ready access to the required data? Such utilities are usually in the form of canned reports developed by software engineers as predefined queries for efficient execution, or in the form of ad hoc queries that can be used to create more flexible reports, as discussed in Section 7.3.2.

6. *Is the data model sound and able to support the front-end features?* Some data tracking systems use the Entity-Attribute-Value (EAV) data model to store all data, and any report will recursively query the same table multiple times reaching multiple layers of data. Other data tracking systems use a conventional normalized relational database table structure or an object-oriented data structure. Each data model has its advantages and disadvantages, and the key issue is to obtain a good understanding of the underlying structure and determine whether it is clearly defined and whether it enables efficient data transactions.

7. *Can the back-end infrastructure support the required functionalities?* One important function in any data tracking system is the audit trail. As described earlier, a typical requirement of a data tracking system is that once data are committed, they are not supposed to be modified. But in biomedical informatics research, it is not uncommon for clinical data to be corrected months later when research or QA or users of the clinical data find and report errors, as discussed in Section 7.3.4.1. Any such data corrections need to be audited. In addition, lab scientists may commit an error in doing an experiment and thus there should be an error handling mechanism. Other issues, that need to be examined by IT professionals, include the system configuration, user privilege setup, data backup, and system security.

8. *Can the back-end infrastructure readily support the modification of existing laboratory workflows and can it expand to accommodate new experiments?* When an existing workflow is modified, data flow changes. If a new step is introduced, it is possible that new data types will need to be tracked. Meanwhile, if an existing step is deleted, the flow of some data types is redirected or no longer tracked. Thus, it is important that the back-end structure ensure data integrity before and after workflow modifications, so that the front-end reporting utility, back-end database direct query, and any

data export utility can be executed smoothly to access the data generated both before and after the modifications.

In addition to the preceding eight factors that we consider to be important in evaluating a commercial product of a data tracking system, several other factors are important to consider when selecting any major IT infrastructure systems. Following on the previous numbering, these factors are as follows: (9) *Are the sales and technical teams competent and eager to help?* (10) *Is the company going to be able to support your institute for long?* (11) *Is the price of the product reasonable?* (12) *Is the price for customization reasonable, given that customization is almost inevitable?* (13) *Are references all positive and "test drive" satisfactory?*

Of all the factors we listed here, the front-end issues need input from lab operators during the evaluation process. After all, it is the lab scientists who will use the tracking system on a daily basis. If they like the front end, some of the challenges we will discuss later in Section 7.5. will be less of a problem. The back-end infrastructure of the data tracking system needs to be sound, and the assessment of it relies on the informatics and bioinformatics professionals. The assessment of the corporate strength and the cost will obviously need input from the organizational administrators.

You need to be prepared to realize that there is no guarantee that at the end of this evaluation process you will find a system that satisfies your needs; there is still a possibility that you will decide to opt for approach number 2, in which you develop your own system. As a matter of fact, debate never ends with regard to which way is better—to buy or to develop [57]. Some academic laboratories and biotech companies, after trials and failures, indeed ended up developing a system of their own.

7.4.2   Develop a System

No doubt, an in-house developed system will better serve any specific organization's needs, and such a system should be easier to maintain and expand when new needs arise. Whereas sometimes you may have a choice to buy or to develop, at other times the only choice is to develop a system by yourself or with a development partner. Development of a data tracking system requires an experienced team. Given the high costs of development, an organization often can only afford to develop a couple of simple modules for its specific needs. Developing a comprehensive system to cover the needs of many experimental platforms may not turn out to be cost effective, unless it is strategically decided that the newly developed system will not be a fully fledged one, but will only minimally meet the data tracking requirements.

1. *Project team formation.* There are two ways to develop a data tracking system: develop it in house or develop it with a partner organization. For the former, the project team should be composed of end users, developers, and biomedical informatics or bioinformatics scientists. End users typically possess the knowledge of the lab operations, but are very weak in information technology. The end users will be able to provide the system requirement information from the user's point of view. Developers, on the other hand, typically do not know much about the lab operations,

but should be professional software developers. A couple of biomedical informatics or bioinformatics scientists on the team can bridge the gaps between the end users and the developers. They typically can understand and translate the lab needs into IT language, but without systematic IT training they are not in a position to develop a solid application system.

To develop a data tracking system with a partner company—typically an existing LIMS company—a couple of business models can be used. One is to follow a vendor–customer model, in which case the vendor (LIMS company) provides professional services to the customer to specifically develop the modules for the customer and maintains and supports the custom modules thereafter. In this model, the costs of development can be high because there is no future possible profit coming out of the development for either the vendor company or the customer.

Another relationship is a partnership, in which case the developer company and the customer organization form a partnership, and the developer company uses the customer as an example case in the development of the data tracking modules. These modules are developed in such a way that they can be adapted to serve other customers. In this way, both partners can benefit from the resale of the modules in the future and therefore alleviate the cost of the development in the long run.

To develop a data tracking system with a partner company, three types of team members are still needed, in which case the end users are from the customer, the developers are from the developer company, and the biomedical informatics or bioinformatics scientists can be from either organization. In addition, a project management team should be formed, with one project manager from either party. Furthermore, because two organizations are involved, communications between the two parties will be very important. It is also critical to understand the common needs and the distinct interests of the two parties so that both parties will benefit from the partnership and end up with a win–win outcome for the project.

2. *System requirement collection.* The system requirements described in Section 7.3 are a good starting point. For development purposes, the collection requirements should be highly detailed and very specific to the operational needs, which will be an essential component of the use case specification for development. For example, for an experimental platform, the whole experimental workflow should be described, and for each step, the operation that is to be tracked and the data types that need to be tracked should be specified. How the data from an experimental instrument are stored should also be specified: simply uploading the original output data file, or parsing the output file to store selected data elements, or simply storing the file location or using a hyperlink. This requirement collection should be done for all data platforms and experimental platforms to be covered. The collection requirement needs detailed input from future end users, and should be documented by the intended developers to make sure that all of the needed information is collected.

The requirements also include the projected number of users of each data platform, the number of concurrent users when the system is in full operation, whether users are all from one site or multiple sites, whether system downtime can be readily scheduled, and so forth.

3. *Planning.* Covering the breadth and the depth of the clinical and experimental platforms in a biomedical informatics research setting requires careful planning. One philosophy is to try to cover everything; another philosophy is to track only essential operations and data elements. The first approach will be very useful in troubleshooting, and at the same time the organization will be ready for any new data analysis technologies that might be developed for data that had already been generated, without having to worry about the possibility that a previously useless data element was not properly tracked, which impedes the application of the new technology. The disadvantage is that it is a lot of work for the lab users to track all of the data—much of it is likely to be wasted and this will definitely intensify the challenge of deploying the product. In addition, developing a system to cover everything is costly.

On the other hand, tracking only essential operations is more practical and less costly to develop and deploy. But it is critical to determine which operations and data elements are essential. For example, is it necessary to track how a routinely used solution is prepared? On one hand, a wrongly prepared solution may lead to the failure of experiments, but on the other hand, the chance of making a mistake at this step might be extremely slim. A properly determined level of tracking will ensure that all of the useful data are captured, that the tracking efforts are manageable, and that possible future regrets are prevented.

The timeline of the development also needs to be well planned and needs to be aligned with the strategic plan of the organization. The milestones for the development project should be identified. A phased product delivery should be planned so that the whole system is developed one module after another, and the modular product should be deployable to meet the laboratory data tracking needs as an intermediate product.

The resources available for the development project should be identified as well. These include the personnel and the funding. Once the project team is formed, efforts should be made to stabilize it. It will be costly and affect progress if a developer is replaced in the middle of the project. The available funding is another key factor in determining the coverage level of the tracking system, scale of the development, and the timeline of delivery. Given the dynamic nature of a research setting, previously budgeted funds may later become unavailable, and new funds may flow in or may be shifted for use in the project.

4. *Use case development.* In software engineering and system architectural design, a use case is a technique for capturing functional requirements of systems and systems-of-systems [58]. In the IT industry there are templates for writing use cases. All of the issues discussed in Section 7.3 and in this subsection so far should be included, together with any other issues that should be covered in a use case. This document should be prepared by all of the participants in the project including the end users and the developers, but

be written up by the developers. A well-prepared use case will facilitate the development process.

5. *System development.* Development of the system based on the documented use case basically only needs to follow IT conventions. The only factor we want to briefly discuss is the dynamic nature of the field of biomedical informatics research. Developers need to be flexible and appreciate that a defined module may need to be modified before, during, and after development.

6. *Testing and delivery.* The testing and delivery procedure should follow IT conventions. After development is completed, an alpha test of the system should be performed by the developers to test all possible application scenarios that have been described in the use case, followed by a beta test by end users. Bugs should be recorded and fixed in a timely fashion, and feature requests should be documented as well for future improvement of the system. A standard QA procedure should be established to be followed every time a new version is released after modifications of the codes in the system.

7.4.3 Pursue a Hybrid Approach

As we have commented earlier, as it stands now, there is no commercial data tracking system that covers all of the data platforms in biomedical informatics research. Thus, to cover all of these operations, buying a commercial off-the-shelf system is not an option. Although developing a comprehensive data tracking system is possible, the cost associated with this approach may be prohibitively high. Therefore, for organizations with such needs, a hybrid approach might be a good choice.

A hybrid approach means that you will try to identify a vendor with a system that can cover most, or a good portion, of your operations, and then develop additional coverage by yourself or with a partner. Thus, this approach may potentially take advantage of both the buy and develop approaches, while reducing the disadvantages of the two approaches previously discussed.

When choosing among the candidate products, it is critical to select a product with a good backbone structure, but not necessarily the one having the most comprehensive coverage of your current operations. Coverage of a data tracking system can be expanded, but the backbone of a system cannot be changed. We discussed major issues associated with the backbone in Section 7.4.1. A good backbone should allow easy expansion of the system to cover your other operations and new experimental platforms, and permit easy modification of existing data tracking modules.

For the modules that you need to develop, they should be developed on the same backbone of the system you purchase. This practice will allow you to have all of the operations tracked by one system, which makes system maintenance and data reporting much easier. If you use a data warehouse as the next step in the data flow, then data loading will be very convenient because you only have one major data source, the data tracking system.

Development can be in house or with a partner. The major issues associated with such development were discussed in Section 7.4.2. In-house development requires that the system you purchase be structured such that it allows external developers to develop new modules for it. Maintenance and support issues are also associated with such a development. For example, if your development triggers a problem in the whole system, whose responsibility is it to fix—yours or the vendor's? If the vendor upgrades its system backbone, whose responsibility is it to ensure the proper functioning of your custom-built module in the new system? These issues should be discussed in advance with the vendor if you plan to opt for the hybrid approach. It would be ideal to the biomedical informatics research organization if the vendor were willing to maintain the new custom-built modules by charging a support fee, but it may not be in the best interest of the vendor.

If you plan to develop new modules with a partner, it is a good idea to choose the original vendor company as the development partner simply because the vendor is more familiar with its own system, although the professional service fee they charge may be high. In addition, this will make it easier to negotiate a maintenance agreement with the vendor for the newly developed modules.

No matter how the new development will be done, you will have intensive communications with the vendor company and, thus, the vendor's attitude toward collaboration, cooperation, and partnership will be a very important factor in your evaluation process before you choose a company with which to work.

7.5   Deployment Challenges and Other Notes

After due diligence, you identified a good data tracking system product, customized it for implementation, and the system is now operating in your laboratories. Or, you developed a data tracking system in house after extensive communication between your developers and your end users, and the system is up and running. You may think you are done, but you are not—many challenges still await you.

7.5.1   Resistance from End Users

Not many biomedical informatics research organizations currently utilize a data tracking system. The need to adopt or develop a data tracking system is often envisioned by the organizational leaders to ensure that at the organizational level, the data are properly organized, stored, and easily accessed across the platforms. The apparent initial beneficiaries are project managers, principal investigators, and upper managers of the organization.

Laboratory staff who carry out the experiments, on the other hand, often see the new data tracking system as a change to the way the experiments are recorded, with extra work involved, at least during the initial implementation stage. They may be used to using a paper notebook, and some of them may only have experience in using Microsoft Office applications such as Word and Excel. Utilizing a data tracking system, therefore, may pose a challenge to them.

Thus, two types of efforts need to be made to reduce this resistance on the part of end users. One is at the mindset level. It is very important to help everybody understand that carrying out any research project is a team effort, and everyone is part of the team. Even though there might be extra work to begin with in deploying the data tracking system, if it enhances the efficiency of carrying out the project as a whole, then consider the extra work as a necessary adjustment of the workload not as extra work. In fact, in the long run, a well-designed data tracking system should reduce the workload of the lab staff.

This brings up the other type of effort needed to meet this challenge of resistance, and in fact this effort should have been started much earlier than the deployment stage. It is very important for the transition to using the electronic data tracking system to be well planned and properly carried out. First, the end users need to be convinced that a data tracking system is essential to their research. It is true that there is a learning curve to begin with, and it appears that extra time is needed to type in the data asked by the tracking system. In addition, it needs to be made known to the end users in advance that no matter how well the system was designed and developed, it has to be debugged in the first weeks or months of implementation. Think about the Microsoft Windows operating systems. After the release of a new operating system, the company releases one patch after another to fix the identified bugs. The situation is so notorious that some experienced PC users do not purchase a newly released operating system at all, but instead wait for several months after the initial waves of bugs have been fixed. Think about the size of Microsoft and the efforts they put into developing a new operating system. No company specializing in data tracking systems can even be remotely comparable to it.

To help convince end users of the benefits of adopting a data tracking system, note that the system should in fact save them time after the initial learning process. The time saving is probably more evident when it is time to report the experimental results. For example, in counting the number of microarray experiments done with a specific type of tissue, when using a manual notebook system, the normal way is to ask every laboratory staff the number of such experiments done. Those staff members will then have to thumb through the notebooks page after page to find those numbers, and then those numbers will need to be added together. When using a data tracking system, all one needs to do is to create an ad hoc query, or even use a predeveloped canned report—the result is simply one click away. In addition, the manual counting process is error prone.

Resistance from end users is common when a data tracking system is newly deployed, and it certainly takes effort to convince end users of the benefits. Sometimes it takes hard line commands from the executive of the organization to enforce adoption of the system.

7.5.2 Training

Given that it is often a top-down implementation, training of the laboratory staff becomes an important step to ensure a successful transition to an electronic data tracking system. The purpose of the training is not only to familiarize the experimental staff, who are usually not computer fluent, with the software, but also to let them see that in fact after they get used to the system, they end up saving time when recording experimental data as well as reporting the results.

The training team is usually composed of experienced trainers from the software development organization, with access to system designers and developers. The trainees should include the IT staff, biomedical informatics or bioinformatics staff, and the end users of the customer organization. Trainees should be given hands-on training. The IT staff often clearly understands how the data tracking system was designed and developed, how the workflow works, and how each button in the interface works. The experimental staff understands where the workflow came from, what data should be supplied when configuring the system, and so forth. The biomedical informatics or bioinformatics staff understands both fields and should be able to bridge the gaps. The trainees should function as a team during the training session so that they can count on each other to get a comprehensive understanding of the whole system. At the same time, no one should stop short of understanding the essentials she or he is supposed to understand by relying on others in the team.

It is important that during training system features be well demonstrated and explained to the trainees so that they can be appropriately utilized. Remember, not all the trainees are strong in IT, and many of them will not take the time to explore the features by clicking around the system. (We refer here to a test system, of course, because blindly clicking around in a production system can be dangerous and thus should be prohibited.) Good features, if unknown to the end users, may not only be wasted but also impose extra burden to the users who then have to develop walk-around steps to make the system work.

7.5.3   Mismatches Between System Features and Real Needs

It is often the case that a commercial data tracking system was designed based on the needs of the initial customers. Some features might have been developed based on "reasonable" expectations. Therefore, not all system features match the needs of subsequent customers. Thus, system customization is inevitable and sometimes critical. However, when such mismatches occur at the fundamental level of the system, the problems can be difficult to resolve. For example, one commercial data tracking system has a built-in feature to request the barcode of a sample vial during an experiment at every step, but in practice many intermediate vials are not barcoded. To solve the problem, the end users have to punch in arbitrary numbers in the place of barcodes, and each time these numbers have to be new since the system does not accept "duplicate barcodes." Mismatches like this may not only occur in commercial systems but also in in-house developed systems, sometimes due to miscommunications between the developers and the end users. The solution to this problem again lies in the flexibility of the system—a data tracking system should allow easy modification of the workflows.

7.5.4   Protocol Changes and Other Evolutions

Biomedical informatics research is very dynamic, and new technologies emerge all the time. A protocol may change with time; for example, in gene expression microarrays, the number of gene probes always increases. The experimental platform may change with time as well due to a variety of reasons. For example, in February 2007, GE Healthcare made a strategic decision to discontinue the production of the CodeLink microarray chips, forcing all of its users turn to other experimental platforms [59].

New experimental platforms need to be supported, for example in genomics, DNA copy number analysis is gaining momentum [59]. In proteomics, antibody protein arrays have become available to researchers for scientific experiments [60]. All of these changes require modification of the existing data tracking system workflows, and even the development of a completely new workflow. Thus, a data tracking system should have a built-in flexibility feature so that the system can grow with the field it serves.

7.5.5 Data Tracking System as a Data Source

Data tracking systems can function as a data source to feed into other analytical applications or a data warehouse [1–3]. This is more a note than a challenge since solutions are readily available. To feed into other applications, data can be retrieved via an ad hoc query or prebuilt canned report. To feed into a data warehouse, however, a large amount of data will be retrieved. This usually can be done by developing a data export utility to directly extract the needed data from the back end. Depending on the nature of the data, for some modules complete loading into the data warehouse is more convenient, and for other modules incremental loading is the only practical choice due to the sheer volume of the data. More details on how data are loaded into a data warehouse will be discussed in the next chapter.

7.6 Summary

In this chapter, we provided an overview of the data tracking system, followed by elaboration of the requirements in the field of biomedical informatics research for data tracking systems. Then we presented three possible approaches for establishing such a system. Finally we listed a few challenges one may face when deploying a data tracking system.

We consider it necessary for a proper data tracking system to be utilized in biomedical informatics research, at a minimum because the scale of the data generated in such research is beyond the capability of manual notebooks, flat files, or spreadsheets. We also discussed several opinions regarding the level of detail the data tracking system should cover. The bottom line is, as it stands now, there is no single commercial data tracking system that covers all of the clinical data collection, tissue banking, genomic research, and proteomic research platforms that an integrative biomedical informatics research organization employs. Thus, establishing a comprehensive tracking system needs the wisdom and collaborative efforts of clinicians, laboratory scientists, biomedical informatics researchers, and software engineers.

References

[1]   Koprowski, S. P., Jr., and Barrett, J. S., "Data Warehouse Implementation with Clinical Pharmacokinetic/Pharmacodynamic Data," *Int. J. Clin. Pharmacol. Ther.*, Vol. 40, 2002, pp. S14–29.

[2]   Hu, H., et al., "Biomedical Informatics: Development of a Comprehensive Data Warehouse for Clinical and Genomic Breast Cancer Research," *Pharmacogenomics*, Vol. 5, 2004, pp. 933–941.

[3]   Parkinson, H., et al., "ArrayExpress—A Public Repository for Microarray Gene Expression Data at the EBI," *Nucleic Acids Res.*, Vol. 33, 2005, pp. D553–555.

[4]   McDowall, R. D., Pearce, J. C., and Murkitt, G. S., "Laboratory Information Management Systems—Part I. Concepts," *J. Pharm. Biomed. Anal.*, Vol. 6, 1988, pp. 339–359.

[5]   McDowall, R. D., Pearce, J. C., and Murkitt, G. S., "Laboratory Information Management Systems—Part II. Implementation," *J. Pharm. Biomed. Anal.*, Vol. 6, 1988, pp. 361–381.

[6]   Cardot, J. M., et al., "LIMS: From Theory to Practice," *Eur. J. Drug. Metab. Pharmacokinet.*, Vol. 23, 1998, pp. 207–212.

[7]   Avery, G., McGee, C., and Falk, S., "Implementing LIMS: a "how-to" guide," *Anal. Chem.*, Vol. 72, 2000, pp. 57A–62A.

[8]   Turner, E., and Bolton, J., "Required Steps for the Validation of a Laboratory Information Management System," *Qual. Assur.*, Vol. 9, 2001, pp. 217–224.

[9]   Klein, C. S., "LIMS User Acceptance Testing," *Qual. Assur.*, Vol. 10, 2003, pp. 91–106.

[10] McDowall, R. D. (Ed.), *Laboratory Information Management Systems: Concepts, Integration and Implementation*, New York: John Wiley & Sons, 1988.

[11] Nakagawa, A. S., *LIMS: Implementation and Management*, Cambridge, UK: Royal Society of Chemistry, 1994.

[12] Paszko, C., and Turner, E., *Laboratory Information Management Systems Revised & Expanded*, 2nd ed., Boca Raton, FL: CRC Press, 2001.

[13] Merchant, M., *Introduction to Laboratory Information Management Systems*: New York: John Wiley & Sons Inc, 2007.

[14] Seamonds, P., and Atteberg, J. M., "Should LIMS Vendors Get a Second Chance to Make a Good First Impression?," *Healthc. Comput. Commun.*, Vol. 4, 1987, pp. 40–42.

[15] Neaves, W., "Selection of a LIMS System in a SMALL LABORATORY," *Canadian Chemical News*, Vol. 41, 1989, pp. 12–14.

[16] Hunkapiller, T. and Hood, L., "LIMS and the Human Genome Project," *Biotechnology (NY)*, Vol. 9, 1991, pp. 1344–1345.

[17] Bund, C., et al., "Validation of a Customized LIMS," *Pharm. Acta Helv.*, Vol. 72, 1998, pp. 349–356.

[18] Friedli, D., Kappeler, W., and Zimmermann, S., "Validation of Computer Systems: Practical Testing of a Standard LIMS," *Pharm. Acta Helv.*, Vol. 72, 1998, pp. 343–348.

[19] Williams, D., "A 5-Step Plan to Evaluate, Pick Laboratory Systems," *Validation Times*, Vol. 1, 1999.

[20] LIMSource, http://www.limsource.com.

[21] LIMS Finder, http://www.limsfinder.com.

[22] Morris, C., et al., "MOLE: A Data Management Application Based on a Protein Production Data Model," *Proteins*, Vol. 58, 2005, pp. 285–289.

[23] Quo, C. F., Wu, B., and Wang, M. D., "Development of a Laboratory Information System for Cancer Collaboration Projects," *Conf. Proc. IEEE Eng. Med. Biol. Soc.*, Vol. 3, 2005, pp. 2859–2862.

[24] Li, H., Gennari, J. H., and Brinkley, J. F., "Model Driven Laboratory Information Management Systems," *AMIA Annu. Symp. Pro.c*, 2006, pp. 484–488.

[25] Viksna, J., et al., "PASSIM—An Open Source Software System for Managing Information in Biomedical Studies," *BMC Bioinformatics*, Vol. 8, 2007, p. 52.

[26] "Cancer Laboratory Information Management System," http://calims.nci.nih.gov/caLIMS.

[27] Beaver, K., *Healthcare Information Systems*, 2nd ed., Boca Raton, FL: Auerbach/CRC Press, 2002.

[28] Healthcare Information and Management Systems Society, http://www.himss.org/ASP/index.asp.

[29] Freezerworks, http://www.freezerworks.com.

[30] "Tissue Banks and Pathology Tools (TBPT) Workspace," https://cabig.nci.nih.gov /workspaces/TBPT?pid=primary.2006-10-24.9768040952&sid= tbptws&status=True.

[31] Perry, D., "LIMS in the Academic World," *Today's Chemist at Work*, Vol. 11, 2002, pp. 15–16, 19.

[32] Steinlechner, M., and Parson, W., "Automation and High Through-Put for a DNA Database Laboratory: Development of a Laboratory Information Management System," *Croat. Med. J.*, Vol. 42, 2001, pp. 252–255.

[33] Xiang, B., et al., "CytoAccess, a Relational Laboratory Information Management System for a Clinical Cytogenetics Laboratory," *J. Assoc. Genet. Technol.*, Vol. 32, 2006, pp. 168–170.

[34] Webb, S. C., et al., "LIMaS: The JAVA-Based Application and Database for Microarray Experiment Tracking," *Mamm. Genome*, Vol. 15, 2004, pp. 740–747.

[35] Maurer, M., et al., "MARS: Microarray Analysis, Retrieval, and Storage System," *BMC Bioinformatics*, Vol. 6, 2005, pp. 101.

[36] Honore, P., et al., "MicroArray Facility: A Laboratory Information Management System with Extended Support for Nylon Based Technologies," *BMC Genomics*, Vol. 7, 2006, pp. 240.

[37] Sanchez-Villeda, H., et al., "Development of an Integrated Laboratory Information Management System for the Maize Mapping Project," *Bioinformatics*, Vol. 19, 2003, pp. 2022–2030.

[38] Monnier, S., et al., "T.I.M.S: TaqMan Information Management System, Tools to Organize Data Flow in a Genotyping Laboratory," *BMC Bioinformatics*, Vol. 6, 2005, p. 246.

[39] Jayashree, B., et al., "Laboratory Information Management Software for Genotyping Workflows: Applications in High Throughput Crop Genotyping," *BMC Bioinformatics*, Vol. 7, 2006, p. 383.

[40] Goh, C. S., et al., "SPINE 2: A System for Collaborative Structural Proteomics Within a Federated Database Framework," *Nucleic Acids Res.*, Vol. 31, 2003, pp. 2833–2838.

[41] Fulton, K. F., et al., "CLIMS: Crystallography Laboratory Information Management System," *Acta Crystallogr. D Biol. Crystallogr.*, Vol. 60, 2004, pp. 1691–1693.

[42] Prilusky, J., et al., "HalX: An Open-Source LIMS (Laboratory Information Management System) for Small- to Large-Scale Laboratories," *Acta Crystallogr. D Biol. Crystallogr.*, Vol. 61, 2005, pp. 671–678.

[43] Amin, A. A., et al., "Managing and Mining Protein Crystallization Data," *Proteins*, Vol. 62, 2006, pp. 4–7.

[44] Baran, M. C., et al., "SPINS: A Laboratory Information Management System for Organizing and Archiving Intermediate and Final Results from NMR Protein Structure Determinations," *Proteins*, Vol. 62, 2006, pp. 843–851.

[45] Cho, S. Y., et al., "An Integrated Proteome Database for Two-Dimensional Electrophoresis Data Analysis and Laboratory Information Management System," *Proteomics*, Vol. 2, 2002, pp. 1104–1113.

[46] Morisawa, H., Hirota, M., and Toda, T., "Development of an Open Source Laboratory Information Management System for 2-D Gel Electrophoresis-Based Proteomics Workflow," *BMC Bioinformatics*, Vol. 7, 2006, pp. 430.

[47] White, W. L., et al., "Protein Open-Access Liquid Chromatography/Mass Spectrometry," *Rapid Commun. Mass Spectrom.*, Vol. 19, 2005, pp. 241–249.

[48] Moloshok, T., "Proteomics LIMS: A caBIGtrade Mark Project, Year 1," *AMIA Annu. Symp. Proc.*, 2006, pp. 1116.

[49] LabVantage, http://www.labvantage.com.

[50] Cimarron Software, http://www.cimsoft.com.

[51] GenoLogics, http://www.genologics.com.

[52] "GeneChip Operating Software (GCOS)," http://www.affymetrix.com/index.affx.

[53] Wikipedia, "Extensibility," http://en.wikipedia.org/wiki/Extensibility.

[54] Ferraiolo, D. F., and D. R. Kuhn, D. R., "Role Based Access Control," paper presented at proceedings of 15th National Computer Security Conference, 1992.

[55] Bohm, M., et al., "Microbeam MOMeNT: Non-Contact Laser Microdissection of Membrane-Mounted Native Tissue," *Am. J. Pathol.*, Vol. 151, 1997, pp. 63–67.

[56] Ellsworth, D. L., et al., "Laser Capture Microdissection of Paraffin-Embedded Tissues," *Biotechniques*, Vol. 34, 2003, pp. 42–44, 46.

[57] Salamone, S., "LIMS: To Buy or Not to Buy?" *Bio-IT World*, June 27, 2004.

[58] Wikipedia, "Use Case," http://en.wikipedia.org/wiki/Use_case.

[59] Cho, E. K., et al., "Array-Based Comparative Genomic Hybridization and Copy Number Variation in Cancer Research," *Cytogenet. Genome Res.*, Vol. 115, 2006, pp. 262–272.

[60] Cutler, P., "Protein Arrays: The Current State-of-the-Art," *Proteomics*, Vol. 3, 2003, pp. 3–18.

CHAPTER 8

Data Centralization

Hai Hu

中医：望、闻、问、切➔诊断。

Observe (wang4), Smell (wen2), Inquiry (wen4), and Touch (qie1) ➔ *Diagnose.*
—Chinese Traditional Medicine

In Chinese traditional medicine, when a doctor sees a patient, he observes the patient's appearance, smells the odor from the patient, asks the patient a number of questions, and touches the wrist artery for pulse performance of the patient. After these four steps, an experienced doctor is able to make a diagnosis of the patient's disease, be it simply a cold or a complicated digestive dysfunction.

An analysis of this case shows that these four exercises are actually all one can do, in a noninvasive manner, to acquire information from the patient using one's natural sensory organs. Chinese traditional medicine adopts an integrative approach in which a patient is treated as one whole system. After the doctor gathers these four types of data, he centralizes them in certain ways and analyzes the centralized data against the knowledge he has accumulated through the years of practice to arrive at a diagnosis for the patient.

From the artificial intelligence viewpoint, the doctor possesses a natural knowledge base, which is based on the facts he has gathered through years of practice, and the rules he has developed through practice. An expert system can be developed as an artificial analogy of this process. The knowledge base should be composed of facts and rules, and newly acquired input information is examined against this knowledge base so that new conclusions can be drawn.

In biomedical informatics research, one major goal is to develop a comprehensive diagnostic system by using a combination of clinical data and high-throughput molecular data for a more economic and accurate diagnosis of the patient. The other major goal is to aid in the development of medicines for disease treatment; to do this, a study of the mechanism of development of the disease is very important. In either case, a large amount of data of different types is generated or collected as described in previous chapters.

The goals of biomedical informatics research call on data centralization and rule development such that when a clinical question is asked, proper data can be retrieved from the centralized data system, to allow biomedical informaticians to use proper data analysis and data mining tools to work toward the answer to the question. Examples of such questions include the following:

- How many subjects have been enrolled in the study?
- Are there enough samples from the control and diseased subjects of matched conditions?
- What biomarkers can be used to tell cancer patients from patients with benign diseases?
- Is this tumor a recurrence of a previous cancer or a new one?
- Is there a molecular basis supporting the pathology diagnoses of these diseases?
- Which genotype profile can be predictive of sudden cardiac death?
- Are abnormally expressed genes at the RNA level also overexpressed or underexpressed at the protein level?

In our opinion, data centralization is not for the mechanical purpose of centralization, but for the purpose of addressing clinical and scientific questions. The former would simply be a response to the need to manage large amounts of data, but the latter will ensure that a fundamentally useful data centralization structure is designed. A good understanding of the data themselves is also a prerequisite of data centralization.

In the preceding chapters, we have described and discussed how disease-centric biomedical informatics data are generated, tracked, and controlled and assessed for quality. These operations are certainly applied across the clinical, genomic, and proteomic platforms. For integrative biomedical informatics research, data centralization is not only necessary for those typically in-house generated heterogeneous data, but is also needed for the publicly available experimental and annotation data that are complementary to internal data, to allow research clinicians and scientists to effectively access the data of different types for both bottom-up and top-down research. One way to centralize such data is to develop a data warehouse (DW).

Note that in this chapter the term *data centralization* is used in the place of the more commonly used term *data integration* because later in the chapter when we discuss DW models there is an "integration" approach and there is also a "federation" approach. Using the term *data integration* here may cause some confusion when we are really referring to "putting data together in an organized manner," which could be done through integration or federation or both approaches. Thus, the more neutral term of *centralization* is chosen here.

8.1 An Overview of Data Centralization

One important approach for centralizing data is through data warehousing. DW technology has been applied to retail, banking, transportation, and other industrial services for about 20 years. There are two widely respected pioneers in the field, William H. Inmon and Ralph Kimball, who define DW from different perspectives. Inmon defines a DW as "a subject-oriented, integrated, time-variant and non-volatile collection of data in support of management's decision making process" [1], whereas Kimball defines it as an integrated collection of several data marts [2]. Note that here a DW refers to all of the data in an enterprise, and a data mart is focused on one subject or on the data in one department of an enterprise.

For biomedical informatics research, the main purpose of developing a DW is not for management's decision making, but for clinicians and scientists to explore the data. Also, the structure of the DW does not have to be integrative; it can also be federative. Based on our understanding of the field, we define DW as a structured collection of clinical, genomic, and proteomic data for easy reporting purposes, accompanied by a set of tools that supports subject-oriented biomedical informatics research.

A DW is different from a normal database: The former is more for query and reporting purposes, whereas the latter is more for transactional operations. Once data are loaded into the DW, be it a complete loading or incremental loading, the data become static and no INSERT, DELETE, or UPDATE transactions are allowed. Only SELECT operations are allowed for reporting the data.

Application of data warehousing to life sciences is relatively new. A search in PubMed, a popular public collection of biomedical literature, using the keywords "data warehouse" or "data warehousing" in mid-year 2005 returned a total of 242 papers with the yearly distribution shown in Figure 8.1. Before 1992, there were only a total of 16 papers on the subject. Up until 1999, almost all such papers were focused on the health care industry. Since the year 2000, with the development of genome sequencing, DW started to be applied to genomic and proteomic research. In the last 3 or 4 years, the number of published papers on this subject became stabilized at around 30 papers per year. About half of them are still focused on health care systems.

When the keyword "data integration" was included in the PubMed search, the returned total number of publications increased to 327, but the yearly distribution has a similar pattern. Note that these numbers may not be very accurate due to the capability of the search engine and other limiting factors in PubMed and the literature itself, but the general trend should hold true.

In health care organizations, such as in a major hospital, a large amount of patient data is collected on a daily basis. This includes demographics, medical history, symptoms, physical exams, routine and diagnostic tests, diagnosis, medica-

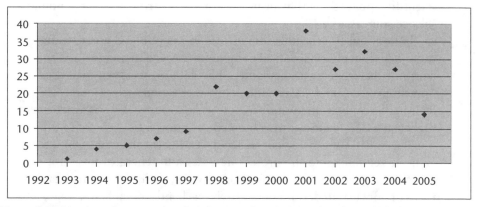

Figure 8.1   Number of papers related to data warehousing as indexed in PubMed for each calendar year from 1993 to mid-2005 as a result of a keyword search using the terms "data warehouse" and "data warehousing" in July 2005.

tions and other treatments, and outcomes. Historically such data were in a paper format or on a medium such as film that was not easy to access. Since the 1990s, when electronic storage of data became more and more popular, DWs started to be developed to integrate the health care data, and currently an increasing number of institutions maintain patient data in clinical DWs [3–10]. Such DWs, existing or in development, allow health care executives and policy makers to assess parameters such as hospital volume, operational costs, and outcomes [11–14]. They also allow clinical researchers to study the diagnoses, treatments, outcomes, and follow-ups and to identify relationships among the data elements in the DW for both clinical and basic research [15–21]. Development of a national clinical DW to centralize the available data from public and private health care providers is also being discussed, although to achieve this goal, substantial hurdles will have to be overcome [22].

With regard to life sciences, most data warehousing efforts are focused on centralizing public data. Through the beginning of 2005, more than 700 public databases had been published in the journal *Nucleic Acids Research* in the special January issues dedicated to databases. Centralizing such data in the public domain is certainly of high value in biomedical informatics research. Most such efforts are subject specific; thus, the DWs developed are specialized and therefore probably fall more into the category of a data mart than a DW. Some organizations, however, do make extended efforts to comprehensively centralize the data in the public domain. One such example is caCORE [23].

caCORE was developed by the National Cancer Institute Center for Bioinformatics serving as a robust infrastructure for data management and centralization that supports advanced biomedical research and development [23]. It is composed of an interconnected set of three components of software and services. Enterprise Vocabulary Services (EVS) provide controlled vocabulary, dictionary, and thesaurus services. The Cancer Data Standards Repository (caDSR) provides a metadata registry for common data elements. Cancer Bioinformatics Infrastructure Objects (caBIO) implements an object-oriented model of the biomedical domain and provides Java, web services, and HTTP-XML programming interfaces. caCORE can be accessed remotely at the NCI website, or the distributed version can be installed locally. The system at the NCI website is continually updated, but the distributed version is only updated twice a year. caCORE has been used to develop scientific applications that bring together data from distinct genomic and clinical science sources.

In addition to centralization efforts in the public domain, industrial organizations including pharmaceutical companies are also making efforts to centralize their corporate heterogeneous data and public data to meet their own research and development needs. Merck's Gene Index browser is one such example [24]. As described later in this chapter, the Windber Research Institute (WRI) is also developing a comprehensive DW for integrative biomedical informatics research [25].

The WRI DW is being constructed as a hybrid structure that integrates internal clinical, genomic, and the proteomic data, and federates this with external public proteomic, genomic, and clinical data. Centralizing external data will not be the focus of our current development. In the earlier developmental stage of the DW [25], however, we did integrate four carefully selected public databases, namely, RefSeq, SwissProt/Tremble (now UniProt), Gene Ontology, and LocusLink (now Entrez

Gene). More importantly, in this earlier version of the DW [25], we integrated clinical data from questionnaires on 800 fields in a breast cancer study, covering demographics, clinical history, family history, lifestyle, risk factor, tissue type, tissue diagnosis, and other annotations. We also integrated internally generated, high-throughput experimental data. A multidimensional On-Line Analytical Processing (OLAP) application and Spotfire application were also developed for data access and visualization.

Currently, the new version of the DW is based on an innovative clinical data module structure with an advanced, newly designed relational OLAP application that is capable of enabling timely access to hundreds of clinical data elements from up to a million subjects. In addition to the OLAP, a set of applications for data retrieval, visualization, analysis, and mining is also envisioned within the biomedical informatics portal structured on top of the DW.

Other kinds of data centralization efforts are presented as search engines; examples include Entrez of NCBI in the United States and the Sequence Retrieval System (SRS) developed by EBI in Europe [26–28]. Entrez contains more than 30 major public databases that can be searched, and the SRS contains more than 130 biological databases. SRS also integrates more than 10 applications. In both Entrez and SRS, search results are returned in their original data formats from the source public databases.

Table 8.1 lists example DWs for biological and biomedical studies, with references and URL links. Some descriptions have been adapted from corresponding websites. caCORE, the WRI DW, Entrez, and SRS are all listed, together with other data repositories that are DW-like in nature.

Biomedical data have their own characteristics and the ways in which the data are used are also very different from practices in the health care, retail, banking, and other industries. A few papers have been published to discuss this unique environment and the special needs for data centralization [34–36]. While some opinions presented in those papers are of value, other comments apply to specific data centralization environments, but may not be generalizable. For example, Koehler et al. stated that "A biological data integration system should support direct import of data from flat files rather than from separate database management systems" and that "When individual data sources have to be updated, it is assumed that all databases to be integrated are reimported and integrated" [34]. Based on our knowledge and practice, we believe that data loading should support multiple data formats. In addition, some of the source data types can accumulate to terabyte level and higher, making it impractical to always perform complete loading. In such cases, data loading will have to be incremental. We will discuss such issues in more detail in Section 8.3.

8.2   Types of Data in Question

As discussed in Chapter 1, translational biomedical informatics research takes data from a broad range of clinical, genomic, and proteomic platforms as well as the knowledge generated in these fields. Without such a broad range of data, the questions raised earlier in this chapter cannot be answered. Currently a systematic col-

Table 8.1   Example DWs for Biological and Biomedical Studies

Name and Reference	Description and URL
caCORE [23]	caCORE is an NCICB effort to provide a robust infrastructure for biomedical research. It has components named EVS, caDSR, and caBIO (see text for details). It integrates or federates data from about 30 NCI and other public sources including sequence, annotations, ontology, pathways, and clinical trials. Flat-file, relational, and Internet Protocol source data are supported. caBIO contributes a DW that integrates several of those data sources. URL: http://ncicb.nci.nih.gov/core
Merck Gene Index browser [24]	The system is composed of a federation of relational databases, a local DW, and simple hypertext links. Data currently integrated include LENS cDNA clone and EST data, dbEST protein and non-EST nucleic acid similarity data, WashU sequence chromatograms, Entrez sequence and Medline entries, and UniGene gene clusters. Flat-file sequence data are accessed using the internally developed Bioapps server.
Windber Research Institute DW [25]	This DW is envisioned to have a hybrid structure that integrates internal clinical, genomic, and proteomic data, which can then be federated with external data. An early phase of development has been completed in which about half of the internally generated types of data have been integrated with four selected public databases. Current development plans are going forward in terms of the envisioned structure. See text for more details.
The Multi-Conditional Hybridization Intensity Processing System (M-CHIPS) [29]	M-CHIPS does not have an underlying transactional database. The data are entered directly into the system, so it is a database of a DW concept. Data of raw intensity, gene annotation, and experimental annotation are stored, and algorithms suitable for statistical analysis of the entire contents are provided. It is implemented as a set of organism-specific databases, namely, *Saccharomyces cerevisiae, Arabidopsis thaliana, Trypanosoma brucei, Neurospora crassa,* and human tumor samples. URL: http://www.dkfz.de/tbi/services/mchips
Open Reading Frame DB (ORFDB) [30]	The ORFDB serves as a central DW enabling researchers to search the human and mouse ORF collection through its web portal ORFBrowser. Researchers can find the Ultimate ORF clones by blast, keyword, GenBank accession, gene symbol, clone ID, Unigene ID, LocusLink ID, or through functional relationships by browsing the collection via the Gene Ontology (GO) browser. The cloned ORFs have been extensively annotated across six categories: Gene, ORF, Clone Format, Protein, SNP, and Genomic links, with the information assembled in a format termed the ORFCard. URL: http://orf.invitrogen.com/cgi-bin/ORF_Browser
Ligand Depot [31]	Ligand Depot is an integrated data resource for finding information about small molecules bound to proteins and nucleic acids. The initial release focuses on providing chemical and structural information for small molecules found as part of the structures deposited in the Protein Data Bank. Ligand Depot accepts keyword-based queries and also provides a graphical interface for performing chemical substructure searches. A wide variety of web resources that contain information on small molecules may also be accessed through Ligand Depot. URL: http://ligand-depot.rutgers.edu
YeastHub [32]	YeastHub is a yeast genome prototype DW based on semantic web technologies including resource description framework (RDF), RDF site summary (RSS), relational-database-to-RDF mapping (D2RQ), and native RDF data repository. This DW allows integration of different types of yeast genome data provided by different resources in different formats including the tabular and RDF formats. Once the data are loaded into the DW, RDF-based queries can be formulated to retrieve and query the data in an integrated fashion. URL: http://yeasthub.gersteinlab.org

Table 8.1   (continued)

Name and Reference	Description and URL
Atlas [33]	Atlas is an integration of the public GenBank, RefSeq, UniProt, Human Protein Reference Database (HPRD), BIND, DIP, Molecular Interactions Database (MINT), IntAct, NCBI Taxonomy, GO, OMIM, Entrez Gene, and HomoloGene databases. The authors classified these databases into four main groups: sequence, molecular interactions, gene-related resources, and ontology. A set of APIs written in C++, Java, or Perl is provided in the toolbox to allow users to retrieve the data based on what they need. URL: http://bioinformatics.ubc.ca/atlas
ONDEX [34]	ONDEX presents biological data in graphs, with nodes for entities and edges for relationships that are defined at the semantic level. The generalized data structure, also called the entity–attribute–value (EAV) model, which is discussed in Section 8.3.7, is used for data storage. Currently parsers of some of the public databases that are of interest to the developer have been developed, including AraCyc, BRENDA, Drastic, TRANSFAC, EC Nomenclature, WorldNet, MeSH, and NCBI TAXONOMY. The system allows for importing and integration of any of the public databases as long as a parser has been developed. URL: http://sourceforge.net/projects/ondex
Entrez [26]	This is a web-based integrated database retrieval system developed by NCBI. It enables text searching of a diverse set of databases using simple Boolean queries. Thirty such databases had been included by 2005 and the number is still increasing. URL: http://www.ncbi.nlm.nih.gov/Database/index.html
SRS [27, 28]	The EBI SRS is an integration system that allows for both data retrieval and provides applications for data analysis. Users can query across databases quickly and efficiently. As of 2002, the server contained more than 130 biological databases and integrated more than 10 applications. URL: http://srs.ebi.ac.uk

lection of patient-centric data across these platforms is not available, at least not to the public. There are a few organizations in the world that are at the cutting edge of collecting and producing such data sets. In this section we provide an overview of the types of data that we think are important to translational biomedical informatics research. This discussion is followed by a section on selected public repositories for these types of data.

8.2.1   in-house Patient-Centric Clinical, Genomic, and Proteomic Data

A comprehensive body of clinical data is important to the analysis and interpretation of genomic and proteomic data. Unfortunately, the types of collected clinical data for this purpose vary from project to project, and standards governing the collection of these data have not been developed. As a result, although genomic and proteomic data from clinical specimens are available in the public domain, the information about the specimens and the donors (normal subjects or patients) is very limited. To collect relatively complete clinical, genomic, and proteomic data sets, researchers will generally almost have to start at the beginning by designing a proper project for clinical data and specimen collection, and then continue to conduct molecular studies using the collected specimens. In Chapters 2 and 3, we discussed clinical operations, and the following types of data obtained from the clinic are considered to be important to biomedical informatics activities.

- *Demographics:* age, sex, ethnicity, geography, family structure, and so forth. Demographics have been shown to be important in human disease studies.

- *Medical exam results and medical history:* lab blood test results, body mass index, previous and current known diseases, current medications, and so forth. For example, it is known that high cholesterol and high blood pressure are associated with cardiovascular diseases. As another example, hormone replacement therapy for treatment of menopausal syndromes has been reported to potentially induce cancers and cardiovascular diseases; recently, the WHO International Agency for Research on Cancer has reclassified this treatment from "possibly carcinogenic" to "carcinogenic" [37].

- *Medical images:* mammograms, ultrasound, MRI, pathology slide images, and so forth. Radiologists and other medical image readers routinely use these images to aid in clinical diagnosis.

- *Family history:* primary and secondary family members' history of diseases. Diseases relevant to the disease in the study should be included. For example, for a breast cancer study, a family history of breast cancer, ovarian cancer, and cervical cancer should be collected.

- *Lifestyle:* exercise patterns and drinking and smoking habits along the temporal dimension. It has been shown that moderate exercise is good for health and is protective against diseases in general. Alcohol and smoking are risk factors to many diseases. The history of the lifestyle data is also important because it is possible that drinking and smoking during certain developmental stages can be more dangerous than doing so during other stages.

- *Risk factors:* often disease specific. For example, age of the first live child birth is known to be important for breast cancer development, and hypertension and high cholesterol level are a risk factor for obesity and cardiovascular diseases.

- *Specimen annotations:* tissue type, sample date, location, diagnosis, and preservation type. The diagnosis is very important to the research since the clinical and molecular study data are often clustered or trained based on the diagnoses of the sample and the patient.

For molecular studies, different organizations focus on different experimental platforms. The common platforms for genomics studies, many of which were discussed in Chapter 5, are microarray gene expression, microarray genotyping, microsatellite genotyping, aCGH, sequencing, FISH, RT-PCR, and so forth. The microarray-based data are structured and often have a size of tens of thousands or more rows of records. For the nonmicroarray-based platforms, the data type for each of them should be defined specifically based on what system is used and what the goal of the project is. For example, RT-PCR can be used as one step for RNA amplification in sequencing, and qRT-PCR can be used to quantify the RNA in the sample to study gene expression. Obviously the data of a results nature are very different in the two PCR experiments.

Regarding proteomics, several experimental platforms were discussed in Chapter 6. Such studies include protein expressions, interactions, and a structural analysis. Qualitative protein expression can be studied using antibody arrays, and quantitative protein expression often involves protein separation (2D gel, HPLC) and identification (mass spectrometry). Standards for some of these platforms such as mass spectrometric analysis are being developed but have not yet matured; for other platforms, development of standards has yet to be started.

8.2.2   Publicly Available Annotation and Experimental Data

Public databases are usually databases developed by universities, governmental, and other nonprofit organizations using grants or other public funds; therefore, the public has free access to them. Typically, public database is a repository of the data focusing on one specific subject, structured from one perspective in which the sponsoring organization is interested, and thus follows a specific development philosophy.

The total number of public databases has increased dramatically in the last few years, as evidenced by the number of corresponding publications in the *Nucleic Acids Research* journal. Starting in 1994, this journal has dedicated a January issue to public databases, covering new listings and selected updates. When the first issue was published, there were only about 30 databases. By 2005 the journal covered 719 databases, excluding ones that are obsolete. All 719 databases have been compiled into the Molecular Biology Database Collection, which also contains other selected databases [38, 39]. The databases are organized in a hierarchical classification that simplifies the process of finding the right database for any given task. The summaries of the databases provide brief descriptions of the databases, contact details, appropriate references, and acknowledgments [39].

Earlier in the chapter, Table 8.1 listed some of the public databases and services that are of a DW or data mart nature. In the life sciences environment, it can be difficult to define a public data collection as a DW, data mart, or database. But one thing we can say for sure is that at least most of these databases are not transactional databases; instead, they were designed for querying or reporting purposes. In that sense, those public databases should be called data marts or DWs, depending on the scope of the data. However, precisely defining those concepts is not the main focus of this book. At times, it is difficult to make such assignments. For example, should the Ligand Depot shown in Table 8.1 be called a data mart in the context of comprehensive biomedical informatics research, or a DW as named by the authors given their scope of study?

Given this difficulty, in the following subsections we continue to ambiguously use the term *public databases* to refer to those public data collections. We discuss some of the most popular public databases and several databases that are less popular but that we think are of special value to biomedical informatics research. At the end of this section, we also discuss some challenges the public databases face that raise serious concerns about centralizing these sources of data.

8.2.2.1   Popular Public Databases

Table 8.2 lists a number of popular public databases with references and URLs. Some descriptions are adapted from corresponding websites. The first eight databases are the most popular, with relatively comprehensive coverage of the data in

Table 8.2   Most Popular Public Databases

Name and Reference	Description and URL
GenBank [40]	GenBank is maintained by NCBI in the United States, the EMBL Nucleotide Sequence Database is maintained by the European Molecular Biology Laboratory (EMBL), and the DNA DataBank of Japan (DDBJ) is maintained by the National Institute of Genetics of Japan [41]. These are the most popular nucleotide sequences and annotations public databases. All three belong to the International Nucleotide Sequence Database Collaborations. Members of this group update and exchange data on a daily basis. Because this international collaboration accepts submissions from research scientists almost automatically with limited verification, the databases are plagued with redundant information and data entry errors. URL: http://www.ncbi.nlm.nih.gov/Genbank
EMBL [42]	See GenBank entry above. URL: http://www.ebi.ac.uk/embl
RefSeq [43]	The NCBI's Reference Sequence collection aims to provide a comprehensive, integrated, nonredundant set of sequences, including genomic DNA, transcript (RNA), and protein products, for major research organisms. URL: http://www.ncbi.nlm.nih.gov/RefSeq
UniProt [44]	UniProt, a protein knowledge base, is the most prominent public database for protein sequences and annotations. UniProt resulted from the merging of the SwissProt/Trembl of SIB (Swiss Institute of Bioinformatics) in Switzerland and EBI (European Bioinformatics Institute) in the United Kingdom, and the PIR (the Protein Information Resources), developed and maintained by the National Biomedical Research Foundation and Georgetown University in the United States. Trembl is a computer translation of the genes in EMBL with annotations provided by a software program. Entries in SwissProt are based on those in Trembl, but are manually annotated and examined by experts in the field to ensure the high quality of the data. URL: http://www.ebi.uniprot.org/index.shtml
Gene Ontology [45, 46]	As a consortium effort, Gene Ontology (GO) aims to develop three structured, controlled vocabularies (ontologies) describing gene products in the categories of their associated biological processes, cellular components, and molecular functions in a species-independent manner. Started as a collaboration between three model organism databases—FlyBase (*Drosophila*), the *Saccharomyces* Genome Database (SGD), and the Mouse Genome Database (MGD)—the consortium has now expanded to include about 20 leading organizations working on many organisms. Applying these ontologies to gene products provides consistent descriptions across different databases, which has largely facilitated scientific research and development. URL: http://www.geneontology.org
Entrez Gene [47]	This is an NCBI-curated cross-reference of genetic loci. Previously known as LocusLink, this database provides a single query interface to curated sequence and descriptive information about genetic loci. It provides information on official nomenclature, aliases, sequence accessions, phenotypes, EC numbers, OMIM numbers, UniGene clusters, homology, map locations, related web sites, and so forth. It is an indispensable source of information for integrative biomedical informatics research. URL: http://www.ncbi.nlm.nih.gov/entrez/query.fcgi?&db=gene
OMIM	NCBI Online Mendelian Inheritance in Man (OMIM) is an authoritative annotated bibliography of human genes and genetic disorders. It can be searched using disease name or gene name. OMIM was designed for use by physicians and genetics researchers, with records written in free text. This unstructured format hinders it from being easily applied to automated data analysis and research. URL: http://www3.ncbi.nlm.nih.gov/omim
PubMed [26]	Developed by NCBI, PubMed was designed to provide access to citations from biomedical literature. It covers biomedical articles dated back to the 1950s, providing abstracts of most of the articles. As the open access policy becomes more popular, more and more full papers are becoming available. URL: http://www.ncbi.nlm.nih.gov/entrez/query.fcgi

Table 8.2   (continued)

Name and Reference	Description and URL
UniGene [26]	A largely automated analytical system for producing an organized view of the transcriptome. URL: http:/www.ncbi.nlm.nih.gov/UniGene?ORG=Hs
DIP [48]	The Database of Interacting Proteins (DIP) catalogs experimentally determined interactions among proteins. URL: http://dip.doe-mbi.ucla.edu
KEGG [49]	Kyoto Encyclopedia of Genes and Genomes (KEGG) is a bioinformatics resource for understanding higher order functional meanings and utilities of the cell or the organism from its genome information. URL: http://www.genome.ad.jp/kegg
BIND [50]	The Biomolecular Interaction Network Database (BIND) is designed to store full descriptions of interactions, molecular complexes, and pathways. URL: http://www.binddb.org/cgi-bin/bind/dataman
STKE	Offered by Science, Signal Transduction Knowledge Environment (STKE) provides a dynamic graphical interface into a cellular signaling database. URL: http://stke.sciencemag.org/cm
PDB [51, 52]	The Protein Data Bank (PDB) is the single worldwide repository for the processing and distribution of 3D biological macromolecular structure data. URL: http://www.rcsb.org/pdb
BRENDA [53]	This is the main collection of enzyme functional data available to the scientific community. URL: http://www.brenda.uni-koeln.de

their specific fields, and they are highly relevant to integrative biomedical informatics research. Thus, more detailed descriptions of these databases are provided. For the remaining databases, brief descriptions are provided.

8.2.2.2   Public Databases of Special Values

Besides the most popular public databases, there are a number of databases that are or potentially will be of special value to integrative biomedical informatics research. Table 8.3 lists some of these databases, in alphabetical order. Descriptions are provided for all of the databases based on the corresponding publications, websites, and the author's knowledge. Some of the databases are not being actively updated, but we have listed them here for their contents.

8.2.2.3   Considerations and Concerns About Using or Integrating Public Data

Although the data in the public databases are of extremely high value to biomedical informatics research, integration of those data is not an easy task. Public databases are developed by different organizations based on different philosophies applying different criteria. The same data may be presented in different formats, and data inconsistencies and redundancies not only exist between different databases but often also within the same database. The error rate varies from database to database. Another issue is that those databases are often developed and maintained using grant funds, and some of them resulted from a graduate or postdoctoral pro-

Table 8.3   Selected Public Databases That Are of Special Value to Biomedical Informatics Research

Name and Reference	*Descriptions and URL*
Atlas of Genetics and Cytogenetics in Oncology and Haematology [54]	The Atlas of Genetics and Cytogenetics in Oncology and Haematology is a peer–reviewed, online journal and database with free access on the Internet. It is devoted to genes, cytogenetics, and clinical entities in cancer, and cancer-prone diseases. The database contains concise and updated information cards on genes involved in cancer, cytogenetics and clinical entities in oncology, and cancer-prone diseases, a portal toward genetics/cancer, and teaching materials in genetics. It is made for and by researchers and clinicians with editors and contributors from all around the world.
	URL: http://www.infobiogen.fr/services/chromcancer
BIOBASE [55]	BIOBASE is a commercial company that provides biological databases and application software for the life sciences industry. Although it charges a fee for using its commercial products, the company offers public access to products that are not maintained as well as its commercial products. BIOBASE offers seven databases to the public, including TRANSFAC, a database on eukaryotic transcription factors, their genomic binding sites and DNA-binding profiles; PathoDB, a database on pathologically relevant mutated forms of transcription factors and transcription factor binding sites; TRANSPATH, a database providing information about the intracellular signal transduction pathways; and PROTEOME, a suite of six protein databases: YPD, HumanPSD, WormPD, GPCR-PD, MycoPath PD, and PombePD. The company also provides a number of applications that are free for public or noncommercial uses, and links to download sites of a number of other public applications.
	URL: http://www.biobase-international.com/pages/
CGED [56]	The Cancer Gene Expression Database (CGED) is a database with data obtained by means of a high-throughput RT-PCR technique. Samples used in experiments were mainly solid tissues of breast, colorectal, hepatocellular, and esophageal cancers. It is worth noting that most of the samples are all from one hospital, which potentially eliminates clinical sample preparation discrepancies among different hospitals. Limited clinical parameters such as metastasis status are also available.
	URL: http://love2.aist-nara.ac.jp/CGED
COSMIC [57]	Developed by Sanger Institute in the United Kingdom, the Catalogue Of Somatic Mutations In Cancer (COSMIC) is designed to store and display somatic mutation information and related details and contains information relating to human cancers. By design, this database contains two features that are very important in biomedical research. First, this database contains information not only from invasive cancer samples, but also from tissues with benign and other diagnoses. Information from cancer cell lines is included as well. Secondly, it contains samples found to be negative for mutations identified during screening. These two features will potentially allow users to assess mutation frequencies in different genes in different cancer types and different tissue types. By midyear 2005 COSMIC contained 20,981 mutations on 529 genes, screened from 115,327 tumors and 1,912 references.
	URL: http://www.sanger.ac.uk/perl/CGP/cosmic
dbSNP [26]	The Single Nucleotide Polymorphism database (dbSNP) is a public-domain archive for a broad collection of SNPs.
	URL: http://www.ncbi.nlm.nih.gov/SNP
HbVar [58, 59]	Developed jointly by academic institutes in the Netherlands, Greece, France, and the United States, HbVar is a relational database aimed at providing up-to-date and high-quality information on the genomic sequence changes leading to hemoglobin variants and all types of thalassemia and hemoglobinopathies. A broad range of information is recorded for each variant and mutation, including sequence alterations, biochemical and hematological effects, associated pathology, ethnic occurrence, and references. Visualization and analysis tools are also available.
	URL: http://globin.cse.psu.edu/globin/hbvar

Table 8.3   (continued)

Name and Reference	Descriptions and URL
HGMD [60]	The Human Gene Mutation Database (HGMD) is a database compiled at the Institute of Medical Genetics, University of Wales School of Medicine, in the United Kingdom (now merged into Cardiff University). HGMD started this effort more than 20 years . ago, and as of 1996 the data became publicly available through the Internet. In recent years the number of entries in the database has increased by about 5,000 per year. By July 2005, the database contained 53,943 mutations in 2,081 genes and provides 1,877 reference cDNA sequences. Data in HGMD are collected through manual and computerized scanning in hundreds of journals for articles describing germline mutations causing human genetic disease. URL: http://www.hgmd.org
IARC TP53 Database [61]	Most human cancers are accompanied by somatic mutation or abnormal expression of the tumor suppressor gene TP53 (also called P53). Of the public databases on TP53 mutations developed so far, the TP53 Database by the International Agency for Research on Cancer (IARC) is considered to be the most extensive. It compiles all TP53 gene mutations identified in human cancers and cell lines that have been reported in the peer-reviewed literature since 1989. The R10 release (July 2005) contains 21,587 somatic mutations, 283 germline mutations and functional data on 426 mutant proteins. URL: http://www-p53.iarc.fr/index.html
ONCOMINE [62]	Featured in the *Journal of the American Medical Association* and Science Netwatch, ONCOMINE is a cancer microarray database with a web-based data-mining platform aimed at facilitating discovery from genome-wide expression analyses. The database was developed at University of Michigan. By midyear 2005, it contained 90 gene expression data sets comprising 71 million gene expression measurements from more than 6,300 microarray experiments. Differential expression analyses comparing most major types of cancer with respective normal tissues as well as a variety of cancer subtypes and clinical-based and pathology-based analyses are available for exploration. Data can be queried and visualized for a selected gene across all analyses or for multiple genes in a selected analysis. Furthermore, gene sets can be limited to clinically important annotations including secreted, kinase, membrane, and known gene–drug target pairs to facilitate the discovery of novel biomarkers and therapeutic targets. URL: http://141.214.6.50/oncomine/main/index.jsp
Stanford Microarray Database [63]	The Stanford Microarray Database (SMD) is a research tool for hundreds of Stanford researchers and their collaborators. In addition, it serves as a resource for the entire biological research community by providing unrestricted access to microarray data published by SMD users and by disseminating its source code. URL: http://genome-www5.stanford.edu
T1Dbase [64]	T1DBase is a public website and database that supports type 1 diabetes (T1D) research. As a joint development effort between the Institute for Systems Biology, Juvenile Diabetes Research Foundation/Wellcome Trust Diabetes and Inflammation Laboratory, and the Juvenile Diabetes Research Foundation International, it is currently focused on the molecular genetics and biology of T1D susceptibility and pathogenesis. The database collects information across human, rat, and mouse species from public sources and from collaborating laboratories. The current data scope includes annotated genomic sequences for suspected T1D susceptibility regions; microarray data; functional annotation of genes active in beta cells; and "global" data sets, generally from the literature, that are useful for systems biology studies. The data are integrated and presented in a form that is useful for T1D researchers. Software tools for analyzing the data are also available. All data are open access and all software is open source. URL: http://t1dbase.org

Table 8.3 (continued)

Name and Reference	Descriptions and URL
The Tumor Gene Family of Databases	The Tumor Gene Family of Databases contains information about genes that are targets for cancer-causing mutations, proto-oncogenes, and tumor suppressor genes. According to its website, its goal is to provide a standard set of facts (e.g., protein size, biochemical activity, chromosomal location) about all known tumor genes. By midyear 2005, the database contained more than 2,600 facts on more than 300 genes. The Tumor Gene Family of Databases is a consortium of more specialized databases as listed below (and more specialized databases may be added).
	The Tumor Gene Database (URL: http://www.tumor-gene.org/TGDB/tgdb.html) is the least selective and most general. However, because of this breadth of information and because of the lack of selectivity of this database, it can be more efficient to use one of the more specialized or selective databases.
	The Breast Cancer Gene Database (URL: http://www.tumor-gene.org/Breast/bcgd.html) is a reviewed, high-quality database of genes involved in breast cancer.
	The Oral Cancer Gene Database (URL: http://www.tumor-gene.org/Oral/oral.html) is a reviewed, high-quality database of genes involved in cancers of the mouth.
	URL: http://www.tumor-gene.org/tgdf.html.

ject. When the funding status changes, the database may be discontinued, merged with others, or sometimes commercialized. Databases of high quality are likely to be favored for longtime supports, but their formats also evolve with time like other databases. Such changes are typically seen as a black box operation—it is close to impossible for outside users to know when and how the changes are to take place.

During an early phase of the development of the WRI DW, we integrated several public databases. Fully aware of these challenges, we established three criteria for a public database to be considered for integration [25]:

1. *Maturity:* The database should be relatively mature, because it is difficult to chase after a moving target.
2. *Popularity:* The database should have been widely accepted in the scientific community.
3. *Essentiality:* The data in the database should be essential to the analysis of our internal data.

Applying these criteria, we finally selected four public databases for integration after an extensive review of dozens of candidate databases. The four selected were RefSeq, Swiss-Prot/Trembl, LocusLink, and Gene Ontology. All of these databases are listed in Table 8.2. Those criteria helped us in developing a relatively stable DW, but it was not stable for long. During and after the phase I development, Swiss-Prot/Trembl merged with PIR to form UniProt, and LocusLink became Entrez Gene. Even though the changes in the formats were not devastating, they certainly imposed challenges to our integrated system and we had to modify the scripts to ensure proper loading.

Given these difficulties with integrating public data and learning our own lessons and those of others, we believe that unorganized efforts to integrate public data are very inefficient and will prove to be a waste of resources. We think that it might be a better idea for a harbored structure, relatively complete, to be established for the public databases by a governmental organization, major university research center, or a nonprofit organization with stable funding. Other institutions can federate such a harbored structure to access many of the public databases through a certain way. Such a harbored structure should provide a database selection option for user institutes since different research settings have different needs for different types of the public data.

8.2.3   Data Format Standards

Data generated on different platforms or by different organizations need to be exchangeable in order to be shared. Thus, data of a similar nature or type (such as microarray data or medical imaging data) need to be in the same format. For this purpose a number of data standardization consortia have been formed to standardize the different types of data. Some standards are relatively mature with better adoption by the clinical and research communities, others are still at the early stage of development.

For clinical data the most well-known standard is Health Level Seven (HL7), currently in version 3 [65]. HL7 originally referred to the nonprofit organization Health Level Seven, accredited by the American National Standards Institute (ANSI) for developing standards to support clinical practice and health care service [65]. The Picture Archiving Computer Systems (PACS) technology enables medical images that in the past could only be presented in the form of films to be presented digitally. For digital imaging data, the Digital Imaging Communications in Medicine (DICOM) standard is dominating [66]. It uses defined tags for annotation of the image. Standards for digital mammograms, MRIs, ultrasounds, and so on, are being developed by specialized working groups appointed by the DICOM committee.

For microarray-based technologies, a standard called MIAME (Minimum Information About a Microarray Experiment) has been developed [67]. Another effort to standardize microarray data and a data exchange format is that of the MAGE group [68]. Shown here is a checklist of the required data fields defined in MIAME as of January 2005 (adapted from the Web site of http://www.mged. org/Workgroups/MIAME/ miame_checklist.html).

Experiment Design

- The goal of the experiment—one line maximum.
- A brief description of the experiment.
- Keywords.
- Experimental factors.
- Experimental design.
- Quality control steps taken.
- Links to the publication, any supplemental websites, or database accession numbers.

Sample Preparation

- The origin of each biological sample and its characteristics.

- Manipulation of biological samples and protocols used.
- Experimental factor value for each experimental factor, for each sample.
- Technical protocols for preparing the hybridization extract and labeling.
- External controls if used.

Hybridization Procedures and Parameters

- The protocol and conditions used for hybridization, blocking, and washing, including any postprocessing steps such as staining.

Measurement Data and Specifications

- Data
  - *Raw data:* Data from a scanner or imager and feature extraction output (providing the images is optional). The data should be related to the respective array designs.
  - *Normalized and summarized data:* Set of quantifications from several arrays on which authors can base their conclusions. The data should be related to the respective array designs.
- Data extraction and processing protocols
  - Image scanning hardware and software, and processing procedures and parameters.
  - Normalization, transformation, and data selection procedures and parameters.

Array Design

- General array design, including the platform type, surface and coating specifications, and spotting protocols used for custom-made arrays, or product identifiers for commercially available arrays. Includes array feature and reporter annotations, normally represented as a table.
- Principal array organism(s).

For proteomic data, the HUPO Proteomics Standard Initiative (HUPO-PSI) is leading the development of the data format standards, including MIAPE (Minimum Information About a Proteomics Experiment), gel electrophoresis data format GelML, the PSI Object Model incorporating the mzData model for mass spectrometry, and a standard data model for the representation and exchange of protein interaction data MIF and so on [69, 70]. In addition to this effort, for proteomics mass spectrometry data, the Institute for Systems Biology developed an XML-based common data format, called mzXML, and HUPO-PSI announced in June 2006 it would combine this format with its mzData to form the newly named dataXML format scheduled for completion by the end of 2006.

For molecular pathways, a format for representing models of biochemical reaction networks called Systems Biology Markup Language (SBML) has been developed in Japan [71]. BioPAX, a consortium formed in 2002 with the goal of developing a common exchange format for biological pathways data, has released its Level 2 ontology files [72].

8.3   DW Development for Integrative Biomedical Informatics Research

Establishment of the data format standards will definitely help data exchange and DW development. At the same time, in developing a DW, a number of important specific issues need to be considered. This section discusses some of these issues although it is not intended to be a description of DW development. For a comprehensive discussion of DW development, see the books by Inmon [1] and Kimball [2]. Several websites also provide fundamentals of data warehousing (http://www. dwinfocenter.org, http://www.1keaydata.com), which contain very helpful information about DW development.

As discussed earlier, data warehousing has been applied to the health care industry for a number of years, and several reviews of clinical DW development have been published [73–75]. There are also a few papers discussing data warehousing in life sciences [34–36], but as we cautioned at the end of Section 8.1, although many ideas presented in these papers are of reference value, some opinions cannot be readily generalized.

Of the major general DW development steps, we focus here on issues that are important or specific to biomedical informatics, or where biomedical informatics has special requirements, based on our own experiences and knowledge. We do not focus on concepts such as decision support and business intelligence that are always associated with DW development. Instead, we use plain scientific language such as data reporting tools, data analysis, and data mining applications when referring to such concepts.

8.3.1   Selection of the Developing Partner—Experiences in the Field

A DW can be developed in house or contracted to an external DW development partner. Even if it is developed in house, the process is likely to involve a team of IT specialists because a DW usually cannot be developed by research scientists or bioinformaticians or biomedical informaticians who typically do not have systematic IT training. In this section we assume that an external DW development partner will be selected to carry out the development, but the same principles apply to the internal DW development process after proper modifications.

Selection of the DW development partner is a critical initial step. If at all possible, select a partner that has developed a DW for life sciences before. The research-oriented life sciences environment is very different from a profit-driven banking or retail industry, such that some experiences gained in the latter may play a negative role in developing a DW for the former. It is very important for your development partner to have a life sciences section, which is indicative of their commitment to the field. Accumulating life sciences knowledge takes time, thus it requires that the development team for the project be relatively stable. Do not select a development partner that hires mainly contractors to work on your project, otherwise you may run into the problem where you spend weeks or months training a developer in terms of domain knowledge only to find out that the developer is leaving soon and you have to train another developer from scratch. To ensure the continuation of the development and therefore the quality of the final DW product, it is important that you try your best to find a development partner that is able to provide a permanent employee team to work on your project.

After a partner is selected, a project team should be composed with members from both the development partner and the user's side. The project team is best served when it is led by someone from the user's side, ideally by one person who has a background in both life sciences and database development. With a good understanding of what the current and future needs are, what the resources and limitations are, the leader can then work with developers to define the specifications and requirements and to coordinate with scientists and DW developers on the details. The leader should also take outsiders' opinions for references especially in their fields of expertise where the leader is lacking knowledge. This approach will ensure that constant communication and error identification and correction occur until the project is finished. Use of a user-led model should guarantee that the product will satisfy the user's needs.

Sometimes no one on the user's side is capable of leading the project team, at which time the team will be developer-led. In this case, the leader needs to be a quick learner and open minded, with a strong coordination ability. The leader needs to keep in mind that the life sciences have unique characteristics and requirements that need to be respected, and the experiences he or she gained in other industries can only be carefully and selectively applied to this field. A model in which developers meet with the users for requirements specifications, then develop the DW by themselves and come back with the finished product will never work for life sciences data warehousing. Numerous rounds of communications and modifications during the development phase are a must in such a DW development.

No matter who is leading the project team, DW development is a joint mission of users and developers. Bidirectional communications are essential to its success.

In developing a DW, information is collected from different sources of data within the user organization. It is important for such compiled information and knowledge to stay within the organization instead of migrating to outside developers or consultants. Outsider developers and consultants are gone when or before the project is finished, but the user organization needs such knowledge to make the best use of the DW and to improve or redesign the DW.

8.3.2 DW Requirements

After the project team is formed, one of its first tasks is to identify and collect the DW requirements. This is not simply a unidirectional gathering of requirements. Instead, this step should be iterative and blend the expertise of both fields and should be bidirectional, with communications going from the users to the developers and from the developers to the users.

The DW requirements should include the goals of the DW, who the users are, and how the DW will be used. Will the DW be used by organizational leaders for management decision making, or by physicians or clinical researchers to aid in clinical practices, or by laboratory scientists for molecular studies, or by biomedical informatics scientists for integrative studies, or by all of the above? Such requirements will not only govern the design of the reporting and query tools, but will also directly or indirectly affect the data source selection, the size of the DW, hardware and software selection, the data loading requirements, and so forth. Therefore, the DW requirements should also include a high-level description of those major issues. In addition, the available resources and limitations of the organization should be incorporated, together with, very importantly, the timeline for the development.

In developing a DW, the developer organization and the user organization have different interests and therefore different priorities. The developers hope to gather the requirements, carve them in stone, develop the DW, and deliver the product. For the developer organization, more data sources typically means more work and therefore more profit. The users, on the other hand, have the ultimate goal of creating a useful and flexible DW. In reality, most users typically have little or no experience in developing a DW, and often they have different opinions among themselves regarding how the DW should be developed. They may, therefore, present a long wish list for developers to work on, which of course changes during the course of the development.

There is a saying that data warehousing is risky, and the estimated failure rate ranges from 5% to 50% to 90%, or 10% to 90% depending on which criteria are used to define success and failure [76–78]. In the life sciences, the situation could be worse given the dynamic nature of these sciences and the fact that data warehousing technology has been applied to these fields only recently. One reason for the failure might be that the project drags on for so long that yesterday's design of the structure cannot meet the needs of today's new technology and the project can never be closed. To guard against this possibility, the budget should be preset on a per-project basis, and payments should be associated with milestone achievements following the timeline, with delay punishment clauses against both sides. The budget should never be time based or open ended. All of these factors should be considered when documenting the DW requirements and preparing the contract.

8.3.3   Data Source Selection

The goal of the DW determines what kind of data should be included. Data source selection directly determines how the DW should be developed. It determines the size, the complexity, and the structural model of the DW, which in turn affects hardware selection, the complexity of the loading scripts, the performance of the system, and eventually the usage of the DW.

Data source selection not only asks the question of which data source should be selected, but also which data elements should be selected from each data source. For one example, for microarray experimental data, are you going to be compliant with the MIAME requirements? Do you have additional specific needs? As another example, if you decide to integrate the data from the public database UniProt, if you are not doing sequence analysis do you need to include the protein sequences? If you are not integrating other public databases do you need all of the database cross-references?

From a practical point of view, a biomedical informatics DW should store the data of a results nature, not the data for tracking purposes. The data fields for quality control, quality assurance, and troubleshooting should remain in the tracking system. It might be a good idea to first classify the data sources and data elements under consideration, according to the goals of the DW, into the categories of "absolutely useful," "likely useful," "unlikely useful," and "not useful," and then based on the available resources decide on which categories of data will be included. In general, the data in the first category should be included, most of the data in the second category should be included, few data in the third category should be included, and no data in the fourth category should be included.

The project team should guard against the urge to cover all of the possibly useful data sources and data elements, which will ultimately render the project unmanageable. Please remember, every data element is associated with a demand for resources and you have to balance what you wish to do with what you can afford to do. In addition, after the DW has been developed, reporting and querying of large amounts of data is resource limited and the least useful data should not be allowed to slow down the performance of the DW.

8.3.4 Hardware and the Database Management Systems Selection

The leading relational database management system (RDBMS) in the life sciences is Oracle. Oracle realized the data warehousing needs in the field and has recently released several specific tools to meet such needs. These tools include DW Builder, Oracle OLAP, and Oracle Data Mining. The advantage of using Oracle for data warehousing is that the vendor has been creating products in the life sciences field for many years and, therefore, has a good understanding of the field and is likely to provide strong technical support when you have a problem. In addition, many data visualization, analysis, and mining tools in the field were either developed in Oracle, or are Oracle compatible, making it very easy to make use of existing tools. That said, users still need to carefully evaluate the functionality of the tools provided by Oracle before counting on them. For example, in our own experience, we did not believe that the Oracle OLAP, which is a multidimensional OLAP, would meet our needs to dynamically cross-examine hundreds of clinical data fields in one of our clinical projects, and we ended up developing a relational OLAP ourselves.

MySQL is an open-source RDBMS owned by the Swedish company MySQL AB. It is favored by academics—especially when there is no ample funding for DW development. It has the usual pros and cons associated with using open-source software, the major disadvantage of which is that there is no reliable technical support. When you encounter a technical problem, you must rely on yourself and your ability to get voluntarily advice from experienced users. MySQL AB currently offers MySQL Enterprise, which provides license-fee technical support. In January 2008, the company announced an agreement to be purchased by Sun Microsystems, with the acquisition expected to be completed before June 30, 2008.

There are a few other RDBMSs that one could consider for DW development. These include Sybase, IBM DB2, Microsoft SQL Server, and Informix. Given the scope of this chapter, no detailed description of these RDBMSs is provided here. Interested readers may refer to other resources for information about them.

Selection of the operating system should be based on the expertise available in the user organization. Two natural choices are UNIX and Windows. UNIX is a very reliable operating system. Windows 2000 and Windows NT are also good choices. Linux may still suffer from lack of technical support, a major disadvantage that open-source system is always born with, but Red Hat (http://www.redhat.com) is filling this gap.

For a hardware structure, at least two separate systems are typically required, with one for development and testing, and the other for production. It would be better if development and testing could be located on two separate systems. For configurations, ideally the production environment will be identical to the development and test environment so that performance can be accurately assessed, and the rolling out from development to production will be the least complicated.

8.3.5   DW Structural Models—Integrated, Federated, or Hybrid

In Inmon's definition [1], DW is an integrated system, that is, the selected data from different original data sources are incorporated into one redesigned single database. The advantage of this system is the operational speed, but the cost is the high maintenance. In Inmon's original consideration, the maintenance is not a major concern, because all the data are from internal data sources. In a biomedical informatics research environment, to make a DW really useful, the data will be selected not only from internal sources but also external ones. It is inevitable that these data sources evolve with time. Integrating internal data sources is not a question (with the exception of data of very large size, which is discussed at the end of this section), and when there is a data source change the DW can be modified accordingly and in a timely, coordinated manner. However, external data sources are out of the control of the organization, making it impossible to coordinate DW modifications with such changes. When one such data source changes, the corresponding loading scripts will have to be modified, otherwise at least some of the information will not be properly loaded. In addition, it often happens that one or many tables in the integrated DW will have to be modified or redesigned to make the system work.

Thus, in a biomedical informatics research environment, a federated data warehousing structure should also be considered. In a federated system, the original source data structures are kept intact either at their home remote site or in the form of a local copy for easy access—ideally, the latter to eliminate the internet trafficking and remote server capability limitations. For each data source, a middleware wrapper is developed to access the data elements of interests, and integration is achieved at the presentation layer. The advantage of this system is that maintenance is relatively easy; the disadvantage is the operational cost. It takes time to access the data across different data sources and integrate them on the fly.

Based on our experience, we propose that a hybrid DW structure will best meet the needs of most biomedical informatics research. The internal data sources should be integrated for the most part for efficiency considerations and because their changes are under the organization's control. The medical image data and other types of data of very large size should be archived, with file location pointers stored in the DW so that the performance of the system will not be impaired. For external data sources, minimal integration efforts should be made. Instead a federated structure should be applied, ideally through a third-party product such as caCORE where the essential public data has been integrated, as discussed in Section 8.2.2.3. This hybrid DW structure should be most cost efficient and maintenance effective.

8.3.6 Data Models: Dimensional Models, Data Marts, and Normalization Levels

A data model is the foundation of the DW system because it directly determines the scalability and performance of the system. Many DWs use a denormalized form such as data marts and dimensional data models, and some also use a highly normalized model such as the third normal form. A few other models such as the entity–attribute–value model and object-oriented data model are also applied. In the following we briefly discuss each of these models.

Data marts and dimensional models are favored by Kimball [2]. A data mart is a subset of the data in the DW focused on one specific subject or departmental needs in one company, and thus Kimball claims that the collection of all of the data marts is a DW. A dimension, on the other hand, refers to a category of information, for example, the geographic location of a patient. A dimension is composed of attributes, which represent specific levels of the information within one dimension. In this example, street address is an attribute of geographic location. Some attributes can be of a hierarchical structure. Again in this example, one hierarchical structure of geographic location is country, state/province, city, street name, and street number.

The highly normalized third normal form data model is favored by Inmon [1]. The third normal form is a common structure in transactional databases in which there is basically no redundancy in the data, which allows for the easiest management of the insert, delete, and update operations that are essential to a transactional database. But for reporting purposes, which typically use SELECT queries, in the third normal form many tables will need to be joined to provide the data needed. If the number of records is high, for example in the millions or more, which is often the case in a DW, such joins may take time and thus hinder the reporting process. In some cases, such as when the expected number of records is not that high, or when resources allow for highly parallel querying and the computational capability can be linearly scaled up with the size of the data, then the third normal form can still be a valid choice of data model for data warehousing.

8.3.7 Data Models: EAV, Entity-Relationship, and Object-Oriented Modules

Clinical data are typically heterogeneous depending on the disease being studied. For example, for breast cancer studies, risk factors and protective factors, such as the age of menarche, the age of menopausal, the age of the first live childbirth, are needed. Data on biomarkers such as ER, PR, and Her2 are also important. For cardiovascular disease studies, physical exercise habits, intake food structure, blood pressure, blood cholesterol level, and so forth, are important. For lung cancers, a person's smoking history is probably one of the most important data elements to capture.

The clinical data can also be dynamic in the sense that the questionnaires are modified constantly based on clinical practices and new research findings. For examples, a question can be ambiguous and should be rephrased, or a new risk factor is identified and should be included. Such modifications need to be reflected in the DW in a timely fashion with minimal impact on the database table structure.

In general, the clinical data are heterogeneous and sparsely distributed. In the health care industry a data model called entity–attribute–value (EAV) is widely used [79–81]. The advantages of the EAV model over the normal relational data model can be explained by using the following example on a breast cancer study with the data described at the beginning of this section. Table 8.4 shows the structure used to capture the ages of menarche and menopause. Three columns are needed, including the patient ID. If we now want to add the age of the first child birth, then a fourth column will have to be added, and Table 8.4 will have to be modified into Table 8.5, or in some cases a new table may need to be created. In either case, the data model requires a structural change.

In the EAV model, the data can theoretically be stored in one table of three columns for entity, attribute, and value, respectively. Table 8.6 shows how the EAV model can be used to store the data in this example with data in the shaded area corresponding to the content in Table 8.5. Clearly, adding one field of data becomes easy, because we need only add more records. Note that in the EAV model, missing data typically are not stored; thus, even though we added three records in Table 8.6 (unshaded) for illustration purposes, in this case only two records are needed.

While the EAV model provides a stable foundation for clinical data storage, such models are not suitable for end users in research or clinical applications. A middle tier should be developed for end users to better appreciate the data. As discussed in Chapter 1 and other preceding chapters, we believe that a patient-centric modular (object) structure is ideal for this purpose. A patient is described by several

Table 8.4   A Normal Relational Data Table Capturing Menarche and Menopausal Ages

Patient ID	Menarche_Age	Menopausal_Age
00010	14	50
00121	11	53
00090	12	49

Table 8.5   Expansion of Table 8.4 to Cover the Age of First Live Child Birth

Patient ID	Menarche_Age	Menopausal_Age	First_Live_Birth_Age
00010	14	50	22
00121	11	53	—
00090	12	49	18

Table 8.6   The EAV Model for the Example Shown in Tables 8.4 and 8.5

Entity	Attribute	Value
00010	Menarche_Age	14
00010	Menopausal_Age	50
00121	Menarche_Age	11
00121	Menopausal_Age	53
00090	Menarche_Age	12
00090	Menopausal_Age	49
00010	First_Live_Birth_Age	22
00121	First_Live_Birth_Age	—
00090	First_Live_Birth_Age	18

modules; each module is composed of attributes and submodules; and each submodule in turn is composed of its attributes and sub-submodules as well; and so forth. Most such modules and submodules are disease independent; however, disease-specific modules are developed as well. Examples include demographics, clinical history, family history, lifestyle, and risk factors, as well as sample annotation and diagnoses results. Based on this layer of objects, a graphical user interface (GUI) can be developed that will allow users to explore the data and decide which attributes from which objects are of interest to them.

A major advantage of this modular clinical data structure is its flexibility, not only for the extension and modification of data elements within one study, but also for easy adaptation to a new study. To support a new study, a number of existing disease-independent modules can be reused, and only a few disease-specific modules will need to be developed.

For genomic and proteomic data, the traditional entity-relationship data models can be used since these data are platform specific and therefore are relatively static. In addition, such data are often generated in a high-throughput fashion, and the large amount of data are certainly loaded more efficiently into a DW that has a minimally layered structure. Thus, object-oriented models are more desirable for such types of data. Certainly a GUI still needs to be developed for users to select the data for reporting purposes. Note that when a new experimental platform becomes available, it is possible that a new object structure will be needed. Therefore, when a DW is designed, the flexibility of the table structure should be built in so that foreseeable future experimental platforms can be covered. Figure 8.2 illustrates the data integration process.

8.3.8 Data Models: Handling of the Temporal Information

In Chapter 1 we discussed the concept that disease is a process, not a state. This demands that biomedical informatics studies of the disease process include time-variant information. For example, smoking is a known risk factor for lung cancer. In general, the more cigarettes one smokes, the higher the risk. But is it possible that smoking during certain developmental stages such as puberty is riskier than smoking at some other age? To collect such data, a questionnaire needs to be carefully designed to cover the time periods of interest and allow the subject to fill in the quantity of cigarettes consumed in different periods of time. Simple questions like "Have you smoked?" or "How many packs of cigarettes have you smoked in your life?" will not be sufficient for this purpose.

The timescale in this example is on the order of years. In other situations, the timescale may be on the order of days or months, and the data collected are time-specific snapshots. For example, a patient comes to a hospital for a breast examination because of a breast lump. She might experience the following series of events:

1. During the initial visit, the patient receives clinical care, is consented to a research program, and a questionnaire is completed during the visit. Blood is drawn for lab exams and for genomic and proteomic molecular experiment studies. Mammograms are taken very shortly following the visit. The patient's disease status is "unknown" at this point.

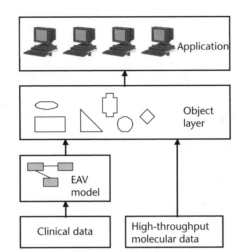

Figure 8.2   Diagram of the structure of a biomedical informatics DW that can integrate internal data. The clinical data are first loaded into an EAV model, which in turn is used to populate the patient modules in the object layer. High-throughput molecular study data are directly loaded into the data modules in the object layer. A GUI is laid onto the object layer to allow end users to access the data.

2. One week later, the patient was called in for a biopsy of the suspicious breast mass because the mammogram reading showed a score of BI-RADS 4.

3. A few days later, the pathology report of the biopsy shows that the patient has invasive breast cancer and the patient's status is now assigned to "alive with disease (AWD)." Surplus breast tissue from the biopsy is now available for molecular studies. A pathology questionnaire with detailed specimen annotation is completed.

4. The patient undergoes a surgical procedure, lumpectomy, to remove the local cancer mass, followed by chemotherapy for 4 months. Mammograms and other imaging tests such as chest x-ray and CT scans, as well as blood samples, are taken periodically during the subsequent months of the treatment.

5. At the end of the treatment cycle, mammograms and blood samples are taken again. Mammograms show that there is no abnormality. The patient status is now changed to "no evidence of disease (NED)." A post-treatment questionnaire is completed.

6. Annual examinations follow and mammograms and blood samples taken. Each year a follow-up questionnaire is completed.

In this example, each event takes place at one or more time points. For research purposes, steps 1 to 3 may be collapsed onto one time spot called "initial visit"; all of the corresponding clinical data and molecular experimental data on those blood and breast tissue samples should be mapped onto that time spot. To study the effect of the treatment, this set of data can provide the baseline for comparison with the data obtained in step 5.

In some biological experiments, a smaller scale time variant is involved. Examples include study of the heat-shock proteins and study of the longitudinal effect of drug treatment on cultured tissues. The timescale in these experiments can be on the order of minutes or hours.

In modeling such time-dependent data, a temporal data model can be developed by defining time-specific EVENTS using rules developed based on the object of study. A unique EVENT_ID can be assigned to each EVENT, which in turn is tagged to any data associated with that EVENT. For the preceding example, for research purposes the first EVENT is the initial visit illustrated in steps 1 to 3, followed by EVENT 2, treatment, in steps 4 through 6, and EVENT 3 and so on for each annual follow-up event.

In real life, time elapses continuously and sometimes we call our world a four-dimensional space. In biomedical informatics research, regardless of its scale as discussed above, the concept of time is more discrete than continuous. A patient goes to see a doctor at a certain time point of his or her life, and all of the clinical information and specimens are taken as a snapshot of time. Experimental data are obtained at certain time points. The importance of developing a temporal data model in biomedical informatics DWs is gradually being recognized, and applications of such models have started to appear in the literature [82, 83].

Two more points require elaboration. First, not all of the data we are concerned with are time variant. Examples include the patient's date of birth, race, and sex. Second, the temporal data model discussed here is not and cannot be substituted by the time stamp typically provided in a LIMS or DW, which records the moment when the data are tracked or loaded. The time in a time stamp may be totally independent of the time of the EVENT we just discussed. Time stamping may meet the needs of a banking or retail industry where the DW is loaded daily for the current balance or inventory, but it is far from sufficient to meet the needs of a biomedical informatics research environment where the experiments done today may be on a sample collected a few years ago—not to mention that the data loading may be performed on a monthly basis or even less frequently.

8.3.9 Data Extraction, Cleansing, Transformation, and Loading

The process of data extraction, cleansing, transformation, and loading (ECTL) can easily take more than 50% of the DW development time. We would like to offer four major comments here. First, do not make the ECTL scripts more complicated than necessary. For example, you should guard against the urge to cover all possible future changes especially when they exist only in someone's—not everyone's—imagination. Future uses can be covered in future improvements as long as the mechanism for future improvement is built in to the system.

Secondly, hard coding should be avoided to make future modifications convenient. This should be common knowledge, but we do know that some DW developers use heavy hardcoding in their scripts.

Thirdly, in terms of data cleansing, no matter how clean the source data are, they are almost guaranteed to have errors. One of the most common errors is a carriage return in a comment field. Others include data type mismatches, typos, and incorrect data values. When such errors are identified, one solution is to modify the scripts to correct the errors for a smooth loading, and the other is to send the errors back to the source data provider for them to correct the errors in the source if possible. Although the first solution is much easier for the developers, the latter is more desired from the data quality point of view.

The fourth comment is about data loading. Loading can be scheduled on a daily, weekly, biweekly, or monthly basis. The loading can also be done over a longer time interval. The loading can be incremental or complete depending on the amount of data in question. Regardless of which method is chosen, the data loading should be finished within the time frame allowed because it often requires the freezing of the transactional databases of the tracking system, and that during loading the DW is not available to general users. When the overall data size becomes very large, incremental loading will be the only option. The loading interval will then depend on the speed at which the data are generated and on the loading time window allowed by the organization.

8.3.10   Tuning and QA

After a DW is developed, its performance should be tuned and scripts checked for quality assurance. It is very important that this step be carried out by someone who is experienced and who was not involved in the development of the DW, so that the system can be examined from a fresh angle. In one case we experienced, a third-party tuning and QA sped up one loading step from 2 hours to 20 minutes after a generic scripting mistake made by a developer was corrected!

8.3.11   Changes—The Dynamic Nature

Life sciences are very active and dynamic, and new findings are made on a daily basis. Yesterday's truth may be proven untrue today, and today's unknown may become known tomorrow. One of the major challenges of a life sciences DW is that it needs to be highly flexible to accommodate these changes. From this point of view, a life sciences DW can be considered to be *alive*.

Consider public databases as an example. Smaller scale databases are not the only databases that are improved with time. Major public efforts, such as SwissProt/Trembl and PIR (currently UniProt) and LocusLink (currently Entrez Gene), which were considered to be relatively stable in structure, also experienced major changes in the last several years. Such structural changes present a real problem in terms of the data integration effort.

At the clinical end, the questionnaires evolve all the time. Some questions need to be rephrased because, although they appeared to be fine in the design phase, when applied to clinical exercises they prove to be ambiguous. Some questions need to be added, for example, when a new risk factor is identified. A new clinical assay may become available and such information can be important to the researchers and thus another new question is required.

From the experimental platform point of view, new systems are developed and existing systems are improved all the time. In gene expression microarrays, we experienced the evolution from the two-colored, home-spotted system to the Affymetrix GeneChips that dominates the current market. Even within one platform, in the last few years, with our increased understanding of the genes and improved manufacturing technologies, the number of gene probes on one chip increased from 10k to 20k, and currently to more than 50k.

All of these changes need to be addressed during DW development one way or another. Accommodating such changes should be one of the requirements in the design of the DW. For example, the microarray module should accommodate any sizes of microarray chips. In the design phase, the involved developers and scientists should be very open minded, and individuals with vision and insight in the relevant fields should be involved in the design phase to conceive a flexible system. Here we should also be sensitive to resource limitations so as to avoid designing a system that is so flexible that implementation of it is far beyond the allowed budget and time frame.

8.4   Use of the DW

The purpose of developing a DW is to use it. So far we have discussed the data tier, which is often called the back end and can be composed of EAV tables, and the modular object middle tier, as shown earlier in Figure 8.2. These tiers of table structure are usually difficult for end users to understand or access, and are often maintained by a database administrator. For regular users, an application tier—also called front end—should be developed. We think that a GUI portal is ideal to serve for this purpose.

Users from different backgrounds may have different levels of need in accessing the DW. A clinical researcher may be more interested in the data of a clinical nature, a genomics scientist may be more interested in DNA and RNA experimental and annotation data, and a proteomics scientist may be more interested in protein expression, interaction, and structural data. Thus different tools should be developed and made available in the application tier.

In an integrative study to identify risk factors and biomarkers of the disease, a biomedical informatics scientist may need to access a broad range of data. For example,

1. He or she may want to know the distributions of the patients enrolled in the study along the dimensions of age, sex, race, body mass index, certain clinical conditions, data on certain potential risk factors, types of specimens available, and so forth.
2. He or she may further want to analyze the data to find out which data elements are significantly associated with a certain disease based on the available diagnoses.
3. He or she may want to verify such findings with the knowledge in the public domain. These data elements may be proven to be new risk factors to the disease.
4. A scientist may also want to choose from all available records in the DW to identify matching subjects and specimens to compose a diseased group and a control group.
5. Then certain high-throughput experiments for genotyping, gene expression, and protein expression can be carried out.
6. Next, he or she may want to perform statistical analysis to identify genes and proteins that are significantly differentially expressed between the two groups of the subjects.

7. And then, he or she may want to check these genes and proteins against the public databases for known subcellular location information and functionality, and their known association with this and other diseases to validate his statistical findings at the biological level.

8. By the end, he or she will be able to determine whether these molecules can be used as biomarkers for diagnosis or mechanistic understanding purpose of the disease.

9. It is also possible that a combination of the risk factors identified in step 3 and the biomarkers identified in step 8 will allow the development of a diagnostic model of the disease or subtypes of the disease, and the possibility will be examined.

In this example, the following tools may be needed, to fulfill each one of the preceding nine tasks,

1. Clinical data reporting.
2. Statistical analysis of the clinical data.
3. Public clinical data mining.
4. Date filtering and experimental design: subject matching, confounding factor identification, efficient use of the samples and experimental resources, and so forth.
5. Platform-specific experimental data analysis.
6. Experimental data reporting and statistical analysis.
7. Data mining of the public gene and protein annotation data.
8. Clinical data mining, artificial neural network modeling and decision making.
9. Artificial neural network modeling and decision making.

To provide this relatively broad range of different types of tools, a portal structure might be a good solution. Thus, all of the tools listed earlier can be accessed through the portal and then launched as needed. Clinical data reporting can be achieved by developing an OLAP tool, because the clinical data are of many dimensions, and a user may need to examine a variety of different combinations of these dimensions of the data before deciding on which subjects and which dimensions to report. Experimental data reporting can be done by using canned reports, or ad hoc queries, because these data are platform specific and thus have a stable structure with limited dimensions. Reporting tools can also be developed for public data federated through a harbored structure as discussed in Section 8.2.2. Data mining and neural network modeling tools can also be accessed through the portal. Detailed descriptions of these tools will follow in the next chapter.

8.5   Example Case

We have discussed a number of major issues involved with integrating biomedical informatics data. In this section we provide a real example of DW development in a nonprofit integrative biomedical informatics research organization.

This organization collaborates with leading medical institutes to enroll subjects in joint translational research programs to enable acquisition of detailed demographics, clinical history, family history, medical images, pathology annotations, and high-quality tissues. These tissues are then used in high-throughput molecular studies of gene expression, genotyping, and protein expression. These operations generate a large amount of data, and to effectively analyze these data, some public genomic and proteomic data are needed.

The organization decided to develop a hybrid DW structure, with the internal data being integrated and external data being federated through a harbored structure like caCORE. To access and analyze the data, an application portal was developed with an OLAP tool for clinical data exploration and reporting, along with canned reports and ad hoc queries for experimental date reporting. Data analysis, data mining, and disease modeling tools were placed on the portal to provide easy access for all users. The portal was developed using a commercially available open workflow system. Currently, this DW is being implemented to meet the research needs of this nonprofit organization and its collaborators. Figure 8.3 shows the current structure of this DW.

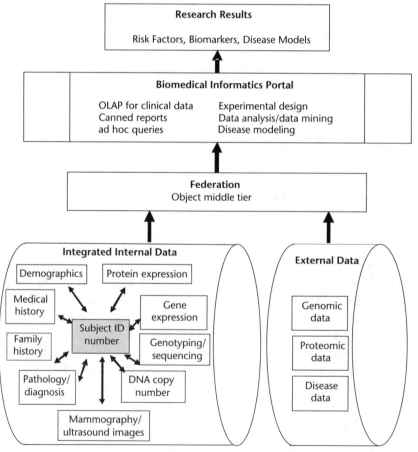

Figure 8.3 Illustration of a DW structure in a nonprofit integrative biomedical informatics research institute. It is a hybrid system in which internal data are integrated and needed external data are federated. An application portal was developed to allow efficient data analysis by accessing the data in the DW and to report the end results.

8.6   Summary

In biomedical informatics research, large amounts of data are generated across the clinical, genomic, and proteomic platforms. To find answers to questions arising from clinical practices and research exercises, these data need to be centralized, and data warehousing is one way to do it. Data warehousing has been applied to the banking, retail, and other industries for many years, but its application to life sciences is relatively new.

In principle, we suggested that the internally generated data be integrated but external and public data be federated. The importance of developing a patient-centric modular structure as a middle data tier was discussed, together with proper handling of the temporal data. Important issues in developing a DW for integrative biomedical informatics research were discussed as well. A real DW example in a nonprofit integrative biomedical informatics research environment was provided.

It is expected that after reading this chapter, a user will have a good understanding of the status of DW application to the field of biomedical informatics research and be able to apply this knowledge to his or her own research environment.

References

[1]   Inmon, W. H., *Building the Data Warehouse*, 3rd ed., New York: John Wiley and Sons, Inc., 2002.

[2]   Kimball, R., and Ross, M., *The Data Warehouse Toolkit*, 2nd ed., New York: John Wiley and Sons, 2002.

[3]   Eggert, A. A., and Emmerich, K. A., "Long-Term Data Storage in a Clinical Laboratory Information System," *J. Med. Syst*, Vol. 13, 1989, pp. 347–354.

[4]   Braly, D., "Show Data Warehouse Benefits to End Users," *Health Manag. Technol.*, Vol. 16, 1995, pp. 22–24.

[5]   Oyama, H., et al., "Virtual Cancer Image Data Warehouse," *Stud. Health Technol. Inform.*, Vol. 39, 1997, pp. 151–154.

[6]   Geisler, M. A., and Will, D., "Implementing Enterprisewide Databases: A Challenge That Can Be Overcome," *Top Health Inf. Manage.*, Vol. 19, 1998, pp. 11–18.

[7]   Berndt, D. J., Hevner, A. R., and Studnicki, J., "CATCH/IT: A Data Warehouse to Support Comprehensive Assessment for Tracking Community Health," *Proc. AMIA Symp.*, 1998, pp. 250–254.

[8]   Koprowski, S. P., Jr., and Barrett, J. S., "Data Warehouse Implementation with Clinical Pharmacokinetic/Pharmacodynamic Data," *Int. J. Clin. Pharmacol. Ther*, Vol. 40, 2002, pp. S14–29.

[9]   Bock, B. J., et al., "The Data Warehouse as a Foundation for Population-Based Reference Intervals," *Am. J. Clin. Pathol.*, Vol. 120, 2003, pp. 662–670.

[10] Therrell, B. L., Jr., "Data Integration and Warehousing: Coordination Between Newborn Screening and Related Public Health Programs," *Southeast Asian J. Trop. Med. Public Health*, Vol. 34 Suppl. 3, 2003, pp. 63–68.

[11] Frank, M. S., "Embodying Medical Expertise in Decision Support Systems for Health Care Management: Techniques and Benefits," *Top Health Inf. Manage.*, Vol. 19, 1998, pp. 44–54.

[12] Li, J., and Hawkins, J., "A System for Evaluating Inpatient Care Cost-Efficiency in a Hospital," *Medinfo*, Vol. 10, 2001, pp. 1171–1174.

[13] Ramick, D. C., "Data Warehousing in Disease Management Programs," *J. Healthc. Inf. Manag.*, Vol. 15, 2001, pp. 99–105.

[14] Studnicki, J., et al., "The Application of Volume-Outcome Contouring in Data Warehousing," *J. Healthc. Inf. Manag.*, Vol. 18, 2004, pp. 49–55.

[15] Prather, J. C., et al., "Medical Data Mining: Knowledge Discovery in a Clinical Data Warehouse," *Proc. AMIA Annu. Fall Symp.*, 1997, pp. 101–105.

[16] Kerkri, E., et al., "Application of the Medical Data Warehousing Architecture EPIDWARE to Epidemiological Follow-Up: Data Extraction and Transformation," *Stud. Health Technol. Inform.*, Vol. 68, 1999, pp. 414–418.

[17] Breault, J. L., Goodall, C. R., and Fos, P. J., "Data Mining a Diabetic Data Warehouse," *Artif. Intell. Med.*, Vol. 26, 2002, pp. 37–54.

[18] Stephen, R., Boxwala, A., and Gertman, P., "Feasibility of Using a Large Clinical Data Warehouse to Automate the Selection of Diagnostic Cohorts," *AMIA Annu. Symp. Proc.*, 2003, p. 1019.

[19] Molina, L., et al., "Completion of Colorectal Cancer Screening in Women Attending Screening Mammography," *Acad. Radiol.*, Vol. 11, 2004, pp. 1237–1241.

[20] Cao, X., et al., "A Web-Based Federated Neuroinformatics Model for Surgical Planning and Clinical Research Applications in Epilepsy," *Neuroinformatics*, Vol. 2, 2004, pp. 101–118.

[21] Coblio, N. A., et al., "Use of a Data Warehouse to Examine the Effect of Fluoroquinolones on Glucose Metabolism," *Am. J. Health Syst. Pharm.*, Vol. 61, 2004, pp. 2545–2548.

[22] Blewett, L. A., et al., "National Health Data Warehouse: Issues to Consider," *J. Healthc. Inf. Manag.*, Vol. 18, 2004, pp. 52–58.

[23] Covitz, P. A., et al., "Cacore: A Common Infrastructure for Cancer Informatics," *Bioinformatics*, Vol. 19, 2003, pp. 2404–2412.

[24] Eckman, B. A., et al., "The Merck Gene Index Browser: An Extensible Data Integration System for Gene Finding, Gene Characterization and EST Data Mining," *Bioinformatics*, Vol. 14, 1998, pp. 2–13.

[25] Hu, H., et al., "Biomedical Informatics: Development of a Comprehensive Data Warehouse for Clinical and Genomic Breast Cancer Research," *Pharmacogenomics*, Vol. 5, 2004, pp. 933–941.

[26] Wheeler, D. L., et al., "Database Resources of the National Center for Biotechnology Information," *Nucleic Acids Res.*, Vol. 33, 2005, pp. D39–45.

[27] Zdobnov, E. M., et al., "The EBI SRS Server-New Features," *Bioinformatics*, Vol. 18, 2002, pp. 1149–1150.

[28] Zdobnov, E. M., et al., "The EBI SRS Server—Recent Developments," *Bioinformatics*, Vol. 18, 2002, pp. 368–373.

[29] Fellenberg, K., et al., "Microarray Data Warehouse Allowing for Inclusion of Experiment Annotations in Statistical Analysis," *Bioinformatics*, Vol. 18, 2002, pp. 423–433.

[30] Liang, F., et al., "ORFDB: An Information Resource Linking Scientific Content to a High-Quality Open Reading Frame (ORF) Collection," *Nucleic Acids Res.*, Vol. 32, 2004, pp. D595–599.

[31] Feng, Z., et al., "Ligand Depot: A Data Warehouse for Ligands Bound to Macromolecules," *Bioinformatics*, Vol. 20, 2004, pp. 2153–2155.

[32] Cheung, K. H., et al., "YeastHub: A Semantic Web Use Case for Integrating Data in the Life Sciences Domain," *Bioinformatics*, Vol. 21 Suppl 1, 2005, pp. I85–I96.

[33] Shah, S. P., et al., "Atlas—A Data Warehouse for Integrative Bioinformatics," *BMC Bioinformatics*, Vol. 6, 2005, pp. 34.

[34] Koehler, J., et al., "Linking Experimental Results, Biological Networks and Sequence Analysis Methods Using Ontologies and Generalised Data Structures," *Silico. Biol.*, Vol. 5, 2005, pp. 33–44.

[35] Schonbach, C., Kowalski-Saunders, P., and Brusic, V., "Data Warehousing in Molecular Biology," *Brief Bioinform.*, Vol. 1, 2000, pp. 190–198.

[36] Blatt, R. J., "Banking Biological Collections: Data Warehousing, Data Mining, and Data Dilemmas in Genomics and Global Health Policy," *Community Genet.*, Vol. 3, 2000, pp. 204–211.

[37] WHO-IARC, "IARC Monographs Programme Finds Combined Estrogen-Progestogen Contraceptives and Menopausal Therapy Are Carcinogenic to Humans," http://www.iarc.fr/ENG/Press_Releases/Pr167a.Html.

[38] Bateman, A., "Editorial," *Nucl. Acids Res.*, Vol. 33, 2005, p. D1.

[39] Galperin, M. Y., "The Molecular Biology Database Collection: 2005 Update," *Nucl. Acids Res.*, Vol. 33, 2005, pp. D5–D24.

[40] Benson, D. A., et al., "Genbank," *Nucleic Acids Res.*, Vol. 33, 2005, pp. D34–D38.

[41] Okubo, K., et al., "DDBJ in Preparation for Overview of Research Activities Behind Data Submissions," *Nucleic Acids Res.*, Vol. 34, 2006, pp. D6–D9.

[42] Kanz, C., et al., "The EMBL Nucleotide Sequence Database," *Nucleic Acids Res.*, Vol. 33, 2005, pp. D29–D33.

[43] Pruitt, K. D., Tatusova, T., and Maglott, D. R., "NCBI Reference Sequence (RefSeq): A Curated Non-Redundant Sequence Database of Genomes, Transcripts and Proteins," *Nucleic Acids Res.*, Vol. 33, 2005, pp. D501–D504.

[44] Bairoch, A., et al., "The Universal Protein Resource (Uniprot)," *Nucleic Acids Res.*, Vol. 33, 2005, pp. D154–D159.

[45] Ashburner, M., et al., "Gene Ontology: Tool for the Unification of Biology. The Gene Ontology Consortium," *Nat. Genet.*, Vol. 25, 2000, pp. 25–29.

[46] Consortium, G. O., "The Gene Ontology (GO) Database and Informatics Resource," *Nucleic Acids Res.*, Vol. 32, 2004, pp. D258–D261.

[47] Maglott, D., et al., "Entrez Gene: Gene-Centered Information at NCBI," *Nucleic Acids Res.*, Vol. 33, 2005, pp. D54–D58.

[48] Salwinski, L., et al., "The Database of Interacting Proteins: 2004 Update," *Nucleic Acids Res.*, Vol. 32, 2004, pp. D449–D451.

[49] Kanehisa, M., et al., "From Genomics to Chemical Genomics: New Developments in KEGG," *Nucleic Acids Res.*, Vol. 34, 2006, pp. D354–D357.

[50] Alfarano, C., et al., "The Biomolecular Interaction Network Database and Related Tools 2005 Update," *Nucleic Acids Res.*, Vol. 33, 2005, pp. D418–D424.

[51] Westbrook, J., et al., "The Protein Data Bank and Structural Genomics," *Nucleic Acids Res.*, Vol. 31, 2003, pp. 489–491.

[52] Berman, H. M., et al., "The Protein Data Bank," *Nucleic Acids Res.*, Vol. 28, 2000, pp. 235–242.

[53] Schomburg, I., et al., "BRENDA, the Enzyme Database: Updates and Major New Developments," *Nucleic Acids Res.*, Vol. 32, 2004, pp. D431–D433.

[54] Huret, J. L., Dessen, P., and Bernheim, A., "Atlas of Genetics and Cytogenetics in Oncology and Haematology, Year 2003," *Nucleic Acids Res.*, Vol. 31, 2003, pp. 272–274.

[55] BIOBASE, http://www.gene-regulation.com.

[56] Kato, K., et al., "Cancer Gene Expression Database (CGED): A Database for Gene Expression Profiling with Accompanying Clinical Information of Human Cancer Tissues," *Nucleic Acids Res.*, Vol. 33, 2005, pp. D533–D536.

[57] Bamford, S., et al., "The COSMIC (Catalogue of Somatic Mutations in Cancer) Database and Website," *Br. J. Cancer*, Vol. 91, 2004, pp. 355–358.

[58] Hardison, R. C., et al., "HbVar: A Relational Database of Human Hemoglobin Variants and Thalassemia Mutations at the Globin Gene Server," *Hum. Mutat.*, Vol. 19, 2002, pp. 225–233.

[59] Patrinos, G. P., et al., "Improvements in the HbVar Database of Human Hemoglobin Variants and Thalassemia Mutations for Population and Sequence Variation Studies," *Nucleic Acids Res.*, Vol. 32, 2004, pp. D537–D541.

[60] Stenson, P. D., et al., "Human Gene Mutation Database (HGMD): 2003 Update," *Hum. Mutat.*, Vol. 21, 2003, pp. 577–581.

[61] Olivier, M., et al., "The IARC TP53 Database: New Online Mutation Analysis and Recommendations to Users," *Hum. Mutat.*, Vol. 19, 2002, pp. 607–614.

[62] Rhodes, D. R., et al., "ONCOMINE: A Cancer Microarray Database and Integrated Data-Mining Platform," *Neoplasia*, Vol. 6, 2004, pp. 1–6.

[63] Ball, C. A., et al., "The Stanford Microarray Database Accommodates Additional Microarray Platforms and Data Formats," *Nucleic Acids Res.*, Vol. 33, 2005, pp. D580–D582.

[64] Smink, L. J., et al., "T1DBase, A Community Web-Based Resource for Type 1 Diabetes Research," *Nucleic Acids Res.*, Vol. 33, 2005, pp. D544–D549.

[65] Health Level 7, http://www.hl7.org.

[66] "DICOM—Digital Imaging Communications in Medicine," http://medical.nema.org/.

[67] Brazma, A., et al., "Minimum Information About a Microarray Experiment (MIAME)—Toward Standards for Microarray Data," *Nat. Genet.*, Vol. 29, 2001, pp. 365–371.

[68] "Microarray and Gene Expression—MAGE," http://www.mged.org/Workgroups/Mage/mage.html.

[69] Hermjakob, H., et al., "The HUPO PSI's Molecular Interaction Format—A Community Standard for the Representation of Protein Interaction Data," *Nat. Biotechnol.*, Vol. 22, 2004, pp. 177–183.

[70] Orchard, S., et al., "Further Steps Towards Data Standardisation: The Proteomic Standards Initiative HUPO 3rd Annual Congress, Beijing, October 25–27, 2004," *Proteomics*, Vol. 5, 2005, pp. 337–339.

[71] "The Systems Biology Markup Language (SBML)," http://sbml.org/index.psp.

[72] "Biopax : Biological Pathways Exchange," http://www.biopax.org.

[73] Gray, G. W., "Challenges of Building Clinical Data Analysis Solutions," *J. Crit Care*, Vol. 19, 2004, pp. 264–270.

[74] Kerkri, E. M., et al., "An Approach for Integrating Heterogeneous Information Sources in a Medical Data Warehouse," *J. Med. Syst*, Vol. 25, 2001, pp. 167–176.

[75] Akhtar, M. U., Dunn, K., and Smith, J. W., "Commercial Clinical Data Warehouses: From Wave of the Past to the State of the Art," *J. Healthc. Inf. Manag,*. Vol. 19, 2005, pp. 20–26.

[76] Power, D., "Bill Inmon Interview: Data Warehouses and Decision Support Systems," http://www.dssresources.com/interviews/inmon/inmon05122005.html.

[77] Imhoff, C., "Failure of Data Warehouse Projects," http://www.b-eye-network.com/blogs/imhoff/archives/2005/03/failure_of_data_1.php.

[78] Greenfield, L., "The Case Against Data Warehousing," http://www.dwinfocenter.org/against.html.

[79] Nadkarni, P. M., et al., "Managing Attribute—Value Clinical Trials Data Using the ACT/DB Client–Server Database System," *J. Am. Med. Inform. Assoc.*, Vol. 5, 1998, pp. 139–151.

[80] Nadkarni, P. M., et al., "Organization of Heterogeneous Scientific Data Using the EAV/CR Representation," *J. Am. Med. Inform. Assoc.*, Vol. 6, 1999, pp. 478–493.

[81] Brandt, C. A., et al., "Managing Complex Change in Clinical Study Metadata," *J. Am. Med. Inform. Assoc.*, Vol. 11, 2004, pp. 380–391.

[82] Yamamoto, Y., Namikawa, H., and Inamura, K., "Development of a Time-Oriented Data Warehouse Based on a Medical Information Event Model," *Igaku Butsuri*, Vol. 22, 2002, pp. 327–333.

[83] Chen, J., et al., "The PEPR Genechip Data Warehouse, and Implementation of a Dynamic Time Series Query Tool (SGQT) with Graphical Interface," *Nucleic Acids Res.*, Vol. 32, 2004, pp. D578–D581.

CHAPTER 9

Data Analysis

Yonghong Zhang, Mick Correll, and Hai Hu

The preceding chapters discussed how biomedical data are collected, generated, tracked, and centralized. In this chapter we discuss how these data are analyzed or mined to verify or disapprove a hypothesis or to extract new knowledge in translational research to ultimately aid in clinical practice.

Data analysis and data mining are two different concepts. The purpose of data analysis is to use validated analytical technologies to transform data to prove or disapprove a hypothesis. In the context of translational research, such a hypothesis might take these forms: Can these genes be used as diagnostic biomarkers for breast cancer? Is the mutation of that protein the reason for developing diabetes and thus should that protein be a drug target? Does excessive alcohol drinking increase the chance of developing stomach cancer? Does cancer progressively develop from a nonsevere disease to an invasive disease and then to a metastatic disease that causes the death of a patient?

Data mining, on the other hand, as its name suggests, can be defined as "the nontrivial extraction of implicit, previously unknown, and potentially useful information from data" [1]. Data mining is especially useful when dealing with large amounts of data. Such technology has been well developed and applied to the business world, including the retail and banking industries, where it is often called *business intelligence,* a term that refers to its ability to extract new knowledge [2, 3]. Instead of being hypothesis driven, data mining is hypothesis generating, a main feature that distinguishes it from data analysis.

In biomedical informatics research, both data analysis and data mining techniques are important. On one hand, all translational projects start from specific clinical questions, and in different research steps, different questions need to be answered by applying data analysis methods. On the other hand, different biomedical research projects in the scientific world have produced a huge amount of data of different types, and mining in this sea of data guarantees the extraction of new knowledge and generation of new hypotheses, which in turn can be addressed by the design of new projects and application of data analysis technologies. In addition, to enable efficient processing of the data, intermediate results from one application need to be smoothly transferred to the input mechanism of the next, thus an ideal infrastructure is an application portal embedded with integrated application software, each of which can be launched successively to fulfill data analysis and mining tasks. This calls on an application workflow structure, and a couple of commercial products are available on the market [4, 5].

Even though biomedical informatics is a relatively new discipline, many data analysis and mining methods developed for other application fields can be readily applied to this field of data processing. These include regression analysis [6], significance test/differential analysis [7], and classification analysis [8]. However, not every data analysis and data mining need in this multidisciplinary subject can be answered by using an existing application or tool, thus new technologies need to be and are being developed to satisfy the needs of biomedical data analysis, mining, and modeling [9]. This is just like the development of BLAST, Smith-Waterman, and ClustalW for bioinformatics sequence analysis.

Given the large amount of data involved in biomedical informatics research, data management sometimes becomes an inevitable factor that needs to be handled in the data analysis and data mining process. Transferring large amounts of data takes time and resources, so sometimes it is beneficial to process data within the database. Thus in-database computation technologies have been developed. For example, Oracle now has built-in statistical functions and a data mining module in it [10].

Analyzing biomedical informatics data is often a complicated process, which requires not only a good understanding of the data collection and generation process, but also a mastering of multiple data analysis technologies. In this chapter, we provide a high-level description of the available data analysis and data mining techniques. We also provide specific examples to illustrate how these techniques are applied to biomedical research and to different types of clinical, genomic, and proteomic data on both individual data platforms and on integrated data sets. Toward the end of the chapter, we provide an overview of the available resources for data analysis and data mining.

Note that there are many experimental platforms and we do not intend to list the data analysis methods for each one of them. Instead, for each data platform, we dissect the data analysis process for a couple of typical experimental technologies to show the principle, which can be applied to data analysis for similar experimental data types. Highly platform-specific data analysis methods are also not the focus of this chapter; examples include handling of multiple probe analysis for Affymetrix GeneChip microarray data in gene expression data analysis software (GDAS) by Affymetrix, protein spot differential in 2D-DIGE analysis, and details in SEQUEST or MASCOT for mass spectrometry data analysis.

9.1 The Nature and Diversity of Research Data in Translational Medicine

9.1.1 Where Data Reside

A defining attribute of translational research studies is their cross-domain nature. In terms of data analysis, this often translates into requiring researchers to access many different sources of data, often in ways that the original system designers had never anticipated. Four distinct types of data are typically used in a translational research project: clinical data, sample data, experimental data, and public-domain data. Each of these sources will often have their own data management systems.

A *clinical data source* will be one or more systems that contain data about a patient or study participant. Example data sources would include an EMR system that contains a unified electronic record about a patient, or in the context of a clinical trial, a clinical data management system that contains data captured as defined by the protocol of a particular study.

A *sample data source* is one that contains data about a biological sample that has been collected from an individual. A collection of biological samples is referred to as a *biobank*. Biobanks are managed by specialized IT systems that track data about where a sample physically resides as well as details on sample collection, preparation, chain of custody, as well as annotation information about the tissue and individual from whom it came.

An *experimental data source* is one that contains the results from a laboratory analysis, for example, from a gene expression profile. Experimental data may reside in one or more systems in a lab. Often, the procedural aspects of the process, for example, how an assay was run, would be contained in a LIMS (refer to Chapter 7), while the actual results themselves may be captured in a custom relational database or frequently just stored as individual files on a computer.

Finally, a *public-domain data source* contains information about genes and proteins, annotation, biological pathways, ontology, disease, and sometimes customer-built knowledge bases. Most of this type of information comes from public databases. Even though public information can be retrieved via a provider's web interface, a local and integrated copy of public databases is usually necessary for large-scale data analysis and studies of system biology.

9.1.2 Operational Versus Analytical Data Systems

Each of the systems just discussed, whether it contains clinical, sample, or experimental data, can be generalized yet again into the single category of being an operational or transactional system. A transactional system is one that has been designed to support the day-to-day business operations of its domain. For example, an EMR system might capture the details of a patient checking into an emergency room with acute appendicitis, whereas a sample management system will know the last time a sample in a vial was accessed. In operational systems a premium is placed on maintaining data integrity and consistency, and on auditing and tracking change history.

In terms of data analysis, however, operational systems present a number of problems. For security and compliance purposes, operational systems often provide only very limited views of data, with narrow and highly regimented means of access. Internally, data are structured and optimized to handle the transactional nature of their environment, and thus are not at all suitable for generating the complex and summarized views necessary for an analysis.

9.1.3 Data Warehouses

For the reasons of data integration and the limitations outlined earlier, projects often require a new data structure to be built that has been designed specifically to support analytical processing. These new structures, called data warehouses, have the following design features:

- An integrated, often summarized, view of multiple data sources;
- Minimization of the number of steps necessary for generation of common reports;
- Fast response time for complex queries.

Building a data warehouse requires connecting to all of the various source data systems, extracting the data, transforming them into a new analysis-friendly format, and loading them into the DW. The extract, transform, and load (ETL) process is common to many industries, and numerous software packages exist specifically to perform ETL tasks. Data warehousing was discussed in detail in Chapter 8.

9.1.4   Data Preprocessing

Beyond the basic transformation steps of making data compatible for loading into a data warehouse, still further preprocessing steps are often required for effective data analysis. Additional preprocessing steps would include the following: missing value handling, outlier removal (clipping), binning, and normalization [11].

9.1.4.1   Missing Value Handling

Missing values are often problematic for statistical and analytical methods. In many cases, the presence of missing or null values can cause an analysis to fail entirely or produce skewed results. Missing values can be handled by removing the entire record from the data set, or by replacing the value with a newly computed value such as the mean, median, minimum, or maximum.

9.1.4.2   Outlier Removal (Clipping)

An outlier is a data point that is outside of the normal or expected range of the data set. Outliers are typically identified by the distance from the mean measured by the number of standard deviations. Similar to null values, outliers can have a deleterious effect on many data analysis tools. For clustering and classification tools, their presence can lead to longer training times, a reduction in discriminating power, or a failure to converge. Some standard methods of handling outliers are to remove the records entirely or to replace the outlier values with a boundary value that is within the desired range.

9.1.4.3   Binning

Binning is the process of reducing the cardinality of a set of values. Binning can be applied to both continuous numeric, as well as categorical data. Binning is accomplished by first defining a number of buckets (bins) and then assigning members to one of the buckets. For continuous numeric data, buckets are defined for a range of values; for categorical data, each member is simply assigned to one of the buckets. For example, the age of a population covers a very broad spectrum, for example, from under 18 to over 80. For a particular analysis, however, age may really only need to be considered as one of these values: under 18, 18–65, or 65 and older.

These definitions are then the basis for the three buckets and we create a new age attribute where the bucket label (name) is used in place of the person's actual age.

9.1.4.4   Normalization

Normalization is the process of scaling continuous numeric data to a new range of values so that comparisons of data sets, for example, gene expression values of individual samples, in downstream analyses are valid. Common types of normalization include (1) global mean normalization, (2) global median normalization, and (3) linear scaling. In global mean normalization, the mean of one or more sets of values is set to a new target value. The value of a given data point is expressed as:

$$x'_i = x_i \cdot c / \overline{x}$$

where is the original value of the data point, is the original mean of the data set, and c is the new mean of the data set. Global median normalization is the same procedure as for global mean normalization except that the median is used instead. It is often preferred over the global mean in that it is less affected by outliers. Linear scaling transforms the data set using a factor or a constant so that the resulting data set falls within a predefined range, such as 0 to 1.

9.2   Data Analysis Methods and Techniques

At long last, having survived the rigors of locating source data, designing and loading a data warehouse, and cleaning data for consistency, we have arrived at the point of analysis. This should be greeted with mild celebration. After all, this is where we can finally start to harvest the fruits of our labor.

In this section we cover common tools of data analysis and data mining. This section can be seen as providing a toolbox of techniques that can be applied to many different types of problems in many different domains.

9.2.1   Generalized Forms of Analysis

Many of the problems we attempt to solve in data analysis can be mapped to one of a few general forms. Next are the generalized problems we are going to cover in this chapter and some examples of how these problems might manifest in a translational research project.

9.2.1.1   Significance Testing

For a significance testing problem, we develop a hypothesis about a relationship between one or more factors across different groups in our population and then use statistical methods to test that hypothesis. The result from our test will be a probability score that a measured difference in a sample reflects a real difference in the population. Example forms of this type of problem include the following:

- Is there a difference in body mass index (BMI) among diabetics and nondiabetics?
- Are the expression levels of a given gene different between responders and nonresponders to a certain drug treatment?
- For a given laboratory test, which of the resulting values were most important in the determining the resulting diagnosis?
- Of the 600,000 genetic markers we tested, which are the most powerful at discriminating between two disease states?

9.2.1.2 Predictive Modeling

For problems of this form, we attempt to build a mathematical model that, based on a set of input parameters, can predict an outcome. We look at two distinct types of predictive modeling, regression and classification, with the simple difference between the two being that the results of a regression model will be a continuous numeric value, and for classification the results will be a predefined set of categorical values. Here is an example of a regression problem:

- Can I construct a model to predict a patient's relative risk for developing adult-onset asthma?

Examples of classification problem include these:

- Among our population of patients at risk for developing diabetes, which ones are most likely to respond to a new intervention campaign?
- Can we use genetic markers to predict which patients are more likely to respond to a certain chemotherapy regimen?

9.2.1.3 Clustering

In a clustering problem we attempt to group similar data into subsets based on a set of input attributes. Consider this example of a clustering problem:

- Based on gene expression profiles, can we identify previously undetermined tumor subtypes?

9.2.2 Significance Testing

The general goal of significance testing is to determine the probability that a measured difference represents a true difference in the data, and not just noise. The first step in performing a significance test is to put forth a hypothesis about one or more of the factors in our data set. To illustrate, let's look in more detail at the earlier example about BMI in a clinical population. For this example, we put forth the hypothesis that there is a difference in BMI for individuals with diabetes as compared to the rest of the population. The tool we will use for our analysis is one of the statistical hypothesis tests. These tests will compute the probability of our hypothesis (also called the *alternative hypothesis*) versus a new hypothesis, the so-called *null hypothesis*. The null hypothesis is the prediction that there is no difference. For our particular example, then, the null hypothesis is that there is no difference in BMI for individuals with diabetes as compared to the rest of the population.

The result of a statistical hypothesis test is a statistic that can be used to calculate the probability or *P value* of the null hypothesis versus the alternative hypothesis. For example, a *P* value of .05 says that there is a 5% chance of the null hypothesis. In a hypothesis test, we define a threshold for significance (such as .05 or .01). If the resulting *P* value is less than our threshold, then we reject the null hypothesis in favor of our alternative; otherwise, the null hypothesis stands.

A number of different statistical hypothesis tests are available, each often with its own variants, so it is critical that we select a test that is appropriate for our data set. Table 9.1 lists some of the factors to consider in selecting the right tool, and the following subsections discuss the most frequently used statistical hypothesis tests.

9.2.2.1   Pearson's Chi-Square Test

Pearson's chi-square test tests whether the observed event frequency is different from the expected frequency. The test examines a 2×2 contingency table of observed and expected frequencies of events and derives a *P* value from the χ^2 distribution.

9.2.2.2   Student's *t*-Test

Two sample test with variants that can be used for paired or unpaired data, with known or unknown variance. Student's *t*-test assumes a normal distribution.

9.2.2.3   ANOVA

ANOVA is used for testing two or more groups and assumes a normal population with equal variance.

9.2.2.4   Wilcoxon Signed-Rank Test

This text is similar to a paired two-sample *t*-test, with the exception that the distribution need not be normal.

Table 9.1   Factors to Consider When Selecting a Hypothesis Test

Factor	Description
Number of groups being tested	Many hypothesis tests can only be applied when there are just two groups being tested.
Paired versus unpaired data	In an unpaired test the variables are assumed to be independent. If our variables are dependent (for example, testing the same group twice), we must use a paired test.
Equal or unequal variance	Variance is a measure of the spread of values for a given variable. Some tests require an equal or similar variance.
Population distribution	Many tests assume a normal distribution (also called a Gaussian distribution or bell curve).

9.2.3   Predictive Modeling

Predictive modeling is the practice of developing a mathematical model that can be used to predict an outcome or a value based on a set of input parameters. Modeling methodologies extend from very simple linear techniques up through highly sophisticated machine learning algorithms. Regardless of the specific form, all models have a few basic properties in common; they all take a series of inputs, termed attributes in this context, and they all produce some form of a result, termed the target attribute. Models come in two distinct varieties, regression and classification. Regression models are those that have a continuous numeric target attribute. Categorical models are those that have a discreet categorical target attribute.

9.2.3.1   Feature Selection

Before moving on to the specifics of different modeling techniques, it is first necessary to discuss the problem of feature selection, that is, determining the set of data to use as input for our model. Translational research presents a number of challenges in predictive modeling, one of which is the fact that the number of attributes is often far greater than the number of samples. As an example, let's look at the problem of classifying tumor types based on gene expression profiles. Using modern DNA microarray techniques, our attributes (genes) will be vastly greater (1,000-fold or more) than our number of samples (tumors). Research has shown that reducing the number of attributes to a small set of informative genes can greatly enhance the accuracy of our models [12]. Feature selection algorithms help us to identify the most informative features in a data set. Here we look at two particular feature selection algorithms that have been shown to be useful in many different domains, information gain and Relief-F.

Information Gain
The information gain method examines each feature and measures the entropy reduction in the target class distribution if that feature is used to partitions the data set [11].

Relief-F
The Relief-F method draws instances at random, computes their nearest neighbors, and adjusts a feature weighting vector to give more weight to features that discriminate the instance from neighbors of different classes [13].

9.2.3.2   Regression

The problem of regression is perhaps best illustrated as an example of curve fitting. From an initial set of data points, we create a function that draws a line that comes as close as possible to all of the points. Now, using our function we can estimate where on the line any new (unknown) data points might fall. In linear regression, we are limited to only being able to use functions that produce straight lines. Linear regression models are simple to calculate and easy to evaluate, their utility is limited however. Figure 9.1 below is an example of linear regression.

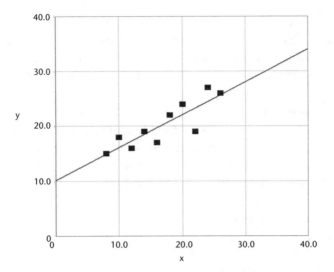

Figure 9.1   Example of linear regression.

In contrast, nonlinear regression makes use of more sophisticated models using nonlinear functions. Like linear methods, we still fit a model to our data; in many cases, however, a standard preexisting model is selected rather than being developed from scratch each time. A classic example of a nonlinear regression model is the generation of a dose–response curve for calculating the EC_{50} value (Figure 9.2).

9.2.3.3   Classification

In a classification problem, our goal is to predict a discreet value based on a set of inputs. To illustrate, let's return to our example of cancer classification based on gene expression profiles. In this instance, our goal is to build a classification model that, based on a gene expression profile, can discriminate between cancerous and normal tissue or between different subtypes of the same cancer. In tackling a classification problem, analysts have a number of very powerful tools at their disposal, and it continues to be an area of intense research. Here we present a number of classification techniques that have been shown to be useful in one or more of the domains that make up translational research.

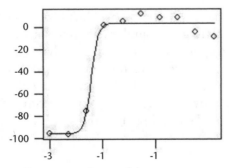

Figure 9.2   Example of a nonlinear regression model.

Bayesian Networks

Bayesian networks are graphical probabilistic models that enable the combination of observed data with prior knowledge (degree of belief data). Bayesian networks can be powerful classifiers and, at the same time, can be intuitive to understand [14].

Logistic Regression

Logistic regression is a generalized linear model that is used to predict a dichotomous target attribute. Some advantages of logistic regression are that it can support both numeric and categorical input attributes and that it can also be used to determine the relative importance of the input attributes on the prediction [15].

Support Vector Machines

Support vector machines (SVM) are a powerful group of learning classifiers. SVMs work by mapping input attributes to a high-dimension feature space and then constructing a hyperplane with maximum separation of positive and negative values [16]. Because of their ability to function well in the presence of a high number of attributes and high levels of noise, SVMs are often the classifier of choice for bioinformatics [17].

Neural networks

Neural networks (also called artificial neural networks) are multilayer statistical learning models that are roughly analogous in structure to the networks of neurons formed in biological systems. Neural networks function by propagating data from a series of input nodes, through one or more layers of hidden nodes, to a set of output nodes. Each node in the network can be a linear or nonlinear model [18].

Decision Trees

Decision trees are widely used classification tools, and here we discuss one particular implementation that makes use of the C4.5 algorithm. The C4.5 method is based on examining the entropy reduction in the target class distribution for each of the input attributes, if that attribute were used to partition the data set. Decision trees can be powerful classifiers that also have the distinct advantage of revealing their methodology (partitioning rules) in an intuitive form [19].

9.2.4 Clustering

As stated previously, a clustering problem is one in which, based on a set of input attributes, we seek to group similar data into subsets. While it certainly has a number of intuitive applications for data analysis, in the context of translational research, one of the more powerful applications of clustering is for class discovery. In the example of tumor classification, clustering algorithms are one technique that can be used to discover previously unrecognized tumor subtypes [20]. We next discuss commonly used clustering algorithms.

9.2.4.1   Self-Organizing Maps

Self-organizing maps (SOM) are a type of clustering algorithm that has been used successfully for class discovery in molecular studies. They are well suited to handling multidimensional data [21].

9.2.4.2   K-Means

K-means is an algorithm that partitions data into a predetermined number of clusters. Items are placed into a cluster on the basis of the similarity between the item and the mean of the cluster. The mean of the cluster is recalculated after a new item is added. This process continues until a steady state is reached. K-means can deal with discrete (categorical) attributes, as well as continuous (numeric) attributes [11].

9.2.4.3   Hierarchical

Hierarchical clustering is a bottom-up approach that works by initially treating each item as its own cluster, and then successively merging the clusters on the basis of a similarity measure until only a single cluster contains the entire data set. A number of different similarity metrics can used including Euclidian, Manhattan, Pearson's correlation, or the uncentered correlation [11].

9.2.5   Evaluation and Validation Methodologies

As we have seen, there are indeed a number of very powerful techniques available for data analysis, but for all their power, care must still be given to understanding the types of errors that can occur and the steps that can be taken to detect and minimize those errors.

9.2.5.1   Type I and Type II Errors

In a statistical analysis, the two primary types of errors are Type I and Type II errors. A Type I error, also called a *false positive*. occurs when we assume a positive result when one does not exist. For a significance test, a false positive occurs when we report the presence of a signal (reject the null hypothesis) when none exists. For a classification problem, a false positive results in the context of a single class when we erroneously assign a member to that group. A Type II error, also called a *false negative*, occurs when we accept a negative result, when in fact a positive result is true. For a significance test, a false negative occurs when we fail to find a signal (accept the null hypothesis) despite the fact that one exists. For a classification problem, a false negative occurs in the context of a single class when we erroneously assign one of its members to a different class. When evaluating performance, we will often want to look at the rate at which these errors occur, for this we use the false-positive rate and false-negative rate.

The false-positive rate is defined by the ratio:

$$\frac{\text{False positive}}{\text{False positive} + \text{False negative}}$$

The false-negative rate is defined by the ratio:

$$\frac{\text{False negative}}{\text{False negative} + \text{False positive}}$$

9.2.5.2   Sensitivity Versus Specificity

Sensitivity and specificity are two valuable metrics we can use in evaluating our results. Sensitivity (a true-positive rate) is defined as the following ratio:

$$\frac{\text{True positive}}{\text{True positive} + \text{False negative}}$$

Specificity (a true-negative rate) is defined as the following ratio:

$$\frac{\text{True negative}}{\text{True negative} + \text{False positive}}$$

9.2.5.3   ROC Graph

A receiver operating characteristics (ROC) graph is a common tool for synthesizing all of the preceding information so we can visualize and evaluate classifier performance. In a ROC graph, the true-positive rate is plotted against the false-positive rate, as seen in Figure 9.3 [22, 23].

   In terms of evaluating performance, we often look for a classifier that rises sharply to the northwest corner of the graph, that is, that quickly maximizes true positives and minimizes false positives.

9.2.5.4   Cross Validation

Cross validation is a robust technique for evaluating models and estimating their generalized error [24]. Cross validation is performed by partitioning the data into multiple subsets, and then repeatedly training and evaluating the performance of a model against the different subsets. Common strategies for cross validation are K-fold, stratified K-fold, and leave-one-out. With K-fold, the data set is randomly split into K equal sized mutually exclusive subsets. The classifier is trained and tested K times. For each iteration the model is built on the entire data set with one group withheld, and then tested against the withheld group (each group withheld once). Stratified K-fold is the same as K-fold with the exception that the sampling of each fold is done so that the proportion of each target attribute remains constant. Leave-one-out is where a single member of the set is left out each time for testing, and all members are left out once. Leave-one-out is the same as K-fold where K is equal to the number of elements in the data set.

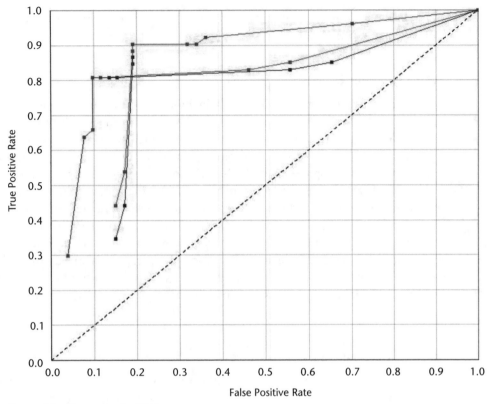

Figure 9.3   Example of a ROC curve.

9.3   Analysis of High-Throughput Genomic and Proteomic Data

With the advancement of detection technologies, high-throughput (HTP) screening has become very popular in biomedical research. These technologies include microarrays for gene expression analysis, single nucleotide polymorphism (SNP) analysis and copy number variation analysis, and spectrometry for proteomics, as discussed in Chapters 4 through 6. The cost for data collection has been greatly reduced per data point. HTP methods provide much higher efficacy in data acquisition. As the trade-off, the specificity, sensitivity, and dynamic range of detection are, in general, significantly worse than those of traditional methods. To achieve higher specificity, sensitivity, and dynamic range in detection, careful experimental design, detailed instrument calibration and configuration, and sometimes additional preprocessing of biological samples are necessary. The overwhelming amount of data collected via HTP also calls for computational infrastructure for data storage, management, and analysis. In this section, data-specific methods, approaches, and pitfalls involved in the analysis of HTP genomic and proteomic data are discussed.

Data analysis needs to address three major issues: quality control, data integration (dealing with data from different sources, for example, the same measure with different methods or different measures), and data mining. One thing that needs to be mentioned here is experimental design. Successful data analysis begins with good experimental design. Things to consider include randomization to reduce or eliminate systematic and nonsystematic errors and determination of an appropriate number of samples.

9.3.1 Genomic Data

Microarray technology is widely used in biomedical researches and is based on hybridization of cDNA synthesized from cRNA extracted from biological samples to complementary nucleotide sequences or oligonucleotides immobilized on slides or glass chips. The goal of most microarray experiments is to survey patterns of gene expression by assaying the level of RNA of thousands or tens of thousands of genes in biological samples. The process involves RNA isolation, amplification, labeling, hybridization, staining, and image acquisition (refer to Chapter 5 for more details on microarray technology). Errors and variation can be introduced during microarray experimentation and affect the analysis and interpretation of the data: experimental design, RNA isolation/purification, array fabrication, and hybridization. QA measures need to be considered to ensure the quality of microarray data. Studies have indicated gene expression microarray technology is relatively robust and consistent with bench-top methods [25, 26].

9.3.1.1 Different Platforms Available

Two types of microarrays are currently available: cDNA and oligonucleotides. Depending on the design, cDNA microarrays can be one color or two colors. Several microarray platforms are available (see Chapter 5). Studies indicate equivalent performance for these platforms [27]. Some labs also spot their own arrays, which may result in high manufacturing variability. This is likely to occur with some suboptimal, in-house, robotically spotted arrays, resulting in poor quality control.

9.3.1.2 Quality Control

Many of the QA issues result from early stages of microarray experimentation and are readily identifiable by examining the output of the evaluation results of the intermediate products, such as gel images for RNA/DNA, and the raw microarray image. A gel image will immediately reveal RNA yields from extraction, amplification, and RNA quality. The visual examination of the array image can quickly identify clues about labeling, hybridization, and staining. Assessment of the brightness, background of the array image, and hybridization saturation including housekeeping genes from different species can be useful in some circumstances. Inclusion of a housekeeping gene from human, rat, and mouse on the Affymetrix Test Chip helped to identify contamination of a human cell line with mouse cells.

9.3.1.3 Image Analysis

The first step of microarray data analysis is the analysis of the raw microarray image. Spots or so-called features representing individual genes have to be identified before any information can be extracted. This is achieved by overlaying a grid over the image. Individual genes (spots or oligonucleotides) on an array are identified by a properly aligned grid. For an Affymetrix GeneChip microarray, the gene expression level is determined by calculating the hybridization signals of all the PM-MM pairs.

Several methods have been used for the analysis of Affymetrix microarrays. The empirical method is the first generation method provided by Affymetrix. It simply takes the difference of the mean of PM and MM average. This method can produce negative values, which makes no sense in biology. The statistical method [28] weighs the probe pairs based on their performance. Affymetrix has recently developed a model-based method, probe logarithmic intensity error (PLIER) estimation [29, 30]. The new algorithm provides higher signal reproducibility and higher expression sensitivity for low expressors. Other model-based methods [31–33] have been developed so that weighing on the probe pairs is determined by examining a group of samples. An approach has also been developed that uses only the PM to determine gene expression [31]. The correlation coefficient between microarrays using all genes on an array can be used to reveal the disparity of array quality and identify problematic arrays [34].

9.3.1.4   Data Normalization and Transformation

Several approaches have been developed to normalize microarray data so that they can be compared. The use of housekeeping genes, such as GAPDH and β-actin, requires additional steps and assumes that these housekeeping genes are expressed at the same level in all samples or experimental conditions. However, user needs to keep in mind that housekeeping genes can indeed change from one condition to another. Data normalization can be done using spike genes. In such a case, RNA/cDNA of known concentration is added to each sample and used as the reference for normalization. Global normalization assumes that the majority of the genes on the array are not differentially expressed so the means of all arrays are the same. Both linear regression and mean/median methods can be used. For arrays that do not have many genes (e.g., custom arrays that feature a very small number of genes), global normalization is not the choice.

Data transformations are necessary for downstream statistical analysis because most statistical tests assume a certain type of data distribution. The type of statistical analysis (parametric or nonparametric) determines how the data should be transformed. The methods include binning for nonparametric tests, inversion, logarithm, and z-score transformations for parametric tests. Parametric analysis is most commonly used and requires the data to be normally distributed. Log transformation is commonly used to achieve Gaussian distribution. However, it should not be used if the downstream analysis relies on a distance measure.

9.3.1.5   Statistical Analysis

As mentioned earlier, in a sense, finding differentially expressed genes is the goal of microarray experiments. These genes are identified by a difference (sometime expressed as a ratio) in the expression level within experimental groups. In some cases, the number of cases in experimental groups is very limited and it is not possible to validate the sample distribution. Fold-change is considered a common way for gene selection. Twofold and threefold changes are usually considered significant depending on the actual number of samples. Note that the fold change approach can be invalid because of high interexperimental variations in microarray experiments. When used as a preliminary screening tool, however, fold change cutoff in conjunction with biological knowledge still serves the purpose of selecting potentially interesting genes that will be validated with additional experiments.

When sample size is large enough, statistical tests should be used for gene selection. Those commonly used include parametric tests (F-test, ANOVA, and t-test) and nonparametric tests (Mann-Whitney test and Kruskal-Williams rank analysis). All statistical tests produce the significance value introduced earlier, the P value, for gene expression comparison. The value is compared to a predetermined acceptance level (α, usually set to 0.05) that determines the false discovery rate (FDR) (Type I error or false-positive discovery; Type II error or false-negative discovery). The FDR can be significantly inflated without a change in α in the case of multiple comparisons. Several procedures are available for FDR correction: the linear step-up approach, rough false discovery rate (RFDR), and Bonferroni correction.

9.3.1.6   High-Level Analysis: Profiling or Pattern Recognition

There is another level of data analysis that has not been discussed thus far. This type of data analysis is not done at the single gene/feature level, but on composite features/genes. It is often called profiling or pattern recognition. In this approach, the clinical or genomic or proteomic meaning of these features is usually not the focus of consideration; instead it is the pattern of the data that is of interest. For example, in the study of a specific disease, a panel of genes may be selected, their expression levels analyzed, and then transformed into a binary value (1 for expressed, 0 for unexpressed) or multiple-level categorical representation values (0 for unexpressed, 1 for low expression, 2 for medium expression, and 3 for high expression). In the training process, this analysis is done on each specimen, producing a profile (or pattern) for each training specimen.

These profiles are then combined to produce a representative profile of the sample set, with a properly defined distance metrics. In an ideal world, one such profile could be generated for normal subjects and another generated for diseased subjects. Then when a subject comes in for diagnosis, a profile is generated and compared with the two representative profiles to determine whether the patient is a normal subject or not with regard to this disease following a predefined algorithm.

9.3.2   Proteomic Data

Protein expression profiling is the study of key functional molecules—proteins in biological systems. It usually involves protein identification, quantification, and functional activity determination. Traditional methods for protein profiling include protein purification, ELISA, and Western blot using protein-specific antibody and protein-specific function (enzymatic activity) assays.

HTP analysis of protein is not as advanced and popular as microarray analysis for gene expression. The main reason lies in the lack of large-scale protein identification and quantization methods suitable for HTP analysis and the huge dynamic range of protein abundance in biology samples. Methodologies used in high-throughput proteomic analysis were discussed in detail in Chapter 6. Mass spectrometry is a HTP method that provides great separation compared to traditional approaches and greatly reduced interrun variation, especially when coupled to HPLC. Here, LC-MS is used as an example to illustrate the procedure and the issues surrounding the analysis of HTP proteomic data.

The goal of proteomic analysis is the same as that of gene expression microarray analysis: to identify differentially expressed genes at the protein level. However, the data are fundamentally different. Data from MS analysis are virtually a list of pairs of m/z intensity; with LC-MS, each pair also has a third value indicating the time point (retention time, RT) on HPLC. In LC-MS, the raw data can be viewed as a 2D gel with one axis for separation by LC (measured in time) and the other for results from MS (measured in m/z). Each peak, representing a peptide of a given charge state, is a group of intensity signals that fit an isotopic distribution along the m/z axis and a Gaussian distribution along the LC axis. One peptide can appear as several individual peaks because of differences in charge state. Major tasks in analyzing HTP proteomic data are feature (spots or peaks that represent proteins and peptides) identification, feature quantization, feature (peak) alignment, and protein identification.

The first step in analyzing LC-MS data is background and noise subtraction. Data filtration (smoothing) may be necessary to facilitate the subsequent step of peak detection. A common approach in peak detection is to identify peaks in a single spectrum and then group similar peaks from adjacent spectra to form the 3D peak. The peptide peaks vary greatly in size because of their abundance in samples; this poses a great challenge. Currently available peak detection methods are sensitive to the detection of peaks with a limited range of size and depend on optimal configuration of detection parameters.

The major challenge in peak alignment lies in RT alignment because of variations in LC. RT alignment needs to address both time shift and jittering (also referred as warping) to achieve optimal LC alignment. The dynamic algorithm by Ono et al. for adjustment of LC jittering appears to be effective and promising [35]. In terms of quantification, a peak is measured by height, area, or volume. Quantification of peptides needs to take into consideration peaks of different charge states. Protein identification is done through tandem MS analysis.

Currently, the major challenge in LC-MS data analysis is the lack of tools for reliable peak detection, peptide quantification, and peptide matching. Undetected peaks, inaccurate peptide quantification, and peptide mismatching impose a detrimental impact on HTP screening and profiling using LC-MS. One general approach is to use an automated pipeline for large-scale processing to identify interesting peptides and then come back to manually verify the accuracy of peak identification, peptide quantification, and peptide matching. Open-source systems available for LC-MS data processing include OpenMS/TOPP [36] and SpecArray [37].

Two XML standards have been developed for exchange of MS data: mzXML [38] and mzData [39]. They are designed with different focuses. Currently, effort has been made to merge the two standards into one. The domain standard is important for data exchange among different platforms and analysis tools, and also makes it convenient to carry along the minimal and adequate experimental information that is required for QA and integration of MS data from different platforms. Tools for conversion between various raw file formats and XML are available.

Tandem MS (MS/MS) analyzes the MS of selected peptides subjected to collision-induced dissociation. Selection can be random or based on the abundance of or size of the peptide. The primary use for MS/MS is protein identification, which is done by searching the result against a protein sequence database. SEQUEST and MASCOT are two commonly used tools for protein identification using MS/MS. Tandem MS counting, referred as spectral counting, has also been used for protein quantification. Because there is no robust and satisfactory tool/platform available, spectral counting provides an alternative and convenient way of protein quantification for LC-MS. It does not require peak detection or sample alignment, and proteins are quantified by the frequency of its peptides being identified by MS/MS. However, there is an undersampling problem in this approach because only a very limited number of ions can be analyzed. Low-abundance proteins in a sample may never be analyzed by MS/MS, and a large sample number is necessary to ensure the statistical significance of the result.

Analysis of 2D DIGE data faces the same challenges as for LC-MS data. Peak detection is based entirely on image processing and is usually handled using manufacturer-provided applications. Samples are usually undigested. Fewer peaks need to be handled compared to LC-MS. The major drawback of 2D DIGE is the large interrun variation that makes the automatic feature extraction from gel and alignment across samples difficult. Note that using different dyes, samples can be run on the same gel. This provides a way of direct comparison for up to three samples.

9.3.3 Functional Determination

After some comparisons and statistical analysis, there is a list of genes that are differentially expressed among the experiment groups. The next question asked then is "What are these genes?" This is the time when functional analysis comes into play. Functional analysis is a significant part of data analysis in biomedical research. The ultimate goal is to understand the biological processes involved in the disease being studied so that targets for diagnosis, treatment, and prevention can be identified. Functional analysis is made possible with the available public and commercial resources.

9.3.3.1 Gene Ontology

The Gene Ontology (GO) [40] provides a controlled vocabulary for describing gene and gene product attributes in any organism. It contains three ontologies and the annotation, which characterizes gene–gene products using terms from the ontologies. Each of the three ontologies represents a key concept in molecular biology: the molecular function of gene products, their role in multistep biological processes, and their localization to cellular components. A gene product might be associated with or located in one or more cellular components; it is active in one or more biological processes, during which it performs one or more molecular functions.

The terms in GO are linked by two relationships: *is_a* and *part_of*. The *is_a* specifies a simple class–subclass relationship, where A *is_a* B means that A is a subclass of B. In the *part_of* relationship, C *part_of* D means that whenever C is present, it is always a part of D, but C does not always have to be present. Using these relationships, the ontologies are structured as directed acyclic graphs that are similar to hierarchies, but differ in that a child term can have many parent terms. Terms must also obey the true path rule: If the child term describes the gene product, then all of its parent terms must also apply to that gene product.

The most common analysis that uses GO to gain insights into the differentially expressed genes is the functional enrichment analysis. Enrichment analysis is designed to find GO terms with an unbalanced distribution between two groups of genes. For interpretation of the data, a GO profile of the differentially expressed genes is compared with that of a reference set, for example, the entire gene list. Change of relative frequency is used to measure enrichment. A number of statistical methods can be used to test the significance of observed enrichment: binomial, Pearson's chi-square test, and hypergeometric tests. Many tools implementing one or more of the methods mentioned are available for enrichment analysis: EasyGO, dChip, DAVID, and GEPAT [41]. A Bayesian approach for searching enriched terms has also been described and a tool implementing it is freely available [42]. In consideration of multiple testing issues, a FDR correction should be considered to control falsely rejected hypotheses.

9.3.3.2 Pathway Analysis

A biological process in GO is not equivalent to a pathway. A biological pathway describes a set of molecular events underlying a biological process. Pathways are built with knowledge about individual molecular events accumulated in the past. The building process requires a significant amount of manual effort because the existing information is often scattered throughout thousands of publications. Pathway analysis allows decomposition of experimental data into a set of known pathways and biological processes.

A number of tools are available for pathway analysis. Ingenuity IPA, GeneGo, GoMiner, and BIOBASE are among them. In pathway analysis, a list of genes/proteins is used as input to search the pathway database. Genes involved in a pathway are overlaid onto the pathway in a graphical representation of the pathway. Some tools also integrate the differential expression in the graphical display, which gives a direct assessment of the agreement of the gene expression profile with molecular events in the pathway and, hence, the likelihood that the pathway is involved in the subject under study.

However, pathway analysis has been hampered by the scarcity of pathway data. A database of metabolic pathways for human tissues has been constructed [43]. Known signaling pathways are scattered among various public and commercial manually curated databases: KEGG has approximately 24 regulatory pathways; the STKE database has about 80 signaling pathways; BioCarta contains about 250 pathways for human, mouse, and rat organisms; and the PathArt database (Jubilant) contains 696 disease-associated pathways describing various biological processes in 26 diseases. Cambridge Cell Networks is undertaking the effort to generate toxicity-associated pathways.

9.4 Analysis of Clinical Data

Clinical data play an important role in translational research. They provide a way to assess factors that could have a significant impact on biomedical research but cannot be evaluated in the lab using molecular or proteomic approaches. Those factors can be clinical, environmental, behavioral, and psychological. Integration of clinical data with biomedical research data will improve patient risk, diagnostic, and prognostic profiling and result in better treatment and patient management. In major research projects such as CBCP, as much clinical information about a patient or participant is collected as possible. Clinical information covers a very broad range: from demographic data to lifestyle-related information, from socioeconomic data to medical history, from laboratory test results to histopathology and diagnostic imaging such as ultrasound and MRI. Clinical data are of different types. Simple data, such as age and body weight, are single values, whereas complex data, such as a pathological report and a mammogram image, provide complicated information that requires specific processing or domain expert interpretation or subjective abstraction of information before the data can be used for analysis or decision making.

One advantage of using clinical data in translational research is that longitudinal clinical information can be collected through follow-up and multiple disease events (such as breast cancer and heart disease) that provide a comprehensive and longitudinal view of patient profile. Clinical information is often collected in its raw format value, with temporal attributes indicating the time or period when the information is valid. Compared to raw clinical data, information extracted from them is more important and used in data analysis by physicians and medical decision-making support applications. One such type of information extraction, temporal abstraction, has been adopted to transform raw clinical data into such meaningful information.

The goal of clinical analysis is to identify clinical information that can serve as a marker for diagnosis and treatment or can assist physicians when they are making decisions. Simple statistical analysis is capable of identifying an individual protein with a certain disease, such as PSA for prostate cancer. More sophisticated analyses would require a wide range of data, including that from molecular analysis, and would use more advanced methodologies, for example, artificial intelligence such as ANNs, SVM, decision trees, and Bayesian networks. The outcome of such sophisticated analyses is data models that make predictions about and classify new data with great accuracy and precision and are suitable for medical decision-making support.

As pointed out earlier in the chapter, clinical data are of different types even after interpretation with domain expertise and temporal abstraction: discrete, categorical, and continuous. It is necessary to transform data from one type to another. Binning might be the most used method. Selection of the best transformation method and parameters (such as number of bins) is important to achieve optimal results in clinical data analysis. Clinical data are prone to missing values and errors, especially for data that are collected with paper-based questionnaires and require human intervention. For instance, information initially collected may not agree with follow-up surveys. To achieve best practices in translational biomedical research, continuous efforts at data QA are required even after data collection.

9.5   Analysis of Textual Data

Text mining has become another popular area of bioinformatics and biomedical research in the last few years. Relationships between biological entities such as genes and proteins, biological processes, and diseases resulting from biomedical research are available but scattered in scientific publications. Construction of knowledge bases by extracting information, such as protein–protein interactions, will be valuable in assisting scientists to understand research data and design new experiments. When extracted and presented in an intuitive way, the otherwise scattered information can reveal information such as indirect gene–protein interactions or a chain of direct interactions that one would otherwise be unaware of [44].

Extraction of relationships among biological/biomedical entities (such as protein–protein, gene–drug, gene–disease, and gene–biological process) bears most of the interest of biomedical textual data analysis. Other goals of textual data analysis include document classification, ontology construction, and gene–protein annotation. Numerous methods and many applications, including commercial ones, have been developed and are available [45]. Tasks in text mining biomedical literature include these areas: biological named-entity recognition (NER), microarray analysis, document retrieval, selective dissemination of information (SDI) services, natural language processing (NLP) and bioinformatics, protein interactions and relationships, and information extraction and text mining of protein annotations [45]. In this section, we will focus on extraction of biological entities and their relation by textual data analysis.

9.5.1   Data Sources

Textual data in biomedical research are found primarily in scientific publications and sometimes hospital medical records. For its availability and ease of access, PubMed, a database currently containing more than 12,000,000 references of biomedical publications, has served as the major source for text mining in biomedical research. Abstracts contain most of the information the authors are trying to convey in a very condensed form as compare to the full article. Most knowledge bases constructed with text mining use MEDLINE abstracts as the data source.

Accessing the full paper is an alternative to using just the abstract, but full papers may not be available to everyone. Researchers may be able to obtain some of them through institutional subscriptions. Some believe certain sections of full-text articles (such as results and figure legends where the authors describe observations in detail) contain more information of interest than the abstracts. For example, the "introduction," "background," "conclusion," and "discussion" sections are the places where author(s) will review and summarize related knowledge and previous findings. Other opinions exist. For example, Martin et al. have suggested comparable results for protein–protein interaction extraction using abstracts and full-text articles [46]. Full-text articles certainly contain richer information than their respective abstracts. In the meantime, they are also more complex. It probably requires more advanced text mining techniques to take advantage of the rich information available from full-text articles.

There are a few other obstacles besides availability that have made using full-text articles in biomedical text mining difficult. First, bulk download of documents is generally not provided by publishers. Document retrieval requires significant manual efforts, which can be automated but only to a certain extent. It is probably impossible to collect the full text of all articles whose abstracts are in PubMed. Second, retrieved documents need preprocessing before they can be used for text mining. Articles are retrieved in either HTML or PDF format. PDF files need to be converted to ASCII or HTML, but the conversion may not be as reliable as one would wish for. For HTML documents, it is advantageous to remove noncontent text that has been provided for other purposes such as navigation.

Another challenge associated with using full-text articles as source texts is the use of images in HTML and PDF files to represent symbols, such as α and ξ, used as part of the name to identify the entity of interest. These images need to be replaced with their spelled-out names.

Structured full texts of scientific publications from some journals have recently become available from the PubMed Central Open Access Initiative (PMC-OAI) [47]. At the end of 2007, PMC-OAI hosted more than 60,000 papers from 383 journals. These papers have the advantage of being very representative of the overall biomedical literature and have already been transformed to XML, so the structure can be automatically extracted. They proved to be very helpful for comparisons between abstracts and other sections of a publication as the source for text mining and also for the evaluation of HTML and PDF conversion tools.

9.5.2 Biological Entity

Biological research is name centered. For instance, proteins are referred to in free text by their names or symbols rather than by the unambiguous identifiers provided by annotation databases. In NLP-based information extraction (IE), the identification of entities in free text, also known as named-entity recognition (NER), is a prerequisite step. Recognition of named biomedical entities in scientific literature is a difficult process. This is because the use of gene and protein names is very complex and domain nomenclature is ever evolving. Genes and proteins may be referred to in free text in a number of ways: as full names (for example, mannan binding lectin), as symbols (such as MBL), and also through typographical variants (e.g., mannan-binding lectin). Many genes also have several synonyms (such as mannose-binding protein and MBP for MBL), or the gene name may be ambiguous and refer to words that also have different meanings depending on the context (for example, MBP for mannose binding protein can also refer to human myelin basic protein). Gene and protein names change with time. When mannose binding lectin gene was first discovered it was referred to as mannose binding protein and MBP; currently, it is referred as MBL, which is more accurate.

In extraction of biomedical entities and biomedical relations (discussed in the next section), the performance on methods and system are generally evaluated using two scores: *precision* and *recall*. They are defined as following:

$$Precision = \frac{True_{matches}}{True_{matches} + False_{matches}}$$

$$Recall = \frac{True_{matches}}{True_{matches} + Missed_{matches}}$$

Precision and recall can be combined to calculate the *F*-measure, which is the weighted harmonic mean of precision and recall:

$$F - Measure = \frac{2 \times Precision \times Recall}{Precision + Recall}$$

There are several approaches to biomedical NER: rule-based [48, 49], dictionary-based [50–52], and model-based [53, 54] approaches. In rule-based approaches, predefined rules are used to describe the composition of the named entities and their context. Surface clues, such as capital letters, symbols, and digits, might be used to extract candidates for gene and protein names. These candidates serve as the core terms and can be further expanded using syntactic rules to include confirming words, such as GENE, PROTEIN, and RECEPTOR, for term refinement. Part-of-speech (POS) tags can also be used to further improve the rules. Rule-based NER usually does not perform well on unseen names, and the construction and tuning of rules can be time consuming.

Dictionary-based NER uses collections of names to identify entities in different categories. Named entities are located in free text by exact matching to names in dictionaries. Dictionary-based NER achieves high precision but depending on the completeness of the dictionaries, the recall can be low. Recall can be improved with fuzzy matching. In biomedical textual analysis, dictionaries of gene, protein, and some other biological names as well as their synonyms can be built in using well-annotated databases.

Model-based or classification-based NER uses machine learning approaches. Commonly used techniques include naïve Bayes, SVM, decision trees, and the Markov model. Using selected features such as word/phrase occurrence, word sequence tag, POS tag, and dictionary match, classifiers are trained on a previously annotated corpus. Model-based NER is sensitive to selection of features used for training and classification and to the quality of the corpus text used in training.

9.5.3 Mining Relations Between Named Entities

Identification of biological entities is the first and crucial step, while the extraction of associations between proteins and their functional features is the goal of the analysis of biological text data. There are two levels of entity relation mining for biomedical literature. At the low level, a relationship between named entities is implied by co-citation at various levels, namely, sentence, paragraph, and document. This co-occurrence approach is not aimed at addressing the specific and precise relationship between entities, but the co-occurrence information is very useful for document navigation and retrieval [55, 56]. Nonetheless, quantitative and statistical methods can be applied to reveal useful information, such as term distribution and information content changes, and assist the data analysis with other data, for example, gene microarrays [57–59] and gene clustering [60, 61]. High-level entity relation extraction focuses on the sentence level and tries to understand the meaning of the sentence. For example, from "*interaction between p34SEI-1 and CDK4 renders cyclin D1-CDK4 complex resistant to inhibition by p16INK4a*," it will be ideal if all of the following relations can be extracted:

Entity A	Relation	Entity B
p34SEI-1	interacts with	CDK4
cyclin D1	forms complex with	CDK4
p16INK4a	inhibits	cyclin D1-CDK4 complex
CDK4 - p34SEI-1 interaction	renders	inhibition of cyclin D1-CDK4 complex by p16INK4a

Relationships extracted to this level are suitable for construction of molecular pathways comparable to and complementary to the well-annotated canonical pathways. Relation extraction uses predicational and propositional information and matches parsed sentences to predefined so-called frames or patterns. General steps include (1) sentence tokenization, (2) verb and noun phrase determination with POS parsing, (3) selection of sentences that contain names of interest, and (4) matching to frames. One system that extracts annotations and detects protein-protein interactions is the information Hyperlinked Over Proteins (iHOP) system [62–64]. The iHOP system uses MEDLINE abstracts as the text source and is based on a knowledge-discovery system called SUISEKI [65]. LexiQuestMine, a dictionary-based NLP tool from SPSS (Chicago, IL), supports custom-built dictionaries and patterns and has been used to extract gene–protein relationships from abstracts and the full text of biomedical publications [46, 59]. Effective relation extraction from biomedical literature depends on the completeness and quality of the predefined frames and NER. Precision and recall range from 60% to 90%, but can be low if the library of frame is suboptimal or the source text is complex.

Literature mining not only enriches but also confirms the traditional evidence-based annotation of gene and protein. Knowledge extraction based on NLP has been adopted for automatic construction of networks of different purposes [69] and can be valuable in finding new gene–gene relationships [44]. Systems have been developed for automated extraction of protein–protein interactions [53, 70], construction of molecular pathways [71], and creation of ontology [60] from biological literature. Information extraction using NLP from medical records has also been reported [72, 73]. Despite significant progression in mining of biological literature, major challenges remain [74].

9.6   Integrative Analysis and Application Examples

In essence, integrative data analysis may have two meanings, emphasizing data integration (centralization) and tool integration, respectively. Here we are focusing on the former. Data integration can be done physically or logically as discussed in Chapter 8. Technically, integrative data analysis can be done in two ways. One way is to extract useful features first from different data platforms as described earlier, and then to integrate those features for integrative analysis. The other way is to integrate the raw data from all of the data platforms and then analyze this huge amount of diversified data.

It is certainly more practical to take the first approach, because whether for data analysis or mining, different data types still require different analytical techniques to be applied. For example, microarray gene expression data contains tens of thousands of dimensions of data (probes) and not all of them are independent of each other in expression even at the gene level. The number of samples is typically far smaller than the number of the probes on the array, which makes it very difficult to apply techniques such as ANN, both due to the computational complexity and the overfitting concern. Molecular expression data would be better subject to differential analysis first to largely reduce the dimension of the data before they are integrated with other types of data for analysis. This would essentially reduce this approach to the same as the first approach, conceptually speaking.

Combining protein expression data with gene expression data is always desirable. Biomarkers identified in one data platform and confirmed in the other are potentially reliable. We know that as gene products it is the proteins that carry out physiological functions in biological systems, but DNA and RNA are also playing critical roles in regulating gene expressions. The recent rapid developments in RNA interference (RNAi) research brought our understanding of such regulatory mechanisms to a new level [75]. However, the mismatch in the maturity of gene and protein expression analysis technologies makes it a challenge to directly compare the data from the two domains. On one hand, we can readily measure the expression of tens of thousands of genes, but on the other hand, we can only semireliably detect hundreds or thousands of proteins at a time in a human specimen that contain hundreds of thousands or even a million proteins (including posttranslational modification variants). As a result, we are still in need of a way to conduct comprehensive integrative analysis of protein and gene expression data. However, partially integrative analysis can be done. For example, concordance analysis between the expressions of genes and proteins (currently detectable) has shown a consistency level of 60% to 70%. It is also possible that proteins with predicted upregulation or downregulation based on gene expression analysis can be pinned in MS or antibody array analyses.

With defined outcome variables (e.g., disease diagnosis), when risk factors and biomarkers are identified from clinical, genomic, and proteomic platforms, ANN, clustering, and logistic regression are powerful tools that can be used to develop disease prediction models. ANN and logistic regression typically require a limited number of inputs, and the former can further identify dependent variables and remove them and thus develop models based only on independent variables. Logistic regression can provide odds ratio analysis for input variables with regard to the outcome. Clustering analysis can accept a large number of input variables; unsupervised clustering can provide a picture of whether the extracted features (from clinical, genomic, and proteomic analyses) can truly cluster the subjects into the outcome groups to which they belong. Supervised clustering, on the other hand, can train the clustering model so that the model can have predictive power, as is possible with ANN and logistic regression.

A good number of genomic and proteomic biomarkers have been identified and applied to clinical practice. Examples in breast cancer include, BRCA1, BRCA2, Her2/Neu, estrogen receptor (ER), and progesterone receptor (PR) [76]. It is now a widely accepted opinion that most cancers are complicated heterogeneic diseases, the development of which cannot be attributed to the mutation or abnormal expression of only a single gene. A panel of genes probably needs to be analyzed for disease diagnosis or prognosis prediction, in line with the concept of "phenotyping determines genotyping." Recently, the American Society of Clinical Oncology recommended using Oncotype DX from Genomic Health for breast cancer assay. Oncotype DX uses a panel of genes to predict the likelihood of breast cancer recurrence, and whether a special type of tumor will respond to chemotherapy [77].

Integrative data analysis demands that new application software be developed and incorporated into the current clinical, genomic, and proteomic knowledge. Efforts are ongoing to develop such a comprehensive system and one such example is a package from BIOBASE, a German company. The software contains TRANSFAC [78], a gene regulation database; TRANSPATH, a pathway database; PROTEOME, a proteomics database; and ExPlain [79], an application for expression data analysis. Gene or protein expression data can be loaded into the software, analyzed against the knowledge databases, and important features can be identified, such as which transcription factors are critical in explaining the observed expression pattern, which genes or gene products are known to the disease being studied, and which gene regulatory pathways are likely involved in producing the observed expression pattern (http://www.biobase-international.com).

Despite the progress being made, challenges remain about how to effectively integrate features being extracted from clinical, genomic, and proteomic data from the same groups of subjects in a specific disease study, how to integrate the data and the knowledge in the public domain regarding this disease including the corresponding clinical knowledge and any other published results of genomic and proteomic studies, and, more comprehensively from a systems point of view, how to include in the research all the known knowledge and data regarding human physiology and all diseases. Integration itself is a challenge, and developing the applications to make use of these integrated data is another major challenge. Despite these difficulties, we believe that integrative data analysis is the future of biomedical research and we believe that the day will come when effective technologies will be developed to meet these challenges.

9.7 Data Analysis Tools and Resources

Many software applications for bioinformatics and biomedical informatics research are published in the literature, such as in the leading journals of *Nucleic Acids*

Research, Bioinformatics, and *BMC Bioinformatics.* The journal *Nucleic Acids Research* publishes a special July web server issue, which is a sister issue to the January database special issue. The July 2007 special issues was the fifth annual issue dedicated to web-based applications for analysis of biological data, and this issue reports on 130 web applications, most of which are new [80]. These 130 applications, together with all other applications published in *Nucleic Acids Research* thus far, and links to many other useful tool and resources for life sciences, are complied by Joanne Fox, Scott McMillan, and Francis Ouellette of the UBC Bioinformatics Centre. This link, named the Bioinformatics Links Directory, is available to the public at http://bioinformatics.ca/links_directory [9]. These resources are compiled by category such as DNA, RNA, Protein, Expression, Human Genome, and Literature. A search engine is also provided to enable quick identification of services from the nearly 1,200 links.

Complementary to applications developed in the academic setting that are freely available, fee-based commercial applications are also available. The following are some examples of the commercial platforms for data analysis and data mining:

SAS
SAS software (http://www.sas.com) is developed by the SAS Institute. It is one of the most popular tools used in decision support and data warehousing. SAS software offers a wide variety of tools and modules and can rapidly draw data from a variety of platforms and applications, drawing together unique data trends about information that can be applied to decision making and application development.

Millions of records can be rapidly analyzed, allowing a constant inflow of data to be repeatedly organized. This allows decision makers the unique ability to evaluate trends and to make sense of vast amounts of data, allowing for accurate and timely decision making.

SPSS Clementine
SPSS Clementine (http://www.spss.com/clementine) is a premier data mining workbench that allows experts in business processes, data, and modeling to collaborate in exploring data and building models. It is a data mining product that offers a highly intuitive, visual interface.

InforSense KDE
InforSense (www.inforsense.com) delivers a unique combination of data integration, predictive modeling, and visualization capabilities within a flexible workflow environment. This enables InforSense to deliver a productized approach to translational informatics that can be replicated across different organizations and disease areas, unlike the professional services-based approach commonly taken. The InforSense Translational Research Solution provides a powerful and flexible framework to integrate and analyze clinical, patient sample, and experimental data for translational research. The solution enables various user groups to integrate data and construct analysis workflows that can then be deployed to a wider scientific audience. This unified system can use any experimental technique to support the identification of biomarkers including Genome Wide Association studies, gene

expression, proteomics and image analysis. The solution also enables users to analyze and compare these techniques, ensuring the best combination of techniques is being used. Built on the powerful InforSense platform, it supports the construction of analytic solutions based on statistical and clustering analysis, which can then be deployed via web portals. The InforSense platform also supports Oracle indatabase processing and data mining functions.

Spotfire

The DecisionSite (http://spotfire.tibco.com/products/decisionsite.cfm) from Spotfire Inc. is a rich, interactive analysis environment for technical analysts. It provides interactive, visual capabilities for data analysis and empowers individuals to quickly and easily see trends, patterns, outliers, and unanticipated relationships in data. It has modules that focus on different tasks in biomedical research data analysis, such as Statistics, Microarray Analysis, and Functional Genomics.

9.8 Summary

In this chapter, we first clarified the concepts of data analysis and data mining and then provided an overview of those techniques as they are applied to biomedical research. Next, we illustrated, using specific example platforms, how these data analysis and data mining techniques are applied to clinical, genomic, and proteomic data analysis and knowledge extraction. We also discussed how integrative data analysis is done across the data platforms, which we believe is the direction for biomedical informatics research.

References

[1]   Cabena, P., and International Business Machines Corporation, *Discovering Data Mining: From Concept to Implementation*. Upper Saddle River, NJ: Prentice Hall PTR, 1998.

[2]   Kudyba, S., Hoptroff, R., and Ebrary Inc., "Data Mining and Business Intelligence: A Guide to Productivity," http://site.ebrary.com/lib/princeton/Doc?id=10019236.

[3]   Walle, A. H., and Ebrary Inc., "Qualitative Research in Intelligence and Marketing: The New Strategic Convergence," http://site.ebrary.com/lib/princeton/Doc?id=10017903.

[4]   Colin, S., and Peter, C., "Case Studies: Commercial, Multiple Mining Tasks Systems: Clementine," in *Handbook of Data Mining and Knowledge Discovery*: Oxford, UK: Oxford University Press, 2002, pp. 564–572.

[5]   Inforsense KDE, http://www.inforsense.com.

[6]   Achen, C. H., *Interpreting and Using Regression*. Beverly Hills, CA: Sage Publications, 1982.

[7]   Mosteller, F., and Rourke, R. E. K., *Sturdy Statistics: Nonparametrics and Order Statistics*. Reading, MA: Addison-Wesley, 1973.

[8]   Jagota, A., *Data Analysis and Classification for Bioinformatics*, Bioinformatics By the Bay Press, 2000.

[9]   Fox, J. A., McMillan, S., and Ouellette, B. F., "Conducting Research on the Web: 2007 Update for the Bioinformatics Links Directory," *Nucleic Acids Res.*, Vol. 35, 2007, pp. W3–W5.

[10] "Oracle Data Mining," http://www.oracle.com/technology/products/bi/odm/index.html.

[11] Han, J., and Kamber, M., *Data Mining: Concepts and Techniques*, 2nd ed., San Francisco: Morgan Kaufmann, 2006.

[12] Wang, Y., and Makedon, F., "Application of Relief-F Feature Filtering Algorithm to Selecting Informative Genes for Cancer," in *Computational Systems Bioinformatics Conference*, Stanford, CA, 2004.

[13] Robnik-Sikonja, M., and Kononenko, I., "Theoretical and Empirical Analysis of Relieff and Rrelieff," *Machine Learning J.*, Vol. 53, 2003, p. 52.

[14] Cooper, G. F., and Herskovits, E., "A Bayesian Method for the Induction of Probabilistic Networks from Data," *Machine Learning*, Vol. 9, 1992, p. 39.

[15] Agresti, A., *An Introduction to Categorical Data Analysis*. New York: John Wiley & Sons, 1996.

[16] Cristianini, N., and Shawe-Taylor, J., *An Introduction to Support Vector Machines and Other Kernel-Based Learning Methods*. New York: Cambridge University Press, 2000.

[17] Burges, C. J. C., "A Tutorial on Support Vector Machines for Pattern Recognition," *Data Mining Knowledge Discovery*, Vol. 2, 1998, p. 47.

[18] Abdi, H., "A Neural Network Primer," *J. Biolog. Syst.*, Vol. 2, 1994, p. 47.

[19] Quinlan, J. R., *C4.5: Programs for Machine Learning*. San Mateo, CA: Morgan Kaufmann, 1993.

[20] Golub, T. R., et al., "Molecular Classification of Cancer: Class Discovery and Class Prediction by Gene Expression Monitoring," *Science*, Vol. 286, 1999, pp. 531–537.

[21] Tamayo, P., et al., "Interpreting Patterns of Gene Expression with Self-Organizing Maps: Methods and Application to Hematopoietic Differentiation," *Proc. Natl. Acad. Sci. USA*, Vol. 96, 1999, pp. 2907–2912.

[22] Tom, F., "ROC Graphs with Instance-Varying Costs," *Pattern Recognition Letters*, Vol. 27, New York: Elsevier Science, 2006, pp. 882–891.

[23] Tom, F., "An Introduction to ROC Analysis," *Pattern Recognition Letters*, Vol. 27, New York: Elsevier Science, 2006, pp. 861–874.

[24] Kohavi, R., "A Study of Cross-Validation and Bootstrap for Accuracy Estimation and Model Selection," paper presented at the International Joint Conference on Artificial Intelligence (IJCAI), 1995.

[25] Guo, L., et al., "Rat Toxicogenomic Study Reveals Analytical Consistency Across Microarray Platforms," *Nat. Biotechnol.*, Vol. 24, 2006, pp. 1162–1169.

[26] Shi, L., et al., "The Microarray Quality Control (MAQC) Project Shows Inter- and Intraplatform Reproducibility of Gene Expression Measurements," *Nat. Biotechnol.*, Vol. 24, 2006, pp. 1151–1161.

[27] Patterson, T. A., et al., "Performance Comparison of One-Color and Two-Color Platforms Within the Microarray Quality Control (MAQC) Project," *Nat. Biotechnol.*, Vol. 24, 2006, pp. 1140–1150.

[28] Affymetrix, "Statistical Algorithms Description Document," 2002, http://www.affymetrix.com/support/technical/whitepapers/sadd_whitepaper.pdf.

[29] Hubbell, E., Liu, W. M., and Mei, R., "Supplemental Data: Robust Estimators for Expression Analysis," Affymetrix, 2005.

[30] Affymetrix, "Guide to Probe Logarithmic Intensity Error (PLIER) Estimation," http://www.affymetrix.com/support/technical/technotes/plier_technote.pdf, 2005.

[31] Li, C., and Wong, W. H., "Model-Based Analysis of Oligonucleotide Arrays: Expression Index Computation and Outlier Detection," *Proc. Natl. Acad. Sci. USA*, Vol. 98, 2001, pp. 31–36.

[32] Irizarry, R. A., et al., "Exploration, Normalization, and Summaries of High Density Oligonucleotide Array Probe Level Data," *Biostatistics*, Vol. 4, 2003, pp. 249–264.

[33] Deng, S., Chu, T.-M., and Wolfnger, R., "A Mixed Model Expression Index to Summarize Affymetrix Genechip Probe Level Data," *Mathematical Subject Classification*, Vol. 62-07, 2005.

[34] Yang, S., et al., "Detecting Outlier Microarray Slides by Correlation and Percentage of Outliers Spots," *Cancer Informatics*, 2006, p. 10.

[35] Ono, M., et al., "Label-Free Quantitative Proteomics Using Large Peptide Data Sets Generated by Nano-Flow Liquid Chromatography and Mass Spectrometry," *Mol. Cell Proteomics*, Vol. 5, 2006, pp. 1338–1347.

[36] Kohlbacher, O., et al., "TOPP—The OPENMS Proteomics Pipeline," *Bioinformatics*, Vol. 23, 2007, pp. E191–E197.

[37] Li, X. J., et al., "A Software Suite for the Generation and Comparison of Peptide Arrays from Sets of Data Collected by Liquid Chromatography-Mass Spectrometry," *Mol. Cell Proteomics*, Vol. 4, 2005, pp. 1328–1340.

[38] Pedrioli, P. G., et al., "A Common Open Representation of Mass Spectrometry Data and Its Application to Proteomics Research," *Nat. Biotechnol.*, Vol. 22, 2004, pp. 1459–1466.

[39] Orchard, S., et al., "Five Years of Progress in the Standardization of Proteomics Data," paper presented at 4th Annual Spring Workshop of the HUPO-Proteomics Standards Initiative, Ecole Nationale Superieure (ENS), Lyon, France, April 23–25, 2007, *Proteomics*, Vol. 7, 2007, pp. 3436–3440.

[40] Ashburner, M., et al., "Gene Ontology: Tool for the Unification of Biology. The Gene Ontology Consortium," *Nat. Genet.*, Vol. 25, 2000, pp. 25–29.

[41] Weniger, M., Engelmann, J. C., and Schultz, J., "Genome Expression Pathway Analysis Tool—Analysis and Visualization of Microarray Gene Expression Data Under Genomic, Proteomic and Metabolic Context," *BMC Bioinformatics*, Vol. 8, 2007, p. 179.

[42] Vencio, R. Z., et al., "Baygo: Bayesian Analysis of Ontology Term Enrichment in Microarray Data," *BMC Bioinformatics*, Vol. 7, 2006, p. 86.

[43] Romero, P., et al., "Computational Prediction of Human Metabolic Pathways from the Complete Human Genome," *Genome Biol.*, Vol. 6, 2005, p. R2.

[44] Natarajan, J., et al., "Text Mining of Full-Text Journal Articles Combined with Gene Expression Analysis Reveals a Relationship Between Sphingosine-1-Phosphate and Invasiveness of a Glioblastoma Cell Line," *BMC Bioinformatics*, Vol. 7, 2006, p. 373.

[45] Krallinger, M., and Valencia, A., "Text-Mining and Information-Retrieval Services for Molecular Biology," *Genome Biol.*, Vol. 6, 2005, p. 224.

[46] Martin, E. P. G., et al., "Analysis of Protein/Protein Interactions Through Biomedical Literature: Text Mining of Abstracts vs. Text Mining of Full Text Articles," in *Knowledge Exploration In Life Science Informatics*, Berlin: Springer, 2004, pp. 96–108.

[47] "Pubmed Central Open Archives Initiative Service," http://www.pubmedcentral.nih.gov/about/oai.html,

[48] Fukuda, K., et al., "Toward Information Extraction: Identifying Protein Names from Biological Papers," *Pac. Symp. Biocomput.*, 1998, pp. 707–718.

[49] Narayanaswamy, M., Ravikumar, K. E., and Vijay-Shanker, K., "A Biological Named Entity Recognizer," *Pac. Symp. Biocomput.*, 2003, pp. 427–438.

[50] Krauthammer, M., et al., "Using BLAST for Identifying Gene and Protein Names in Journal Articles," *Gene*, Vol. 259, 2000, pp. 245–252.

[51] Egorov, S., Yuryev, A., and Daraselia, N., "A Simple and Practical Dictionary-Based Approach for Identification of Proteins in Medline Abstracts," *J. Am. Med. Inform. Assoc.*, Vol. 11, 2004, pp. 174–178.

[52] Hanisch, D., et al., "Playing Biology's Name Game: Identifying Protein Names in Scientific Text," *Pac. Symp. Biocomput.*, 2003, pp. 403–414.

[53] Ono, T., et al., "Automated Extraction of Information on Protein–Protein Interactions from the Biological Literature," *Bioinformatics*, Vol. 17, 2001, pp. 155–161.

[54] Wilbur, W. J., et al., "Analysis of Biomedical Text for Chemical Names: A Comparison of Three Methods," *Proc. AMIA Symp.*, 1999, pp. 176–180.

[55] Jenssen, T. K., et al., "A Literature Network of Human Genes for High-Throughput Analysis of Gene Expression," *Nat. Genet.*, Vol. 28, 2001, pp. 21–28.

[56] Stapley, B. J., and Benoit, G., "Biobibliometrics: Information Retrieval and Visualization from Co-Occurrences of Gene Names in Medline Abstracts," *Pac. Symp. Biocomput.*, 2000, pp. 529–540.

[57] Blaschke, C., Oliveros, J. C., and Valencia, A., "Mining Functional Information Associated with Expression Arrays," *Funct. Integr. Genomics*, Vol. 1, 2001, pp. 256–268.

[58] Rubinstein, R., and Simon, I., "MILANO—Custom Annotation of Microarray Results Using Automatic Literature Searches," *BMC Bioinformatics*, Vol. 6, 2005, p. 12.

[59] Bremer, E. G., et al., "Text Mining of Full Text Articles and Creation of a Knowledge Base for Analysis of Microarray Data," in *Knowledge Exploration In Life Science Informatics*, Berlin: Springer, 2004, pp. 84–95.

[60] Blaschke, C., and Valencia, A., "Automatic Ontology Construction from the Literature," *Genome Inform.*, Vol. 13, 2002, pp. 201–213.

[61] Homayouni, R., et al., "Gene Clustering by Latent Semantic Indexing of MEDLINE Abstracts," *Bioinformatics*, Vol. 21, 2005, pp. 104–115.

[62] Hoffmann, R., and Valencia, A., "A Gene Network for Navigating the Literature," *Nat. Genet.*, Vol. 36, 2004, pp. 664.

[63] Hoffmann, R., and Valencia, A., "Implementing the iHop Concept for Navigation of Biomedical Literature," *Bioinformatics*, Vol. 21, Suppl. 2, 2005, pp. 252–258.

[64] Blaschke, C., et al., "Extracting Information Automatically from Biological Literature," *Comp. Funct. Genom.*, 2001, pp. 4.

[65] Blaschke, C., and Valencia, A., "The Potential Use of SUISEKI as a Protein Interaction Discovery Tool," *Genome Inform.*, Vol. 12, 2001, pp. 123–134.

[66] Aubry, M., et al., "Combining Evidence, Biomedical Literature and Statistical Dependence: New Insights for Functional Annotation of Gene Sets," *BMC Bioinformatics*, Vol. 7, 2006, p. 241.

[67] Miotto, O., Tan, T. W., and Brusic, V., "Supporting the Curation of Biological Databases with Reusable Text Mining," *Genome Inform.*, Vol. 16, 2005, pp. 32–44.

[68] Theodosiou, T., et al., "Gene Functional Annotation by Statistical Analysis of Biomedical Articles," *Int. J. Med. Inform.*, Vol. 76, 2007, pp. 601–613.

[69] Yuryev, A., et al., "Automatic Pathway Building in Biological Association Networks," *BMC Bioinformatics*, Vol. 7, 2006, p. 171.

[70] Albert, S., et al., "Computer-Assisted Generation of a Protein-Interaction Database for Nuclear Receptors," *Mol. Endocrinol.*, Vol. 17, 2003, pp. 1555–1567.

[71] Friedman, C., et al., "GENIES: A Natural-Language Processing System for the Extraction of Molecular Pathways from Journal Articles," *Bioinformatics*, Vol. 17 Suppl 1, 2001, pp. S74–S82.

[72] Rao, B. R., et al., "Mining Time-Dependent Patient Outcomes from Hospital Patient Records," *Proc. AMIA Symp.*, 2002, pp. 632–636.

[73] Heinze, D. T., Morsch, M. L., and Holbrook, J., "Mining Free-Text Medical Records," *Proc. AMIA Symp.*, 2001, pp. 254–258.

[74] Erhardt, R. A., Schneider, R., and Blaschke, C., "Status of Text-Mining Techniques Applied to Biomedical Text," *Drug Discov. Today*, Vol. 11, 2006, pp. 315–325.

[75] Fire, A., et al., "Potent and Specific Genetic Interference by Double-Stranded RNA in *Caenorhabditis elegans*," *Nature*, Vol. 391, 1998, pp. 806–811.

[76] Hanahan, D., and Weinberg, R. A., "The Hallmarks of Cancer," *Cell*, Vol. 100, 2000, pp. 57–70.

[77] Harris, L., et al., "American Society of Clinical Oncology 2007 Update of Recommenda-
       tions for the Use of Tumor Markers in Breast Cancer," *J. Clin. Oncol.*, Vol. 25, 2007,
       pp. 5287–5312.

[78] Matys, V., et al., "TRANSFAC and Its Module Transcompel: Transcriptional Gene Regula-
       tion in Eukaryotes," *Nucleic Acids Res.*, Vol. 34, 2006, pp. D108–D110.

[79] Kel, A., et al., "Composite Module Analyst: A Fitness-Based Tool for Identification of Tran-
       scription Factor Binding Site Combinations," *Bioinformatics*, Vol. 22, 2006,
       pp. 1190–1197.

[80] Benson, G., "Editorial," *Nucleic Acids Res.*, Vol. 35, 2007, p. W1.

CHAPTER 10

Research and Application: Examples

Susan Maskery and Darrell L. Ellsworth

10.1 Introduction

Previous chapters have focused on the nuts and bolts of biomedical informatics in a translational medicine setting. In this chapter we switch gears to examine how biomedical informatics techniques have been implemented in translational medicine research programs. Typically, translational medicine projects involve a close collaboration between scientists and clinicians and focus on expediting advances in human disease research to improve patient treatment. Because translational research requires multitudes of human data (e.g., specimens, medical records, outcome data, experimental data), accurate tracking of biological and medical data for each de-identified participant is vital. Biomedical informatics not only enables this logistical step, but also specializes in analyzing clinical along with biological data.

The core pillars of biomedical informatics—clinical data collection, human biological specimen collection, genomic studies, proteomic studies, data tracking (laboratory information management systems), data centralization, data analysis, data visualization, and data mining methods—have been described in detail in previous chapters. Here we attempt to integrate these components by describing how biomedical informatics is implemented at two institutions focused on translational research. We focus on clinical and biological data collection from human subjects, genomic and proteomic studies, data centralization, unique data analysis algorithms, and research results enabled by strong centralized biomedical informatics capabilities. In particular, we focus on a population genetics approach used by deCODE Genetics to develop drugs and diagnostics for complex diseases such as cardiovascular disease and diabetes, and on the collection and synergistic analysis of detailed clinical, biological, and lifestyle information at Windber Research Institute (WRI) with the goal of improved risk prediction, diagnosis, and treatment of breast cancer and cardiovascular disease.

The company deCODE Genetics was chosen as an example in biomedical informatics because of their success in applying population-wide methods to discover genes that predispose patients to common diseases such as cancer, asthma, diabetes, heart attack, and stroke. According to deCODE's website [1], by early 2008, they had discovered 15 genes/drug targets for 12 common diseases, had enrolled more than 3,000 patients in over 30 clinical trials, and had three diagnostic tests in clinical use. In the deCODE profile, we will describe their three primary databases (genetic, medical, and genealogic), their primary experimental methods (linkage analysis and association studies), and highlight the development of a drug to prevent myocardial infarction (also known as heart attack) and a diagnostic to predict diabetes risk. deCODE genetics is a good example of how biomedical informatics can be applied to human disease research based on clinical data, sample collection, and genomic studies to enable target gene identification and subsequent drug development.

The next organization we profile is WRI. Recognizing that most of the complex human diseases develop over the course of multiple years and are the result of poorly understood interactions between the environment and each person's individual genetic makeup, a premium is placed on gathering comprehensive biological data (tissue and blood samples), lifestyle and epidemiological data (age, ethnicity, occupation, reproductive history, comorbidities), clinical data (disease diagnoses, diagnostic data, treatment regimens), and careful sample selection for proteomic and genomic studies. WRI is chosen as an example organization for this chapter because of its strong biomedical informatics infrastructure. Currently, the primary focus of WRI, as part of the Clinical Breast Care Project (CBCP), is breast disease and breast cancer research. However, programs in gynecological disease and cardiovascular disease are also ongoing at WRI. In the detailed WRI section we illustrate WRI's approach to combining biological, clinical, and environmental information from participants in the CBCP and the Integrative Cardiac and Metabolic Health Program (ICMHP) to research risk factors for progression in these diseases.

10.2   deCODE Genetics

deCODE Genetics uses a population genetics approach to study the genetics of many common diseases (e.g., heart disease, stroke, asthma, diabetes, schizophrenia, cancer) seen in the Western world. In this section we highlight pioneering work in clinical and biological data collection, integration, and centralization; genomic studies; the development of analysis software to link genealogical analysis to high-throughput genomic studies; and examples of drug and diagnostic products that deCODE Genetics has developed based on their genetic research programs. Figure 10.1 places the deCODE sections discussed in this chapter into the context of other chapters.

10.2.1   Data Repository Development and Data Centralization

deCODE conducts population genetics research using the Icelandic biobanking effort, which involves the collection and storage of genetic samples from more than 100,000 volunteers (over half the Icelandic population). These samples are cross-referenced to a genealogy databank that contains 80% of the population that has ever lived in Iceland. This databank enables deCODE scientists to trace the detailed ancestry of most Icelanders back to the 9th century [2]. Additionally, because of the centralized nature of health care in Iceland, it is possible to cross-reference genealogy data with medical information that has been stored nationally in

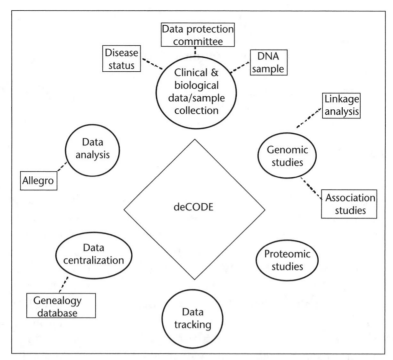

Figure 10.1 Specific aspects of deCODE Genetics, in particular, their clinical data, biological data, and sample collection protocols, genealogy database, data analysis methods, and genomic studies, are placed into the context of the book chapters. Like all pharmaceutical companies, deCODE also has extensive data tracking and proteomic components, but these are not discussed in this chapter.

computer format for the past 20 years. Hence, deCODE is able to combine medical, genetic, and genealogic information on a population scale that is unlike any other medical data repository in the world. Using this platform scientists at deCODE have discovered novel gene targets for cardiovascular disease (heart attack and stroke) [3–6], breast cancer [7], prostate cancer [8], schizophrenia [9], asthma [5], and diabetes [10–12].

10.2.1.1 Clinical Data Collection: Patient Consent and Deidentification

Special consent laws have been developed in Iceland to enable deCODE to conduct human subject research on a population scale. The standard procedure for obtaining human blood samples for genomic analysis is described in [13] and reviewed briefly here. The National Bioethics Committee of Iceland and the Data Protection Commission (DPC) of Iceland must first approve any study between deCODE and clinical collaborators. Once a study has been approved, the clinical collaborator of deCODE will compile a list of its patients that fit a clinical definition of the disease of interest and submit that list to the DPC. The DPC will encrypt this information such that all patient identifiers are removed. This deidentified and encrypted set will be sent to deCODE, which will then compare these patients to an encrypted genealogic database hosted at deCODE. Patients who are part of a large genealogic pedigree are selected for genetic analysis. An encrypted list of patients selected for genetic analysis is sent back to the DPC, which reidentifies the patients and sends a request to the original physician to contact the patient and the patient's extended family to inquire about participation in the research study. Patients and family members who are willing to participate in the study are consented and blood is collected for genetic analysis. Blood samples are then deidentified and encrypted at the DPC and sent back to deCODE for analysis.

10.2.2   Genomic Studies

10.2.2.1   Linkage Analysis

Before going further into the case study of deCODE's success at identifying disease-associated genes, we first introduce the techniques of genetic linkage and association that are important to deCODE's genomic studies. Genetic linkage analysis is used to locate genes associated with human diseases to approximate chromosomal regions within the genome. When two genes are in proximity along a chromosome, they tend to be inherited together (or cosegregate) more often than would be expected by chance. Genes affecting a particular disease can be localized by identifying linkage with a genetic marker of known location, usually a microsatellite marker. Linkage methods were first applied to Mendelian diseases (diseases caused by mutations in a single gene) by examining two hypotheses. The null hypothesis (H_0) is that a disease-susceptibility gene is not linked to a given genetic marker, whereas the alternative hypothesis (H_1) is that a specific chromosomal region contains a disease-susceptibility gene and this gene is close to (linked to) a known genetic marker. The strength of evidence for linkage (H_1) relative to the evidence for no linkage (H_0) is then determined by calculating the following likelihood ratio (LR) and corresponding Log Odds (LOD) score [14]:

$$LR = \text{Probability Data}\left(\text{Data}|H_1\right)/\text{Probability}\left(\text{Data}|H_0\right) \qquad (10.1)$$

$$LOD\ score = \log_{10}\left(LR\right)$$

Often several large families may be required to have sufficient statistical power to show significant evidence for linkage, but assuming there is no genetic heterogeneity (i.e., mutations in different genes are responsible for the same disease in different individuals), data can be pooled across multiple affected families.

In cases with complex diseases, such as heart disease or cancer, many genetic and environmental factors may affect disease development and phenotype. This makes inheritance patterns difficult to define and potentially variable among families. The method described earlier requires a priori knowledge of such parameters. However, methods that do not require such knowledge, known as nonparametric or model-free methods, have been developed to study complex diseases [15, 16].

Nonparametric techniques for genetic linkage have been widely used in an attempt to locate genes that confer increased susceptibility to complex diseases [17–19]. The objective is to determine whether related individuals who are affected with a given disease, for example, affected sibling pairs, inherit copies of particular genomic regions more often than would be expected by chance. This approach is based on the premise that if two siblings are both affected by a particular disease, they probably inherited identical copies of certain chromosomal regions containing the disease-susceptibility genes from their parents.

To locate genes influencing complex diseases using affected sib-pair methods, linkage is determined by comparing the observed and expected numbers of sibling pairs sharing zero, one, or two alleles identical by state using a simple chi-square test with two degrees of freedom [20]. Alternatively, one can infer the probability that chromosomal regions are identical by descent and then compute a statistic such as the maximum likelihood of odds score (MLS) [21]. Both of these approaches use two-point linkage statistics that evaluate linkage between a genetic marker and a theoretical disease-susceptibility gene.

In contrast to two-point linkage methods, multipoint linkage methods consider many markers simultaneously, which helps to more rapidly locate genes that influence disease. Multipoint methods usually utilize many genetic markers along an entire chromosome to infer a linkage statistic at every point along the chromosome [22, 23]. This approach attempts to extract the maximum amount of information from the genetic data and thus may have a lower chance of detecting spurious associations, particularly when densely spaced markers are utilized for detecting linkage.

10.2.2.2 Association Studies

Association studies have the same goal as linkage studies: the identification of genes related to disease. However, they do not rely on related individuals (extended families or sib-pairs) and often use SNPs instead of microsatellite markers. A SNP is a change in one DNA base; the DNA sequence 5′-GCATCTGA-3′ and 5′-GCACCTGA-3′ is an example of a SNP. Such single nucleotide changes are far more abundant than microsatellites—there are millions of SNPs in the human genome. Because of this there has been a gradual shift toward using association studies with SNPs and away from linkage analysis using microsatellites.

Association studies compare the frequencies of markers between unrelated individuals who exhibit a particular disease (cases) versus those who do not (controls). When conducting an association study, one form of a genetic marker (an allele) is deemed to be associated with a given disease if that allele occurs at a significantly higher frequency in the case group relative to the controls [24].

The correlated occurrence of a disease and a genetic polymorphism in a given population may be due to a gene that actually contributes to the disease. In this case, a true-disease susceptibility gene would be identified. However, sometimes the gene in question does not influence the disease, but occurs on the same chromosome and is close to a true disease-susceptibility gene. If these genes are so close together that certain forms of each gene tend to be inherited together, the markers may exhibit linkage disequilibrium and the true disease-susceptibility gene would have to be determined. False associations can also occur due to population admixture (the mixing of individuals with different genetic backgrounds) [25].

deCODE Genetics is now attempting to locate genes influencing complex human diseases through large-scale linkage and association analyses that use hundreds of genetic markers throughout the genome. Many large families, each encompassing several generations, are being studied to see how common diseases, for example, cardiovascular disease, are passed from one generation to the next.

10.2.2.3   Limitations

An important limitation of many efforts that try to identify genes associated with complex diseases is statistical power—the actual chance of detecting a true linkage or association using the collection of patients (families or individuals) currently available. Many studies do not have a sufficient number of families to have a reasonable chance of identifying disease-susceptibility genes. However, deCODE is uniquely positioned to capitalize on the extensive pedigree information available in the Icelandic population and to take advantage of the thousands of people available for study.

Furthermore, genes influencing a complex disease are more likely to be identified in isolated populations where geographic or cultural isolation restricts immigration and, hence, the flow of new genes into the population. Isolated populations are usually more homogeneous than the general human population and thus may be advantageous for genetic studies due to reduced etiological, phenotypic, and genetic heterogeneity. Although isolated populations may be useful for detecting genetic effects associated with complex diseases because of the influence of fewer genes and environmental factors, not all genes contributing to a particular disease in the human population worldwide will be identifiable because some susceptibility genes may not be present in the isolated population.

The ability to effectively use isolated populations to identify disease-associated genes and to detect genetic effects may be influenced by the number of ancestors who originally established or founded the population, the size of the population and rate of growth, the number of generations during which the population has remained in isolation, and the extent of gene flow into the population over time. Other isolated populations, such as the Pima Indians of Arizona, the Old Order Amish of Lancaster County, Pennsylvania, and the Finnish population, have been used successfully to identify potential disease-susceptibility genes [26–28].

10.2.2.4   Analysis Tool

deCODE scientists developed Allegro, a computational tool for multipoint linkage analysis of large pedigree families, to facilitate its large-scale genomic studies. This software has much of the functionality of other linkage analysis software packages such as GeneHunter, but has faster run times and fewer memory requirements than comparable packages [29, 30].

10.2.3   Application

10.2.3.1   Drug Development Based on Identification of Genotype for Myocardial Infarction Risk

Using myocardial infarction (MI) as an example to illustrate the use of linkage and association methods to identify genes that influence complex diseases, deCODE conducted a genome-wide linkage analysis using 713 people from 296 Icelandic families with multiple generations represented in each family [6]. Using 1,068 microsatellite markers throughout the genome, several linkage analyses were conducted that first examined all individuals, then only people with early onset disease, and then men and women separately. None of these analyses resulted in a significant LOD score, but the most promising region occurred on chromosome 13 at 13q12-13 (LOD score = 2.86). The refined chromosomal region of interest was 7.6 Mb (7.6 million DNA bases) in size and contained 40 known genes.

To identify which gene in this region may contribute to MI, a follow-up association study was conducted using 120 microsatellite markers in this region and 802 unrelated people with MI and 837 healthy controls. The haplotype with the strongest association to MI contained two genes, *ALOX5AP* and a gene of unknown function. Because *ALOX5AP* appeared to be a good candidate gene based on information about its function, the DNA sequence for much of the gene was determined in 93 affected people and 93 controls. Some of the SNPs identified by the DNA sequencing efforts were then studied in larger numbers of people. One haplotype from markers in the *ALOX5AP* gene, called HapA, was found to be associated with an increased risk of MI [6].

The discovery that HapA was associated with an increased risk for stroke in a separate population [4] further increased the likelihood that this is a true association. The gene *ALOX5AP* encodes the protein 5-lipoxygenase–activating protein (FLAP). A competitive inhibitor of FLAP was tested in a clinical population with a history of MI and with a risky genetic profile for MI (HapA genotype and other genotypes that subsequent studies showed were associated with risk for MI) to test the hypothesis that blocking the effect of FLAP could decrease the levels of multiple biomarkers for MI risk. The FLAP inhibitor tested appears to lower biomarkers associated with arterial inflammation such as leukotriene B4, myeloperoxidase, C reactive protein (CRP), and serum amyloid A [31]. A clinical study to see if administration of this FLAP inhibitor impacts clinical outcomes for patients at risk for MI is under development [31].

10.2.3.2 Development of a Diagnostic to Detect a Diabetes Risk Genotype

Identification of a susceptibility gene for type 2 diabetes represents another example of the utility of linkage and association methods for identifying genes associated with complex diseases. Nearly 7% of the population in the United States is currently affected by diabetes, which costs ~$100 billion per year in direct health care costs. Experts predict that by the year 2025, approximately 300 million people throughout the world will have diabetes [32]. Most patients with diabetes have adult-onset diabetes, or type 2 diabetes, which develops in adulthood because the body can no longer produce sufficient amounts of insulin or because the body can no longer use insulin properly.

To identify genes that influence development of type 2 diabetes, deCODE selected people with diabetes from more than 2,400 diabetics in the Icelandic population. In the first phase of the study, a genome-wide linkage analysis consisting of 906 microsatellite markers was performed on 763 patients (individuals previously diagnosed with diabetes or patients with impaired fasting glucose were included) and 764 close relatives. The best evidence for linkage was a LOD score of 1.84 on chromosome 5q when all type 2 diabetics were considered. However, when the diabetic patients were stratified into obese (BMI $\geq$ 30 kg/m^2) and nonobese (BMI < 30) groups, the LOD score increased to 2.81 in the nonobese diabetics. When additional markers were genotyped in this region, the LOD score became significant (3.64, $P = 2.12 \times 10^{-5}$) and was centered on the 5q34-q35.2 region. Other regions showing suggestive evidence of linkage included chromosomes 6q (LOD score of 1.8), 10q (LOD = 1.69), and 12q (LOD = 1.44) [12].

The genomic region on chromosome 10q was of interest for further study because this region had previously been linked to type 2 diabetes in Mexican Americans [33]. The next phase of the investigation used an association approach in which 228 microsatellite markers were genotyped across a 10.5-Mb region on chromosome 10q [11]. All markers were assayed in 1,185 Icelandic individuals with type 2 diabetes and 931 unrelated controls. Several variants (alleles) of a microsatellite marker (DG10S478) were associated with an increased risk of type 2 diabetes. The results were subsequently replicated in a Danish female cohort consisting of 228 type 2 diabetics and 539 controls and in a European-American cohort of 361 diabetics and 530 controls [11]. The DG10S478 marker is located in the transcription factor 7–like 2 gene (TCF7L2), which assists in the expression of other genes that function in cell proliferation and differentiation. Although recent studies support the role of the TCF7L2 gene in susceptibility to type 2 diabetes in large cohorts of U.S. women and men [34, 35], the exact mechanisms by which this gene contributes to disease pathogenesis have yet to be determined.

On April 15, 2007, deCODE announced that it now provides a trademarked test, deCODE T2, to detect the high-risk "T" allele of SNP rs7903146 in the TCF7L2 gene [36]. A person with two copies (homozygous carrier) of this variant is predicted to be at increased risk (1.8 times the average risk) for developing type 2 diabetes [34]. The test is being marketed to physicians as a method to identify prediabetic patients at especially high risk for developing diabetes who may derive the greatest benefit from aggressive treatment (e.g., lifestyle changes, drug therapy) [36].

10.3 Windber Research Institute

Windber Research Institute hosts a tissue and data repository that can store biological, experimental, and clinical data related to breast disease and breast cancer. Ongoing work is expanding the repository to store these data types for other diseases as well. As of January 2008, the tissue repository contained 50,282 biological specimens stored on site. Specimens are primarily blood and blood by-products (42,414 samples) or tissue (7,868 samples), contributed by 8,260 individuals. In this section we highlight clinical data collection and biorepository development, genomic studies, data analysis algorithm development, and the knowledge inferred by these studies. Figure 10.2 places the WRI sections discussed in this chapter into the context of other chapters.

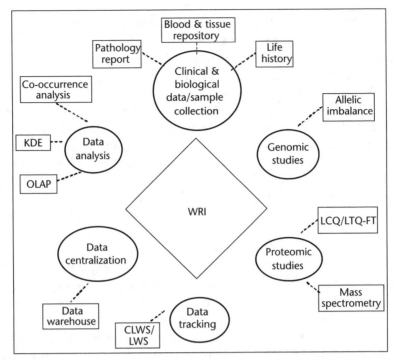

Figure 10.2 Specific aspects of WRI, in particular, their clinical data, biological data and sample collection, data warehouse, data tracking system, data analysis methods, and experimental genomic and proteomic studies, are placed into the context of the book's chapters.

10.3.1 Clinical Data Collection and Storage

10.3.1.1 The Clinical Breast Care Project

The Clinical Breast Care Project, which is focused on breast disease and breast cancer research, is a collaborative program between WRI and Walter Reed Army Medical Center (WRAMC). As of January 2008, the CBCP had 4,028 patients enrolled. The majority of patients come from the Breast Care Center at WRAMC, but patients are also recruited from other civilian (Anne Arundel Medical Center, Annapolis, Maryland, and Joyce Murtha Breast Care Center of Windber Medical Center, Windber, Pennsylvania) and military (Malcolm Grow, Andrews Air Force Base, Maryland, and Landstuhl, Kichberg, Germany) institutions.

Because patients are recruited at breast care centers at these facilities, they tend to be at higher risk for breast cancer than the general population. Currently there are 941 patients with invasive or in situ breast cancer, 96 patients with atypical disease, 1,240 patients with benign breast disease, and 1,676 patients who have not had a breast biopsy recruited through the CBCP. Each patient who is enrolled in the CBCP completes a comprehensive lifestyle questionnaire and in the case of a biopsy or other breast-related surgery, a pathology checklist is completed.

10.3.1.2 Integrative Cardiac and Metabolic Health Program

In addition to the CBCP, WRI also has established the Integrative Cardiac and Metabolic Health Program (ICMHP) in collaboration with the Integrative Cardiac

Health Program at WRAMC and the Dr. Dean Ornish Program for Reversing Heart Disease at Windber Medical Center. To be eligible to participate in this program, patients must have either a diagnosis of coronary artery disease or two or more risk factors for heart disease. Currently more than 290 patients have been recruited into the ICMHP research protocols.

As part of the Ornish program, participants make comprehensive lifestyle changes designed to successfully manage heart disease without relying on lipid-lowering drugs or surgical procedures. The program lasts for an entire year and is divided into two parts. The first part is an intensive 12-week intervention during which participants learn how to effectively change their lifestyles. Once the first part of the program is complete, the participants transition to the second phase, where they have less interaction with program staff but are still expected to meet the program guidelines.

Extensive data are collected from participants enrolled in the lifestyle change program at three examinations: baseline, after 3 months, and at the conclusion of the program (1 year). Interviews are conducted with participants to collect information on demographic factors such as age, ethnicity, gender, cardiovascular history, and medication use. A thorough physical examination includes height and weight measurements to calculate BMI, a graded exercise test to assess cardiovascular fitness, blood lipid profiles, systolic and diastolic blood pressure, and psychological screening to evaluate mental health. In addition, each participant is asked to keep a weekly Personal Awareness Log, which includes daily documentation of diet, exercise frequency and duration, stress management frequency and duration, and group attendance, to collect information on their adherence to the guidelines of the lifestyle change program. Currently, 219 ICMHP participants have completed the 1-year program.

10.3.2 Data Tracking

In Chapter 7, three approaches for establishing a data tracking system were discussed. WRI opted for the hybrid approach: off-the-shelf software, purchased from Cimarron Software, to track laboratory data from microarray, genotyping, and proteomics platforms and codevelopment with Cimarron Software, of a module to track clinical data and tissue banking activity. In the past couple of years, WRI witnessed the dynamic nature of biomedical informatics research as several experimental platforms evolved or were phased out. This posed serious challenges to the maintenance of the laboratory data tracking system that could effectively support all the data platforms.

The clinical data collection and tissue banking activities are tracked by a module called CLWS (Clinical Laboratory Workflow System) codeveloped with Cimarron Software. A screenshot of the CLWS is shown in Chapter 7. Because this data tracking system was codeveloped by WRI, the institute could place multiple quality control measures on clinical data tracking including data collection through nurse interviews (core questionnaire) or directly by a pathologist (pathology checklist), double data entry into the database, and the planned implementation of a QA metric to flag suspicious entries. Another application, the QA Issue Tracking System (QAIT), has been developed to facilitate communication among research and clinical data handlers to resolve QA problems in clinical data.

10.3.3 Data Centralization

WRI opted to develop a hybrid data warehouse for centralization of the internally generated and the public data needed in data analysis [37]. The details of this DW are discussed in Chapter 8. Currently, WRI is furthering the development of the clinical component of the data warehouse with a modular data model that enables multiple clinical projects to be readily supported.

10.3.4 Genomic and Proteomic Studies

10.3.4.1 Allelic Imbalance to Characterize Genomic Instability

Allelic imbalance (AI) studies examine patterns of changes to the physical structure of the chromosomes. This technique has been used at WRI to characterize genomic alterations in breast disease and cancer.

AI in Breast Disease
Progression of breast cancer has long been viewed as a nonobligatory sequence of changes in tissue histology from normal epithelium to a malignant tumor. During the process of breast cancer development, genetic changes are thought to accumulate in a random fashion, but little is known about the timing of when these critical mutations occur and how such genetic changes can influence progression of the disease.

To investigate the timing of critical genetic changes in human breast disease, patterns of AI have been examined in tissue samples that represent various stages along the continuum of breast cancer development to study the evolution of genomic instability. The samples were first subjected to laser microdissection to separate the diseased cells from all of the surrounding normal tissues. The DNA from these cells was then isolated and 52 genetic markers known as microsatellites, which represent 26 chromosomal regions throughout the genome, were assayed to assess patterns of AI.

This study showed that preinvasive ductal carcinoma in situ (DCIS) lesions contain levels of genomic instability that are very similar to that of advanced invasive tumors, suggesting that the biology of a developing cancer may already be predetermined by the in situ stage. Conversely, levels of AI in atypical ductal hyperplasia (ADH) lesions are similar to those in disease-free tissues, which may be why patients with ADH who receive prompt treatment usually have a good prognosis [38].

AI in Breast Cancer
An important problem in treating patients with breast cancer is trying to determine which patients will respond to treatment and which patients will not respond well. One way is to stratify breast cancer patients into two groups: those who are expected to have a favorable outcome and those who likely will have a less favorable outcome (such as disease recurrence or premature death). The structural characteristics of the cancer cells that can be seen by a pathologist can be used for patient

stratification. Currently, three pathological groupings of tumors are used based on the characteristics of the tissue histology. Patients who will likely do well have well-differentiated tumors, patients predicted to have an unfavorable outcome have poorly differentiated tumors, but there is a third group with intermediate-grade tumors whose prognosis is difficult to predict.

To determine whether molecular profiles can discriminate breast disease by pathological grade, patterns and levels of AI were examined in 185 laser-microdissected specimens representing well-differentiated (grade 1; $n = 55$), moderately differentiated (grade 2; $n = 71$), and poorly differentiated (grade 3; $n = 59$) breast tumors. Overall levels of AI were significantly higher in grade 3 compared to grade 1 tumors ($P < 0.05$) and tumors classified as grade 1 or grade 3 showed distinct genetic profiles. This study showed that genetic information could accurately categorize approximately 70% of the tumors into high- or low-grade groups and suggests that many of the intermediate-grade tumors may actually represent extremes of the well-differentiated and poorly differentiated groups. Thus, molecular signatures of breast tumors may be useful for more accurate characterization of invasive breast cancer, which has the potential to improve treatment in those patients where defining the best treatment approach has been difficult [39].

AI in Metastases

Metastatic breast cancer is usually an aggressive disease in which a substantial number of patients experience recurrence of cancer and thus tend to have poor outcomes. To better understand important molecular mechanisms that control metastasis, levels and patterns of AI were assessed between primary breast tumors and metastatic tumors, which were descended from the primary tumors and were now growing in the axillary lymph nodes. Higher overall levels of chromosomal changes in the primary tumors compared to the metastatic lymph node tumors suggest that spread of metastatic cells to the lymph nodes can occur early in carcinogenesis, occurring before significant levels of AI accumulate in the primary tumor [40]. By applying phylogenetic analysis methods to the genomic data, researchers showed that metastases in the axillary lymph nodes can be genetically quite different from each other, suggesting that these metastases are derived from progenitor cells that independently colonized the axillary nodes [41]. Some of these progenitor cells appeared to acquire metastatic potential early in the disease process and formed metastases with relatively few genomic changes. However, some of the other metastases evolved late in tumorigenesis and harbored many chromosomal alterations present in the primary tumor. The extent of genetic differences among metastatic tumors may influence how these tumors behave and respond to treatment. The ability to quantify these differences thus may be helpful in improving the treatment of patients with metastatic breast cancer.

10.3.4.2 Proteomic Analysis of Cardiovascular Risk Factor Modification

The genomic and proteomic efforts in the ICMHP are focusing on understanding the early development of cardiovascular disease at a molecular level and the identification of markers associated with clinical improvement of cardiovascular disease during intensive lifestyle changes. Although previous research has shown that changes in diet and exercise can have positive health effects in patients with coronary heart disease (CHD), little is known about the molecular events associated with changes in traditional risk factors during lifestyle interventions for reversing CHD. Researchers in the ICMHP are attempting to characterize changes in plasma proteins that are associated with improved cardiovascular risk factor profiles using a high-performance LC/LTQ-FT mass spectrometer.

To date, plasma samples ($n = 30$) collected at three time points throughout the yearlong lifestyle change program have been analyzed from 10 subjects by immunodepletion to remove the 12 most abundant plasma proteins. The samples were then digested with trypsin, separated on a reverse-phase column by online liquid chromatography, and analyzed on an LTQ-FT mass spectrometer equipped with a nanospray source. Preliminary analysis detected more than 3,500 peptide features for each data set and several hundred peptide features with a twofold (+2) difference in expression ($P < 0.05$) between the time points. Further analysis of these data sets will focus on quantifying differences in protein expression throughout the program in a larger cohort of patients and examining protein expression in a matched control population not participating in the lifestyle change program.

10.3.5 Data Analysis, Data Mining, and Data Visualization

10.3.5.1   Knowledge Development Environment

Using the Knowledge Development Environment (KDE) of InforSense Ltd., a biomedical informatics portal was jointly developed by WRI and InforSense. This portal runs off of the WRI data repository to enable physicians and scientists to explore (i.e., data mine, analyze, visualize) the data repository hosted by WRI. These tools have already been detailed in Chapters 8 and 9, and are mentioned briefly in this chapter as an example of tool development for translational research at WRI. The reader is directed to Chapters 8 and 9 to learn more about these tools.

10.3.5.2   Pathology Co-Occurrence Analysis

Access to the well-documented data set of CBCP pathology reports, in which the review and documentation of all samples uses a consistent and highly expanded classification scheme [37], has enabled researchers at WRI to explore patterns in breast cancer/breast disease pathology in an unprecedented manner. Visual analysis of breast disease pathology slides had already shown that invasive breast cancer often co-occurs with many other breast diseases as illustrated in Figure 10.3.

The co-occurrence project was initiated to discover and quantify patterns in pathology co-occurrence with the hope that these patterns could guide experiments into the development of breast cancer and aid in the classification of invasive or in situ cancer. Development of new algorithms and utilization of commercial software systems enabled this quantitative search. Multiple methods identified co-occurrence patterns that pointed to a difference in the presentation of low-grade (DCIS noncomedo) and high-grade (DCIS comedo) malignant lesions based on menopausal status or on the presence or absence of other breast disease pathologies [42, 43].

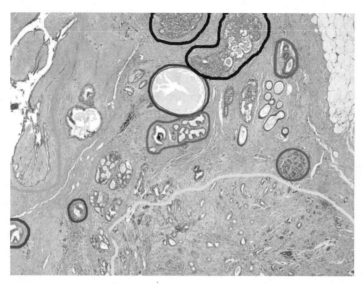

H&E, 4x objective (field width 5.5 mm)

Figure 10.3 Example of multiple pathologies found in co-occurrence with invasive ductal carcinoma H&E stained FFPE slide from a breast biopsy. Circled are multiple pathologies including: invasive ductal carcinoma, ductal carcinoma in situ, atypical ductal hyperplasia, florid ductal hyperplasia, a papilloma, columnar cell change with calcifications, a cyst, and a normal lobule. (*From:* [43]. © 2008 ELSEVIER. Reproduced with permission.)

One method uses a co-occurrence score (S_{DD}) derived from the Jaccard coefficient [42]. The S_{DD} score was calculated for the 2,775 unique diagnosis pairs found in the study patient population. Significance was assessed by permutation tests and the Bonferroni correction for multiple comparisons was applied. From this test we found 7 significant disease co-occurrences with in situ or invasive ductal carcinoma and 11 significant disease co-occurrences with in situ or invasive lobular carcinoma as illustrated in Table 10.1.

We applied this co-occurrence technique to examine of variations in diagnosis co-occurrence between premenopausal and postmenopausal women [42]. Meno-

Table 10.1 Primary Diagnoses

Primary Diagnosis	Co-Occurring Diagnoses				
IDC	DCIS C	DCIS NC	—	—	—
DCIS C	Microcalcs	—	—	—	—
DCIS NC	Microcalcs	ISPC	CCH	ADH	—
ILC	LCIS	—	—	—	—
LCIS	Apo. Met.	Microcalcs	Cysts	MPPs	CCH
LCIS	Scl. Aden.	Mod. IDH	DCIS NC	ADH	—

Key: IDC, infiltrating ductal carcinoma; DCIS C, ductal carcinoma in situ comedo; DCIS NC, ductal carcinoma in situ non comedo; Microcalcs, microcalcifications; ISPC, in situ papillary carcinoma; CCH, columnar cell hyperplasia; ADH, atypical ductal carcinoma; ILC, infiltrating lobular carcinoma; LCIS, lobular carcinoma in situ; Scl. Aden., sclerosing adenosis; Apo. Meta., apocrine metaplasia; MPPs, multiple peripheral papillomas; Mod. IDH, moderate intraductal hyperplasia.

pause is a known risk factor for breast cancer: 77% of breast cancers occur in women older than 50 years [44]. However, breast cancer in premenopausal women is generally more aggressive than breast cancer in postmenopausal women [45]. Consequently, it is hypothesized that patterns in pathology co-occurrence may be different in these two populations and, further, the co-occurrence analysis techniques applied to the entire CBCP patient population may identify these differences. To find variations in co-occurrence patterns between populations, the absolute difference (AD) of the dual diagnosis co-occurrence scores for pathology pairs common to the two populations was used.

The S_{DD} values with a large absolute difference between the two populations were identified and analyzed for significance with cross-tabulation analyses. Cross-tabulation analysis answers this question: In our CBCP population, do postmenopausal women with diagnosis 1 have diagnosis 2 at a greater frequency than premenopausal women with diagnosis 1? For example, the pair columnar cell hyperplasia (CCH) and invasive ductal carcinoma (IDC) cross-tabulation analysis can answer this question: In our study population, do premenopausal women with CCH have IDC at a different frequency than postmenopausal women with CCH? CCH is chosen as diagnosis 1 in this case because it is the less severe pathology. All cross-tabulation analyses are conducted in this manner, such that diagnosis 1 is always the less severe pathology than diagnosis 2. Dual diagnoses identified in the AD matrix and that are significantly different between premenopausal and postmenopausal groups by cross-tabulation analysis are tabulated in Table 10.2 [42]. A similar analysis performed on the population stratified by ethnicity, parity (carried a pregnancy to term), and BMI did not show clear differences in breast disease co-occurrence in these stratified groups.

Table 10.2   Cross-Tabulation of Identified Diagnoses in Premenopausal Versus Postmenopausal Populations

Women with Columnar Cell Hyperplasia		
	No IDC	*IDC[a]*
Premenopause (N = 40)	95% (N = 38)	5% (N = 2)
Postmenopause (N = 60)	62% (N = 37)	38% (N = 23)
Women with Florid Ductal Hyperplasia[b]		
	No DCIS C	*DCIS C[a]*
Premenopause (N = 52)	100% (N = 52)	0% (N = 0)
Postmenopause (N = 82)	84% (N = 69)	16% (N = 13)
	No IDC	*IDC[a,b]*
Premenopause (N = 52)	98% (N = 51)	2% (N = 1)
Postmenopause (N = 82)	74% (N = 61)	26% (N = 21)
Women with Multiple Peripheral Papillomas		
	No DCIS NC	*DCIS NC[a]*
Premenopause (N = 35)	88% (N = 31)	11% (N = 4)
Postmenopause (N = 46)	57% (N = 26)	43% (N = 20)

From: [42]. © 2006 IEEE. Reproduced with permission.
[a] Pearson chi-square test; $p < 0.01$.
[b] Bonferroni correction applied; $p < 0.025$ significant.

The previous analysis uses frequentist, also known as traditional, statistical methods. A Bayesian analysis also was run on the same data set. In general, Bayesian networks encode the joint probability distribution of all the variables in a domain. For this analysis the domain is breast pathology diagnoses from all WRAMC CBCP pathology reports. The Bayesian network is built using conditional probabilities inferred from the domain. These networks use conditional independence assumptions to make a tractable representation of tens to hundreds of variables. In this example, Bayesian networks are used to provide insight into the co-occurrence of breast pathology diagnoses in a graphical and intuitive manner. By inputting current knowledge into the model (i.e., a pathology diagnosis) the probability of multiple outcomes (other likely pathologies) can be calculated.

Bayesian network analysis of the pathology report data set, including grade for invasive and in situ ductal carcinomas, and menopausal status was conducted to build a network of diagnoses that can predict the simultaneous presence of other diagnoses. To build the network, the present/not present occurrences of 72 breast disease and cancer diagnoses from 1,232 pathology reports were used. The resulting network has 35 diagnosis nodes (Figure 10.4). Each arc represents a co-occurrence prediction and each node represents a diagnosis. From Figure 10.4 it is evident that menopausal status and CCH can predict the co-occurrence of DCIS grade 1 (DCIS G1). Further, evidence of DCIS G1 predicts the co-occurrence of IDC G1. CCH also can predict the co-occurrence of atypical ductal hyperplasia (ADH), which in turn can predict the co-occurrence of DCIS G2, a predictor of both IDC G1 and IDC G2. No hyperplasia pathologies are found that co-occur with DCIS G3.

In summary, both Bayesian and non-Bayesian quantitative analyses show patterns in breast disease co-occurrence and menopausal status in conjunction with in situ and invasive breast cancer. Common co-occurrence themes are seen from both analyses in relation to higher co-occurrence of noncancerous lesions (ADH, ductal hyperplasia, CCH) with low- and moderate-grade DCIS (DCIS noncomedo) compared to high-grade DCIS (DCIS comedo).

10.3.6 Outcomes Summary

To conclude this section on WRI, we link the genomic AI analysis of invasive and noninvasive breast lesions to the informatic analysis of breast pathology co-occurrence. The genomic analyses described previously [39] suggest that high-grade (grade 3) and low-grade (grade 1) lesions are distinct entities that are separable based on patterns of AI. Co-occurrence analysis shows that low- and moderate-grade DCIS co-occur with multiple breast pathologies. In contrast high-grade DCIS appears to occur without other breast pathology lesions. These different patterns in co-occurrence suggest that very different tissue microenvironments are present and support high-grade versus nonhigh-grade in situ breast cancer development. From the genetic (allelic imbalance) and informatic (pathology co-occurrence) studies a similar pattern is seen and further experiments will be designed to explore the genetic and tissue environment factors that may be driving these quite possibly different diseases: high-grade and low-grade cancer development.

We should note that these studies are not the first to observe differences between high-grade and low-grade DCIS. Breast pathology textbooks have reported patholo-

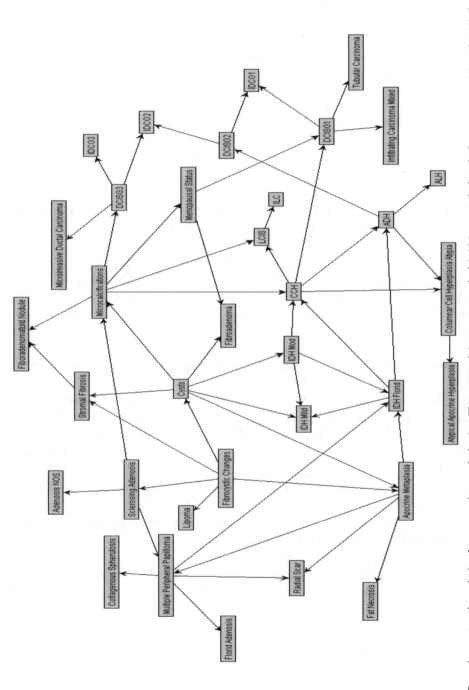

Figure 10.4 Bayesian network analysis of co-occurring pathologies. The network is constructed of 1,232 expanded pathology reports. Note that 1) the same grade IDC and DCIS co-occur with each other, 2) DCIS grades 1 and 2 co-occur with other pathologies including various hyperplasias, 3) DCIS grade 3 does not co-occur with other pathologies. Abbreviations: NOS–not otherwise specified; IDH–intraductal hyperplasia; Mod–moderate; CCH–columnar cell hyperplasia; LCIS–lobular carcinoma in situ; ILC–invasive lobular carcinoma; ADH–atypical ductal hyperplasia; ALH–atypical lobular hyperplasia; IDC–invasive ductal carcinoma; DCIS–ductal carcinoma in situ; G1–grade 1; G2–grade 2; G3–grade 3.

gies that often co-occur with DCIS in general [46]. Research by other groups has noted that allelic loss increases with histological grade [47]. Furthermore, the ability to discriminate high-grade from low-grade DCIS by genomic characterization, and the implication of separate genomic pathways for these two lesions, has previously been reported [48]. However, the expanded clinical and epidemiological data available in the WRI data repository will enable researchers at WRI to expand on the results detailed in this chapter. The challenge facing WRI researchers is taking these results to the next level: the identification of DCIS characteristics (genomic, proteomic, and tissue microenvironment) and patient characteristics (epidemiological, comorbidities, reproductive history) that predict likely recurrence or progression to invasive breast cancer.

10.4 Conclusions

Both of the case studies presented in this chapter highlight medical and multidisciplinary scientific contributions necessary to enable translational research into human disease. Because of the multiple sources of data (clinical, "omic," epidemiological, and so on) and typically large quantity of data used in translational research, the new discipline of biomedical informatics is arising to facilitate this type of research. In this chapter we detailed how clinical data collection and storage, genomic analyses, novel algorithm development, and most importantly access to large repositories of human data for analysis enabled both deCODE and WRI to make novel discoveries in human disease.

In this chapter we also have demonstrated how using data from multiple sources enables the discovery of previously unknown molecular correlates to human disease. In the case of deCODE we saw how identification of previously unknown genes led to the discovery of new drugs and new diagnostics that are making their way through clinical trials into clinical use. Without access to both human sample data (DNA), clinical data, and genealogic information, and the ability to integrate these three data sources, deCODE would not have been able to discover multiple genetic associations to complex human diseases. The data and tissue resource at WRI has enabled genomic analysis and data-mining studies that show an emerging picture of the genomic and tissue environment factors that can differentiate between high-grade and low-grade cancer. WRI now faces the challenge of translating this knowledge into a clinically useful tool.

Where this chapter looked at how biomedical informatics enabled research that could be translated into clinical use, the next chapter will look at how the clinic can motivate translational research projects.

References

[1] http://www.decode.com.

[2] Gulcher, J., and Stefansson, K., "Population Genomics: Laying the Groundwork for Genetic Disease Modeling and Targeting," *Clin. Chem. Lab. Med.*, Vol. 36, 1998, pp. 523–527.

[3]   Helgadottir, A., et al., "A Variant of the Gene Encoding Leukotriene A4 Hydrolase Confers Ethnicity-Specific Risk of Myocardial Infarction," *Nat. Genet.*, Vol. 38, 2006, pp. 68–74.

[4]   Helgadottir, A., et al., "Association Between the Gene Encoding 5-Lipoxygenase-Activating Protein and Stroke Replicated in a Scottish Population," *Am. J. Hum. Genet.*, Vol. 76, 2005, pp. 505–509.

[5]   Hakonarson, H., et al., "Profiling of Genes Expressed in Peripheral Blood Mononuclear Cells Predicts Glucocorticoid Sensitivity in Asthma Patients," *PNAS*, Vol. 102, 2005, pp. 14,789–14,794.

[6]   Helgadottir, A., et al., "The Gene Encoding 5-Lipoxygenase Activating Protein Confers Risk of Myocardial Infarction and Stroke," *Nat. Genet.*, Vol. 36, 2004, pp. 233–239.

[7]   Stacey, S. N., et al., "The BARD1 Cys557Ser Variant and Breast Cancer Risk in Iceland," *PLoS Med.*, Vol. 3, 2006, p. E217.

[8]   Amundadottir, L. T., et al., "A Common Variant Associated with Prostate Cancer in European and African Populations," *Nat. Genet.*, Vol. 38, 2006, pp. 652–658.

[9]   Stefansson, H., et al., "Association of Neuregulin 1 with Schizophrenia Confirmed in a Scottish Population," *Am. J. Hum. Genet.*, Vol. 72, 2003, pp. 83–87.

[10] Helgason, A., et al., "Refining the Impact of TCF7L2 Gene Variants on Type 2 Diabetes and Adaptive Evolution," *Nat. Genet.*, Vol. 39, 2007, pp. 218–225.

[11] Grant, S. F., et al., "Variant of Transcription Factor 7–Like 2 (TCF7L2) Gene Confers Risk of Type 2 Diabetes," *Nat. Genet.*, Vol. 38, 2006, pp. 320–323.

[12] Reynisdottir, I., et al., "Localization of a Susceptibility Gene for Type 2 Diabetes to Chromosome 5q34-Q35.2," *Am. J. Hum. Genet.*, Vol. 73, 2003, pp. 323–335.

[13] Gulcher, J., Kong, A., and Stefansson, K., "The Genealogic Approach to Human Genetics of Disease," *Cancer J.*, Vol. 7, 2001, pp. 61–68.

[14] Ott, J., *Analysis of Human Genetic Linkage,* Baltimore, MD: John Hopkins University Press, 1991.

[15] Weeks, D. E., and Lange, K., "The Affected-Pedigree-Member Method of Linkage Analysis," *Am. J. Hum. Genet.*, Vol. 42, 1988, pp. 315–326.

[16] Amos, C. I., "Robust Variance-Components Approach for Assessing Genetic Linkage in Pedigrees," *Am. J. Hum. Genet.*, Vol. 54, 1994, pp. 535–543.

[17] Chen, W., et al., "Autosomal Genome Scan for Loci Linked to Blood Pressure Levels and Trends Since Childhood: The Bogalusa Heart Study," *Hypertension*, Vol. 45, 2005, pp. 954–959.

[18] North, K. E., et al., "Linkage Analysis of Factors Underlying Insulin Resistance: Strong Heart Family Study," *Obes. Res.*, Vol. 13, 2005, pp. 1877–1884.

[19] Hauser, E. R., et al., "A Genomewide Scan for Early-Onset Coronary Artery Disease in 438 Families: The GENECARD Study," *Am. J. Hum. Genet.*, Vol. 75, 2004, pp. 436–447.

[20] Bishop, D. T., and Williamson, J. A., "The Power of Identity-by-State Methods for Linkage Analysis," *Am. J. Hum. Genet.*, Vol. 46, 1990, pp. 254–265.

[21] Holmans, P., "Asymptotic Properties of Affected-Sib-Pair Linkage Analysis," *Am. J. Hum. Genet.*, Vol. 52, 1993, pp. 362–374.

[22] Kruglyak, L., et al., "Parametric and Nonparametric Linkage Analysis: A Unified Multipoint Approach," *Am. J. Hum. Genet.*, Vol. 58, 1996, pp. 1347–1363.

[23] Kruglyak, L., and Lander, E. S., "Complete Multipoint Sib-Pair Analysis of Qualitative and Quantitative Traits," *Am. J. Hum. Genet.*, Vol. 57, 1995, pp. 439–454.

[24] Khoury, M. J., Beaty, T. H., and Cohen, B. H., *Fundamentals of Genetic Epidemiology,* New York: Oxford University Press, 1993.

[25] Lander, E. S., and Schork, N. J., "Genetic Dissection of Complex Traits," *Science*, Vol. 265, 1994, pp. 2037–2048.

[26] Stengård, J. H., et al., "Apolipoprotein E Polymorphism Predicts Death from Coronary Heart Disease in a Longitudinal Study of Elderly Finnish Men," *Circulation*, Vol. 91, 1995, pp. 265–269.

[27] Ginns, E. I., et al., "A Genome-Wide Search for Chromosomal Loci Linked to Bipolar Affec-
      tive Disorder in the Old Order Amish," *Nat. Genet.*, Vol. 12, 1996, pp. 431–435.

[28] Imperatore, G., et al., "Sib-Pair Linkage Analysis for Susceptibility Genes for Microvascular
      Complications Among Pima Indians with Type 2 Diabetes. Pima Diabetes Genes Group,"
      Diabetes, Vol. 47, 1998, pp. 821–830.

[29] Gudbjartsson, D. F., et al., "Allegro, a New Computer Program for Multipoint Linkage
      Analysis," *Nature Genetics*, Vol. 25, 2000, pp. 12–13.

[30] Gudbjartsson, D. F., et al., "Allegro Version 2," *Nature Genetics*, Vol. 37, 2005,
      pp. 1015–1016.

[31] Hakonarson, H., et al., "Effects of a 5-Lipoxygenase-Activating Protein Inhibitor on
      Biomarkers Associated with Risk of Myocardial Infarction: A Randomized Trial," *JAMA*,
      Vol. 293, 2005, pp. 2245–2256.

[32] King, H., Aubert, R. E., and Herman, W. H., "Global Burden of Diabetes, 1995–2025:
      Prevalence, Numerical Estimates, and Projections," *Diabetes Care*, Vol. 21, 1998, pp.
      1414–1431.

[33] Duggirala, R., et al., "Linkage of Type 2 Diabetes Mellitus and of Age at Onset to a Genetic
      Location on Chromosome 10q in Mexican Americans," *Am. J. Hum. Genet.*, Vol. 64, 1999,
      pp. 1127–1140.

[34] Florez, J. C., et al., "TCF7L2 Polymorphisms and Progression to Diabetes in the Diabetes
      Prevention Program," *N. Engl. J. Med.*, Vol. 355, 2006, pp. 241–250.

[35] Zhang, C., et al., "Variant of Transcription Factor 7–Like 2 (TCF7L2) Gene and the Risk of
      Type 2 Diabetes in Large Cohorts of U.S. Women and Men," *Diabetes*, Vol. 55, 2006,
      pp. 2645–2648.

[36] http://www.decodediagnostics.com/t2.php.

[37] Hu, H., et al., "Biomedical Informatics: Development of a Comprehensive Data Warehouse
      for Clinical and Genomic Breast Cancer Research," *Pharmacogenomics*, Vol. 5, 2004,
      pp. 933–941.

[38] Ellsworth, R. E., et al., "Timing of Critical Genetic Changes in Human Breast Disease,"
      Ann. Surg. Oncol., Vol. 12, 2005, pp. 1054–1060.

[39] Ellsworth, R. E., et al., "Correlation of Levels and Patterns of Genomic Instability with
      Histological Grading of Invasive Breast Tumors," *Breast Cancer Res. Treat.*, Vol. 107,
      2008, pp. 259–265.

[40] Ellsworth, R. E., et al., "Allelic Imbalance in Primary Breast Carcinomas and Metastatic
      Tumors of the Axillary Lymph Nodes," *Mol. Cancer Res.*, Vol. 3, 2005, pp. 71–77.

[41] Becker, T. E., et al., "Genomic Heritage of Axillary Lymph Node Metastases in Breast Can-
      cer Patients," *Ann. Surg. Oncol.*, 2008, 15(4): 1056–63.

[42] Maskery, S. M., et al., "Co-Occurrence Analysis for Discovery of Novel Breast Cancer
      Pathology Patterns," *IEEE Trans. on Inf. Technol. Biomed.*, Vol. 10, 2006, pp. 497–503.

[43] Maskery, S. M., et al., "A Bayesian Derived Network of Breast Pathology Co-Occurrence,"
      J. Biomed. Inform., 2008, 41(2): 242–50.

[44] *Cancer Facts and Figures 2005*, Atlanta, GA: American Cancer Society, 2005.

[45] Early Breast Cancer Trialists' Collaborative Group, "Polychemotherapy for Early Breast
      Cancer: An Overview of the Randomised Trials," *The Lancet*, Vol. 352, 1998,
      pp. 930–942.

[46] Rosen, P., *Rosen's Breast Pathology*, 2nd ed., Philadelphia, PA: Lippincott Williams and
      Wilkins, 2001.

[47] Fujii, H., et al., "Genetic Progression, Histological Grade, and Allelic Loss in Ductal Carci-
      noma *in situ* of the Breast," *Cancer Res.*, Vol. 56, 1996, pp. 5260–5265.

[48] Vos, C. B., et al., "Genetic Alterations on Chromosome 16 and 17 Are Important Features
      of Ductal Carcinoma *in situ* of the Breast and Are Associated with Histologic Type," *Br. J.
      Cancer*, Vol. 81, 1999, pp. 1410–1418.

CHAPTER 11

Clinical Examples: A Biomedical Informatics Approach

Michael N. Liebman

As stated in Chapter 1, biomedical informatics can play a key role in driving the evolution of patient care by addressing those issues that appear when a physician is faced with a patient and the need to make clinical choices that will impact the patient, the patient's quality of life, and the patient's family. Bridging the gap between clinical need and the available technologies requires being able to define a clinical problem within a biomedical informatics framework, that is, with data, analytical tools, and interpretive tools [1]. Three examples are presented in this chapter that attempt to provide this perspective: (1) the use of Her2/neu as a diagnostic for Herceptin treatment in breast cancer, (2) stratification of patients progressing through perimenopause, and (3) analysis of blood coagulation disorders including DIC.

11.1 Understanding the Role of Biomarkers and Diagnostics

The introduction of high-throughput, omics-based technologies has led to the identification and publication of more than 4,000 biomarkers but relatively few of them have potential relevance as diagnostics and even fewer as causal diagnostics [2]. It is important to clarify the differences among these concepts in light of the goal of using them to improve patient care.

A *biomarker* refers to a measurable quantity that reflects a change in state of a biological process and can range from the presence/absence/increase/decrease of a molecular entity to the presence/absence of a fever in a patient. The association of a biomarker with a specific disease process typically reflects a correlative relationship between marker and condition.

A *diagnostic* is a biomarker that more specifically describes one of several stages in the premanagement of the disease. For example, from a patient perspective, there are five major stages starting with presymptomatic detection and extending to postintervention, where diagnostics are relevant: risk detection, early detection of disease, stratification for intervention, adherence, and control [3]. A diagnostic can play a significant role in clinical decision making and typically requires FDA review and approval although many are used in an off-label manner.

Many diagnostics are viewed as potential therapeutic targets but specificity and selectivity are lacking when compared to causal diagnostics.

A *causal diagnostic* differs from a simple diagnostic in that it is directly implicated in the mechanism of the disease stage as noted earlier. A causal diagnostic can more directly be considered a potential therapeutic target with a much higher degree of confidence than can a simple diagnostic. Causal diagnostics also require FDA review and approval as noted for simple diagnostics.

11.2   Understanding the Difference Between Pathways and Networks

Pathway is a term that is conventionally used to describe the intermolecular interactions that cluster to form a biological process that appears to function as a unit. This term is used to describe processes, such as glycolysis (i.e., glycolytic pathway) and coagulation (i.e., coagulation pathway), that are used to train biochemists and molecular biologists. Note that pathways are a construct that is based on the integration of observed intermolecular relationships and physiological processes that are actually dynamic. As a result, not all interactions/components of a "pathway" may be active at the same time and under the same conditions because the pathway is only a convenient way to cluster the observations into a concerted representation, not a result of direct genetic and biological determinants.

Network is a term that describes a broader concept than pathway in that it reflects sets of interactions that may operate under different conditions and elements that span multiple, defined pathways. Therefore, network is a more general term than pathway, and pathways are examples of specific types of networks but do not comprise all possible elements and/or interactions. This distinction is critical for understanding the difference between the true causal relationship and the correlative relationship between experimental observations and the existing knowledge base, which is conventionally derived from annotation and curation of data related to pathways, not networks.

11.3   How Biomarkers/Diagnostics and Pathways/Networks Are Linked

Having defined biomarkers, diagnostics, and causal diagnostics as well as the difference between pathways and networks, it is appropriate to discuss their interrelationship before we present the clinical examples in this chapter.

It should be apparent that biomarkers can be identified in a simple pathway analysis of experimental data. To create diagnostics and causal diagnostics, however, it is necessary to extend our understanding of the molecular interactions beyond simple pathways, as they have been presented in biochemistry and molecular biology, into broader networks of interactions that function to yield physiological response. The potential that any identifiable biomarker can be subject to modulation by interceding pathways that can affect that response separates biomarkers from causal diagnostics. The expansion of the analysis to incorporate networks, beyond pathways, enhances the potential to explore the sensitivity and specificity of network nodes (e.g., enzymes or genes) as diagnostics rather than just biomarkers. The three examples discussed later in this chapter are focused on exploiting these differences to effect translational medicine and patient care through a better understanding of disease mechanisms.

Among the most critical characteristics that typical physiological systems may exhibit and which are needs that exist for accurate modeling of pathway behavior are complex, concurrent interacting pathways; deficient existing models of pathway architecture because of missing pathway components or linkages, or incorrect linkages; missing or unavailable experimental data, or inconsistent data quality; the need to develop and evaluate hypotheses about pathway linkages, sensitivity of components, and so on, with limited data; the need to evaluate the risk of secondary effects (e.g., side effects) of specific target selections prior to experimental development; and the need to identify appropriate control points to modulate physiological responses with minimal risk.

The integrated use of biomarkers and networks focuses on the ability to analyze the system-based behavior of the stated problem. A significant opportunity in biomedical informatics is that of looking beyond the conventional view of downstream analysis to also include upstream analysis: For example, when researchers observe differences in gene or protein expression levels in patients (e.g., disease versus normal), the differences in these perspectives is as follows:

- *Downstream:* What are the predictable effects of these differences? Can biomarkers predict the likelihood of these effects and can these biomarkers potentially become diagnostics? What pathways will be effected and what is the predicted impact? Can we determine critical points for intervention?
- *Upstream:* What are the predictable causes of these differences? Can biomarkers predict the observed differences and can these biomarkers potentially yield new diagnostics? Can these biomarkers potentially become *new therapeutic targets?*

As we will see in the following three clinical examples, this discrimination will be useful in better understanding both the effects of a disease or perturbed state as well as what is producing that state.

11.4   Breast Cancer

Breast cancer is a disease for which the use of mammography, ultrasound, and self-examination remain the cornerstones for early detection and observed improvement in patient survival. Treatment for this disease has been hallmarked by the drugs tamoxifen and Herceptin, although it has been recognized that treatment with tamoxifen is limited to 5 years in most patients to minimize risk of cardiovascular impact.

Herceptin's success in breast cancer treatment and its apparent, although still uncertain, specificity for the Her2/neu growth factor, has led to its evaluation in other cancers as well. The requirement for overexpression of Her2/neu for use of Herceptin appears to be obvious because studies have indicated a statistically significant improvement in survival rates in patients who overexpress this gene and are treated with Herceptin. The overall situation for breast cancer patients may be somewhat more complex, and the application of a broader, biomedical informatics perspective to this problem has generated several new research opportunities and directions.

As mentioned, overexpression of Her2/neu is presently a requirement for prescribing Herceptin in the treatment of breast cancer patients [4]. Overexpression appears to occur in only 25% of all breast cancer patients, and is viewed as a biomarker of greater aggressiveness in the tumors. Herceptin is an antibody, trastuzumab, thought to target Her2/neu, although recent reviews have questioned the mechanism of action of this drug in treating breast cancer. (Note that its potential effectiveness in this subset of patients has not been questioned.) It is notable, however, that among patients receiving Herceptin, only 40% respond positively to treatment. Thus (25% overexpressers) × (40% response rate) yields an effective treatment in approximately 10% of all breast cancer patients. This lack of perfect responsiveness in the patients overexpressing Her2/neu raises several issues [5]:

1. Some patients may receive Herceptin who will not respond. Does this impact or delay other potential treatment options?
2. Some patients may not receive Herceptin who may be potentially responsive because of the diagnostic screening test. Are they being undertreated?
3. Is there a problem with the screening process involving the Her2/neu test by either FISH or immunohistochemistry (IHC)?
4. Are adjunct markers available that can improve specificity and sensitivity?
5. Are there opportunities to identify better biomarkers for use as diagnostics that might actually be causal diagnostics?

In the Clinical Breast Care Project, as described in earlier chapters of this book, certain clinical procedures were uniquely performed, including the evaluation of Her2/neu levels by both FISH and IHC. This dual characterization revealed an enigmatic observation. In more than 25% of all patients tested by both methods, the results were not in concordance regarding overexpression of Her2/neu. In these patients, the observation further delineated that an individual could be IHC (+) and FISH (–) but never the reverse. Note that FISH effectively measures gene copy number, whereas IHC reflects the level of protein expression, two functionally related but disparate biomarkers. Although this observation may be specific to a subgroup of breast cancer patients, it is well recognized in many laboratories where both proteomic and genomic analyses are performed on the same biospecimens that there frequently is a discrepancy between the two measurements, suggesting that there might be a common control mechanism that differentiates between the two biological processes. This observed difference in measurement is therefore of clinical interest [e.g., in determining how to appropriately classify patients who are FISH (–) and IHC (+)] and of interest at the molecular level (e.g., in understanding whether there is a common mechanism supporting the differences between protein and gene expression levels).

The problem should be approached on two different levels when considering the integration of the clinical and molecular research perspectives. The current standard of care requires the clinical evaluation of Her2/neu expression levels by either FISH or IHC to determine if a patient is overexpressing this gene for treatment with Herceptin. One approach involves identifying additional biomarkers that may be used in conjunction with the accepted diagnostic to improve the specificity and sensitivity of either FISH or IHC. A successful result from this approach would require FDA approval for modification of an existing diagnostic. This analysis is outlined in Project 1 in Figure 11.1. The true clinical problem involves the response of patients to Herceptin, regardless of whether the Her2/neu test is used. To accomplish this, all patients who have received Herceptin will be evaluated in terms of their response, and samples will be analyzed independent of Her2/neu overexpression to identify potential biomarkers/diagnostics that may prove more causal, thus enhancing potential specificity and sensitivity. A successful result from this approach would require full FDA review as a new diagnostic and be a significantly more involved process than that outlined earlier (see issue 1 in previous list).

- How does the differentially expressed her2/neu gene copy number affect common pathways/networks?
- How do differentially expressed her2/neu protein levels affect common pathways/networks?
- What is the impact on networks/pathways, that is, would the signal flow through affected pathways be increased or decreased (e.g., by observed up- or downregulation)?
- Are these biomarkers or potential diagnostics?
- Would these critical sites/targets be suitable for drug development?

In summary, how do observed changes affect the cellular information flow?

As the network is formed of the intermolecular interactions, including both the observed differences in gene expression and those interactions that have been

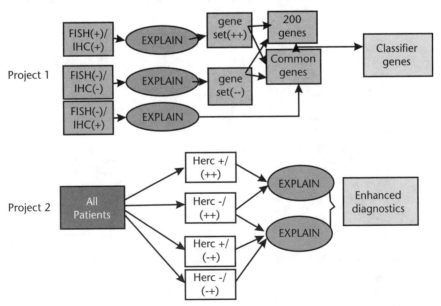

Figure 11.1   Defining the analysis of her2/neu into tactical (Project 1) and strategic (Project 2) components.

curated from the literature (by BIOBASE), it is possible to see that the processes involved in the difference between these patients bridges the conventional pathways through genes or proteins that link these pathways but may not be part of any single pathway (Figure 11.2). These linkages become a focal point for identifying new control points in the biological processes, potentially providing new insight into how complex biology is controlled by elements that have not been previously considered.

It is further critical, therefore, to be able to explore the full literature concerning this linkage point to understand what has been experimentally or theoretically predicted or observed. Such linkage to curated information from the literature is also available through the use of data and knowledge base repositories such as those provided by BIOBASE and others as outlined in Chapter 8 and in Figure 11.3, which is related to the specific example described here.

- Can coregulation of multiple genes be explained by common transcription factor (TF) activity?
- Are the regulation of gene expression and protein expression differentiable at the regulatory pathway level?
- What other genes might be impacted by common regulators?
- Can one identify networks that link potential regulators?
- Is there an observable branch point between gene and protein expression processes as noted in Her2/neu?
- Can TFs or upstream components serve as drug targets or diagnostic markers?

The questions about coregulation and the role of transcription factors in the activation of multiple pathways and/or control of specific networks of interactions has been further examined and the results displayed for the Her2/neu patients in Figure 11.4. In this figure, the common, integrated network of molecular interactions, as noted earlier in this example, is detailed in the central element of the figure, while

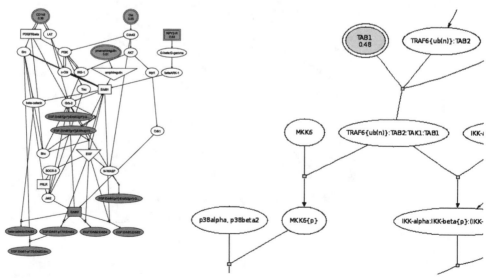

Figure 11.2 Identifying network (pathway) linking genes (shaded) by combining the curated literature with the observed list of differentially expressed genes.

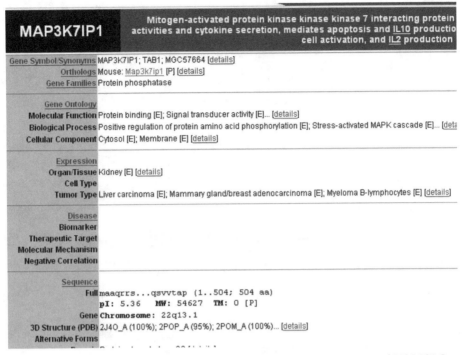

Figure 11.3   Curated data set for linking gene noted in Figure 11.2. (Courtesy of BIOBASE Corporation.)

the enlarged displays on the left and right reveal that those patients who are FISH (+) and those who are ICH (+) exhibit additional, specific patterns based on the integration of the experimentally observed gene expression data and those interactions extracted from the knowledge base.

This approach is generalizable to the identification and validation of biomarkers and provides the critical opportunity to move from the simple identification of conventional pathway biomarkers to causal diagnostics. A key tool to enable this transition/evolution is the ability to both form the network representation of information, as detailed earlier, and to also simulate the behavior of the individual nodes (i.e., genes/proteins) to identify those nodes that provide specificity and sensitivity to the overall process. The methods used for such representation and simulation are described in the two clinical examples that follow in this chapter.

11.5   Menopause

Menopause is an example of the contrast between a "state" and a "process" as outlined in Chapter 1. Although women are termed either "premenopausal" or "postmenopausal" (or sometimes "perimenopausal"), this transition is one that can extend over a 10- to 12-year time period and reflects normal development. Thus it serves as a potentially significant background to other diseases that may present in this time frame. In addition, this transition may be impacted by environment and lifestyle factors as well. It is well established that risk for a number of diseases

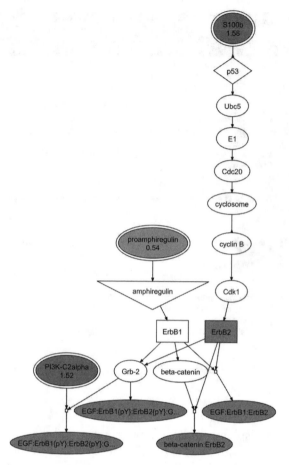

Figure 11.4 Network generated by the integration of experimental data with curated literature data, with specificity for FISH (shaded with border) and IHC (shaded without border) experiments noted.

increases significantly postmenopause and so it is of particular interest to better understand, define, classify, and analyze this complex transition.

The time frame of reproductive potential in the human female is marked by its beginning, termed *menarche,* at approximately age 12, and continues until *menopause,* at approximately age 51. This 39-year time frame is modulated individually by an approximate 30-day hormonal cycle and normal accretion of hormonal changes that occur over time along with interaction with environment and lifestyle. In addition, pregnancy, childbirth, and lactation, to name only a few natural events, produce significant impact beyond the normal aging process itself. Limited quantitative analysis of this normal progression, beyond measurement of serum hormone levels as a woman approaches menopause, has been carried out. An accurate quantitative model of this process would be invaluable in assessing an individual's risk for breast cancer, ovarian cancer, cardiovascular disease, osteoporosis, and Alzheimer's disease; in evaluating fertility and infertility issues; in determining suitability for hormone replacement therapy; and in providing insight into the interactions of these endocrine effects on other endocrine-sensitive processes, including diabetes, psychological responses, and other responses to environment and lifestyle.

The female reproductive aging process is a continuous process that begins early in a woman's life and gradually leading to its final stage, menopause. The hallmark of menopause is a major decline in ovarian function manifested by a marked decrease in estrogen production. The onset of menopause follows gradual changes in the menstrual cycle that define the so-called perimenopausal period, accompanied by gonadotropin hormone changes ([mainly an increase in follicle-stimulating hormone [FSH]). The transition from normal menstrual cycles to perimenopause and subsequently postmenopause lays the ground for disorders (breast and ovarian cancer, heart disease, osteoporosis) according to genetic and environmental factors determining individual disease predisposition. At the center of the pathogenetic mechanisms of postmenopausal diseases lies estradiol, which predisposes to certain conditions and protects from others. Understanding and modeling the hormonal changes during the normal menstrual cycle and then extending the model to include peri- and postmenopause are essential to the accurate evaluation of estrogen production and assessment of individual disease risks.

Only a few published papers focus on modeling the menstrual cycle. These studies use differential equations to describe estradiol and progesterone concentrations changing upon FSH and luteinizing hormone (LH) gonadotropin-dependent regulation. These modeling approaches attempt to establish a basis for quantitatively associating steroid hormone levels with FSH and LH concentrations, without considering in detail the molecular pathways involved in hormonal control, and without including the enzymes responsible for steroid hormone production into their models.

Estrogen production is not a simple linear process starting from cholesterol and stopping at estradiol (Figure 11.5). Instead, there are at least two positive and one negative feedback responses. The negative feedback response comes from estradiol-dependent inhibition of FSH actions, when estradiol levels are very high. The two positive feedback loops involve estradiol (which promotes its own production as well as progesterone's production when present in low to moderate amounts), and progesterone, which upregulates its own concentration (Figure 11.6).

The number of ovarian premature follicles is fixed at birth and gradually decreases each time follicles mature and release oocytes. At perimenopause, the follicular number has decreased substantially, and those present respond poorly to FSH and LH, resulting in cycle irregularity and erratic ovulation. There is a gradual decrease in progesterone and estrogen, but hormone fluctuations are common. This period can last from 3 to 10 years before menopause. Irregular menstrual cycles are the most common first sign of perimenopause, along with increasing levels of FSH. As the number of follicles keeps decreasing, estrogen production continues to fall. At some point, the estrogen-based feedback mechanisms associated with LH secretion are disrupted, leading to nonovulatory cycles. At the onset of menopause, when ovulation ceases entirely, LH starts rising again.

Menopause is due mainly to declining ovarian function, as the pool of primordial follicles is exhausted. The feedback control mechanisms of the hypothalamic-pituitary-ovarian axis are disrupted, leading to increased levels of FSH, but with unchanged levels of hypothalamic GnRH. Estradiol and progesterone production is sharply reduced due to cessation of the menstrual cycle and mature follicular

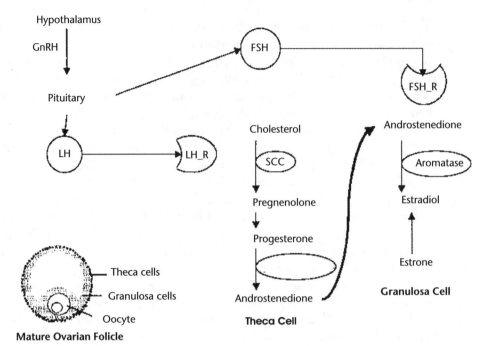

Figure 11.5   The mature ovarian follicle contains the two cell types responsible for estradiol and progesterone production. Theca cells produce progesterone and androgens. Androstenedione is retrieved by granulosa cells and converted to estradiol. The enzymes responsible for these processes are shown inside ovals. Theca cells express LH receptors (LH_R) and respond to LH released by the pituitary gland. Similarly, granulosa cells have receptors (FSH_R) for the pituitary hormone FSH. FSH and LH release is regulated by the hypothalamic hormone GnRH.

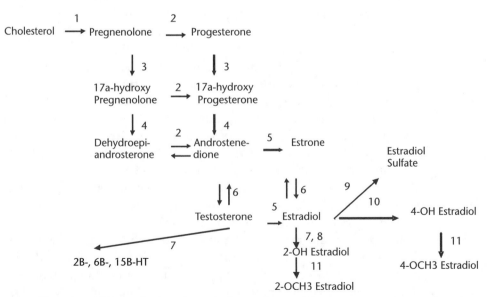

Figure 11.6   Steroid biosynthesis and metabolism pathway, with enzymes noted as numbered nodes.

development. The increased levels of FSH have no effect on estrogen production, because there is limited expression of FSH receptors in the follicles, rendering them insensitive to FSH. Ovarian steroidogenesis during menopause is restricted to androgen production. It is established that menopausal theca cells are responsive to LH and produce androstenedione and testosterone. Most of the circulating androgens come from the adrenal gland. During menopause, estrone is exclusively produced at remote sites (mainly adipose tissue) by the conversion of androstenedione. The rate of this conversion correlates to body size (amount of adipose tissue).

Our interest in the quantitative evaluation of complex biological processes such as the menstrual cycle requires us to develop flexible models that enable accurate representation of the underlying biological pathways, through incorporation of only a limited amount of data [6–8]. This ability is typically necessary in dealing with biological pathways because of the potential lack of complete information about all components and their interactions, as well as limited experimental observations, measured under a variety of conditions and of varying potential quality. Stochastic activity networks, a stochastic extension of Petri nets, are appropriate for modeling such processes that can be viewed as discrete-event systems of probabilistic nature (Figure 11.7). In this study, stochastic activity networks (SANs) have been implemented using the UltraSan/MOBIUS software environment, which allows for representation and modeling of biological pathways that can be either simulated or solved analytically. The user's manual and information about how to retrieve the software are available at http://www.mobius.uiuc.edu. We have previously evalu-

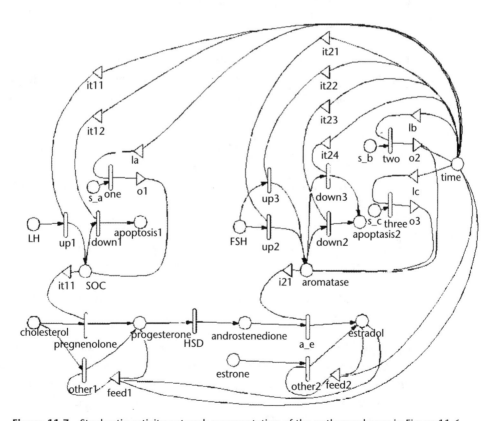

Figure 11.7 Stochastic activity network representation of the pathway shown in Figure 11.6.

ated the use and sensitivity of this approach in studying the behavior of normal and abnormal coagulation processes.

UltraSan/MOBIUS was originally developed as a tool for model-based performance and dependability evaluation of computer and communication systems, and was later used for modeling purposes in biology and biomedical research. The UltraSan/MOBIUS environment contains five process elements: places, activities, gates, arcs, and tokens (see Figure 11.7). Places appear graphically as circles and represent the state of the modeled system. In terms of biological pathway modeling, places correspond to molecular species such as enzymes and hormones. Places contain tokens that correspond to numbers of molecules. The number of tokens defines the marking of the place, which is always a discrete number. Activities (hollow ovals) represent actions of the modeled system that take a nondeterministic amount of time to complete. The duration of the activities is controlled by a probability distribution function, which can depend on place markings. The activities allow the flow of tokens from places that are connected at their left side, to places connected to the right. Gates (triangles) are distinguished in input and output gates that include predicates and functions. In particular, input predicates define the conditions on which the activities are enabled, and the functions of both gate types determine the marking changes occurring in places connected to activities, after these activities are completed. Arcs are used to connect the components to one another in an orderly fashion.

As a stochastic activity network executes, it undergoes state (marking) changes according to a marking change algorithm. The steps for implementing this algorithm are as follows:

- The predicates of the input gates and the markings of the places are examined.
- Activities are enabled if the predicates of the connected input gates are true, and only when there is at least one token to each of the incoming connected places.
- These conditions should be true throughout the duration of the activity. The order of priority with which the activities are enabled and executed depends on their probability distribution functions.
- After activity completion, the connected input places have their markings decremented.
- All input gate functions are executed.
- All connected output places have their marking incremented.
- The functions of the connected output gates are executed.

In the UltraSan/MOBIUS environment, the user monitors certain important parameters of the modeled system (such as hormone concentrations or enzymatic activity) by declaring reward variables, which can relate to place markings or activity durations. During analytical solution or simulation of the network, UltraSan/MOBIUS estimates and provides the mean and variance for each reward variable over a period of time. Figure 11.8 shows experimental observations of estradiol and progesterone production using the stochastic model shown in Figure 11.7, and Figure 11.9 shows simulated output.

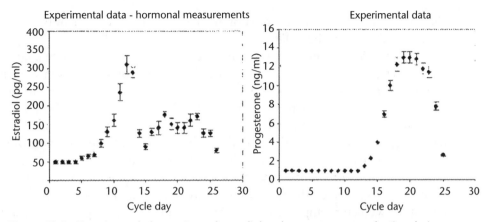

Figure 11.8   Experimental observations of estradiol and progesterone production during an average menstrual cycle (input into the stochastic model shown in Figure 11.7).

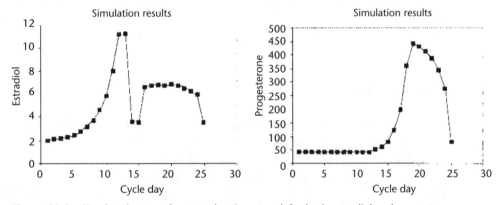

Figure 11.9   Simulated output from stochastic network for both estradiol and progesterone over a menstrual cycle.

A detailed description of the modeling process involved in this study has been presented elsewhere, but the key components are discussed next as are the future directions that this modeling approach uniquely enables.

Modeling a normal menstrual cycle, as outlined earlier, shows the robustness of the system's ability to incorporate system-level data (e.g., hormone levels as input and output of the total system) without relying on experimentally determined kinetic data that may be of variable quality and measured under varying conditions.

The complex network (pathway) was constructed in segments and recombined to create the full steroid metabolism pathway, showing the ability to segment complex processes, modeling the segments at varying levels of resolution based on available experimental data and integrating the results to provide a robust model.

To represent the complete biological process being modeled, which extends beyond the 30-day menstrual cycle to a period of up to 12 years, requires extending the modeling approach to incorporate stochastic changes during that time period in the simulation that retain memory of the previous menstrual cycle when modeling the next cycle. This is critical to support the combination of phenotypic data with genotypic data as outlined later.

The temporal simulation of the perimenopause transition can be characterized using a set of parameters that treats estradiol production as a biological signal and uses signal processing methods to analyze the long-term variation in this process.

Genotypic analysis generates profiles of SNPs, as outlined in Figure 11.10 for each enzyme reaction, although very few of these polymorphisms occur with significant frequency in the general population. This impact of these genotypic differences can be simulated and compared to the normal variation as outlined in earlier.

Stratification of women based on their genotypic makeup can be compared with stratifications based on their temporal behavior and variations to develop a classification for women to improve the determination of postmenopausal disease risk for these subclasses. It is hoped that the use of this classification will improve clinical decision making about symptomatic treatment versus disease risk (e.g., breast cancer or cardiovascular disease risk with hormone replacement therapy) by supporting the development of enhanced risk–benefit analyses at a level that is not completely individualized but is stratified within the patient subclasses. This stratification can be extended to examine the risk of comorbidities and to refine clinical decision making about treatments for comorbid conditions.

11.6 Coagulation/DIC

Many coagulation-based disorders exist beyond the conventional hemophilias, for example, disseminated vascular coagulopathy (DIC), that present significant health risks and are poorly understood at a mechanistic or molecular level. Even the well-characterized hemophilias present a challenge because of the range of severity that they present and the variation in treatment and response from individual to individual. There have been many studies of the kinetics of the underlying processes

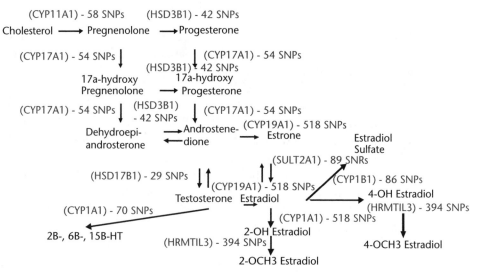

Figure 11.10 Superposition of literature observed SNPs for each enzyme represented in the pathway of Figure 11.6.

in coagulation, including both the extrinsic and intrinsic pathways, and the potential to utilize the broad base of experimental data to refine modeling approaches and extend them to clinically novel areas such as DIC presents both an opportunity and a challenge.

The basic procedure described in our previous studies with the trypsin system was used for modeling blood coagulation [9]. The system to be modeled needs to first be described in terms of interactions and stoichiometry, and then experimental kinetic observations are required to refine the initial model to a final working model. The first step in applying this procedure required the delineation of the process from vascular injury through clot formation. Extrinsic blood coagulation is initiated by vascular injury, which exposes tissue factor to the bloodstream. This exposure results in activation of the extrinsic pathway, which is shown as the bold set of reactions in Figure 11.11. Once thrombin is produced by the initial cascade of zymogen activation reactions, it then participates in many feedback reactions, including activation of the intrinsic pathway, which can supplement the extrinsic pathway (Figure 11.12). The extrinsic and intrinsic pathways cooperate to produce cross-linked fibrin (i.e., the blood clot) from fibrin, thus effecting repair of the injury.

The initial SAN representation of the coagulation system is presented in Figure 11.13 [10]. The figure shows five pathway segments that combine to yield the representation of the entire system. The segments include (1) initiation, (2) Factor VIII–Factor IX complex formation, (3) Factor V–Factor X complex formation, (4)

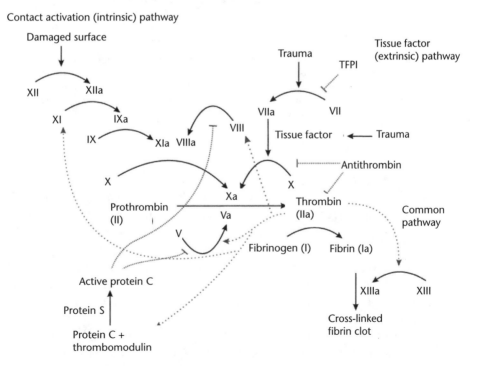

Figure 11.11 Blood coagulation cascade, showing intrinsic and extrinsic pathways. (Courtesy of Wikipedia.)

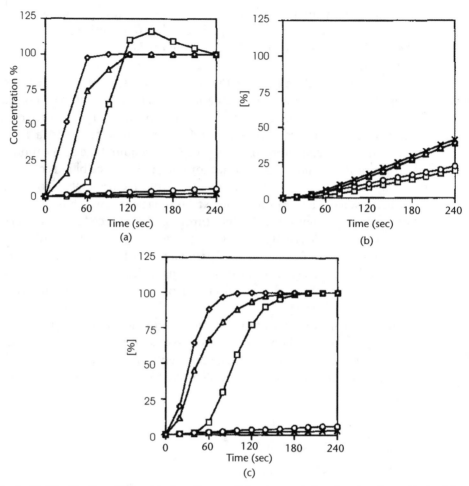

Figure 11.12 Kinetics of the extrinsic pathway of blood coagulation showing Factor Va (—Q-), Factor VIIIa (-A-), factor IXa (-O), factor Xa (- x -), and thrombin (—_i) versus time with (a) the experimental kinetics 122, (b) the initial SAN model kinetics, and (c) the final SAN model kinetics. Experimental values of thrombin that are greater than 100% in (a) represent the superactive intermediate meizothrombin, and were not modeled in (b) or (c).

clot formation, and (5) the intrinsic pathway. Each zymogen, enzyme, and complex is represented by a distinct place. These places are connected to activities by arcs, representing the reactions and stoichiometry of the coagulation system as presented in Figure 11.11. For example, the representation presented shows that tissue factor and Factor VII interact to form a 1:1 complex. Once the complex is formed, Factor VII is activated to Factor VIIa. This activated complex can then activate Factor IX or Factor X as represented in Figure 11.11, respectively. Thus, each of the reactions present in Figure 11.11 has a corresponding schematic representation in one of the segments of Figure 11.13.

One of the key features of the UltraSan tool is the potential to construct a composed model from individual SANs. The model developed for coagulation provides an example of this process. Five separate SANs were created to simplify the overall representation and to readily isolate the SAN representing the intrinsic pathway.

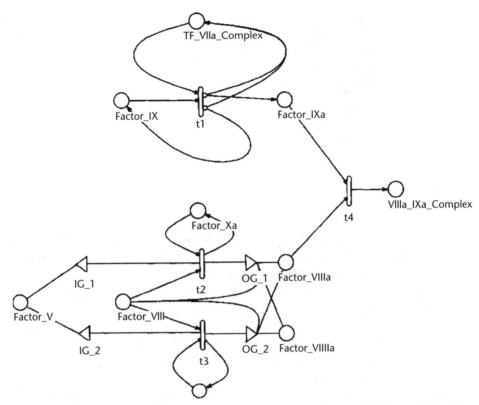

Figure 11.13   Final representations of the VIIIa_IXa_Binding, Va_Xa_Binding, and Clot_Formation SANs, which produce the dynamic working UltraSan model of the blood coagulation system producing the simulation results presented.

The presence of multiple feedback reactions and several enzymes, each activating multiple reactions, makes the representation of the complete extrinsic pathway difficult to develop as a single system, particularly since model completion requires iterative model refinements. The composed model for coagulation incorporates the five SANs, which represent the subsegments of the pathway constructed such that at least one common place exists for overlap of the joined SAN pairs. These common places are necessary to complete the composed model of coagulation and are presented in Table 11.1.

Completion of a competent model for normal blood coagulation enables its use for studying various natural single-site mutations to provide information on how the system responds upon incorporation of these changes. The most prevalent inherited bleeding abnormalities of the coagulation system are hemophilia A and B, caused by X-linked, recessive, genetic defects in Factors VIII and IX, respectively. The primary clinical observations in these diseases include prolonged or spontaneous bleeding, and depend on the severity of the respective disease, that is, on the expression level of the defective gene.

These two distinct genetic diseases provide a logical test for evaluating the sensitivity of our coagulation model for disease modeling because both involve perturbation to factors that are key components of our model. Hemophilia A simulations are presented in Figure 11.14, in which three graphs show the results

Table 11.1 Common Places for Each of the Five SANs of the Coagulation Composed Model

Common Places
Factor IX
Factor_ IXa
Factor XI
Thrombin
Factor_ V
Factor Vilna
Factor_ Xa
TF_VIIa Complex
VIIIa_IXa_Complex
Va_Xa Complex

The subnets are numbered as follows: (1) intrinsic, (2) VIIIa_ IXa_Binding, (3) Va_Xa_Binding, (4) Clot_ Formation, and (5) initiation.

of simulations of mild (25% Factor VIII activity), moderate (3% Factor VIII activity), and severe (1% Factor VIII activity) hemophilia A. The deviation from normal levels of factor VIII is due to mutation or nonexpression and does not contribute to clot formation. The simulation under these separate conditions show that the varying degrees of severity impact coagulation by altering the resulting thrombin curve, which is a directly proportional time course, while moderate and severe conditions also significantly limit total production.

An analogous study was performed with the factor IX defect hemophilia B. The results of this study are presented in Figure 11.15 and show that when the amount of useful factor IX is decreased by 50%, the thrombin activation curve shows a similar delay in clot formation to the results presented for mild hemophilia A, but also with a limiting thrombin production level to the rate of clot formation. As the severity of the disease increases (i.e., as Factor VIII decreases), the amount of thrombin generated decreases in the amount formed, and the lag in time required to achieve a specific level increases dramatically. Thus, mild hemophilia A only shifts the time course, whereas moderate and severe conditions also significantly limit total production.

Disseminated intravascular coagulinopathy (DIC) is a condition that presents a significant clinical challenge in that the patient is both producing too much clot as well as in a high state of clot lysis (i.e., effective imbalance in homeostasis). This condition is frequently observed upon significant blood loss due to trauma or surgery, but curiously its occurrence is also associated with a much wider range of comorbidities ranging from septicemia to cancer to infection. The patient is managed with difficulty because of the contraindications against using either pro- or anticoagulants in this unstable condition. Patients are often treated with a "watch and wait" follow-up but the condition can be serious.

Although significant loss of blood volume and resulting potential changes in coagulation factor concentrations are viewed as the primary cause of DIC, it is notable that it occurs in patients who do not experience such loss of blood volume. It has been suggested that a mutation in Factor VII may be a cause for this condition and to evaluate this potential, the network was used to simulate the impact of Factor VII mutations (Figure 11.16).

It is apparent, from these simulations that alterations/mutations in Factor VII alone are not sufficient to produce the observed condition of DIC. Studies are under way to utilize the combined network representation of both the coagulation and

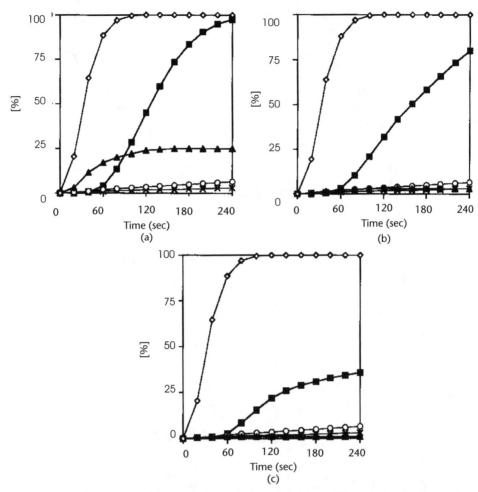

Figure 11.14   UltraSan/MOBIUS model simulation of the three different classifications of hemophilia A: (a) mild, (b) moderate, and (c) severe. The simulations show Factor Va (-O-), Factor VIIIa (-A-), Factor IXa (-C -), Factor Xa (- x), and thrombin (-E-) versus simulation time.

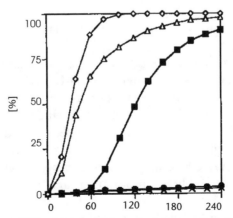

Figure 11.15   UltraSan/MOBIUS model simulation of mild hemophilia B showing Factor Va (-Q—), Factor VIIIa (Factor IXa (O), Factor Xa (- x), and thrombin (- ❑ -) versus simulation time.

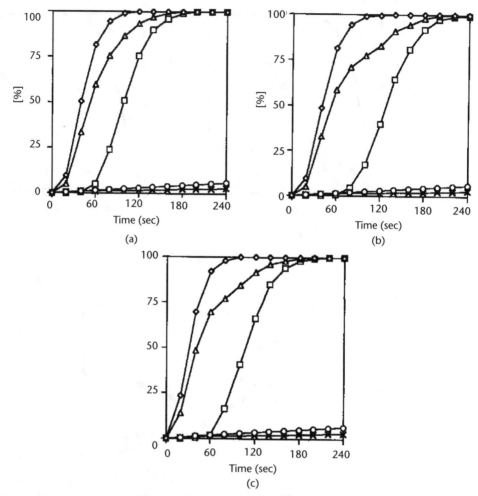

Figure 11.16 Results of sensitivity experiments for Factor VII. (a) 25% reduction in tissue factor–Factor VII binding, (b) 25% reduction in Factor VII activation, and (c) 25% reduction in both binding and activation, showing Factor Va (Factor VIIIa (-A-), Factor IXa (O-), Factor Xa (— x), and thrombin (-C) versus simulation time.

fibrinolysis pathways in an effort to evaluate the potential for a two-mutation condition.

The working hypothesis is that coupled mutations in these two pathways may place an individual at significant risk for DIC because it lowers the dynamic range in homeostasis that is critical to support the interactions between coagulation and fibrinolysis that normally occur. In such a patient, small perturbations could easily exceed the capacity of the system to compensate and thus place the patient in this unbalanced and uncontrollable state. A goal of such studies is the potential development of a diagnostic screen that could identify those patients at high risk for DIC and further help establish appropriate means for monitoring and controlling their potential risk.

This example is intended to show the potential for using such in silico approaches to evaluate multiple hypotheses that can then lead to laboratory validation and potential development of new diagnostics and therapeutics, particularly in clinically difficult problems without adequate animal models.

11.7 Conclusions

This chapter dealt with three examples of clinical problems and how the use of a biomedical informatics perspective can be used to address clinical needs and contribute to our understanding of the molecular basis of the problem. This may only involve expanding the perspective on the problem to incorporate a broader view of the patient and his or her needs (e.g., Her2/neu as a diagnostic for determination of Herceptin treatment eligibility and the differences between FISH and IHC testing) by incorporating issues of false-positive and false-negative testing, testing inconsistencies, over- and undertreatment, FDA approval issues, and so forth. More frequently it will involve reexamining the problem through the use of tools, algorithms and approaches that may have been developed in other disciplines to handle *problems of the same class*—not necessarily specifically the same problems. Many problems in this category also require analysis of the completeness and accuracy of available data to support the analytical methods. For this reason, the key factor in using biomedical informatics in simulation and analysis remains its close interaction with experimental evidence and remembering that the goal is not to replace experimental validation, but rather to help refine the definition of the next experiment and provide a mechanism for which its results can be used to refine the hypothesis.

References

[1] Langheier, J., et al., *Methods, Systems, and Computer Program Products for Developing and Using Predictive Models for Predicting a Plurality of Medical Outcomes, for Evaluating Intervention Strategies, and for Simultaneously Validating Biomarker Causality*, Patent WO/2006/072011, http://www.wipo.int/pctdb/en/wo.jsp?WO=2006/072011.

[2] Ludwig, J. A. and Weinstein, J. N., "Biomarkers in Cancer Staging, Prognosis and Treatment Selection," *Nat. Rev. Cancer*, Vol. 5, No. 11, 2005, pp. 845–856.

[3] Lester, D., and Liebman, M. N., *Coping with Cancer*, Hauppauge, NY: Nova Publishers, 2008.

[4] Moasser, M. M., "Targeting the Function of the HER2 Oncogene in Human Cancer therapeutics," *Oncogene*, Vol. 26, 2007, pp. 6577–6592.

[5] Liebman, M. N., et al., "Analysis of HER2/neu as a Diagnostic/Biomarker Using ExPlain to Examine Signaling Pathways and Transcription Factors," paper presented at ISMB, Vienna, July 2007.

[6] Reddy, V. N., et al., "Qualitative Analysis of Biochemical Reaction Systems," *Comput. Biol. Med.*, Vol. 26, 1996, pp. 9–24.

[7] Reddy, V. N., et al., "Modeling Biological Pathways. A Discrete-Event Systems Approach," *Inst. Syst. Res., ACS Symp. Ser.*, Vol. 576, 1994, pp. 221–234.

[8] Tsavachidou, D., and Liebman, M. N., "Modeling and Simulation of Pathways in Menopause," *J. Am. Medical Infor. Assoc.*, Vol. 9, No. 5, 2002, pp. 461–471.

[9] Mounts, W. M., and Liebman, M. N., "Analysis of Enzyme Pathways with Petri Nets and Stochastic Activity Nets," *Int. J. Computer Simulation*, 1996, pp. 1–7.

[10] Mounts, W. M., and Liebman, M. N., "Qualitative Modeling of Normal Blood Coagulation and Its Pathological States Using Stochastic Activity Networks," *Int. J. Biological Macromolecules,* Vol. 20, 1997, pp. 265–281.

About the Editors

Hai Hu is the deputy chief scientific officer and senior director of Biomedical Informatics of the Windber Research Institute. Before joining the institute he was group leader and senior bioinformatics scientist at AxCell Biosciences. He obtained his PhD in biophysics from the State University of New York at Buffalo, and subsequently completed postdoctoral training at the Johns Hopkins University. His educational background includes physics (BS), speech signal processing (MS), applied mathematics/statistics, and computer engineering. He has coedited two books including the current one, and published more than 30 peer-reviewed papers and book chapters on subjects including biomedical informatics, bioinformatics, proteomics, and genomics. He serves as a peer-reviewer for a number of journals including *Bioinformatics*, *Proteomics*, and *Circulation Research*. He also serves on the editorial board of two journals. In addition, he has presented at numerous national and international scientific and business conferences, serving as bioinformatics program chair or session chair in several of them. He holds a joint faculty appointment at the Uniformed Services University of the Health Sciences, and also serves as invited professor of the Shanghai Center for Bioinformation Technology.

Michael N. Liebman is the managing director of Strategic Medicine, Inc and is also a senior institute fellow at the Windber Research Institute after serving as its executive director since November, 2003. Previously, he was the director of computational biology and biomedical informatics at the Abramson Family Cancer Research Institute of the University of Pennsylvania Cancer Center since September, 2000. He served as the global head of computational genomics at Roche Pharmaceuticals, and as the director of bioinformatics and pharmacogenomics at Wyeth Pharmaceuticals. He was also the director of genomics for Vysis, Inc and the director of bioinformatics at the Amoco Technology Company. He has served on the faculty of Mount Sinai School of Medicine in Pharmacology and Physiology/Biophysics. He serves on 12 international scientific advisory boards, consults for 5 pharma/biotech companies, and has been on the economic development programs in the Philadelphia Life Sciences Sector and the State of Illinois Biotechnology Commission. He is an invited professor at the Shanghai Center for Bioinformation Technology and is currently the chair of the healthcare task force for the SMART program, and on the human health and medicinal chemistry commission of the IUPAC. His research focuses on computational models of disease progression; stressing risk detection, disease process modeling, and analysis of lifestyle interactions.

Richard J. Mural is the chief scientific officer of the Windber Research Institute (WRI). He received his BS degree in zoology from the University of Michigan and his Ph. D. from the University of Georgia. Dr. Mural has authored more than 70 papers on a range of subjects from bacteriophage molecular genetics, models of leukemogenesis, protein engineering, and bioinformatics to the genomics of mosquitoes, mice, and humans. Before joining WRI he held positions at the Frederick Cancer Research Center, the Oak Ridge National Laboratory, and Celera Genomics. Dr. Mural is an associate editor of *Genomics* and is on the editorial board of *Briefings in Bioinformatics*. He has served on numerous review panels and advisory boards. In 1992 Dr. Mural received an R&D 100 Award from *Research and Development Magazine* and was listed as an "unsung hero" of the Human Genome Project by *Science* magazine in 2001.

About the Contributors

Lee Bronfman is a healthcare executive with more than 20 years' experience developing and implementing innovative projects and programs. She is adept at conceptualizing and leading initiatives. Her areas of expertise include: management and supervision, research, customer service, public speaking. training and development, policy development, and coaching and mentoring. During Lee's career she has been the director of education and the director of nursing for a hospital, a corporate management development specialist and a certified research protocol coordinator. Lee managed the research for the Clinical Breast Care Project – a military/civilian partnership funded by the Department of Defense to study breast cancer and breast disease. In her role as administrative director for the CBCP, Lee provides executive level project oversight. She executes grants, major awards and commitments of awarding agencies and translates policies and procedures into effective practices within the context of the overall project. Lee is an accomplished public speaker with excellent facilitation skills. Her strong background in management brings a real-life perspective to her presentations. Her problem-solving skills make her an excellent consultant and she has published articles on reengineering, customer service, backpacks and their effect on children's spines, the CBCP's Core Questionnaire, and a chapter on the Clinical Perspective for a textbook on Biomedical Informatics. Ms. Bronfman is a Certified Clinical Research Professional and holds an MA in Adult Education and Human Resource Development from the George Washington University and a Bachelor of Science degree from D'Youville College.

Henry Brzeski has been involved in molecular biology for the last 30 years. As computer technology advanced he took a great interest in bioinformatics and used it both in his own research and in the teaching of bioinformatics to undergraduates in the UK. He moved to the US and there he was able to merge his experience with bioinformatics with the medical aspects that were available in breast cancer research at the Windber Research Institute. He is now using informatics and data mining technologies and applying them to intelligent solutions in business.

Mick Correll is the director of healthcare product management at Inforsense LLC. In his career thus far, he has focused on the design, management, and implementation of informatics solutions for the pharmaceutical, biotech, and healthcare industries. While at Inforsense, he has been actively involved in a number of pioneering translational research projects at leading medical research centers in the US and abroad. Prior to joining Inforsense, Mick was a bioinformatician at Lion Bioscience Research Inc, where he was the principle architect of a globally distributed gene annotation and analysis platform. Mick also served as the head of professional services for Lion Bioscience Inc in North America. He holds a BS in computer science and a BA in molecular, cellular, and developmental biology from the University of Colorado at Boulder.

Darrell L. Ellsworth is the senior director of the Integrative Cardiac and Metabolic Health Program at the Windber Research Institute. Dr. Ellsworth received his PhD from Texas A&M University in human genetics, served as a research assistant professor in the Institute for Molecular Medicine at the University of Texas, and was a research geneticist at the National Heart, Lung, and Blood Institute, National Institutes of Health. He has been actively involved in the design, execution, and management of large multi-center collaborative research projects focusing on genetic influences on complex diseases such as heart disease, obesity, and breast cancer at Windber Research Institute. Dr. Ellsworth has published more than 50 articles, book chapters, and abstracts in peer reviewed publications such as *The Lancet Oncology, Nature Genetics, Circulation, Annuals of Surgical Oncology, Obesity Research*, and *The International Journal of Obesity.*

Leigh Fantacone-Campbell is the pathologists' assistant and sites coordinator for the Henry M. Jackson Foundation Clinical Breast Care Project. She received her BS degree in biology from the University of Central Florida and her master of science in Pathology from the University of Maryland, Baltimore. She spent two years working in surgical and autopsy pathology for Inova Fairfax Hospital in northern Virginia before transitioning into breast cancer research.

Emily Gutchell is a data analyst in risk management services at MedStar Health, a non-profit healthcare delivery system of eight hospitals and other healthcare services in the Baltimore/Washington area. She received a B.A. in english from the State University of New York at Albany. Ms. Gutchell has ten years experience in data reporting focused on quality control and quality improvement in patient safety, and experience in data integrity coordination for research. She worked as a coordinator of biomedical informatics on the Clinical Breast Care Project where she developed standard operating procedures for completion and quality review of research questionnaires.

Jeffrey Hooke is the chief pathologist for the Clinical Breast Care Project (CBCP) at the Walter Reed Army Medical Center, overseeing the pathologic analysis and archiving of CBCP tissue and serum specimens. He earned his medical degree from Tufts University School of Medicine in 1992. He completed residency training in pathology at Walter Reed Army Medical Center in 1997. Following his residency, Dr. Hooke remained at Walter Reed as a staff pathologist and served as medical director of the Infectious Diseases Laboratory for four years. Dr. Hooke is trained in both anatomic and clinical pathology, and received subspecialty certification in medical microbiology in 1999. Dr. Hooke continues to practice actively in the surgical pathology service at Walter Reed.

V.S. Kumar Kolli is the senior director of proteomics of Windber Research Institute. He obtained his master's degree in chemistry in 1987 from Osmania University, Hyderabad, India, then secured a research fellowship from Council of

Scientific and Industrial Research (CSIR) to perform his doctoral research work in Mass Spectrometry at the Indian Institute of Chemical Technology (IICT), Hyderabad, India and received his Ph.D degree in Chemistry (1992) from Osmania University, Hyderabad, India. He joined the Complex Carbohydrate Research Center (CCRC) at the University of Georgia, Athens for postdoctoral research, and utilized advanced mass spectrometric techniques to address the structural problems of glycoconjugates. His current research interests are mainly centered on developing new proteomics methods to facilitate the high-throughput molecular profiling research for identifying biomarkers from various disease related clinical samples using the state-of-the-art proteomics instrumentation.

Leonid Kvecher is the data manager of the Windber Research Institute (WRI). He received his BS in chemistry as well as MS in computer science from Drexel University. Mr. Kvecher has more then 10 years experience in oracle database administrating, data warehousing, data managing, programming, and data mining for different industries. Before joining WRI he held positions at the Fleet Bank (Bank of America), the AxCell Biosciences, and Shared Medical Systems (Siemens Medical Solutions). He is coauthor in more than 10 papers on a range of subjects from data mining, data modeling, and data preparation to data warehousing, laboratory workflow systems, and QA/QC procedures.

Susan M. Maskery is a postdoctoral fellow in biomedical informatics at Windber Research Institute. She earned her B.S. degree in chemical engineering from the University of Michigan and her M.S. and Ph. D. degrees in chemical engineering from Rutgers, the State University of New Jersey. Her research interests include data-mining clinical datasets for hypothesis generation and modeling, and simulation of biological processes. Dr. Maskery's research has been published in journals from many disciplines such as: *BMC Neuroscience, Annual Review of Biomedical Engineering*, and *The Journal of Biomedical Informatics*.

Colonel Craig D. Shriver became program director of the Walter Reed Army Medical Center General Surgery residency in June 1998, became director of the Clinical Breast Care Project (CBCP) in February 2000, and became chief of general surgery at Walter Reed in April 2001, all positions which he presently holds. Dr. Shriver is director and principal investigator of the CBCP and along with Nick Jacobs, FACHE of the Windber Medical Center, is a co-founder of the CBCP at Windber Research Institute, made possible through the support of The Honorable John P. Murtha.

After completing his surgical oncology fellowship in 1993, he was assigned to Walter Reed Army Medical Center as a staff general surgeon. He took over as chief of surgical oncology in 1995, becoming general surgery residency program director in 1998, and Chief of General Surgery in 2001. In February 2000 he was selected by the command to become director of the congressionally-mandated CBCP, a military-civilian coalition on the forefront of providing excellent clinical care and cutting-edge breast cancer research.

Yaw-Ching Yang is a research scientist with over 10 years experience in genomics, genetics, molecular biology, and medical research. Dr. Yang received his Ph.D. degree in genetics from Texas A&M University. He then completed his postdoctoral research projects at Michigan Tech University, and then moved to the Albert Einstein College of Medicine as postdoctoral research associate where he studied and became an expert in genomic technology. After he completed his postdoctoral trainings, Dr. Yang was hired as senior scientist at Genome Therapeutic Corporation (GTC) in Waltham, Massachusetts. He established both spotted and Affymetrix microarray platforms at GTC and supported projects in drug discovery and functional genomic study. Dr Yang then joined the Windber Research Institute (WRI) in 2004. He successfully established GE CodeLink, Affymetrix GeneChip, an array base comparative genomic hybridization (aCGH) platform, and supports all projects using these genomic technologies. He has published his works with collaborators in peer review journals and presented his work at scientific conferences.

Yonghong Zhang is a senior staff scientist at the Windber Research Institute (WRI). Dr. Zhang received his BS degree from Beijing Agricultural University, his MS in computer science from University of Chicago and his Ph. D. in Immunology/Microbiology from Rush University. Dr. Zhang served as a data analyst and data manager for the Microarray Core Facility of Children's Memorial Research Center before joining WRI. He has been actively involved in analysis of clinical and high throughput genomic/proteomic data, data management and QA/QC, algorithm and tool development, and text mining in biomedical research.

Index